Sovereign Debt Restructuring and the Law

The book sheds light on the perhaps most important legal conundrum in the context of sovereign debt restructuring: the holdout creditor problem. Absent an international bankruptcy regime for sovereigns, holdout creditors may delay or even thwart the efficient resolution of sovereign debt crises by leveraging contractual provisions and, in an increasing number of cases, by seeking to enforce a debt claim against the sovereign in courts or international tribunals.

Following an introduction to sovereign debt and its restructuring, the book provides the first comprehensive analysis of the holdout creditor problem in the context of the two largest sovereign debt restructuring operations in history: the Argentine restructurings of 2005 and 2010 and the 2012 Greek private sector involvement. By reviewing numerous lawsuits and arbitral proceedings initiated against Argentina and Greece across a dozen different jurisdictions, it distils the organizing principles for ongoing and future cases of sovereign debt restructuring and litigation. It highlights the different approaches judges and arbitrators have adopted when dealing with holdout creditors, ranging from the denial of their contractual right to repayment on human rights grounds to leveraging the international financial infrastructure to coerce governments into meeting holdouts' demands. To this end, it zooms in on the role the governing law plays in sovereign debt restructurings, revisits the contemporary view on sovereign immunity from suit and enforcement in the international debt context, and examines how creditor rights are balanced with the sovereign's interest in achieving debt sustainability. Finally, it advances a new genealogy of holdouts, distinguishing between official and private sector holdouts and discussing how the proliferation of new types of uncooperative creditors may affect the sovereign debt architecture going forward.

While the book is aimed at practitioners and scholars dealing with sovereign debt and its restructuring, it should also provide the general reader with the understanding of the key legal issues facing countries in debt distress. Moreover, by weaving economic, financial, and political considerations into its analysis of holdout creditor litigation and arbitration, the book also speaks to policymakers without a legal background engaged in the field of international finance and economics.

Sebastian Grund is a Legal Counsel at the International Monetary Fund (IMF). This book was written before his employment with the IMF, and the views expressed herein are those of the author and do not necessarily represent the views of the IMF, its Executive Board, or IMF management.

Routledge Research in Finance and Banking Law

The European Sovereign Debt Crisis
Breaking the Vicious Circle Between Sovereigns and Banks
Phoebus L. Athanassiou and Angelos T. Vouldis

Global Finance in the 21st Century
Stability and Sustainability in a Fragmenting World
Steve Kourabas

Banking Regulation in Africa
The Case of Nigeria and Other Emerging Economies
Folashade Adeyemo

Crypto-Finance, Law and Regulation
Governing an Emerging Ecosystem
Joseph Lee

Regulation and Governance of Mutual Funds
United Kingdom and United States of America Perspectives on Investor Protection
Mohammed Khair Alshaleel

Regulation of Debt Collection in Europe
Understanding Informal Debt Collection Practices
Cătălin-Gabriel Stănescu

The Regulation of Megabanks
Global Systemically Important Banks and their Legal Frameworks
Katarzyna M. Parchimowicz

Regulating Open Banking
Comparative Analysis of the EU, the UK and Taiwan
Chang-Hsien Tsai and Kuan-Jung Peng

For more information about this series, please visit: www.routledge.com/Routledge-Research-in-Finance-and-Banking-Law/book-series/FINANCIALLAW

Sovereign Debt Restructuring and the Law

The Holdout Creditor Problem in Argentina and Greece

Sebastian Grund

Routledge
Taylor & Francis Group
LONDON AND NEW YORK

First published 2023
by Routledge
4 Park Square, Milton Park, Abingdon, Oxon OX14 4RN

and by Routledge
605 Third Avenue, New York, NY 10158

Routledge is an imprint of the Taylor & Francis Group, an informa business

British Library Cataloguing-in-Publication Data
A catalogue record for this book is available from the British Library

Library of Congress Cataloging-in-Publication Data
A catalog record for this book has been requested

ISBN: 978-0-367-77460-8 (hbk)
ISBN: 978-1-032-42236-7 (pbk)
ISBN: 978-1-003-36187-9 (ebk)

DOI: 10.4324/9781003361879

Typeset in Times New Roman
by Apex CoVantage, LLC

To Katharina, you are my sovereign.

Contents

Preface xii
Acknowledgements xiii
Acronyms, Abbreviations, and Defined Terms xv

1 Sovereign Debt and Its Restructuring 1
1.1. Sovereign Debt – An Overview 1
1.2. Sovereign Debt Restructuring 3
1.2.1. Introduction 3
1.2.2. Definition and Types of Sovereign Debt Restructurings 4
1.2.3. Legal and Transactional Aspects of Sovereign Debt Restructurings 5
1.2.3.1. Restructuring Principles and Processes 5
1.2.3.2. Debt Restructuring Methods 6
1.2.3.2.1. Debt Restructuring Versus Debt Rescheduling 6
1.2.3.2.2. Debt Restructuring Techniques: Sticks and Carrots 7
1.2.3.3. Scope of Debt Restructurings 7
1.2.3.3.1. Domestic Versus Foreign Sovereign Debt Restructurings 7
1.2.3.3.2. Creditor Classes, Ranking, and Priority 8
1.2.4. Holdout Creditor Problems in Sovereign Debt Restructurings 9
1.2.5. The Evolution of Sovereign Debt Restructuring Practice 10

2 Holdout Creditor Problems and Foreign Law Debt: The Argentine Debt Restructurings in Courts and Tribunals (2001–2016) 31

2.1. Argentina's Sovereign Debt Restructurings (2001–2010) 31

2.1.1. Background 31

2.1.2. The 2005 Debt Restructuring 31

2.1.3. The 2010 Debt Restructuring 32

2.2. Holdout Litigation After Argentina 32

2.2.1. Holdout Litigation in Foreign Domestic Courts 32

2.2.1.1. United States 32

2.2.1.1.1. Lightwater v Argentina 33

2.2.1.1.2. EM v Banco Central de la República Argentina 34

2.2.1.1.3. NML Capital v Argentina 35

2.2.1.2. Germany 38

2.2.1.2.1. BVerfG Decision of 8 May 2007 38

2.2.1.2.2. BGH Decision of 25 November 2010 39

2.2.1.2.3. BGH Decision of 24 February 2015 40

2.2.1.2.4. BVerfG Decision of 3 July 2019 40

2.2.1.3. Italy 41

*2.2.1.3.1. Italian Supreme Court (*Corte Suprema di Cassazione*) 41*

2.2.1.4. United Kingdom 42

2.2.1.4.1. UK Supreme Court 42

2.2.1.5. France 42

*2.2.1.5.1. French Supreme Court (*Cour de Cassation*) 43*

2.2.1.6. Switzerland 44

2.2.1.6.1. Swiss Federal Supreme Court 44

2.2.2. Holdout Litigation in International Courts and Tribunals 45

2.2.2.1. International Tribunal for the Law of the Sea 45

2.2.2.2. International Court of Justice 46

2.2.3. Interim Conclusions: Enforcing Sovereign Debt in Foreign Courts 47

2.2.3.1. Adjudicatory Sovereign Immunity 47

2.2.3.1.1. *The Commercial Activity Exception: 'Once A Trader Always A Trader' and the Mixed Activity Conundrum* 47
2.2.3.1.2. *Recognition of Foreign Judgements* 49
2.2.3.2. *Immunity from Enforcement* 50
2.2.3.2.1. *The Immunity of Public Claims from Creditor Attachment* 50
2.2.3.2.2. *The Immunity of Central Bank Reserves from Attachment* 51
2.2.3.2.3. *ARA Libertad and the Immunity of (Military) Vessels* 53
2.2.3.3. *Third-Party Injunctions: A New Super Remedy to Circumvent the Immunity Defence?* 54
2.3. *Holdout Arbitration After Argentina* 56
2.3.1. *International Investment Arbitration Before ICSID Tribunals* 56
2.3.1.1. *Abaclat and Others v Argentine Republic* 56
2.3.1.1.1. *Sovereign Bonds as Investment* 57
2.3.1.1.2. *Jurisdiction over Mass Claims* 58
2.3.1.1.3. *The Dissenting Opinion by Professor Abi-Saab* 58
2.3.1.2. *Ambiente Ufficio v Argentine Republic* 59
2.3.2. *Interim Conclusions* 60
2.3.2.1. *Sovereign Bond Arbitration Against Argentina – Producing a Monster?* 60
2.3.2.2. *ICSID Jurisdiction and the Rejection of the Salini Test* 61
2.3.2.2.1. *Contribution to the Development of the Host State* 61
2.3.2.2.2. *Duration* 62
2.3.2.2.3. *Risk-Sharing* 63
2.3.2.2.4. *Territorial Link* 64
2.3.2.2.5. *The Admissibility of Mass Claims* 64
2.4. *Settling a Decade of Holdout Lawsuits Against Argentina* 65
2.4.1. *The 2016 Election and Argentina's Return to International Financial Markets* 65

2.4.2. *Settling with the Vulture Holdouts* 65

2.4.3. *Settling with the Retail Holdouts* 68

3 Holdout Creditor Problems and Domestic Law Debt: The Greek Debt Restructuring in Courts and Tribunals (2012–2020) 98

3.1. *Introduction* 98

3.2. *The Greek Sovereign Debt Crisis: 2009–2015* 98

3.3. *The Greek Debt Restructuring of 2012* 99

3.3.1. *Debt Restructuring Negotiations: The Role of the Troika and the IIF* 99

3.3.2. *Restructuring Greek Law Bonds* 100

3.3.3. *Restructuring Foreign Law Bonds* 101

3.4. *Holdout Creditor Litigation After Greece in Foreign Courts* 102

3.4.1. *Germany* 102

3.4.1.1. *BGH Judgment of 8 March 2016* 102

3.4.1.2. *BGH Judgment of 19 December 2017* 103

3.4.1.3. *BVerfG Judgment of 6 May 2020* 104

3.4.2. *Austria* 105

3.4.2.1. *OGH Judgment of 20 May 2014* 105

3.4.2.2. *OGH Judgment of 27 January 2016* 105

3.4.2.3. *OGH Judgements of 25 April 2017 and 22 January 2019* 106

3.4.2.4. *OGH Judgment of 21 February 2020* 106

3.4.3. *Interim Conclusions* 107

3.4.3.1. *Sovereign Immunity in Domestic Law Restructurings* 107

3.4.3.2. *(Some) Hypothetical Problems with Enforcing Greek Sovereign Debt in Germany and Austria* 108

3.5. *Holdout Litigation After Greece in European Courts* 109

3.5.1. *Court of Justice of the EU (CJEU)* 109

3.5.1.1. *Accorinti v ECB* 109

3.5.1.2. *Fahnenbrock v Hellenic Republic* 110

3.5.1.3. *Hellenic Republic v Kuhn* 111

3.5.2. *European Court of Human Rights (ECtHR)* 112

3.5.2.1. *Mamatas v Greece* 112

3.5.3. *Interim Conclusions* 113

3.5.3.1. *Sovereign Debt Restructurings in European Courts: Novel Judicial Challenges* 113

3.5.3.2. *The (Tenuous) Link Between Sovereign Immunity and Jurisdiction Under EU Law* 114

3.5.3.3. *Jurisdiction Under the Brussels I Regulation 116*
3.5.3.4. *Property Right Guarantees for Sovereign Bondholders in Unilateral European Sovereign Bond Restructurings 116*
3.5.3.5. *The (Preferential) Treatment of Eurosystem Claims in Euro Area Sovereign Debt Restructurings 118*
3.6. *Holdout Arbitration After Greece 118*
3.6.1. *Poštová banka v Hellenic Republic 119*
3.6.2. *Interim Conclusions: Closing Pandora's Box? 120*

4 Holdouts in Foreign Versus Domestic Law Debt Restructurings: Walking Back from Argentina and Greece 142
4.1. *Introduction 142*
4.2. *The Role of Governing Law in Sovereign Debt Restructurings 142*
4.3. *The Legal Basis for Sovereign Debt Instruments: Contracts Versus Statutes 143*
4.4. *Sovereign Immunity Revisited 145*
4.5. *The Protection of Sovereign Creditors' Property Rights 146*

5 A Genealogy of Holdout Creditors: The Future of Sovereign Debt Restructuring 155
5.1. *The Proliferation of Holdout Creditors 155*
5.2. *Private Sector Holdouts 156*
5.2.1. *Vulture Funds 156*
5.2.2. *Banks 160*
5.2.3. *Asset Management Funds (Real Money Investors) 161*
5.2.4. *Retail Investors 162*
5.2.5. *Commodity Traders 164*
5.3. *Official Sector Holdouts 166*

6 Concluding Remarks 180

Bibliography 183
Statutes, Treaties, and Judicial Authorities 206
Index 218

Preface

Nations have been issuing debt for many centuries to finance their expenditures. Ranging from costly wars and hegemonical endeavours to establishing and maintaining large social welfare systems, public debt has been essential in facilitating the emergence and growth of the modern state. Contrary to some long-held beliefs, however, countries may become unable to repay the monies they have borrowed domestically or internationally. In the absence of a normative framework to regulate sovereign insolvency, the resolution of sovereign debt crises is governed by a set of inchoate rules, held together by a loose web of judicial precedents, international agreements, and political decisions. The perhaps most important legal implication of this non-system of sovereign debt is that, under certain circumstances, lenders may hold out from a sovereign debt restructuring to obtain a better deal than their fellow creditors, often underpinned by (the threat of) legal action.

This book seeks to provide guidance on the holdout creditor problem against the backdrop of the two largest sovereign debt restructurings in history, Argentina's 2005/2010 restructuring and the Greek Private Sector Involvement of 2012. In both Argentina and Greece, holdout creditors challenged the respective governments' restructuring measures in domestic courts and international arbitration tribunals with the goal of extracting better terms than those offered by the sovereign and accepted by the restructured creditors. Litigation and arbitration dragged on for more than a decade after Argentina's debt workout and over eight years in the case of Greece. It should be mentioned that Argentina implemented another sovereign debt restructuring in 2020, which will, however, not be covered in this book.

With the last lawsuits having been largely concluded in 2020, to the best of my knowledge, this book presents the first study to review the seminal judicial decisions rendered across almost a dozen different jurisdictions in the wake of the two restructurings. While the transactional techniques applied in the respective debt operations shared many similarities, the Argentine restructuring mainly covered *foreign* law instruments while the Greek PSI concerned *domestic* law securities. This difference allows for a direct comparison of the pertinent legal issues arising with respect to the restructurings of the two types of public debt. Finally, looking beyond Argentina and Greece, the book offers a genealogy of holdout creditors, distinguishing between different categories of private and public creditors that may pursue holdout strategies and, thus, pose obstacles to fast and effective debt restructurings.

Acknowledgements

This monograph is a revised and updated doctoral thesis written at the University of Vienna, which was funded by the Graf Hardegg'sche Foundation and awarded the Austrian Prize for Restructuring Management and Insolvency Law 2020. As part of my doctoral studies, I spent time as a visiting researcher at the University of New South Wales and completed course work and trainings at the London School of Economics, the European University Institute, Maastricht University, the European Central Bank, and the Federal Reserve Bank of New York.

I am greatly indebted to many people that supported my research. First and foremost, I would like to thank my supervisor Professor August Reinisch as well as the members of my doctoral committee, Professor Ross Buckley and Professor Kunibert Raffer.

This book has benefitted from countless informal exchanges with academics, practitioners, and policymakers, who provided background knowledge and inspiration. I cannot mention all of them here, so I will limit myself to those who had the greatest influence on my writing. I want to thank Professor Mitu Gulati, who very early in my research encouraged me to submit some of my findings in one of the leading journals in the field and who provided directions when I most needed them. The numerous conversations with Lee Buchheit allowed me to connect the practical with the theoretical legal aspects of restructuring of sovereign debt. His passion was contagious and invigorated my desire to specialize in this field. Professor Anna Gelpern introduced me to the world of sovereign debt restructuring conferences and was always available to delve into the most challenging sovereign debt questions. Jeromin Zettelmeyer did a fantastic job in explaining to a lawyer the economics of international debt crises.

At the European Central Bank (ECB), I want to express my gratitude to all the colleagues that I have worked with in the Directorates General Legal Services and International and European Relations. Among the numerous colleagues who have accompanied me on my academic journey, I am especially thankful to Chiara Zilioli and Niall Lenihan who were excellent mentors and role models. At the International Monetary Fund (IMF), I would like to thank colleagues in the Legal Department, the Monetary and Capital Markets Department as well as the Western Hemisphere Department for their invaluable comments on the manuscript.

Finally, I am deeply indebted to my family – to my parents, Beatrix and Georg; my brother Benjamin; and my grandmothers, Inge and Irmtraud. Their tireless backing of my endeavours has made all this possible. And I owe eternal gratitude to my wife, Katharina, for her love and unwavering support.

This book was written before my employment with the IMF. The views expressed herein are mine and do not necessarily represent the views of the IMF, its Executive Board, or IMF management. Nothing contained in this book should be reported as representing the views of the IMF, its Executive Board, member governments, or any other entity mentioned herein. The law is as of 2 November 2021.

Acronyms, Abbreviations, and Defined Terms

AMF	Arab Monetary Fund
AoA	Articles of Agreement of the International Monetary Fund
BGH	*Bundesgerichtshof* (German Federal Court of Justice)
BIS	Bank for International Settlements
BIT	Bilateral Investment Treaty
BVferG	*Bundesverfassungsgericht* (German Federal Constitutional Court)
CAC	Collective Action Clause
CDS	Credit Default Swap
CJEU	Court of Justice of the European Union
CFR	Charter of Fundamental Rights
DM	*Deutsche Mark* (German Mark)
ECB	European Central Bank
ECtHR	European Court of Human Rights
EFSF	European Financial Stability Facility
EGC	(EU) General Court
EMEs	Emerging Market Economies
ESCB	European System of Central Banks
ESCI	European Convention on State Immunity
ESM	European Stability Mechanism
EU	European Union
EUR	Euro
FRBNY	Federal Reserve Bank of New York
FSIA	Foreign Sovereign Immunities Act
G10	Group of Ten
G20	Group of Twenty
GBA	Greek Bondholder Act 4050/2012
GBP	Pound Sterling
GDP	Gross Domestic Product
GFC	Global Financial Crisis of 2008–2009
HIPC	Heavily Indebted Poor Countries
ICJ	International Court of Justice
ICMA	International Capital Market Association
ICSID	International Centre for Settlement of Investment Disputes

IEO	Independent Evaluation Office
IFI	International Financial Institution
IIA	International Investment Agreement
IIF	Institute of International Finance
ILC	International Law Commission
IMF	International Monetary Fund
ISDA	International Swaps and Derivatives Association
ISDS	Investor-State Dispute Settlement
ISIN	International Securities Identification Number
LIA	Lending into Arrears
LICs	Low-Income Countries
LOLR	Lender of Last Resort
MDB	Multilateral Development Bank
MoU	Memorandum of Understanding
OECD	Organisation for Economic Co-operation and Development
OGH	*Oberster Gerichtshof* (Austrian Supreme Court)
PCIJ	Permanent Court of International Justice
PSI	Private Sector Involvement
SDNY	United States District Court for the Southern District of New York
SDRM	Sovereign Debt Restructuring Mechanism
SFSC	Swiss Federal Supreme Court
SOE	State-Owned Enterprise
TFA	Task Force Argentina
TFEU	Treaty on the Functioning of the European Union
UK	United Kingdom
UN	United Nations
UNCSI	United Nations Convention on State Immunity
UNCTAD	United Nations Conference on Trade and Development
USD	US Dollar
VCDR	Vienna Convention on Diplomatic Relations
VCLT	Vienna Convention of the Law of Treaties
WTO	World Trade Organization

1 Sovereign Debt and Its Restructuring

1.1. Sovereign Debt – An Overview

Since time immemorial, government borrowing has been a crucial feature of the international economy as well as a cornerstone of the global growth and development process.[1] Countries have raised debts to wage war, finance public infrastructure, and more recently, preserve costly social welfare systems.[2] Sovereign debt is also a pivotal factor in world affairs.[3]

Macroeconomic theory suggests that a country with above average growth prospects should attract capital for both investment and consumption smoothing.[4] As a matter of (international) law, states have an unlimited capacity to borrow,[5] and virtually all modern nations make use of this right to borrow.

Empirically speaking, the volume of sovereign debt issuances has firmly accelerated within the last three decades. In the wake of the COVID-19 pandemic, total volume of outstanding sovereign debt has reached a record level of 100% of world GDP – in other words, the amount of public debt outstanding is almost the equivalent of a whole year of economic output.[6] In emerging economies, which are generally more vulnerable to elevated levels of government, debt-to-GDP ratios reached 64% on average in 2021, an increase of almost 10 percentage points compared to 2019.[7]

While sovereign debt has allowed governments around the globe to spur growth and cultivate their social, economic, and political development, borrowing excesses harbour risks. The first cases of sovereign default can be traced back to the Greece tyrant Dionysius I of Syracuse (432–367 BC).[8] Sovereign debt crises have remained recurring and frequent features of the global economy well into modernity. As Reinhart and Rogoff's seminal book *This Time is Different* posits, most countries that were able to raise debts have undergone one or more default episodes in the course of the past two centuries.[9]

This book refrains from delving deeper into the controversies in the economic literature on optimal sovereign debt management strategies. It instead focuses on the *legal* problems associated with a given state's inability to repay its debts in full and on time. The notion that sovereign insolvencies are 'non-legal issues,' as suggested by Drago-Porter-Convention of 1907,[10] no longer holds true. Foreign governments have lost their absolute immunity from litigation in foreign

DOI: 10.4324/9781003361879-1

courts concerning unpaid public debts, though international law prohibits the use of force or similar measures to compel repayment.[11]

To understand what happens at the end of a sovereign debt contract when the government defaults, however, we must first trace its beginnings.

Conceptually, 'sovereign debt' has been referred to as 'oxymoron'[12] or 'Janus-faced' asset class.[13] On the one hand, the term 'debt' defines a legal relationship where the borrower has promised to repay the amount stated in the contract plus interest to the lender. The principle of pacta sunt servanda applies to financial promises rendered by sovereigns just as much as it does in a legal relationship under private law.[14] On the other hand, the sovereignty of states[15] under international law confers a unique status of immunity[16] upon nations. The sovereignty fiction emanates from the well-established principle of equality of nations: *par in parem non habet imperium*.[17]

This tension has shaped sovereign debt markets for the better part of at least four decades and filled millions of pages in books, academic journals, and policy reports. Five critical developments are worth highlighting in this respect, many of which I will revert back to in the course of this study:

- First, many (poorer) sovereign nations surrendered their legal power over debt contracts to attract foreign capital: while in the past, most sovereign loans were governed by the debtor's own domestic laws and, therefore, subject to the local law advantage, today's *international* sovereign debt is almost exclusively governed by neutral laws, most notably New York or English law.[18] It was this legal transformation that empowered creditors to mitigate the risk[19] of investing in developing and emerging economies by securing stronger judicial enforcement channels. By the same token, sovereigns that were long barred from international capital markets gained access to it, including previously excluded developing nations that had been dependent on concessional financing from the official sector for decades.
- Second, underpinning this development, the principle of sovereign immunity morphed from a relative to an absolute concept.[20] Before the 1970s, the doctrine of absolute state immunity essentially barred litigation against sovereign borrower in a foreign court. Nowadays, with the demise of the principle of absolute sovereign immunity *from suit*, foreign creditors may entertain legal actions against a debtor state in the courts of a foreign state subject to the (foreign) laws of that jurisdiction.[21] This said, immunity *from execution* continues to provide protection to certain key assets of the sovereign, such as diplomatic instrumentalities or central bank reserves.
- Third, following the debt crises of the 1980s and 1990s, sovereign issuers gradually turned away from syndicated lending by global banking houses. While syndicated bank loans were the prime source of sovereign funding during the 1970s, when petrodollars were channelled through the US banking system to emerging market sovereigns,[22] governments started to issue most of their (private) debts in the form of tradable debt securities on international

markets. Within a few years, bonds eclipsed loans as the funding instrument of choice for state.[23]

- Fourth, related to the rise of securities as a financing instrument, the number of legal disputes pertaining to sovereign bonds has skyrocketed in recent years.[24] Indeed, as empirical evidence suggests, holdout litigation and arbitration are no longer negligible nuisances during debt workouts.[25] Holdouts' relative increase in leverage over the sovereign has been particularly obvious after the Argentine debt restructuring, where, after a decade of fierce litigation, the government eventually accepted the holdouts' claims for full repayment.[26] Similarly, the Greek government expected aggressive speculative holdout litigation by hedge funds and, therefore, decided to pay them in full rather than risking drawn-out litigation in London.[27]
- Last, traditional official sector lending, which mainly came from richer Western countries during the 20th century through bilateral or plurilateral channels, has increasingly lost its significance compared to the funding of sovereign budgets through commercial debt. New lenders have entered the stage. On the bilateral side, China and other emerging economic powerhouses, like India, Saudi Arabia, or Brazil, now provide a significant share of official sector funding. On the private sector side, the increasing variety of lenders, including large asset managers, retail investors, and commodity traders, has gradually altered the creditor base for many nations. This shift may provide some new coordination challenges to the existing debt restructuring architecture, especially in poorer countries that depend on more unconventional sources of financing like pre-sales of commodities.

1.2. Sovereign Debt Restructuring

1.2.1. Introduction

The history of sovereign default and restructuring is as old as the history of sovereign debt itself.[28] While some trace the first public debt crises back to the Greek empires around 400 BC,[29] others consider that the first regular borrowing agreements with states were concluded – and some of them subsequently breached – between AD 1000 and 1400.[30] During the 16th century, when the nation state became entrenched in Europe, leaders started to accumulate significant amount of (foreign) debts, ranging in volume between 20% and 60% of GDP.[31] Costly wars were financed with debt and waves of defaults followed.[32]

The trend since the Middle Ages has been clear: more debts and more restructurings. Between 1820 and 2012, 251 sovereigns defaulted on their public debts.[33] The frequency of default indeed accelerated with the globalization of financial markets. Pre–World War II, several international debt crises occurred, such as the crash of 1825 and the 'first world debt crisis' in 1873, when the New York stock markets collapsed and the Ottoman Empire, Egypt, Greece, Tunisia, and eight Latin American countries defaulted.[34]

Between 2005 and 2015, at least 14 countries have undertaken 18 debt restructurings.[35] From Greece to Grenada and Argentina to Cameroon, several governments in countries with different levels of economic development asked their creditors for public debt rescheduling or restructuring.[36] Between 2014 to 2020, there were at least a dozen government debt restructurings involving private financial claims.[37] While the COVID-19 pandemic has not yet triggered a wave of defaults, as some had feared in its early stages, the risk of sovereign debt distress in LICs and EMEs has risen to unprecedented levels.[38]

Some regions have been more prone to fiscal and financial instability than others.[39] While many European countries defaulted on their public debts in the 19th and early 20th century, Latin American and the Caribbean countries alone implemented 25 restructurings in the past 35 years.[40] Moreover, there were periods of severe stress where the frequency of default shot up. Some recent examples include the Latin American debt crises in the 1980s, the Argentine default of 2001, and the euro area crisis starting in 2010.[41]

1.2.2. Definition and Types of Sovereign Debt Restructurings

The term 'sovereign debt restructuring' is neither defined under international nor domestic law. In the literature, it has, by way of example, been referred to as 'the mechanism used by sovereign states to prevent or resolve debt issues and achieve debt sustainability levels'[42] or as 'a set of operations through which debtor countries seek debt relief from their creditors in the form of maturity extensions, face value reductions and/or lower interest rates.'[43] At its heart, a sovereign debt restructuring relates to the modification of the *payment* terms of sovereign debt instruments.[44]

Sovereign debt restructurings can either be voluntary (i.e., with creditors consenting to the proposed changes)[45] or involuntary (i.e., by means of unilateral modifications or by debt repudiation). In the context of private debt instruments, such as bonds, involuntary restructurings usually trigger a contractual event of default,[46] conferring upon creditors the right to accelerate all outstanding interest and principal payments, and sue the government or initiate arbitration proceedings.

Prior to a restructuring, a key question is whether the government is indeed unable (or unwilling) to pay all its debts in full and on time. From an economic viewpoint, two concepts may be applied to ascertain solvency, or lack thereof, in the context of sovereign debtors. The IMF's Executive Board has defined 'public debt sustainability' as follows:

> [i]n general terms, public debt can be regarded as sustainable when the primary balance needed to at least stabilize debt under both the baseline and realistic shock scenarios is economically and politically feasible, such that the level of debt is consistent with an acceptably low rollover risk and with preserving potential growth at a satisfactory level.[47]

Sovereign borrowers may be deemed insolvent when one or both tests are negative. From a legal perspective, however, the contractual documentation would require an event of default to occur for legal consequences to be triggered.[48] Hence, the economic and legal perspectives on the sovereign's inability to repay its debts ought not to be confused.

Assessing debt sustainability is far from straightforward and usually warrants a mix of technical analysis and sound judgement.[49] At the international level, in the context of both its surveillance and lending mandate, the IMF regularly assesses the sustainability of a sovereign's financial situation.[50]

To this end, the IMF's debt sustainability analysis (DSA) follows a probabilistic approach to determine whether a given country's public debt is stable under a feasible set of policies.[51] The IMF DSA has no intention to establish a bright line rule between liquidity problems and solvency problems, also because both may ultimately result in an unsustainable debt situation. However, it still has significant practical relevance. If a country were to seek access to Fund resources, the Fund is precluding from lending if debt is assessed as unsustainable, unless the member takes steps to restore debt sustainability.[52]

1.2.3. Legal and Transactional Aspects of Sovereign Debt Restructurings

1.2.3.1. Restructuring Principles and Processes

The overriding objective of any debt restructuring operations lies on rapidly reaching agreement to restore public debt sustainability.[53] In a country with a diverse debtor profile, official sector debt relief, usually via the Paris Club[54] but possibly also through other mechanisms,[55] will usually precede private sector negotiations.[56] Once official sector creditors have agreed on a deal, private creditors will be invited to negotiations, which usually involve the formation of creditor committees.[57] The IIF, which was first brought into play in the early 1980s, now plays an important role in coordinating private creditors.[58]

While sovereign debt restructuring is essentially based on a 'non-system,'[59] various (soft law) principles exist that guide debt restructuring procedures in practice.[60] One key issue is whether a restructuring is pre-emptive or post-default.[61] From an empirical perspective, pre-emptive restructurings make up about a third of all restructurings, result in lower haircuts, are faster, and lead to less severe macroeconomic outcomes.[62] From a legal perspective, the main distinction between pre-emptive and post-default restructuring is that the sovereign has never formally breached its repayment terms if it restructures pre-emptively.[63] Consequently, post-default restructurings are typically more litigation-prone, as no contractual default even has been triggered that would allow creditors to pursue legal action.[64]

Restructurings remain, by and large, dominated by an ad hoc process, which is devised by the sovereign in consultation with its legal and financial advisors on a case-by-case basis. This process may be coarsely divided into three different stages:[65]

- First, following the determination of debt being unsustainable during the *initiation stage*, usually through the IMF's DSA,[66] the debtor typically prepares a restructuring plan in line with the financing parameters of an IMF-supported program,[67] depending on the specific circumstances of the case.[68] In cases of exceptional access to the IMF's resources, the Fund also has to make a judgement that the restructuring 'makes the debt sustainable and is likely to be successful in the sense of attracting sufficient creditor participation and avoiding disruptive legal challenges.'[69]
- During the *negotiation stage*, private creditor committees tend to play a critical role and can influence restructurings in different – positive and negative – ways.[70] Creditors' collective objective will be to maximize the recovery on the instruments they hold, while ensuring that no fellow creditor is given more – as Buchheit et al note, 'debt restructuring is a zero-sum game.'[71]
- In the *closing stage*, the sovereign debtor seeks to maximize creditor participation and mitigate collective action (i.e., holdout creditor) problems.[72] During this phase, it will become clear whether a restructuring proposal struck the right tone and whether the government successfully employed the restructuring tools.[73] This book will focus on that closing stage and the legal problems associated with it.

1.2.3.2. Debt Restructuring Methods

1.2.3.2.1. DEBT RESTRUCTURING VERSUS DEBT RESCHEDULING

From a transactional perspective, one may broadly distinguish debt operations that reduce the face value of the instrument (*debt restructuring*) or such that amend the timetable of repayments (*debt rescheduling* or 'reprofiling'):[74]

- A debt restructuring, thus, typically includes forgiveness of (part of) the outstanding principal amount ('principal haircut').[75]
- A debt rescheduling or reprofiling usually entails the application of below-market interest rates as well as moratoriums on outstanding and forgiveness of accrued interest rates.[76]

Principal (not interest) haircuts are usually reluctantly accepted by commercial creditors, rejected by bilateral creditors,[77] and excluded vis-à-vis multilaterals, such as the World Bank or the IMF.[78] From a contractual viewpoint, however, most debt reprofilings will require the same level of creditor support (eg, super-majority in many bonded debt instruments), for they usually affect the payment terms of the debt instrument.[79]

It should also be noted that in the context of the IMF's 2016 reform of its revised Exceptional Access Policy framework,[80] debt reprofilings were introduced as an alternative to private and official debt restructurings under certain circumstances. Normally, a reprofiling would have to be undertaken before the approval of a Fund arrangement, though there may be circumstances under which more flexibility is warranted, and the conclusion of the debt operation may be delayed.[81]

1.2.3.2.2. DEBT RESTRUCTURING TECHNIQUES: STICKS AND CARROTS

The overarching goal of restructuring negotiations is to induce creditors to provide debt relief.[82] To achieve a satisfying level of participation, a balance needs to be struck between coercive and conducive measures vis-à-vis creditors, especially in large-scale bond restructurings where multiple types of investors with different incentives and interests are present.[83] To this end, sovereign issuers tend to employ a variety of legal (and financial) techniques, commonly referred to as 'sticks' and 'carrots.'[84]

- Carrots or sweeteners aim at encouraging creditor participation in an exchange of debt instruments. These tools can range from posting collateral security or collateral from creditworthy entities[85] and even cash payouts to issuing GDP-linked bonds in exchange for the old (illiquid) bonds.[86] Other carrots in bond restructurings include providing a menu of options for creditors,[87] loss reinstatement clauses,[88] or value recovery instruments.[89] In the context of restructuring bilateral or multilateral debt, such contractual techniques are of limited relevance – negotiations in more institutionalized fora, such as the Paris Club, or informal settings, such as bilateral meetings, have become the ordinary method to resolve public debt issues.[90] In those settings, moral suasion and even (geo-)political considerations regularly drive the outcome of restructurings.[91]
- Sticks involve coercive elements.[92] For instance, transactional techniques, such as exit consents,[93] threats of non-payment,[94] or minimum participation thresholds[95] allow the issuer to reduce the attractiveness of holdouts. Especially, exit consents have been the subject of much debate following two seminal judgements in English and New York courts, respectively.[96] Even though both these cases concerned corporate bond restructurings, they also influence the design of exit consents in sovereign bond restructurings and, importantly, reveal important jurisdictional differences between the world's two premier financial centres.[97] The main take-away should be that while they reduce the incidence of holdout problems, exit consents and other legal sticks are no panacea. The Argentine and Greek debt exchanges mark cautionary tales in that respect.[98]

1.2.3.3. Scope of Debt Restructurings

1.2.3.3.1. DOMESTIC VERSUS FOREIGN SOVEREIGN DEBT RESTRUCTURINGS

A perennial issue for sovereign debt restructuring is the treatment of debt governed by domestic and foreign law, respectively.[99] While countries usually incur both types of financial obligations, there may be differences in the government's decision whether and how to reduce the respective types of liabilities.[100] To that end, different factors may need to be considered. For one, the investor base for a given debt class may influence the government's decision – restructuring domestic debt that is predominantly held by local financial institutions may endanger domestic financial stability, potentially wiping out the benefits of reducing public debt levels. For another, from a legal perspective, domestic restructurings leave the issuer with more discretion since the modification of payment and other terms may be implemented unilaterally and retroactively within certain constitutional limits.[101] As discussed in Chapter 3, the Greek PSI of 2012, where most affected debt instruments were governed by local law and, thus, amenable to retroactive changes to payment terms by the sovereign, serves as a case in point.[102]

The sovereign's legal discretion stems, on the one hand, from the fact that the applicable law could offer more defences to the sovereign debtor vis-à-vis litigious creditors.[103] On the other hand, claims brought before the sovereign debtor's own court may not be justiciable given the political nature of legislative measures or there may be a risk of judicial bias in favour of the sovereign debtor.[104] By contrast, as the Argentine debt restructuring discussed in Chapter 2 suggests, a restructuring of foreign law debt may typically be challenged in foreign courts as well as international investment arbitration tribunals.[105] A country that is heavily reliant on foreign capital may, thus, reconsider exposing itself to costly litigation that could hamper its access to international debt markets for a long time.

1.2.3.3.2. CREDITOR CLASSES, RANKING, AND PRIORITY

Another critical consideration in sovereign debt restructurings pertains to the ranking of creditors: who gets paid first and how much? Domestic insolvency laws incorporate the principle that, for purposes of determining the priority of distribution, creditors should be ranked by categories but that within those categories or classes, all creditors are treated equally (pari passu).[106] In the absence of bankruptcy procedures, however, sovereign debt restructurings are not subject to a predetermined and binding ladder of creditor priorities or classes; the debtor's assets and future revenue streams are, at least theoretically, 'up for grabs.'

To ensure intercreditor equity, the contractual terms governing international sovereign bonds may stipulate that all holders of external indebtedness are generally ranked equally or that the debtor may not pledge security of any kind to other creditors.[107] Similarly, foreign sovereign loans – both such extended by official bilateral as well as private creditors – tend to be unsecured, albeit collateralized loans have become more common in the 2010s.[108] By contrast, domestic debt instruments are usually not captured by pari passu or negative pledge clauses contained in external debt instruments, allowing for a different treatment of domestic debt holders.[109]

Broadly speaking, at least two important exceptions exist to the equality of sovereign creditors:

- First, certain IFIs and multilateral creditors enjoy preferred creditor status (PCS).[110] In essence, intergovernmental international financial institutions, such as the World Bank, the IMF, or the ESM, enjoy PCS, which means that they are excluded from the sovereign debt restructuring process.[111] As quasi-lenders of last resort (LOLR), the IMF and the ESM provide financing when the majority of other, especially private, lenders are unwilling to assume the borrower's default risk.[112] In return, to safeguard their own resources and avoid debtor moral hazard, like the concept of debtor-in-possession (DIP) financing in domestic bankruptcy, the PCS is generally accepted by the international community as well as private creditors.[113]

- Second, official lenders, such bilateral lenders, or their central banks, which provide financing bilaterally, may at times insist on being treated as preferred creditors. One important example was the Eurosystem's successful insistence not to be included in the Greek PSI in 2012.[114] While the private sector has not been content with official lenders' preferential treatment in restructurings, the official sector's central role in providing concessional bilateral financing and lending on a last resort basis is widely acknowledged.[115]

Against this backdrop, it may seem surprising that the empirical literature is inconclusive on the seniority structure of sovereign debt. Schlegl et al, for instance, show that bilateral official creditors are, at least in some cases, junior to private creditors, notwithstanding the official sector's frequent assertion of seniority over private lenders.[116] However, given the lack of transparency in bilateral sovereign lending as well as rapid changes of the bilateral creditor base, significant uncertainty remains as to the allocation of losses among different creditor groups in sovereign debt restructurings.[117]

1.2.4. Holdout Creditor Problems in Sovereign Debt Restructurings

The holdout creditor problem, which I will frequently return to in the remainder of this book, refers to a situation in which a certain percentage of the creditors to a sovereign debtor refrain from the participation in a debt restructuring operation, thereby thwarting, or at least delaying, the debt resolution, or alternatively, free-riding on the restructuring process with an objective of receiving full payment.[118] Put differently, holdout inefficiencies arise when recalcitrant creditors coerce benefits from the sovereign debtor, which go beyond is generally considered fair or equitable.[119] The holdout creditor problem is, therefore, a collective action problem in which potentially rational individual action – to the extent it succeeds in blocking a solution accepted by most creditors – produces suboptimal outcomes at a group level.[120] Opportunistic creditors usually 'withhold their essential vote in hope of procuring a side payment from the transaction's proponents,'[121] free-riding on the other creditors' acceptance of the proposed debt plan.[122] The consequence is that '[holdouts] plague the readjustment of [public] debt claims, to the detriment of the creditors as well as the debtor.'[123]

Holdout creditor problems in the sovereign debt context became a major focus for policymakers in the 1990s when international sovereign bonds, often referred to as Eurobonds, replaced syndicated loans as the primary form of external commercial debt to EMEs and LICs.[124] Bondholders were much more dispersed than bank lenders, and critically, bond indentures usually did not include sharing clauses, which, in loans, ensure that any individual member of the syndicate would have to share the benefits of litigation and attachment with the whole group proportionally. However, due to concerns in the bondholder community, who opposed limiting their enforcement rights while also hoping that bonds would be restructured less frequently thank bank loans, sharing clauses never migrated to international sovereign bonds.[125]

As mentioned earlier, domestic bankruptcy laws typically resolve holdout problems by providing for majority voting across different classes of creditors and guaranteeing pari passu treatment of all (unsecured) creditors.[126] Historical evidence suggests, however, that safeguarding collective creditor action is equally paramount in the sovereign debt space to both avoiding deadweight losses for the debtor and ensuring intercreditor equity.[127] Moreover, the complex legal instruments many sovereigns rely on mean that collective action problems can arise on several levels: (i) with respect to the restructuring of individual securities, (ii) when restructurings concern other instruments than bonds, and (iii) with respect to the restructuring of the aggregate of outstanding debt instruments.[128]

Indeed, countries that have limited access to international capital markets have increasingly borrowed from a broader variety of lenders, ranging from private banks[129] and bondholders[130] to (foreign) SOEs,[131] governments,[132] and (at least indirectly) central banks.[133] Even if the number of individual creditors is smaller, their refusal to restructure may still pose obstacles to resolve the debt crisis.[134]

At the margins, whether a creditor is holding out or merely bargains hard during restructuring negotiations is not always clear-cut, especially ex ante. While trying to cast a wide net, this book will investigate cases in which holdouts have, in fact, hampered restructuring efforts or where a tangible risk exists that they may do so in the future. For instance, while hedge funds[135] and retail investors have actively engaged in holdout strategies in recent restructurings, other creditors, such as commodity traders[136] or official sector lenders,[137] have sought to extract preferential treatments in debt operations in a more subtle manner.

Regardless of the type of creditor that may engage in such tactics, holdout behaviour, if successful and widespread, may discourage a large share of sovereign creditors from agreeing to a restructuring. After all, why should they accept a rescheduling or even a write-down of their claims if others, by way of refusal to negotiate, are likely to strike a better deal down the road?[138]

This book seeks to analyse holdout creditors holistically. In a first step, it documents the role of uncooperative bondholders in the Argentine and Greek debt restructurings in Chapter 2 and Chapter 3, including an analysis of the main legal principles inherent to modern holdout litigation and arbitration in Chapter 4. In a second step, Chapter 5 advances a new genealogy of holdout creditors, extending the analysis new types of holdouts that may disrupt future debt restructurings.

1.2.5. The Evolution of Sovereign Debt Restructuring Practice

Considering the legal predicaments associated with debt workouts, it might surprise that a fair number of restructurings in the past three decades have been relatively successful in restoring debt sustainability.[139] These include Pakistan's restructuring of 1999, Belize's debt workouts of 2006–2007 and 2012–2013,[140] or Jamaica's restructuring of 2010 (at least temporarily).[141] Similarly, an IMF study on the restructuring of sovereign debt owed to commercial creditors between 2014 and 2020, finds that 'recent restructurings have generally proceeded smoothly, were largely pre-emptive, and had a shorter average duration and higher average creditor participation, mainly due to the use of CACs.'[142] These empirical findings are somewhat in tension with the more popular argument in the pertinent literature that the absence of a sovereign debt restructuring mechanism renders crisis resolution difficult.[143]

Following the infamous lost decade in Latin America during the 1980s and Mexico's Tequila crisis in 1995, the 2000s and 2010s have not seen waves of defaults but isolated cases. As Gelpern notes, by the late 1990s, 'sovereign debt restructuring was the work of a reasonably integrated regime, even if it was not recognised as such.'[144] Albeit informal in nature, the system relied heavily on cross-conditionality and negotiation sequencing.[145] Cross-conditionality was achieved by rendering debt relief by Paris Club members as well as private investors dependent on the member implementing an IMF supported program of macroeconomic reforms.[146] The Iraqi debt restructuring of 2004–2005 served as a case in point, as Paris Club debt relief was required for the successful completion of a Fund-supported program.[147]

Moreover, due the IMF's strict non-toleration policy with respect to official sector arrears and the comparability of treatment principle by the Paris Club, the success of Paris Club negotiations and emergency liquidity assistance by the Fund were closely intertwined.[148] As a result, private investors and bilateral official creditors could, or indeed had to, align their expectations to the outcome of a Paris Club deal.[149] Holdout problems flamed up occasionally when syndicated loans were restructured, but they remained a nuisance rather than a systemic issue.[150] However, the rise of sovereign *bond* financing unearthed more serious creditor coordination challenges. Challenges that had many observers worried could disrupt the resolution of future sovereign debt distress,[151] while others welcomed it as deterrence for states to default in the future.[152] At least since Argentina's 2001 bond default, the prospect of holdouts leveraging their contracts against sovereign debtors, their agents, as well as international payments and settlements providers[153] revived the architecture debate.[154]

Despite some improvements in the contractual framework in the past 30 years,[155] the existing sovereign debt architecture is still often characterized as a non-system, a term used to highlight the absence of binding rules governing the reorganization of sovereign financial liabilities.[156] Against this backdrop, a plethora of scholarly proposals has emerged on how to reform and institutionalize sovereign debt restructurings,[157] ranging from emulating Chapters 9 or 11 of the US Bankruptcy Code[158] to establishing an 'International Debt Restructuring Agency.'[159] Similarly, policymakers weighed in. Starting with the Group of 77's proposal for the creation of an International Debt Commission to the IMF's SDRM in 2002[160] and the UN's Basic Principles on Sovereign Debt Restructuring Processes of 2015, the list of reform ideas is long and diverse.[161] With some exceptions, however, intellectual efforts have far outpaced tangible reform.[162]

Private sector groups, such as the IIF, have promoted principles and standards that ought to guide sovereign debt restructurings, whilst rejecting statutory solutions.[163] The IIF has usually supported contractual reform and ad hoc negotiation frameworks. Other than initiatives of a number of governments as well as NGOs, which tend to emphasize that a sovereign nation has a 'right to restructure,'[164] private groups contend that sovereigns may only interfere with private creditors' claims as ultima ratio measure.[165]

There are two important exceptions to the ad hoc approach: the Paris Club[166] and the London Club[167] were created to institutionalize the process of sovereign debt restructuring by providing for a for negotiations between the (formerly) largest groups of creditors and government borrowers.[168]

While the Paris Club continues to coordinate official sector debt relief,[169] including in the context of initiatives such as the G20 Common Framework for Debt Treatments, the London Club has de facto seized to exist.[170] In the wake of the Brady Plan, as part of which loans were securitized and became tradeable in secondary markets, a few hundred international banks were replaced as the prime commercial creditors to sovereigns by millions of bondholders.[171] Today, private creditor coordination is largely organized through creditor committees that facilitate negotiations with sovereign debtors ahead of a restructuring.[172]

Notes

1 Compare, for an overview of sovereign debt and crises, Carmen Reinhart and Kenneth Rogoff, *This Time Is Different: Eight Centuries of Financial Folly* (Princeton: Princeton University Press, 2009).

2 For an overview of the role of sovereign debt in modern economies, see Ali Abbas, Alex Pienkowski, and Ken Rogoff (eds), *Sovereign Debt: A Guide for Economists and Practitioners* (Oxford: Oxford University Press, 2019).

3 Kevin Gallagher, 'Financial Crisis and International Investment Agreements: The Case of Sovereign Debt Restructuring' (2012) 3(3) Global Policy 362; Robert Kolb, *Sovereign Debt – From Safety to Default* (Hoboken: Wiley, 2011) 3.

4 See, for example, Mark Aguiar and Manuel Amador, 'Sovereign Debt' in Gita Gopinath, Elhanan Helpman and Kenneth Rogoff (eds), *Handbook of International Economics* (Amsterdam: Elsevier, 2014). However, as Reinhart et al show, in advanced economies, a negative correlation exists between debt-to-GDP ratios and growth; see Carmen Reinhart, Vincent Reinhart, and Kenneth Rogoff, 'Public Debt Overhangs: Advanced Economy Episodes Since 1800' (2012) 26(3) Journal of Economic Perspectives 69.

5 The Case of the S.S. 'Lotus' (*France v Turkey*), PCIJ, Series A, No 10, 18–19.

6 See IMF, 'Fiscal Monitor – Strengthening the Credibility of Public Finances' (October 2021) xi <www.imf.org/en/Publications/FM/Issues/2021/10/13/fiscal-monitor-october-2021> accessed 2 November 2021.

7 Ibid 8.

8 See Rodrigo Olivares-Caminal, 'Sovereign Debt Litigation' in Anne Peters (ed), *Max Planck Encyclopaedia of Public International Law* (Oxford: Oxford University Press, 2020).

9 Carmen Reinhart and Kenneth Rogoff, *This Time Is Different: Eight Centuries of Financial Folly* (Princeton: Princeton University Press, 2009)..

10 The Drago doctrine considered sovereign debt to be an obligation of honour that does not allow for (military) intervention to compel repayment. For a discussion, see

Holger Schier, *Towards a Reorganisation System for Sovereign Debt* (Leiden/Boston: Martinus Nijhoff Publishers, 2007) 6–7.

11 The UN Charter (Article 2(4)) stipulates that '[a]ll Members shall refrain in their international relations from the threat or use of force against the territorial integrity or political independence of any state, or in any other manner inconsistent with the Purposes of the United Nations.' See Art 2(4) Charter of the United Nations (done at San Francisco, United States, on 26 June 1945) (United Nations [UN]) 1 UNTS XVI, 59 Stat 1031, TS 993, 3 Bevans 1153, 145 BSP 805, 892 UNTS 119. Some scholars have gone as far as boiling the sovereign creditor-debtor relationship to the legal scaffolding that surrounds it; see, for example, Hayk Kupelyants, *Sovereign Defaults Before Domestic Courts* (Oxford: Oxford University Press, 2018).

12 Lee Buchheit and Mitu Gulati, 'Responsible Sovereign Lending and Borrowing' (2013) 73 Law and Contemporary Problems 63, 65. In German, the term 'debt' (*Schuld*) equates the English word 'sin,' thus implicating a (negative) moral aspect to owing money. The Greek finance minister Yanis Varoufakis has referred to this grammatical particularity in the context of the Greek debt crisis, remarking that 'here was a tendency in Germany among strong creditors to demand penitence from weak debtors for their debt-guilt and to punish them if they did not seek redemption.' See The Economist, 'As We Forgive Our Debtors' *The Economist* (London, 16 June 2015).

13 Barry Eichengreen, Asmaa El-Ganainy, Rui Pedro Esteves, and Kris James Mitchener, 'Public Debt Through the Ages' in Abbas et al (n 2) 7 et seq, noting this:

> [i]n the best of times it relaxes the domestic constraint on savings, smooths consumption, and finances investment. Investors see it as a safe haven, as delivering 'alpha,' and as a means of portfolio diversification [while] in the worst of times it is associated with debt overhangs, banking collapses, exchange-rate crises, and inflationary explosions.

14 Of course, originally, the pacta sunt servanda doctrine only refers to international treaty, as the word 'pacta' suggests. However, in scholarship, the pacta sunt servanda principle is almost used synonymously with the principle of maintenance of contracts.

15 Kelsen refers to 'sovereignty' as the 'legal authority of the States under the authority of international law.' He adds, 'a State's legal authority may said to be "supreme" insofar as it is not subjected to the legal authority of any other sates.' Consequently, 'the State's sovereignty under international law is its legal independence from other States.' Hans Kelsen, 'The Principle of Sovereign Equality of States as a Basis for International Organisation' (1944) 53(2) The Yale Law Journal 207, 208. Black's Law Dictionary defines 'sovereignty' as a 'supreme, absolute and uncontrollable power by which any independent state is governed.' See Bryan A Garner, *Black's Law Dictionary* (London: Thomson Reuters, 2014, 10th ed).

16 For an analysis of public debt and sovereign immunity, see Georges R Delaume, 'Three Perspectives on Sovereign Immunity – Public Debt and Sovereign Immunity: The Foreign Sovereign Immunities Act of 1976' (1977) 71(3) The American Journal of International Law 399.

17 For a recent analysis of the non-intervention principle in contemporary international law, compare Maziar Jamnejad and Michael Wood, 'The Principle of Non-Intervention' (2009) 22(2) Leiden Journal of International Law 345; John P Grant and J Craig Barker (eds), *Encyclopaedic Dictionary of International Law* (Oxford: Oxford University Press, 2009, 3rd ed). A more critical view is taken by Yang, who argues that the *par in parem non habet imperium* maxim has nothing to do with sovereign immunity or even international law. Rather, the maxim is one of the grounds on which Dante argues that the rule of a single person is necessary for the well-being of humankind. See Xiaodong Yang, *State Immunity in International Law* (Cambridge: Cambridge University Press, 2012) 52.

18 Schier (n 10) 6.

19 See Gregory Smith, *Where Credit Is Due: How Africa's Debt Can be a Benefit, Not a Burden* (London: Hurst Publishers, 2021).

20 The legal doctrine of sovereign immunity constitutes one of the foundational principles of inter-state relations and – reminiscent of the principle of non-intervention into domestic affairs – limits foreign judicial, executive, and legislative bodies to bind citizens in another state. Section 1.5 discusses sovereign immunity and explains in broad brushstrokes its relevance for cross-border financing.

21 See, for an in-depth study, for example, Julian Schumacher, *Enforcement in Sovereign Debt Markets* (PhD thesis, Humboldt University, Berlin 2015) unpublished manuscript.

22 Mark Wright, 'Sovereign Debt Restructuring: Problems and Prospects' (2012) 2(1) Harvard Business Law Review 166; David E Spiro, *The Hidden Hand of American Hegemony: Petrodollar Recycling and International Markets* (Ithaca: Cornell University Press, 1999).

23 However, bonds were anything but a novelty: sovereigns had issued bonds in the 18th and 19th century to finance their state activities, albeit on a far smaller scale. See, for example, Ross Buckley, 'The Facilitation of the Brady Plan: Emerging Markets Debt Trading from 1989 to 1993' (1997) 21 Fordham International Law Journal 1802, 1820–1822. Intentional or not, the shift from loan to bond financing had important implications for the holdout creditor problem. The legal specificities of a bond as multiparty debt instruments render it more vulnerable to collective action problems, especially outside the four corners of a bankruptcy system, where a third party may enforce majority voting. At the same time, bonds have a higher default risk than loans in the context of government debt. Miles instance notes that '[b]ondholders are too dispersed to negotiate with during a liquidity shortfall' and finds that 'empirical pricing of loans and bonds as assets reveals that bonds incorporate the greater risk of default into their spreads'; see William Miles, 'The Pricing of Risk in Emerging Credit Markets: Bonds versus Loans' (2000) 6(2) International Advances in Economic Research 221.

24 For empirical evidence, see Schumacher (n 21).

25 See, for example, Ran Bi, Marcos Chamon, and Jeromin Zettelmeyer, 'The Problem That Wasn't: Coordination Failures in Sovereign Debt Restructurings' (2011) IMF Working Paper No 11/265 <www.imf.org/external/pubs/ft/wp/2011/wp11265.pdf> accessed 2 November 2021.

26 See Chapter 2 'Holdout Creditor Problems and Foreign Law Debt: The Argentine Debt Restructurings in Courts and Tribunals (2001–2016).'

27 See Chapter 3 'Holdout Creditor Problems and Domestic Law Debt: The Greek Debt Restructuring in Courts and Tribunals (2012–2020).'

28 For historical background, see Kim Oosterlinck, 'Sovereign Debt Defaults: Insights from History' 29(4) Oxford Review of Economic Policy 697.

29 Olivares-Caminal (n 8) (describing default cases in Syracuse, Miletus, and Cnidus between 400–300 BC).

30 Eichengreen et al (n 13) 10 (observing that '[o]nly after 1500 were territorial states able to borrow long term').

31 Ibid 11.

32 See, for example, Mauricio Drelichmann and Hans-Joachim Voth, 'Lending to the Borrower from Hell: Debt and Default in the Age of Philip II' (2011) 121 The Economic Journal 1205. Zahavi summarizes this period as follows:

> Edward III, the King of England, repudiated his debts in 1339; the King of France went bankrupt in 1598, 1648, and 1661. Spain repudiated its debts in 1557, after borrowing heavily to pay for the wars of the sixteenth century. And revolutionary France suspended its payments on foreign obligations in 1793 and annulled two-thirds of its domestic and foreign debt in 1797.

See Netanella Tani Zahavi, *Sovereign Debt: Analyses and Remedies* (PhD thesis, 2005) 14, unpublished manuscript (on file with author).

33 Michael Tomz and Mark Wright, 'Empirical Research on Sovereign Debt and Default' (2013) 5 Annual Review of Economics 247.

34 Zahavi (n 32) 32.

35 Tim Strickland, 'Sovereign Debt Restructuring: Recent Issues and Reforms' (2014) Reserve Bank of Australia Bulletin, December – Quarter 73 <www.rba.govau/publications/bulletin/2014/dec/pdf/bu-1214-9.pdf> accessed 2 November 2021 (These countries are Argentina (2005, 2010), Belize (2007, 2013), Cameroon (2005), Dominica (2004), Dominican Republic (2005), Ecuador (2009), Greece (2012), Grenada (2005), Côte d'Ivoire (2010, 2012), Jamaica (2010, 2013), Nicaragua (2008), Paraguay (2004), Seychelles (2010), and St Kitts and Nevis (2012).) More recent data shows that between 2014 and 2020, 13 individual sovereign restructurings by 9 different governments were executed. See IMF, 'The International Architecture for Resolving Sovereign Debt Involving Private-Sector Creditors – Recent Developments, Challenges, Reform Options' (2020), IMF Policy Papers <www.imf.org/en/Publications/Policy-Papers/Issues/2020/09/30/The-International-Architecture-for-Resolving-Sovereign-Debt-Involving-Private-Sector-49796> accessed 2 November 2021.

36 Those countries took different approaches in negotiating with their creditors. Some resolved their sovereign debt crisis with surprising ease, such as in the case of Cameroon, whilst others – as evidenced by this thesis on the Argentine restructuring – fight court battles for over a decade against their lenders. See Paris Club, 'Annual Report 2008' 14 <www.clubdeparis.org/sections/communication/rapport-annuel-d/annual-report-2008/downloadFile/file/AnnualReport2008.pdf> accessed 2 November 2021.

37 See IMF (n 35) 8 (including Argentina (2020), Barbados (2019), Belize (2017), Chad (2018), Ecuador (2020), Grenada (2015), Mongolia (2017), Mozambique (2019), and Ukraine (2015)).

38 United Nations (UN), 'COVID-19 and Sovereign Debt' (14 May 2020) UN Department of Economic and Social Affairs (DESA) Policy Brief No 72 <www.un.org/development/desa/dpad/publication/un-desa-policy-brief-72-covid-19-and-sovereign-debt/> accessed 2 November 2021.

39 Odette Lienau, 'The Longer-Term Consequences of Sovereign Debt Restructuring' in Rosa Lastra and Lee Buchheit (eds), *Sovereign Debt Management* (Oxford: Oxford University Press, 2014) 99.

40 Andrew Powell, 'Bipolar Debt Restructuring: Lessons from LAC' (*Vox Lacea*, 24 February 2017) <http://vox.lacea.org/?q=debt-lessons-LAC> accessed 2 November 2021.

41 This said, the volume of sovereign debt in default has generally decreased since the Greek restructuring of 2012. See David Beers, Elliot Jones, and John Walsh, 'Database of Sovereign Defaults, 2020 (June 2020) Bank of Canada Technical Report No 13 <www.bankofcanada.ca/wp-content/uploads/2020/06/san2020-13.pdf> accessed 2 November 2021.

42 Yuefen Li, Rodrigo Olivares-Caminal, and Ugo Panizza, 'Avoiding Debt Crises: Lessons from Recent Default' in Carlos Braga and Gallina Vincelette (eds), *Sovereign Debt and the Financial Crisis* (Washington, DC: The World Bank, 2011) 245.

43 Annamaria Viterbo, *Sovereign Debt Restructuring: The Role and Limits of Public International Law* (Turin: Giappichelli, 2020) 2.

44 Kupelyants (n 11) 86.

45 Most sovereign bond contracts contain majority action provisions, which provide that a (super-)majority of bondholders can override a minority of holdouts.

46 For a standard event of default clause in an international sovereign bond, see United Mexican States, 'USD 110,000,000,000, Global Medium-Term Notes, Series A' (*Base Prospectus*, 3 February 2016) <www.bourse.lu/programme/Programme-Mexico/2395> accessed 2 November 2021.

47 See, for example, IMF, 'Staff Guidance Note for Public Debt Sustainability Analysis in Market-Access Countries' (May 9, 2013) IMF Policy Papers 4 <www.imf.org/external/np/pp/eng/2013/050913.pdf> accessed 2 November 2021. The ECB has a slightly different definition, according to which, a sovereign may be considered solvent when the net present value (NPV) of the government's future primary balances is at least as high as the NPV of outstanding government debt (flow concept) or when the present value of liabilities is smaller than the present value of asset (stock concept). See ECB, 'Debt Sustainability Analysis for Euro Area Sovereigns: A Methodological Framework' (April 2017) Occasional Paper Series No 185, 8 <www.ecb.europa.eu/pub/pdf/scpops/ecbop185.en.pdf?abccaa198c0d791777fe3dfb148873f5> accessed 2 November 2021 (also pointing at the important role the government's liquidity situation plays in avoiding market hysteria and thus ensuring debt sustainability).

48 See Julianne Ams, Reza Baqir, Anna Gelpern, and Christoph Trebesch, 'Sovereign Default' in Abbas et al (n 2) 275–327.

49 Moreover, different institutions may have recourse to different methodologies to assess debt sustainability. This has become particularly evident in the wake of the Greek debt crisis, where the IMF and Europe reached remarkably divergent conclusions in regard to the sustainability of Greek public debt. See, for example, Julian Schumacher and Beatrice Weder di Mauro, 'Diagnosing Greek Debt Sustainability: Why Is It so Hard?' (Fall 2015) Brookings Papers on Economic Activity 280 <www.brookings.edu/wp-content/uploads/2016/06/SchumacherTextFall15BPEA.pdf> accessed 2 November 2021.

50 See IMF, 'Debt Sustainability Analysis' (November 2015) <www.imf.org/external/pubs/ft/dsa/> accessed 2 November 2021. However, the Fund itself acknowledges that the line between liquidity and solvency is inherently blurry, noting that '[i]n practice, a clear-cut distinction between solvency and liquidity risks is impossible, since borrowing costs and market access depend on (actual and perceived) solvency.' See IMF, 'Review of the Debt Sustainability Framework for Market Access Countries' (February 2021) IMF Policy Papers <www.imf.org/en/Publications/Policy-Papers/Issues/2021/02/03/Review-of-The-Debt-Sustainability-Framework-For-Market-Access-Countries-50060?> accessed 2 November 2021.

51 See IMF, 'Sovereign Debt Restructuring – Recent Developments and Implications for the Fund's Legal and Policy Framework' (26 April 2013) 12 <www.imf.org/external/np/pp/eng/2013/042613.pdf> accessed 2 November 2021; IMF, 'Review of the Debt Sustainability Framework for Market Access Countries' (n 50) 6. The Fund also distinguishes between debt sustainability for low-income countries and for countries with access to international debt markets, given that different econometric methods and assumptions are required to factor in different stages of economic and financial development. For low-income countries, see 'Joint World Bank-IMF Debt Sustainability Framework for Low-Income Countries' (17 March 2021) Factsheet <www.imf.org/en/About/Factsheets/Sheets/2016/08/01/16/39/Debt-Sustainability-Framework-for-Low-Income-Countries> accessed 2 November 2021.

52 See Sean Hagan, 'Sovereign Debt Restructuring: The Centrality of the IMF's Role' (July 2020) Peterson Institute for International Economics Working Paper 20–13 <www.piie.com/system/files/documents/wp20-13.pdf> accessed 2 November 2021.

53 Marcus Miller and Dania Thomas, 'Eurozone Sovereign Debt Restructuring: Keeping the Vultures at Bay' (2013) 29(4) Oxford Review of Economic Policy 745.

54 See Viterbo (n 43) 90–103 for background on the Paris Club.

55 See, for example, the Common Framework for Debt Treatments beyond the Debt Service Suspension Initiative (DSSI), an agreement of the G20 and the Paris Club to coordinate debt treatments for low-income countries. It includes both Paris Club members as well as non-Paris Club G20 creditors, notably China, India, and Saudi Arabia. For an overview, see IMF, 'Questions and Answers on Sovereign Debt

Issues' (8 April 2021) <www.imf.org/en/About/FAQ/sovereign-debt> accessed 2 November 2021.

56 The Paris Club usually requires comparability of treatment between official and private sector debt restructurings, which it defines as follows:

> A debtor country that signs an agreement with its Paris Club creditors should not accept from its non-Paris Club commercial and bilateral creditors terms of treatment of its debt less favourable to the debtor than those agreed with the Paris Club.

See Club de Paris, 'The Six Principles' (2016) <www.clubdeparis.org/en/communications/page/the-six-principles> accessed 2 November 2021.

57 See, for a discussion, for example, Viterbo (n 43) 199 et seq.

58 The IIF was founded in 1983, and according to its bylaws, it is 'committed to being the most influential global association of financial institutions.' See Institute of International Finance (IIF), 'By-Laws' (January 2020) <www.iif.com/Portals/0/Files/general/2020_IIF_Bylaws.pdf?ver=2020-02-27-151109-237> accessed 2 November 2021. At first, though, the IIF was mere a data hub. In 1983, the IMF's Deputy Counsel noted that 'the IIF could provide a forum [to coordinate major commercial banks], although . . . the indented function of this institute is only to act as a clearinghouse for information on the position of debtor countries.' See Rea F Graeme, 'Restructuring Sovereign Debt' (1983) 77 American Society of International Law Proceedings 312, 316. By 2019, the IIF was considered by some the 'most powerful lobby group in the world.' See Jasper Blom, 'What We Can Learn from the Institute of International Finance' (*Open Democracy*, 24 January 2019) <www.opendemocracy.net/en/banking-on-public-power-what-we-can-learn-from-institute-of-international-finance/> accessed 2 November 2021.

59 Anna Gelpern, 'Sovereign Debt: Now What' (2016) 41(2) Yale Journal of International Law Online 45.

60 Procedural principles are as follows: the creditor takes the initiative to restructure and submits to a global negotiation, and all parties agree to negotiate in good faith. Regarding the substantive principles, restructurings should be guided by the following principles: debt relief, original terms restored in the event of a default, the PCS of IFIs; equal burden sharing among creditors in the same group; elaboration of an adjustment plan under the auspices of the IMF. See Mauro Megliani, *Sovereign Debt: Genesis, Restructuring, Litigation* (Berlin: Springer, 2015) 252.

61 See, for the content of such restructuring proposal, for example, Lee Buchheit, Guillaume Chabert, Chanda DeLong, and Jeromin Zettelmeyer, 'How to Restructure Sovereign Debt: Lessons from Four Decades' in Abbas et al (n 2), explaining this:

> [t]he sovereign debtor, as the party seeking to modify the terms of its existing debt contracts, is responsible for preparing proposals – often captioned as indicative restructuring scenarios – that lay out both the overall quantum of debt relief the sovereign will be seeking from private creditors as well as the methods (haircuts, maturity extensions, coupon adjustments, etc.) used to convey that relief.

The Greek PSI of 2012 was a pre-default restructuring, while the Argentine restructurings of 2005 and 2010 were post-default deals. While the Argentine operation resulted in significantly more (and more successful) legal challenges, Greece, too, was sued by domestic and foreign investors, as Chapter 3 and Chapter 4 explain in more detail.

62 See Tamon Asonuma and Christoph Trebesch, 'Sovereign Debt Restructuring: Preemptive or Post-Default' (2016) 14(1) Journal of the European Economic Association 175 (describing different types of restructurings).

63 For an overview, see Ams et al (n 48).

64 The lawsuits covered in Chapter 2 and Chapter 3 in the context of the Argentine and the Greek debt restructurings were all initiated post-default.

65 Hagan (n 52).

66 See IMF (n 50).

67 According to the IMF, the 'DSA also plays the essential role of determining the envelope of financial resources that is available for debt service payments to official and private creditors by charting out the program's medium-term paths for key macroeconomic, policy, and financing variables.' See IMF 'Sovereign Debt Restructuring – Recent Developments and Implications for the Fund's Legal and Policy Framework' (n 51) 8.

68 Negotiations with the official sector will usually precede those with commercial creditors since the Paris Club requires at least comparable treatment between official and private sector debt relief. Hagan (n 52) notes in this context that 'private creditors have generally relied on the IMF's assessment of the limits of economic adjustments and, by extension, the residual amount of financing to be borne by creditors in the form of debt relief.'

69 See IMF, 'Sovereign Debt Restructuring – Recent Developments and Implications for the Fund's Legal and Policy Framework' (n 51) 8.

70 See Buchheit et al (n 61) 9 (noting that committees can help address coordination problems and influence the collective bargaining power of creditors but may also reduce the debtor's flexibility to deal with heterogenous creditors).

71 Ibid.

72 Hagan (n 52):

> [w]hile this free rider or 'collective action' problem has always existed, its dimensions have grown over the past 30 years because of the changing composition of the creditor community and, in particular, the shift from bank credit to sovereign bonds, the holders of which not only are numerous but also have diverse interests.

73 See Chapter 1.2.3.2. 'Debt Restructuring Methods.'

74 Compare Buchheit et al (n 61) 344, noting this:

> the IMF endorsed the use of a reprofiling technique in 2016 for cases of exceptional access to Fund resources, when debt is not sustainable with a high probability, since reprofiling shifts the maturities of these debts outside the period of the IMF program.

Also see, for a comprehensive overview of debt restructuring procedures at the international level, Charlotte Rault, *The Legal Framework of Sovereign Debt Management* (Berlin: Nomos, 2017).

75 See, for example, Alison Wirtz, 'Bilateral Investment Treaties, Holdout Investors, and Their Impact on Grenada's Sovereign Debt Crisis' (2015) 16(1) Chicago Journal of International Law 249, 253.

76 See, for an overview, for example, Rodrigo Olivares-Caminal, *Legal Aspects of Sovereign Debt Restructuring* (London: Sweet & Maxwell, 2009). Also compare Joana Dreger, 'Why Is Sovereign Debt Restructuring a Challenge? The Case of Greece' (2012) Bruges European Economic Policy Briefings 24/2012, 21 <http://aei.pitt.edu/58456/> accessed 2 November 2021. While debt reschedulings are typically NPV-neutral, they may also entail losses to the instrument's present value.

77 For an overview of different contractual techniques, see, for example, Buckley (n 23). Of course, in the absence of strict legal definitions, some authors also consider 'sovereign debt restructuring' an umbrella term that comprises NPV cuts and reschedulings. For instance, China has traditionally refused reductions in principal payments and instead favoured rescheduling by increasing the repayment period; see Kevin Acker, Deborah Brautigam, and Yufan Huang, 'Debt Relief with Chinese Characteristics' (June 2020) SAIS-CARI Working Paper Series No 39 <https://static1.squarespace.com/static/5652847de4b033f56d2bdc29/t/603533452 59d4448e01a37d8/1614099270470/WP+39+-+Acker%2C+Brautigam%2C+Huang+-+Debt+Relief.pdf> accessed 2 November 2021.

78 Given that the international creditor community respects the PCS, several multilaterals enjoy that their claims are de facto excluded from sovereign debt restructuring; see Buchheit et al (n 61) 11–12. However, there are examples in which multilateral lenders have agreed to debt reprofiling, such as the EFSF medium-term debt relief in 2018 that extended the average maturity of all multilateral loans by ten years from 32.5 to 42.5 years; see ESM, 'Explainer on EFSF Medium-Term Debt Relief Measures for Greece' (*Press Release*, 22 November 2018) <www.esm.europa.eu/press-releases/explainer-efsf-medium-term-debt-relief-measures-greece> accessed 2 November 2021.

79 For instance, in a bilateral or a private syndicated *loan*, an extension of maturities as part of a debt reprofiling will typically require consent by all affected creditors. Similarly, in a *bond* restructuring supported by majority action provisions, the reprofiling will require the same share of bondholders to vote in favour of a deal as a restructuring (haircut) since standard provisions do not differentiate between maturity extensions and reductions of principal or coupon payments. See, for example, Mexico's sovereign bond prospectus governed by New York law, which include CACs that require a (super-)majority of noteholders to approve any amendments to maturity date, interest rate, and other payment terms; United Mexican States (n 46).

80 See IMF, 'The Fund's Lending Framework and Sovereign Debt – Further Considerations' (April 2015) <www.imf.org/~/media/Websites/IMF/Imported/external/np/pp/eng/2015/_040915pdf.ashx> accessed 2 November 2021. The Fund justifies this approach by noting that '[a]lthough a reprofiling is a form of debt restructuring, it was recognized that, in these circumstances, it will likely be less costly to the debtor, the creditors, and the system than a definitive debt restructuring.'

81 Ibid 53–54 (noting that '[i]n three pre-default cases (Jamaica 2010 and 2013; Greece 2012), prior actions were established requiring the authorities to finalize the debt restructuring before approval of the arrangement').

82 Lee Buchheit, 'Sovereign Debt Restructuring: The Legal Context' (2013) BIS Papers No 72 – Sovereign Risk: A World Without Risk-Free Assets? Proceedings of a Seminar on Sovereign Risk Including Contributions by Central Bank Governors and Other Policy-Makers, Market Practitioners and Academics, Basel, 8–9 January 2013.

83 For a case study of the Argentine 2020 debt restructuring, see Andres De La Cruz and Ignacio Lagos, 'CACs at Work: What Next? Lessons from the Argentine and Ecuadorian 2020 Debt Restructurings' (2021) 16(2) Capital Markets Law Journal 226.

84 See Bi et al (n 25) 3. Sticks and carrots are typically used *before* holdout problems emerge and are, hence, not the focus of this book. Nonetheless, given their practical importance, they must not be ignored.

85 Ibid.

86 See, for an overview, Lee Buchheit and Elena Daly, 'Minimising Holdout Creditors: Carrots' in Lastra and Buchheit (n 39) 3–13. In the Greek debt restructuring part of the exchanged debt instruments are GDP-linked notes, which promise additional coupon payments in the event of economic stabilization.

87 A menu of options gives creditors the ability to choose restructuring options, all of which can be calibrated so as to have an equivalent net present value at the time the restructuring closes; see ibid 6.

88 Loss reinstatement features provide that if a debtor government were to restructure its bonds again in the (near) future, some or all of the principal amount that was forgiven in the first round will be reinstated. In other words, the debt relief provided by the creditors to the debtor will be reversed, providing a powerful incentive for the government to avoid another restructuring. Loss reinstatement was, for instance, used in Ecuador (2000), Seychelles (2010), St Kitts and Nevis (2012), and Belize (2013). See Lee Buchheit, Guillaume Chabert, Chanda DeLong, and Jeromin Zettelmeyer in Abbas et al (n 2) 348.

89 Ibid.

90 There are, of course, exceptions, such as Russia's refusal to settle its debt dispute with Ukraine within the Paris Club framework in 2015. See, for more details, Chapter 5.3. 'Official Sector Holdouts.'

91 For the role of moral suasion in debt restructurings, see IMF, 'Issues in Restructuring of Sovereign Domestic Debt' (November 2021) <www.imf.org/-/media/Files/Publications/PP/2021/English/PPEA2021071.ashx> accessed 2 November 2021.

92 Buchheit et al (n 61).

93 See, for example, Bi et al (n 25):

> 'Exit consents' refer to changes in the non-payment terms of the bonds, such as cross default, listing, and acceleration clauses, which can typically be undertaken with a simple majority of bondholders. These changes destroy value by impairing the liquidity and litigation prospects associated with a particular bond, and hence make it less attractive for creditors to hold out.

94 A threat of non-payment is usually the bluntest measure that a sovereign issuer may take. While threats of outright default have become rare, they may be used at an early stage of the negotiations to set the stage and indicate that the government considers that a deep restructuring is necessary. To be sure, actual non-payment usually provides (commercial) creditors with the right to accelerate payment of interest and principal, declare a cross-default, and ultimately sue the issuer.

95 These thresholds condition the exchange to a critical level of creditor participation. This reassured creditors that a successful exchange would improve the debtor's finances and achieve a measure of burden-sharing, while also raising the spectre of generalized default if participation fell short. See Gelpern (n 59) 62.

96 See *Assenagon Asset Management SA v Irish Bank Resolution Corp Ltd* (formerly Anglo Irish Bank Corp Ltd), 27 July 2012, United Kingdom; England and Wales; High Court [EWHC] 2090; Chancery Division [ChD]. In this case, it was found that where an issuer sought to amend existing bonds in a manner that would substantially destroy their value in order to persuade noteholders to exchange such existing bonds, the resolution passed by the majority bondholders to amend the bonds was invalid. For background, see, for example, Keegan S Drake, 'The Rise and Fall of Exit Consents' (2014) 64 Duke Law Journal 1589 (reviewing the Delaware case *Katz v Oak Industries*, which adopted a more deferential approach towards exit consents, and *Assenagon*, and proposing a framework to reconcile the two cases). Also see Kupelyants (n 11) 255 (noting that the court has taken a non-interventionist approach by extending the application of a disenfranchisement clause to beneficial holders of bonds not only in a proprietary sense but also in an economic sense). By contrast, the *Marblegate* judgment by the Second Circuit Court of Appeals in 2017 confined the scope of Section 316(b) of the US Trust Indenture Act to formal amendments to core payment terms. For an in-depth analysis of the judgment and its implications, see Marcel Kahan, 'The Scope of Section 316(b) After *Marblegate*' (2018) 13(2) Capital Markets Law Journal 136, concluding this:

> The different degree of protection afforded to minority bondholders with respect to changes in core payment terms under US (stronger) and English (weaker) law and drafting conventions relate to the different degrees of protection afforded under US (weaker) and English (stronger) law and drafting conventions against coercive exit consents.

97 For a discussion of the current state of exit consents, see Isabelle Sawhney, 'The Hidden Law Guiding the Sovereign's Use of Exit Consents' (27 April 2019) SSRN <https://papers.ssrn.com/sol3/papers.cfm?abstract_id=3363957> accessed 2 November 2021 (proposing 'two situations that may be the tipping point for permissible strategies: When bondholders are left with no practical ability to receive payment, and when core payment terms are amended').

98 By contrast, financial incentives (i.e., carrots) have become a common feature in sovereign debt restructurings, affecting negotiation dynamics and outcomes.

99 See, among others, IMF (n 35) 28 (noting that 'the perennial issue of information asymmetry and lack of clarity on the perimeter of and treatment of claims in the debt restructuring continues to add friction to restructurings').

100 For instance, domestic law debt may be reduced through other means than restructurings; see Carmen Reinhart and Kenneth Rogoff, 'The Forgotten History of Domestic Debt' (2011) 121(552) The Economic Journal 319.

101 See, for example, Kupelyants (n 11); Mitu Gulati and Lee Buchheit, 'Use of the Local Law Advantage in the Restructuring of European Sovereign Bonds' (2018) 3(2) University of Bologna Law Review 172.

102 See, for an overview of the post-PSI litigation in Greece, Sebastian Grund, 'Restructuring Government Debt Under Local Law: The Greek Case and Implications for Investor Protection in Europe' (2017) 12(2) Capital Markets Law Journal 253. Also see, for an analysis of the local law advantage in future restructurings, Yannis Manuelides, 'Using the Local Law Advantage in Today's Eurozone (with Some References to the Republic of Arcadia and the *Mamatas* Judgment)' (2019) 14(4) Capital Markets Law Journal 469. Barbados's 2018 domestic debt restructuring essentially copied the Greek approach and retrofitted a statutory voting mechanism into domestic law bonds. See Anthony Myrvin, Gregorio Impavido, and Bert van Selm, 'Barbados' 2018–19 Sovereign Debt Restructuring – A Sea Change?' (February 2020) IMF Working Paper No. 20/34 <www.imf.org/en/Publications/WP/Issues/2020/02/21/Barbados-201819-Sovereign-Debt-RestructuringA-Sea-Change-49044> accessed 2 November 2021. Barbados also used a novel exit consent strategy for the restructuring of its foreign law loans. Also see Andrew Shutter, 'Barbados Sovereign Debt Restructuring 2018–2019 – Like the Island, Small but Perfectly Formed' (2020) 15(2) Capital Markets Law Journal 250 (noting that the Barbados restructuring was the 'first use in the Caribbean of local law legislation to introduce a class voting system across existing local law sovereign bonds'). Also see IMF (n 91) 15.

103 The fact that the Greek Constitution as well as the ECHR allowed the government to interfere with creditors' property, even if only under narrowly circumscribed limits, affords anecdotal evidence. See Decision 1116–1117/2014 (21.3.14) of the Greek Council of State; *Mamatas v Greece,* App No 63066/14, App No 64297/14, App No 66106/14, 21st July 2016, European Court of Human Rights [ECHR]. For a discussion, see Ioannis Glinavos, 'Casenote – Decision 1116–1117/2014 (21.3.14) of the Greek Council of State (Συμβούλιο της Επικρατείας)' (2014) unpublished manuscript <www.academia.edu/23043745/Casenote_Decision_1116-1117_2014_21.3.14_of_the_Greek_Council_of_State_> accessed 2 November 2021; Dimitris Tsibanoulis and Iakovos Anagnostopoulos, 'The Greek PSI and the Litigation Surrounding It' (2014) 2 International Review of Financial Services 18 (noting that the Greek Council of State, the highest administrative court in the land, in its decision 1116/2014 published on March 31 2014 and addressing some of the petitions for the annulment of the PSI, upheld the legality of the [debt restructuring] programme); Manuelides (n 102) (shows that the ECtHR held that the Greek PSI was proportionate).

104 Olivares-Caminal (n 76) 17 (pointing to the examples of Greek and Argentina, where domestic courts were reluctant to entertain foreign bondholders' challenges against public measures to avert default).

105 This said, domestic debt restructurings may, too, be challenged before international investment arbitration tribunals. See later for the case of Greece in Chapter 3.6. 'Holdout Arbitration After Greece.'

106 IMF, 'Orderly & Effective Insolvency Procedures' 1999 <www.imf.org/external/pubs/ft/orderly/> accessed 2 November 2021.

107 International sovereign bonds (i.e., bonds issued or guaranteed by a government or central bank under a law other than the law of the issuer (or where a foreign court has

jurisdiction over claims arising under the bond)) are, in most instances, unsecured, and the sovereign covenants to treat all holders of such bonds equally (pari passu), regardless as to the issuance date or nature of the holder. A standard pari passu clause in a New York law governed sovereign bond reads as follows:

> The global bonds will rank equally in right of payment with all other indebtedness issued in accordance with the fiscal agency agreement and with all other unsecured and unsubordinated Indebtedness of Panama, but Panama will have no obligation to effect equal or ratable payment or payments at any time with respect to any such other Indebtedness and, in particular, will have no obligation to pay other Indebtedness at the same time or as a condition of paying sums due on the global bonds and vice versa.

See Republic of Panama, 'USD 1,250,000,000 4.000% Global Bonds Due 2024' Prospectus Supplement (15 September 2014) <www.sec.gov/Archives/edgar/data/76027/000119312514344533/d788677d424b5.htm> accessed 2 November 2021. To be sure, differences may exist between domestic law and foreign law loans and bonds: while the local law advantage confers more discretion on the issuer to differentiate between different classes of creditors, foreign law instruments usually contain pari passu clauses. For the definition of 'international sovereign bonds,' see IMF, 'Progress Report on Inclusion of Enhanced Contractual Provisions in International Sovereign Bond Contracts' (March 2015) IMF Staff Report <www.imf.org/external/np/pp/eng/2015/091715.pdf> accessed 2 November 2021. Also see Lee Buchheit, 'The Search for Intercreditor Parity' (2002) 8(1) Law and Business Review of the Americas 73 and Rodrigo Olivares-Caminal, 'The definition of indebtedness and the consequent imperilling of the *pari passu*, negative pledge and cross default clauses in sovereign debt instruments' (2017) 12(2) Capital Markets Law Journal 164.

108 Notably, African sovereigns have begun to conclude loans with commodity traders, in which assets, physical commodities, or future revenue streams are pledged as collateral in the event of default. See IMF (n 35) (noting that '[t]he enforceability of collateral depends on the type of collateral and the governing law of the jurisdiction where it is located').

109 See Reinhart and Rogoff (n 100).

110 From an economic viewpoint, a higher ranking usually results in a higher recovery value or a complete carve-out from a debt restructuring. Given the absence of codified sovereign bankruptcy rules, whether a (multilateral) creditor has de facto or de jure PCS very much depends on the contract and practice. However, there may also be instances in which private creditors are legally preferred to official creditors; for example, if the private instrument is collateralized or otherwise secured and provides the private creditor with special and preferred access to the sovereign's assets. See, for a recent paper on IFIs' PCS in Tito Cordella and Andrew Powell, 'Preferred and Non-Preferred Creditors' (2021) 132 Journal of International Economics 1.

111 Note, however, that the IMF's de facto PCS is, for instance, reflected in the ESM Treaty, which, in Recital (13), stipulates that 'Heads of State or Government have stated that the ESM loans will enjoy preferred creditor status in a similar fashion to those of the IMF, while accepting preferred creditor status of the IMF over the ESM.' See Treaty Establishing the European Stability Mechanism (European Union [EU], Brussels 2 February 2012).

112 According to Cordella and Powell (n 110) 18, '[IFIs'] critical characteristic is that they can commit to lend at the risk-free interest rate and they can credibly limit the amount they lend; this is what makes lending at the risk-free interest rate sustainable.'

113 DIP lenders provide funding after the commencement of bankruptcy procedures, and given the risk they incur by lending to a bankrupt entity, they have a high statutory ranking than other (unsecured) creditors. On the international plane, there are two key

reasons for conveying preferential treatment to official sector lenders: (i) these lenders will often continue provide funds when sovereigns have lost access to other sources of (private) financing, and (ii) official sector loans are usually made on a concessional basis. For an in-depth discussion of the PCS at the sovereign finance level, see, for example, Annamaria Viterbo, 'Supranational Creditors: A Threat to the Equal Status of Bondholders?' (2015) 10(2) Capital Markets Law Journal 193.

114 At the same time, official sector lenders may provide financing not only via loans but (indirectly) through the purchase of foreign sovereign bonds traded on the secondary market. As a result, they are bound to the same contractual framework as other private creditors, which renders it difficult from a transactional perspective to separate sovereign holdings from private holdings for the purpose of granting preferential treatment. Moreover, private creditors may challenge PCS treatment of sovereigns that have acquired bonds that belong to the same pool and are governed by the same contractual framework. See IMF, 'Reforming the Fund's Policy on Non-Toleration of Arrears to Official Creditors' (2015) IMF Policy Papers <www.imf.org/external/np/pp/eng/2015/101515.pdf> accessed 2 November 2021.

115 See, for example, Tito Cordella and Andrew Powell, 'Preferred and Non-Preferred Creditors' (March 2021) IDB Working Paper Series 1215 <https://publications.iadb.org/publications/english/document/Preferred-and-Non-Preferred-Creditors.pdf> accessed 2 November 2021.

116 Schlegl et al find that a pecking order has emerged in last three decades that puts the IMF and multilateral creditors first, bondholders second, bank creditors third, and trade creditors last. See Matthias Schlegl, Christoph Trebesch, and Mark Wright, 'Sovereign Debt Repayments: Evidence on Seniority' (*VoxEU*, 11 August 2015) <http://voxeu.org/article/sovereign-debt-repayments-evidence-seniority> accessed 2 November 2021. However, as Steinkamp and Westermann show, granting seniority to official sector lenders may 'crowd-out' private sector creditors, thereby increasing the interest rates of countries with a large stock of debt owned by senior creditors. Sven Steinkamp and Frank Westermann, 'The Role of Creditor Seniority in Europe's Sovereign Debt Crisis' (2014) 29(79) Economic Policy 495.

117 See, for example, Sebastian Horn, Carmen Reinhart, and Chrisoph Trebesch, 'Hidden Defaults' (2022) World Bank Policy Research Working Paper No 9925 <https://openknowledge.worldbank.org/bitstream/handle/10986/36965/Hidden-Defaults.pdf?sequence=1&isAllowed=y> accessed 2 April 2022 (showing that between 2000 and 2019, China has rarely agreed to debt restructurings with face value reductions when compared to the Paris Club or private creditors and usually only extended maturities).

118 Lee Buchheit has described the nature of the 'problem' that arises when certain creditors hold out:

> [i]t is only by virtue of the indulgence shown by the majority of creditors that the sovereign [debtor] has the money to pay-or settle on preferential terms-the claims of the more exacting few. This resentment can be aggravated where the [vulture fund] bought [its] claim on the secondary market at a small fraction of its face value, while the original [creditors] advanced 100 cents on the dollar. It is like giving up your seat on a crowded bus to an elderly woman only to watch a teenager jump on it.

See, for the quote, Jill Fisch and Caroline Gentile, 'Vultures or Vanguards: The Role of Litigation in Sovereign Debt Restructuring' (2004) 53(1) Emory Law Journal 1047, 1093. The IMF describes the holdout creditor problem as follows:

> even if creditors as a group recognize that it is in their best interests to agree to a restructuring as soon as possible, individual creditors may be incentivized not to participate ('hold out') in the hope of recovering payment on the full contractual

> claim. If the perceived holdout risk is significant, creditors who would otherwise have agreed to participate in a restructuring may be unwilling to do so for inter-creditor equity and liability reasons. Full payment of these holdout creditors would also reduce the sovereign's available resources to pay the restructured creditors, thus undermining a negotiated settlement by further increasing the incentive to hold out. This coordination failure can, therefore, lead to a disorderly restructuring despite it being in the creditors' collective best interest to reach a smooth and negotiated agreement.

See IMF, 'Strengthening the Contractual Framework to Address Collective Action Problems in Sovereign Debt Restructuring' (2014), IMF Policy Papers 12 <www.imf.org/external/np/pp/eng/2014/090214.pdf> accessed 2 November 2021.

119 Richard Euliss, 'The Feasibility of the IMF's Sovereign Debt Restructuring Mechanism: An Alternative Statutory Approach to Mollify American Reservations' (2003) 19(1) American University International Law Review 107, 121.

120 See Mancur Olson, *The Logic of Collective Action: Public Goods and the Theory of Groups* (Cambridge: Harvard University Press, 1965). In the economic and political sciences literature, the term 'collective action problem' generally describes a situation in which 'rationally acting self-interested individuals generate an outcome damaging their interests as a group.' Compare Lisa Brahms, 'Legitimacy of Global Governance of Sovereign Default: The Role of International Investment Agreements' (2013) Working Papers by the Center for International Political Economy No 16, 2 <www.polsoz.fu-berlin.de/polwiss/forschung/oekonomie/ipoe/index.html> accessed 2 November 2021. Applied to (sovereign) debt restructurings, it implies that potential gains for individual creditors to defect from a debt workout may be higher than acting in line with the collective of creditors.

121 As Roubini and Setser remark, '[e]very individual creditor would be better off if it got paid in full while other creditors bore the burden of the restructuring.' Nouriel Roubini and Brad Setser, *Bailouts or Bail-Ins? Responding to Financial Crises in Emerging Economies* (Washington, DC: Peterson Institute for International Economics, 2004) 292. Similarly, Bratton contends that the incentive to hold out arises from the fact that a debt restructuring 'makes the bondholders better off as a group.' See William W Bratton, 'Pari Passu and a Distressed Sovereign's Rational Choices' (2004) 53 Emory Law Journal 823, 829.

122 For holdout problems in corporate debt restructurings, see Eric Posner and Glen Weyl, 'A Solution to the Collective Action Problem in Corporate Reorganization' (2013) University of Chicago Coase-Sandor Institute for Law & Economics Research Paper No 653 <https://papers.ssrn.com/sol3/papers.cfm?abstract_id=2321904> accessed 2 November 2021 (arguing that even in the corporate context, collective action problems pose serious obstacles to equitable outcomes of debt restructuring operations under Chapter 11 of the US Bankruptcy Code). For sovereign restructurings, see Christopher Wheeler and Amir Attaran, 'Declawing the Vulture Funds: Rehabilitation of a Comity Defense in Sovereign Debt Litigation' (2003) 39 Stanford Journal of International Law 253, 253 (analysing the policy solution to resolve collective action problem in the sovereign lending context); Anne Krueger, *A New Approach to Sovereign Debt Restructuring* (Washington, DC: IMF, 2002) 2 (suggesting the implementation of a – statutory – Sovereign Debt Restructuring Mechanism to better coordinate creditors during restructuring operations); Steven Schwarcz, 'Sovereign Debt Restructuring: A Bankruptcy Reorganization Approach' (2000) 85 Cornell Law Review 956 (proposing a comprehensive bankruptcy regime for States as a panacea to collective action issues).

123 Jeffrey Sachs, 'Conditionality, Debt Relief and Developing Country Debt Crisis in Jeffrey D Sachs (ed), *Volume 1: The International Financial System: Developing Country Debt and Economic Performance* (Chicago: University of Chicago Press, 1989) 6.

124 Lee Buchheit and Mitu Gulati, 'Sovereign Bonds and the Collective Will' (2002) 53 Emory Law Journal 1324, 1340 (analysing the history of collective action issues in both corporate and sovereign bonds); Samuel E Goldman, 'Mavericks in the Market: The Emerging Problem of Hold-Outs in Sovereign Debt Restructuring' (2000) 5 UCLA Journal of International Law & Foreign Affairs 159.

125 Lee Buchheit, 'Changing Bond Documentation: The Sharing Clause' (1998) 17 International Financial Review 17 (advocating the inclusion of sharing clauses in bonds to reduce holdout problems). This said, trust indentures, as opposed to fiscal agency agreements, curb the individual bondholder's right to file suit against the issuer, thereby discouraging litigation. See Lee Buchheit, 'Trustees Versus Fiscal Agents for Sovereign Bonds' (2018) 13(3) Capital Markets Law Journal 410, 413 (noting that '[i]n a sovereign debt workout, the prospect of having to rely on the trustee for enforcement actions should make bonds issued under trust structures less attractive to creditors intent on pursuing their recoveries through litigation').

126 See, for example, for an analysis of domestic bankruptcy procedures, Philipp Wood, *The Law and Practice of International Finance* (London: Sweet & Maxwell, 2008).

127 Compare Ousmène Jaques Mandeng, 'Intercreditor Distribution in Sovereign Debt Restructuring' (2004) IMF Working Paper, WP/04/183, 18 <www.imf.org/external/pubs/ft/wp/2004/wp04183.pdf> accessed 2 November 2021 (noting that 'sovereign debt restructuring does not rely on a common basis for comparing individual creditor action and proposing a code of conduct for consenting creditors to strengthen inter-creditor group collective action').

128 Roubini and Setser (n 121) 292. The IMF's SDRM proposal, for instance, sought to confront the issue of bondholder coordination head-on, proposing a majority voting mechanism that aggregates the claims of all eligible creditors regardless of the instrument and, thereby, enable a majority of bondholders to cram down dissenting holdouts; see Krueger (n 121) (responding to fears that this would allow countries to regularly default on their debt, Krueger notes that 'it is very unlikely that alleviating the collective action problem somewhat would significantly weaken the credit culture or create moral hazard').

129 See, for example, the case of Mozambique, which borrowed significant amounts from a consortium of international banks, including Credit Suisse and VBT Bank. The debts were, however, hidden, as the government used off-balance sheet entities to organize the loan agreement. Ultimately, the hidden debts were uncovered, and Mozambique has since been engaged in a legal dispute with the international lenders. See Daniel Bradlow, 'Prudent Debt management and Lessons from the Mozambique Constitutional Council' (*AfronomicsLaw*, 5 August 2020) <https://papers.ssrn.com/sol3/papers.cfm?abstract_id=3676342> accessed 2 November 2021.

130 The hedge fund Elliott Management LLC, which invests in distressed sovereign debt to sue for a recovery of the instrument's full face value, has become particularly infamous.

131 Especially, Chinese SOEs have lent heavily to sovereigns in Africa and South America. In note, the asset manager Franklin Templeton describes Chinese lending mechanisms as follows:

> The three policy banks are the most conspicuous, and of these China Development Bank and the Export-Import Bank of China have been more active in BRI lending than the Agricultural Development Bank. Also involved to a lesser extent are the non-policy state banks (eg, ICBC, CCB, Bank of China, ABC), the state-owned funds (China Investment Corp, Silk Road Fund), and international financing institutions (Asian Infrastructure Investment Bank, New Development Bank, Asian Development Bank).

See Franklin Tempelton, 'The Evolution of China's Lending to Emerging Markets' (April 2021) <www.franklintempleton.com/content-ftthinks/common-pdf/

fixed-income/evolution-of-china-lending-to-emerging-markets-us.pdf> accessed 2 November 2021.

132 See Chapter 5.3. 'Official Sector Holdouts.'

133 See *Accorinti v European Central Bank*, Judgment, Case T-79/13, [2015] Court of Justice of the European Union [CJEU]; GC of the European Union [EGC] and for a discussion of the case, see Chapter 3.5.1.1. 'Accorinti v ECB.'

134 This transformation of the creditor is particularly evident in certain low-income countries, where Paris Club loans used to be the main source of foreign capital for decades, while in contrast, commercial debt and bilateral loans by new lenders are at least as important as concessional instruments. See Sum-Jim Ho, 'Sovereign Debt Column: Is This Time Different for Sub-Saharan Africa?' (Winter 2019–2020) 10 Cleary Gottlieb Emerging Markets Restructuring Journal <www.clearygottlieb.com/-/media/files/emrj-materials/issue-10-winter-2019_2020/sovereign-debt-column–is-this-time-different-for-subsaharan-africa-pdf.pdf> accessed 2 November 2021.

135 Criticizing the role of distressed debt funds in the sovereign debt space, Martin Wolf, 'Holdouts Give Vultures a Bad Name' *Financial Times* (London, 2 September 2014). Also see for a critique of vultures in Martin Guzman, José Antonio Ocampo and Joseph E Stiglitz (eds), *Too Little, Too Late: The Quest to Resolve Sovereign Debt Crises* (New York: Columbia University Press, 2016).

136 See, for example, Ho (n 134) (noting that 'Africa has attracted an increasingly diverse set of lenders as a result of its natural resources,' including commodity traders like Glencore, which now hold considerable amounts of commodity-backed debt in Africa). For an analysis of commodity traders' role in sovereign debt restructurings, see Chapter 5.2.5. 'Commodity Traders.'

137 See, for example, Anna Gelpern, 'Examining Belt and Road: The Lending Practices of the People's Republic of China and Impact on the International Debt Architecture' (18 May 2021) Testimony Before the House Committee on Financial Services, Subcommittee on National Security, International Development and Monetary Policy <https://docs.house.gov/meetings/BA/BA10/20210518/112661/HHRG-117-BA10-Wstate-GelpernA-20210518.pdf> accessed 2 November 2021. For discussion, see Chapter 5.3. 'Official Sector Holdouts.'

138 See Anne O Krueger and Sean Hagan, 'Sovereign Workouts: An IMF Perspective' (2005) 6(1) Chicago Journal of International Law 203, 211, noting the following:

> to the extent that holdouts have a credible postdefault holdout strategy, creditors who are otherwise willing to engage in the debt restructuring process may be more reluctant to do so because of concerns regarding intercreditor equity' and that 'creditors contemplating whether to accept a restructuring offer will clearly be concerned that the holdout strategy may be used to interrupt payments to them once the debt has been restructured.

139 See, for example, Bi et al (n 25) 2–6 (arguing that creditor coordination problems have been exaggerated in the pertinent literature).

140 In Belize, for instance, the debt restructuring was characterized by a high representation of creditors in a committee, the use of CACs, as well as commitments on the government's side to augment contract enforceability in the future. See, in particular, Tamon Asonuma, Gerardo Peraza, Kristine Vitola, and Takahiro Tsuda, 'Sovereign Debt Restructurings in Belize: Achievements and Challenges Ahead' (2014) IMF Working Paper WP14/32 (July 2014) <www.imf.org/external/pubs/ft/wp/2014/wp14132.pdf> accessed 2 November 2021.

141 See, notably, David Grigorian, Trevor Alleyne, and Alejandro Guerson, 'Jamaica Debt Exchange' (2012) IMF Working Paper WP/12/244 (October 2012) <www.imf.org/external/pubs/ft/wp/2012/wp12244.pdf> accessed 2 November 2021, noting this:

> [t]he sovereign debt restructuring operation in Jamaica undertaken in early-2010 was a unique experiment that perhaps offered less by way of upside, if compared

> to the conventional sovereign debt exchanges, but provided credible assurances against further downfall and financial sector distress.

Also see Megliani (n 60) 368–369.

142 See IMF (n 35). CACs are the single most important contractual restructuring device in international sovereign bonds, as they allow the sovereign issuer to modify reserved matters, that is, terms of the bond relating to payment (principal and interest), if a (super-)majority of creditors consents, thereby mitigating holdout inefficiencies.

143 See, among others, Joseph E Stieglitz and Martin Guzman, 'A Rule of Law for Sovereign Debt' (*Project Syndicate*, 15 June 2015) <www.project-syndicate.org/commentary/sovereign-debt-restructuring-by-joseph-e-stiglitz-and-martin-guzman-2015–06?barrier=accessreg> accessed 2 November 2021 (arguing that '[a] "soft law" framework containing these features, implemented through an oversight commission that acted as a mediator and supervisor of the restructuring process, could resolve some of today's inefficiencies and inequities'). But also see IMF (n 35) 20 (the Fund also notes, however, that 'sovereign debt restructurings in a few LICs were protracted, incomplete, and non-transparent').

144 Gelpern (n 59) 106.

145 Ibid 110.

146 Ibid 53. For the IMF's role in debt restructurings, see Hagan (n 52) and earlier Daniel K Tarullo, 'The Role of the IMF in Sovereign Debt Restructuring' (2005) 6(1) Chicago Journal of International Law 287.

147 IMF, 'Iraq – First Review Under the Stand-By Arrangement and Financing Assurances Review Staff Report; Staff Supplement; Press Release on the Executive Board Discussion; and Statement by the Executive Director for Iraq' (2008) <www.elibrary.imf.org/view/journals/002/2008/303/article-A001-en.xml> accessed 2 November 2021:

> The Paris Club agreed on November 21, 2004 to a debt reduction for Iraq, equivalent to 80 percent in net present value (NPV) terms, to be achieved in three stages. The first and second stages, each comprising a 30 percent debt reduction in NPV terms, went into effect in November 2004 and in December 2005 (following approval of the first SBA), respectively.

148 IMF (n 114).

149 See earlier IMF (n 147) for the example of the Iraq debt restructuring, where an 80% NPV reduction was achieved through a Paris Club agreement. Gelpern (n 59) 110 (noting that cross-conditionality was flexible enough to accommodate diverse stakeholders and diverse versions of inter-creditor equity).

150 This said, while most commercial creditors ultimately participated in London Club renegotiations, they were not always fond of them. As Buchheit notes, '[s]yndicated loans showed themselves to be uncomfortably susceptible to rescheduling during the 1980s,' while 'Eurobonds and floating rate note issues of most countries were consciously excluded from the restructuring excursive and were paid on time in full.' He further observes that '[t]his is one important reason why investors are prepared to buy emerging market bonds, even if they might recoil at the idea of buying interests in syndicated bank loans to the same borrowers.' Lee Buchheit, 'Cross-Border Lending: What's Different This Time' (1995) 16(1) Northwestern Journal of International Law & Business 44, 48.

151 See, most notably, Krueger (n 122) (proposing an SDRM), and Sean Hagan, 'Designing a Legal Framework to Restructure Sovereign Debt' (2004) 36 Georgetown Journal of International Law 299 (explaining the legal mechanics behind an SDRM).

152 The rationale was that bonds may be more difficult to restructure than loans, thereby disincentivizing sovereigns from defaulting. This issue was particularly prevalent under New York law securities, which – in contrast to their English law counterparts – have traditionally not included CACs that reduce holdout inefficiencies. For background, see, for example, Barry Eichengreen, 'Restructuring Sovereign Debt' (2003) 17(4) Journal of Economic Perspectives 75.

153 The risk of holdouts obtaining court orders that block payments by holdouts first materialized in the aftermath of the Peruvian debt restructuring in 2000; see Robert A Cohen, 'Sometimes a Cigar Is Just a Cigar: The Simple Story of Pari Passu' (2011) 40 Hofstra Law Review 11.

154 IMF, 'Sovereign Debt Restructuring – Recent Developments and Implications for the Fund's Legal and Policy Framework' (26 April 2013) 12 <www.imf.org/external/np/pp/eng/2013/042613.pdf> accessed 2 November 2021 (noting that 'collective action problems could either make restructuring unsuccessful due to the holdout strategy or cause delay due to uncertainty about creditor participation').

155 See IMF (n 118).

156 See, for example, Jose Antonio Ocampo, 'A Brief History of Sovereign Debt Resolution and a Proposal for a Multilateral Instrument in Guzman et al (n 135) 189–194; Gelpern (n 59) 48. For additional proposals, see Lex Rieffel, *Restructuring Sovereign Debt: The Case for Ad Hoc Machinery* (Washington, DC: Brookings Institution Press, 2003); Patrick Bolton and Olivier Jeanne, 'Structuring and Restructuring Sovereign Debt: The Role of a Bankruptcy Regime' (2007) 115(6) Journal of Political Economy 905.

157 See Kenneth Rogoff and Jeromin Zettelmeyer, 'Bankruptcy Procedures for States: A History of Ideas, 1976–2001' (2002) 49(3) IMF Staff Papers 470; Hal Scott, 'How Would a New Bankruptcy Regime Help?' (2002) 33(1) Brookings Papers on Economic Activity 334. Also see Ross Buckley, 'The Bankruptcy of Nations: An Idea Whose Time Has Come' (2009) 43(3) The International Lawyer 1189; Udabir Das, Michael Papaioannou, and Christoph Trebesch, 'Sovereign Debt Restructurings 1950–2010: Literature Survey, Data and Stylized Facts' (2012) IMF Working Paper, WP/12/203 <www.imf.org/external/pubs/cat/longres.aspx?sk=26190.0> accessed 2 November 2021; Christoph Paulus (ed), *A Debt Restructuring Procedure for Sovereigns – Do We Need a Legal Procedure?* (London: Hart, 2014).

158 See Kunibert Raffer, 'Applying Chapter 9 Insolvency to International Debts: An Economically Efficient Solution with a Human Face' (1990) 18(2) World Development 301; Jeffrey Sachs, 'Do We Need an International Lender of Last Resort?' (1995) Frank D Graham Lecture at Princeton University (on file with author).

159 Rogoff and Zettelmeyer (n 157).

160 Brad Setser, 'The Political Economy of the SDRM' in Barry Herman, José Antonio Ocampo, and Shari Spiegel (eds) *Overcoming Developing Country Debt Crises* (Oxford: Oxford University Press, 2010) (emphasizing the difficulties in convincing stakeholders of the SDRM's advantages, noting that '[t]he IMF put forward a proposal that its architects knew was sure to be stillborn').

161 See Rogoff and Zettelmeyer (n 157); Gelpern (n 59); United Nations General Assembly Resolution 69/319: Basic Principles on Sovereign Debt Restructuring Processes (United Nations General Assembly [UNGA]) UN Doc A/RES/69/319.

162 One such exception is the introduction of enhanced contractual clauses in international sovereign bonds to mitigate holdout inefficiencies; see IMF (n 119).

163 See, in particular, IIF, 'Principles for Stable Capital Flows and Fair Debt Restructuring' (October 2020) Report on Implementation by the Principles Consultative Group <www.iif.com/Portals/0/Files/content/Regulatory/10_23_2020_pcg_report_2020.pdf> accessed 2 November 2021.

164 See, for a discussion, Vassilis Paliouras, 'The Right to Restructure Sovereign Debt' (2017) 20 Journal of International Economic Law 115 (arguing that 'at least part of this policy space is related to a state right to restructure sovereign debt'). Also see Bianco, Giuseppe, 'How Neutral Is the Law of Sovereign Debt' (2017) 9(3) ESIL Conference Paper Series (ESIL Research Forum, Granada, 30–31 March 2017) <https://papers.ssrn.com/sol3/papers.cfm?abstract_id=3045246> accessed 2 November 2021; Blom (n 58).

165 See Raymond Ritter, 'The Principles for Stable Capital Flows and Fair Debt Restructuring in Emerging Markets' (April 2009) ECB Occasional Paper Series No 103

<www.ecb.europa.eu/pub/pdf/scpops/ecbocp103.pdf> accessed 2 November 2021, noting this:

> [t]he Principles for Stable Capital Flows and Fair Debt Restructuring in Emerging Markets, which have been jointly agreed between sovereign debtors and their private creditors, have proved to be an effective instrument for crisis prevention and crisis resolution in the international financial system.

166 Over time, the Paris Club moved from offering debt reprofilings under the Classic Terms for all countries to providing special debt relief for highly indebted lower to middle income countries (Houston Terms) and for highly indebted poor countries (Naples Terms), including under the IMF and World Bank HIPC initiative (Cologne Terms). IMF (n 119) 12. Formally, debt relief is granted on the basis of Agreed Minutes, which are signed by the heads of the participating delegations, which recommend to their governments to provide debt relief.

167 According to Das et al (n 157) 16, despite its name, the term 'London Club' 'loosely describes the case-by-case restructuring routine developed between major Western banks and developing country governments.' The London Club was the private sector's response to the syndicated loan crisis of the 1980s that received the official sector's blessing, and while its setup was more informal than that of the Paris Club, there are some important similarities. For instance, London Club lenders, too, demanded that debtor states have an IMF arrangement in place before agreeing to a rescheduling. See Pamela Blackmon, 'Determinants of Developing Country Debt: The Revolving Door of Debt Rescheduling Through Paris Club and Export Credits' (2014) 35(8) Third World Quarterly 1423. The IIF, as the main representative of the financial sector in all matters sovereign debt, was usually involved in the London Club, although its role was limited to coordinating smaller banks. See Jasper Blom, 'The Institute of International Finance: From Poacher to Gatekeeper' (2021) 23(1) Business and Politics 153, 165 (noting that the national differences in handing Mexico's 1982 crisis made it more difficult for the private sector to reach consensus, offering an opportunity for the IIF to become the advocacy group for the global banking community).

168 The two Clubs should facilitate negotiations without curtailing the sovereign debtor's rights under international law or limiting the creditors' capacity to file suit. Kenneth HF Dyson, *States, Debt, and Power: 'Saints' and 'Sinners' in European History Integration* (Oxford: Oxford University Press, 2014) 376. For an in-depth review of both Clubs and their evolution, see Viterbo (n 43) 90 et seq and, for an older perspective, see Karen Hudes, 'Coordination of Paris and London Club Reschedulings' (1985) 17(3) New York University Journal of International Law and Politics 553.

169 The Paris Club is still embedded in the sovereign debt architecture as the main forum to bring together a number of important lenders. However, the rise of new bilateral creditors, notably China and India, has gradually eroded the Club's influence. In the wake of the COVID-19 pandemic, the G20 have sought to integrate Paris Club procedures and bilateral debt relief measures through the 'Common Framework.' See IMF (n 55), noting this:

> [t]he Common Framework for Debt Treatments beyond the DSSI is an agreement of the G20 and Paris Club countries to coordinate and cooperate on debt treatments for up to 73 low income countries that are eligible for the Debt Service Suspension Initiative (DSSI).

And that the framework 'includes not only members of the Paris Club but also G20 official bilateral creditors such as China, India, Turkey or Saudi Arabia that are not members of the Paris Club.'

170 Anna Gelpern, 'Hard, Soft, and Embedded: Implementing Principles on Promoting Responsible Sovereign Lending and Borrowing' (2012) Georgetown Law Faculty

Publications and Other Works 1860, 13 <https://scholarship.law.georgetown.edu/facpub/1860/> accessed 2 November 2021. The main reason was that banks no longer represented the major creditors to emerging market issuers. Moreover, the London Club was controversial. For example, there was an information gap between smaller banks in the syndicate and larger banks, which sat at the negotiation table and presented a fait accompli to unrepresented creditors once a deal was reached. Disagreements about fees, too, resulted in bitter fights between creditors. See Zahavi (n 32) 59.

171 See Ross Buckley, 'The Transformative Potential of a Secondary Market: Emerging Markets Debt Trading from 1983 to 1989' (1997) 21(4) Fordham Journal of International Law 1152, 1237 (noting that 'the [new bond] market facilitated the exit of certain banks from LDC lending [as it] enabled regional U.S. and Continental European banks to dispose of their LDC debt portfolios in the late 1980s and early 1990s').

172 For instance, disparate Argentine investors united under the umbrella of the Global Committee of Argentina Bondholders (GCAB) to pool negotiating leverage and demand a better deal. They represented about USD40 billion in US, European, and Japanese creditors, amounting to approximately 45% of total bonds in default; see Anna Gelpern, 'After Argentina' (2012) Peterson Institute for International Economics Policy Briefs No PB05–02 <https://piie.com/publications/policy-briefs/after-argentina> accessed 2 November 2021. This said, initially more than 30 creditor committees were established in Argentina, raising some difficult regarding their recognition by both the government and international financial institutions providing financing to Argentina. See IRC Task Force on IMF and global financial governance issues, 'The IMF's Role in Sovereign Debt Restructurings' (September 2021) ECB Working Paper No 262, 22 <www.ecb.europa.eu/pub/pdf/scpops/ecb.op262~f0e9e1e77e.en.pdf> accessed 2 November 2021. In Greece, several big banks, mainly of German and French origin, coordinated their negotiating position with the aid of the IIF. According to *Reuters*, the banks and other steering group members held about 30% of the EUR206 billion of bonds in circulation; see Alex Chambers and Lefteris Papadimas, 'Athens, Creditor Group Turn Up Heat on Greek Bondholders' *Reuters* (London, 6 March 2012) <www.reuters.com/article/us-greece-bonds-idUSTRE82412N20120306> accessed 2 November 2021. Also see Chapter 3.3.1. 'Debt Restructuring Negotiations: The Role of the Troika and the IIF.'

2 Holdout Creditor Problems and Foreign Law Debt

The Argentine Debt Restructurings in Courts and Tribunals (2001–2016)

2.1. Argentina's Sovereign Debt Restructurings (2001–2010)

2.1.1. Background

Argentina's sovereign default of 2001 presaged a new era of sovereign finance. Notwithstanding the country's longstanding history of defaulting on government debt obligations – Argentina had reneged on (parts of) its government debt three times in the last 32 years[1] – the debt crisis in the early 2000s resulted in the largest-ever sovereign bankruptcy in history, today only surpassed by the Greek PSI of 2012.[2]

Not only was Argentina's external debt exceptionally large in volume, but its structure was very complex, too.[3] As was feared, creditor coordination proved considerably more complex in Argentina than in previous emerging market sovereign debt workouts, where the bulk of commercial debt was structured as syndicated loans, while Argentina had issued more than a hundred series of international debt securities.[4] Concerns that holdout creditor problems would seriously undermine a quick and orderly resolution of the country's financial crisis materialized shortly. Ultimately, some holdouts successfully blocked Argentina's return to international capital markets for a period of 15 years, and the aftershocks of the 2001 default linger on well into the 2020s.

2.1.2. The 2005 Debt Restructuring

Argentina's first debt swap took place in 2005: it involved 152 varieties of paper denominated in 6 currencies and governed by the laws of 8 jurisdictions, held by more than 700,000 creditors scattered across the international financial community.[5] The offer[6] was presented in January 2005 as part of an 'International Global debt exchange,' and while it was accepted by a majority of investors, the proportion of holdout investors (24% of creditors of outstanding credit) as well as the haircut size (roughly 70% on a net present value basis) were historically high.[7]

To encourage higher creditor participation, Argentina passed the so-called Lock Law (*Ley 26,017*), which would become a major point of contention in the holdout litigation in New York courts described later[8] and perhaps the biggest liability

DOI: 10.4324/9781003361879-2

in the government's restructuring strategy.[9] Experts at the time considered Argentina's confrontational approach towards holdouts as risky.[10]

2.1.3. The 2010 Debt Restructuring

Against the backdrop of a low participation rate and a fairly high number of outstanding holdout claims, Argentina concluded another round of negotiations with bondholders in 2010.[11] It included reopening discussions with previously shunned distressed debt funds. Although the terms and conditions of the second offer were less attractive than the 2005 exchange, the low trading price of Argentine bonds and the government's persistent refusal to settle with the holdouts enticed many creditors to participate in the debt workout, pushing participation north of 90%.[12]

By the same token, the non-exchanged debt was held by creditors who were both motivated and experienced in holdout cases. Indeed, in 2010, many of these funds had already obtained money judgements in US, and other courts and had launched collection proceedings across the globe, as discussed in the subsequent sections.[13] Both the background noise these trials created and the prospect of holdouts attaching the proceeds from a new bond issuance continued to pose serious obstacles for Argentina's return to international capital markets,[14] until a final settlement was reached in 2016.[15]

2.2. Holdout Litigation After Argentina

2.2.1. Holdout Litigation in Foreign Domestic Courts

The following subsections analyse holdout litigation cases against Argentina in the wake of the 2001 default and the subsequent debt swaps. The onus lies on major jurisdictions whose laws are frequently chosen for the purpose of sovereign debt issuances.[16] There is no intention to exhaustively cover all the thousands of legal challenges that were initiated against the country[17] but rather single out the seminal judgements that inform cross-border sovereign debt restructuring practice and discuss both the courts' decisions as well as the implications the judgements may have going forward.

2.2.1.1. United States

This section sheds light on cases of holdout litigation in US federal courts following Argentina's default on bonds governed by New York law. More than 50% of holdout investors after the 2010 debt restructuring deal held debt securities governed by the law of New York, putting these cases at the centre of the Argentina holdout saga. This section does not provide an exhaustive analysis of litigation in the US but rather covers the seminal judgements with a view at distilling the courts' legal reasoning as well as the implications for holdout litigation as a matter of US and, specifically, New York law.[18]

2.2.1.1.1. LIGHTWATER V ARGENTINA[19]

The *Lightwater* litigation was one of the first legal challenges to Argentina's debt moratorium of December 2001. Given that the litigation was initiated *before* Argentina launched its restructuring negotiations, the litigating creditors may not be qualified as holdouts in the narrow sense. Still, *Lightwater* represented an important example of opportunistic creditor action by specialized creditors, often dubbed 'vulture funds'[20] – a behaviour that was copied by hundreds of other creditors in the decade during which Argentina sought to resolve its debt problems.

The plaintiffs in *Lightwater* claimed principal and interest payments of bonds Argentina defaulted on in late 2001.[21] Argentina put forward three defences against the plaintiff's motion: (i) international comity, (ii) champertous behaviour on the plaintiffs' side, and (iii) the act of state defence. The court rejected all defences and granted summary judgment amounting to USD700 million:

- First, regarding defence of *international comity*, Argentina had argued that it should be given an opportunity to achieve an overall debt restructuring. Given the severe economic crisis facing the government, the principles of international comity require the court to stay the plaintiff's actions. Relying on the principles established in *Pravin*,[22] the court found that it is in the strong interest of the US (government) to ensure the enforcement of foreign debt obligations and declined to grant a stay of proceedings to allow for the completion of debt restructuring negotiation.[23]
- Second, the US District Court for the Southern District of New York (SDNY) declined the applicability of NY Judiciary Law § 489, also known as law of champerty, which prohibits the practice of purchasing claims for the purpose of commencing litigation.[24] Citing previous decisions,[25] the court in *Lightwater* noted that 'where a bond is purchased with the intent to collect on that bond, the statute is *not* violated even though there is also an intention to collect by a lawsuit if necessary' (emphasis added).[26]
- Third, weighing in on the act of state defence, prominently discussed in the *Allied Bank* case,[27] Judge Griesa held that '[a]n act of a nation in failing to make payments on bonds held in other countries does not constitute an act of state dealing with property located within the nation.'[28] A defaulted sovereign borrower could, thus, not invoke the act of state defence in instances where the situs of the bondholders is outside its territory.[29]

While the District Court denied a stay on *litigation*, it stayed the judgment's *execution* with a view at facilitating debt restructuring negotiations to commence without the threat of bondholder execution attempts in line with principles of international comity.[30] However, since the stay was temporary and the Argentine debt problem was nowhere near the point of resolution, the order had little practical effect and judgment creditors soon initiated enforcement proceedings.

2.2.1.1.2. EM V BANCO CENTRAL DE LA REPÚBLICA ARGENTINA[31]

Against the backdrop of enforcement constraints, Argentina's creditors became both increasingly impatient and creative in their legal strategies to enforce money judgements they had obtained in *Lightwater* and similar cases. The *EM v BRCA* litigation concerned holdouts' attempts to attach assets of Argentina's central bank, *Banco Central de la República Argentina* (BCRA), held at the New York branch of the Federal Reserve Bank (FRBNY).

The 2015 *EM v BRCA* litigation followed an earlier attempt by the same hedge fund to attach the FRBNY account in 2007, when the Argentine central bank used its reserves held at the FRBNY to repay the IMF. In that earlier case, the Court of Appeals for the Second Circuit rejected the holdouts' claims, noting that repaying the IMF was not a commercial activity.[32]

However, in 2010, Judge Griesa of the SDNY held that BCRA had held the funds on behalf of the Argentine state and was, therefore, the government's alter ego.[33] In 2011, the SDNY decision was reversed by the Second Circuit on appeal, which noted that '[foreign central banks] are given "special protections" befitting the particular sovereign interest in preventing the attachment and execution of central bank property.'[34]

Not all legal issues were settled, though. The 2015 *EM v BCRA* case, which concerned execution attempts into reserves held at the FRBNY, focused on the following two legal issues:

- First, EM and NML, the two vulture funds and plaintiffs in the case, sought declaratory judgment that BCRA was Argentina's alter ego and that, therefore, BCRA was liable for Argentina's debt.[35] More specifically, the court had to decide whether Argentina's waiver of sovereign immunity in its international bonds could also be imputed to BCRA as its alter ego.
- Second, plaintiffs argued that since reserves of the BCRA held at the FRBNY could be used for payments of obligations undertaken with international monetary authorities and the IMF, they should also be accessible to satisfy private creditor claims.[36] The legal question at stake was whether BCRA had waived its sovereign immunity by engaging in commercial activity in New York through its account at the FRBNY, given that the central bank – in contrast to the government – had never explicitly waived its immunity.[37]

In regard to the alter ego claim, the Second Circuit opined that Argentina would have had to control BCRA so extensively that 'a relationship of principal and agent was created.'[38] The US Supreme Court had established the standard under US federal law for the alter ego test in the *Banec*,[39] which focused on four criteria to assess the entanglement between the government and its central bank.[40] Applying the *Banec* test, the Second Circuit rejected the plaintiffs' claims as it could not find evidence that the Argentine government had used its influence over these directors to interfere with BCRA's ordinary business affairs.[41] The court also failed to detect signs of extensive control of BCRA's day-to-day operations by the government branch.[42] In summary, BCRA was no sham to hide assets.[43]

On the issue of BCRA's liability for the (numerous) judgements rendered against Argentina by New York courts, the court focused on the issue whether the commercial activity exception in § 1605(a)(2) FSIA applied to the central bank.[44] While the plaintiffs had alleged that BCRA carried relevant commercial activities by purchasing dollars through their account at the FRBNY, the Court of Appeals concluded that the plaintiffs' 'capacious understanding of the commercial activity exception was inconsistent with the FSIA's presumption that foreign states and instrumentalities enjoy sovereign immunity.'[45] This would imply that any allegedly wrongful use of dollars outside the US by the central bank could compromise its sovereign immunity, with potentially far-reaching effects for foreign central banks operating in the US and holding accounts in New York City.[46]

2.2.1.1.3. NML CAPITAL V ARGENTINA[47]

The *NML* case, dubbed 'sovereign debt's trial of the century' by the Financial Times,[48] lay at the heart of the Argentine holdout litigation. The judgment shook the foundations of modern sovereign debt restructuring and heralded profound changes in the international financial architecture.[49] The trial's importance stems from at least two reasons:

- First, US courts entertained an unconventional interpretation of the pari passu clause. Akin to the plaintiff in the *Elliott* litigation,[50] NML Capital convinced US courts in all instances that Argentina had violated the pari passu clause in Argentina's bonds by not paying all bondholders ratably.[51]
- Second, the *NML* decision established a new avenue for sovereign debt enforcement, at least for instruments governed by New York law: creditors were granted an injunctive relief against Argentina, which effectively left the government with two options – either pay all creditors (holdout and restructured creditors) in full or default on all debt obligations. Argentina opted for the latter and defaulted on its external debt in 2014.

The holdouts ultimately got their way when the newly elected government by President Mauricio Macri decided to pay them off in early 2016 to regain international investors' confidence. The *NML v Argentina* litigation saga had several phases and spanned more than a decade (from 2005 to 2016); considering its importance, the following sections will cover the legal proceedings in detail.[52]

District Court for the Southern District of New York NML Capital, a subsidiary of the hedge fund Elliott Management, had bought Argentine bonds for a steep discount in the wake of the Argentine default of 2001 with a face value of roughly USD1.6 billion, making up more than a fifth of all remaining holdout claims after the 2010 restructuring. At first, NML sought to obtain money judgements[53] from the SDNY to attach Argentine assets located in the US or other jurisdictions.[54]

Litigation records indicate that the first such judgment in NML's favour was rendered by the SDNY in 2005,[55] and several others followed.[56]

NML Capital went to great lengths to try to seize Argentine assets on the basis of these judgements – both in the US and abroad.[57] The Argentine government saw itself forced to ground the presidential plane after NML had obtained court orders to seize the jet. NML even targeted Argentine dinosaur fossils on exhibition in Europe for attachment.[58] Several of the early money judgements were used in asset seizure motions in various European courts.[59]

Following years of costly but relatively unsuccessful execution proceedings against Argentina,[60] NML's lawyers revamped their strategy. From 2011 onwards, NML asserted that Argentina's debt default and the subsequent restructuring measures were in breach of the pari passu clause in the 1994 Fiscal Agency Agreement (FAA), the contractual instrument governing Argentina's global bonds.[61] Judge Griesa eventually agreed with the plaintiff and granted a motion for partial summary judgment,[62] declaring this:

> [t]he Republic violates Paragraph 1(c) of the FAA whenever it lowers the rank of its payment obligations under NML's Bonds below that of any other present or future unsecured and unsubordinated External Indebtedness, including (and without limitation) by relegating NML's bonds to a non-paying class by failing to pay the obligations currently due under NML's Bonds *while at the same time making payments currently due to holders of other unsecured and unsubordinated External Indebtedness* or by legislative enactment.
>
> (emphasis added)[63]

The SDNY, moreover, claimed that, given Argentina's persistent violations of the pari passu clause, it had the authority to issue injunctive remedies against Argentina under Rule 65(d) of the US Federal Rules of Civil Procedure[64] as well as the court's inherent equitable powers. Judge Griesa argued that these injunctions were necessary to accommodate the plaintiff's legitimate interests having its securities enforced. Indeed, in the court's opinion, 'NML [was] irreparably harmed by and has no adequate remedy at law for the Republic's ongoing violations of Paragraph 1(c) of the FAA [the pari passu clause].'[65]

Another crucial feature of the injunction was that it also applied to third parties that were not directly involved in the bond dispute.[66] This meant that paying agents, clearing houses, or other financial agents processing Argentina's bond payments would act in contempt of a US court[67] if they were to assist the government in circumventing the pari passu injunction.[68]

Court of Appeals for the Second Circuit Like the SDNY, the Second Circuit found that the two sentences of the pari passu clause in the FAA 'protect[ed] investors against any form of discrimination: the issuance of other superior debt (first sentence) and the giving of priority to other payment obligations (second sentence)' (emphasis added).[69]

With respect to the injunctive relief, the Second Circuit rejected Argentina's claim that 'plaintiffs cannot now rely on "equity" to interfere with payments to third parties who have obviously developed reasonable expectation of that regular source of income.'[70] It rather held that the injunction could not only be an alternative to a summary judgment but also be granted in a situation where no adequate monetary remedy was available.[71] In the court's view, the only requirement was that the balance of equities must tip in the plaintiff's favour.[72] This was fulfilled here, as 'monetary damages [were] an ineffective remedy for the harm plaintiffs have suffered as a result of Argentina's breach [because] Argentina will simply refuse to pay any judgments.'[73] The injunctive remedies were also not considered incompatible with the FSIA, as they did not transfer any dominion or control over sovereign property to the court; they did not even require Argentina to pay any bondholder any amount of money or limit the other uses to which Argentina may put its fiscal reserves.[74]

Finally, the Second Circuit examined the practical effects of enabling a holdout creditor to pressure a sovereign debtor into paying the government bonds' face value. In its amicus brief, the US government had argued that the equitable remedy granted by the District Court would allow 'a single creditor to thwart the implementation of an internationally supported restructuring plan.'[75] The court, however, rejected this line of reasoning, noting that it was 'up to the sovereign – not any "single creditor" – whether it will repudiate that creditor's debt in a manner that violates a pari passu clause.'[76]

After the Court of Appeals remanded the injunctions due to lack of specificity, the District Court issued amended injunctions on 21 November 2012.[77] In 2013, the matter was back in the Court of Appeals, and this time, it allowed the defendant (Argentina) to propose an alternative payment formula and schedule for the outstanding bonds.[78]

US Supreme Court The Supreme Court of the US (SCOTUS) played a relatively minor role in the *NML* litigation: it denied two petitions for certiorari to review the Second Circuit's affirmance of the injunctions that enjoined Argentina and its agents.[79] Following the SCOTUS ruling in June 2014, the remedies passed by the SDNY and affirmed by the Second Circuit attained legal force. The Argentine debt saga returned to international newspapers' headlines.[80] And justifiably so: for the first time in history, a sovereign defaulted on its public debts as a direct consequence of a foreign court decision.

While SCOTUS refused to review the injunction orders, it did look at the limits the FSIA imposed on US Courts to order extraterritorial, post-judgment discovery.[81] Argentina asserted that NML's motions to discovery of Argentina's property, affirmed by the Second Circuit, violated the FSIA.[82] The order, it submitted, transgressed the FSIA because it permitted discovery of Argentina's extraterritorial assets.[83] NML's objective was to 'locate Argentina's assets and accounts, learn how Argentina moves its assets through New York and around the world, and accurately identify the places and times when those assets might be subject to attachment and execution.'[84] Both lower courts held that, since Argentina expressly waived its immunity in the debt instruments, the concerns expressed dealing with jurisdictional discovery under the FSIA were not relevant.[85]

Rules of post-judgment discovery under US law are intricate and largely irrelevant for this study. What should, however, be taken away from the SCOTUS ruling that private creditors have powerful rights to identify foreign sovereign property under US law. The judges confirmed that holders of government debt governed by New York law may obtain the information necessary to locate executable assets both in the US *and* abroad. Crucially, the Supreme Court remarked that 'there [was] no provision in the FSIA limiting or forbidding discovery in aid of execution of a foreign-sovereign judgment debtor's assets.'[86]

2.2.1.2. Germany

This section focuses on four seminal decisions rendered by German courts in the wake of the Argentine default of 2001. Overall, Argentina had issued government bonds with a face value of DM1 billion at German capital markets and 648 retail bondholders filed suit in Germany against Argentina after the default.[87] The two cases discussed subsequently were representative for the outcome of the vast majority of these lawsuits: while the holdout bondholders obtained enforceable judgements, there were few Argentine assets amenable to execution, and thus, satisfaction of the bondholders' pecuniary claims, in Germany.

2.2.1.2.1. BVerfG DECISION OF 8 MAY 2007[88]

The *Bundesverfassungsgericht* (BVerfG), the German Federal Constitutional Court, was called upon to adjudicate claims by German (retail) holdouts following Argentina's default in the *Argentina Necessity Case.*[89] Argentina invoked the necessity defence under customary international law, codified in Article 25 of the ILC Draft Articles,[90] to fend off holdout suits filed in German civil courts.[91] The BVerfG negated the defence and ruled in favour of the creditors.

Argentina argued that the debt moratorium was vital for Argentina to avert imminent peril during a state of emergency.[92] The plaintiffs rejected the necessity defence for the following reasons: first, when the plaintiffs filed suit, Argentina had no longer found itself in a state of emergency.[93] Second, Argentina had itself contributed to the situation of necessity, which would exclude the applicability of the defence.[94] Third, other municipal courts also held that the debt moratorium was not justified under international law.[95]

In its majority decision, the BVerfG sided with the plaintiffs and concluded that there was no general rule of international law according to which a state was entitled to suspend its repayment obligations vis-à-vis private individuals in the event of a state emergency.[96] On the one hand, there were no rules for sovereign insolvency – there was no international *lex specialis* for such an event.[97] On the other hand, while states could have recourse to the defence of necessity in inter-state disputes, the doctrine had no scope for application in purely private legal relationships.[98]

In reaching its conclusion, the BVerfG reviewed international and domestic law. Referring to the practice of the International Centre for the Settlement of Investment Disputes (ICSID), it found that both state practice and *opinio iuris* were missing to prove the existence of the defence of necessity in private legal relationships.[99] Similarly, the BVerfG's analysis of national case law did not yield evidence for an internationally recognized rule that would endorse Argentina's claims.[100] Finally, taking into account the existing legal literature,[101] the court found that the majority view in the literature rejected the existence of a legal basis for necessity in the relationship between states and their private creditors.[102]

There was one dissenting opinion, in which Judge Lübbe-Wolff offered a remarkably different perspective.[103] She emphasized that the majority decision, which rejected the necessity defence, ignored core principles of international law. Against the backdrop of Article 38 of the ICJ Statute, which defines the sources of international law, Lübbe-Wolff noted that the necessity defence was accepted under both customary international law (for inter-state relationships) *and* the general principles of law (for private legal relationships).[104]

On the question of economic necessity, Judge Lübbe-Wolff posited that under international case law,[105] Argentina's debt moratorium may be qualified as a state act that could be defended as a 'necessary' state measure.[106] Furthermore, she claimed that a majority of scholars believed that private bondholder rights vis-à-vis a debtor country could offer more protection than the rights, which sovereigns possessed in international relations.[107]

Finally, the dissenting opinion contended that municipal courts in certain jurisdictions have stayed enforcement attempts against Argentina to ensure the success of the debt restructuring.[108] While these courts had not directly referred to the concept of (financial) necessity, the rationale of staying creditor litigation to facilitate a debt workout was strikingly similar to the rationale underpinning the necessity defence.[109]

2.2.1.2.2. BGH DECISION OF 25 NOVEMBER 2010[110]

In this case, plaintiffs had sought to attach 'receivables' of several German companies owed to Argentina for exports, relying on several money judgements they had obtained after the BVerfG denied the necessity defence.[111] The highest German court in civil and criminal matters, the *Bundesgerichtshof* (BGH), held that holdout creditors could not seize such receivables of Argentina against third-party debtors, in this case German companies, stemming from tax and customs claims.[112] This was because German courts, due to the territoriality principle, lacked jurisdiction under German civil procedural law for the enforcement of claims located outside of Germany.[113] Moreover, since there was no international agreement between the Argentina and Germany to regulate bilateral tax and customs duties, international jurisdiction could also not be concluded on the basis of other sources of (international) law.[114]

2.2.1.2.3. BGH DECISION OF 24 FEBRUARY 2015[115]

Almost 14 years after Argentina's default, yet another holdout lawsuit reached the BGH in 2015 to assess the validity and enforceability of private bondholders' claims against Argentina as a matter of German civil law.[116] The decision first assessed Argentina's defence, namely that international law would allow insolvent countries to halt debt repayments to investors who acted in an uncooperative fashion during debt restructuring negotiations. Although the BGH explicitly denounced holdout tactics, it held Article 25 of the *Grundgesetz*, in conjunction with customary international law, did not per se prohibit such (holdout) behaviour.[117] Citing the BVerfG's 2007 ruling on necessity,[118] the BGH again concluded that there was neither a codified bankruptcy system for states nor a general rule of international law that would allow for the suspension of debt repayments to holdout creditors.[119]

Argentina moreover asserted that the global financial crisis of 2007/2008 as well as the euro area crisis of 2010–2012 made the BVerfG's judgment from 2007 redundant. The measures adopted by European countries and policymakers to rescue Greece and Cyprus have, in Argentina's view, cultivated a rule of international law that required states' private creditors to accept debt cuts if an economic state of emergency were to occur.[120] Until such debt reorganization agreement was reached, sovereign debtors might delay debt repayments if the objective was to stabilize their domestic economies.[121]

The BGH was not convinced. It stressed that both the BVerfG as well as the UN General Assembly made clear that – *de lege lata* – states could not rely on a debt restructuring mechanism or any other mechanism of such kind. After all, the UN had passed a resolution in 2014 with the very purpose of establishing a sovereign debt restructuring mechanism in the long run.[122] Referring to the *Abaclat* arbitration case before the ICSID, the BGH, moreover, reiterated that the suspension of payments was deemed illegal under international (investment) law, providing further evidence international law against the defendant's legal opinion.[123] US courts did not even discuss the issue of financial necessity and the lawfulness of debt moratoria under international law.[124] Consequently, the BGH upheld the holdout's claim.

2.2.1.2.4. BVERFG DECISION OF 3 JULY 2019

In the latest decision on the Argentine bondholder claims in German courts, the BVerfG rejected a constitutional complaint lodged by Argentina against the 2015 BGH decision.[125] The Second Chamber of the Constitutional Court found that the BGH had correctly concluded that there was no rule under international law that would regulate the insolvency of states.[126] Specifically, since its 2007 rejection of the financial necessity defence, there had not been any new developments that would allow Argentina to renege on its financial obligations, for neither the UN or UNCTAD initiative had (yet) morphed into a rule of customary international law pursuant to the ICJ Statute.[127] Finally, the proliferation of CACs *after* the

Argentine default was no proof that there had always been a general system under private law that suggested the existence of general principles of law that may be binding to domestic courts.[128]

2.2.1.3. Italy

In the post-restructuring litigation before Italian courts, the majority of plaintiffs can be qualified as retail holdouts.[129] According to Schumacher, 13 retail holdout cases were filed in Italian courts.[130] This section focuses on the analysis of the most prominent trial in *Borri v Argentina* (2005),[131] in which the highest Italian civil court (*Corte Suprema di Cassazione*) thwarted attempts by creditors to obtain enforceable judgements against the Argentine Republic.

2.2.1.3.1. ITALIAN SUPREME COURT (*CORTE SUPREMA DI CASSAZIONE*)[132]

The plaintiff was an Italian citizen who had purchased Argentine government bonds with a face value of approximately EUR 183,000 in 1998. When Argentina suspended its payments to international creditors, the plaintiff sued Argentina in Italy, demanding full payment following an event of default under the bond indenture. Several lower Italian courts issued injunctions that obligated Argentina to pay a certain fraction of the total outstanding value of the bonds.[133]

Argentina appealed, invoking its immunity from suit under international law and arguing that the debt moratorium of 2001 was based on domestic Argentine legislation,[134] hence a sovereign measure (*acta iure imperii*).[135] The Italian bondholders countered the claim by contending that Argentina's bond sales on the New York capital market were fiscal acts and, hence, of commercial nature (*acta iure gestionis*) that did not afford Argentina immunity.[136]

The Italian Supreme Court first declared that state immunity indeed constituted a principle of customary international law directly applicable under Article 10(1) of the Italian Constitution.[137] Referring to Italian case law, the court further noted that reference must be made to the legal acts' nature *and* purpose, respectively.[138] On this basis, in accordance with well-established principles of customary international law, the issuance of bonds on international market amounted to a commercial legal act for which Argentina may not invoke immunity before municipal courts.[139]

However, the court observed Argentina suspended repayments to bondholders by virtue of new budget laws that had the explicit purpose of safeguarding basic needs of the Argentine population.[140] The legislation exhibited 'clear signs of the exercise of sovereign power,' qualifying as *acta iure imperii* and rendering them immune to scrutiny by a foreign municipal court.[141] While the bondholders' property rights also fell squarely into the category of human rights, the Supreme Court found that curtailing them did not impinge on the 'universal values of human dignity.'[142] Adding a caveat, the Italian Supreme Court clarified that its assessment was rendered in light of an unprecedented economic crisis that Argentina had faced when passing the emergency legislation. Under such circumstances, and only then, it considered the protection of basic human rights of the Argentine people to be superior to the protection of investor rights.[143] Thus, as *acta iure imperii*, Argentina's moratorium and debt restructuring measures could not be challenged in Italian courts.

2.2.1.4. *United Kingdom*

2.2.1.4.1. UK SUPREME COURT[144]

The UK Supreme Court's (UKSC) decision in *NML v Argentina (UK)* was closely connected to the *NML* litigation in US courts discussed earlier.[145] Unlike rulings rendered by other (European) courts in the wake of Argentina's crisis, *NML v Argentina (UK)* primarily concerned the recognition and enforcement of foreign judgements against sovereign states in the UK.[146] NML applied for the recognition of the US money judgements in order to enforce it in the UK, thereby broadening the scope of potentially Argentine (commercial) assets to such located in the world's (second) financial centre, London.[147]

Lord Phillips, who wrote the majority opinion, first clarified that judicial immunity did not apply to commercial transaction under both pertinent case law[148] and the UK State Immunity Act 1978 (SIA).[149] He specified that while the SIA did not make provision for the enforcement of foreign judgements,[150] section 31 of the UK Civil Jurisdiction and Judgments Act of 1982 (the Act) regarding the recognition of foreign court decisions was applicable.[151] In Lord Phillip's view, this provision replaced the exemptions from immunity contained in the SIA, which 'provides an alternative scheme for restricting state immunity in the case of foreign judgments.'[152]

The majority opinion further held that suits relating to judgements issued by foreign courts must be distinguished from legal action that included a review of the merits in English court.[153] According to the SIA, English judges had no legal power to (re)investigate whether a foreign court had rightly concluded that a state activity was commercial.[154] Accordingly, the English courts may accept the foreign court's assessment of the commercial nature of a foreign state act.[155] Consequently, since the SDNY had denied Argentina's immunity, the UKSC recognized the judgment as a matter of English law. Regarding English courts' jurisdiction, the UKSC further noted that Argentina's bonds contained broad immunity waivers, and that '[this] unambiguous waiver of immunity . . . was tantamount to a submission to the jurisdiction [of English courts].'[156] Hence, all requirements set out in section 2(2) of the SIA to establish international jurisdiction of UK courts were met, opening the gates for the attachment of Argentine assets located in Britain.

While there were no execution proceedings in the United Kingdom because of that decision, NML relied on it to seize an Argentine navy vessel in Ghana's capital a few months later.[157]

2.2.1.5. *France*

In its worldwide hunt for assets, the NML Capital also sought to attach Argentine assets located in France. The judgements rendered by French courts focus in particular on the types of assets foreign creditors may attach if a sovereign debt issuer has waived its immunity from enforcement. International bonds issued by Argentine government in the 1990s contained sovereign immunity waivers, which included explicit waivers of execution immunity.[158] However, despite Argentina's express waivers, the French Supreme Court (*Cour de Cassation*) dismissed a series of execution measures launched by the NML Capital between 2009 and 2013.

2.2.1.5.1. FRENCH SUPREME COURT (*COUR DE CASSATION*)

NML v Argentina I This first case before French courts concerned the immunity of diplomatic assets from holdout attachment. Based on a money judgment obtained in New York courts against Argentina, the NML Capital sought to attach deposits in a French bank account owned by Argentina's diplomatic missions in France. The key question at stake was whether Argentina's contractual sovereign immunity waiver would also extend to diplomatic assets.

The *Cour de Cassation* threw out the suit, holding that the protection of foreign diplomatic missions vital to ensure the receiving state's due representation in France.[159] The lower courts had previously sided with the plaintiff, arguing that the 1994 FAA underpinning Argentina's bonds also covered diplomatic assets. Referring to the text Vienna Convention on Diplomatic Relations (VCDR) 1961,[160] the Court of Appeals emphasized that sums deposited in the diplomatic embassy's bank accounts were not protected under international law if the receiving country had expressly waived immunity from enforcement.[161]

The French Supreme Court, however, rejected this interpretation. Instead, it held that a sovereign immunity waiver, in order to be effective, must expressly specify the types and categories of diplomatic assets exempted from the general immunity set out in Article 32 of the VCDR.[162] The French Supreme Court argued that a special regime existed under customary international law, which required waivers to be both *specific* and *explicit*.[163]

In a second plea, the plaintiff argued that the enforcement judge had imposed a disproportionate burden on the creditor by requiring him to identify whether the sums deposited in a foreign state's bank account had in fact been assigned to diplomatic purposes.[164] The French Supreme Court also denied this claim, arguing that the funds' ultimate use was irrelevant to assessing their possible protection under the rules of international law. The fact that these funds were attributable to Argentina's diplomatic representation in France was sufficient to shield them from enforcement attempts by private creditors.[165] Specifically, in the court's view, it should have been obvious from the name stated on the account, namely 'Embassy of Argentina,' that the funds could not be subject to enforcement measures in France due to the principle of diplomatic immunity.[166]

NML Capital v Argentina II In three decisions published on 28 March 2013, the French *Cour de Cassation* further expanded the requirement of an asset-specific waiver to all assets of a foreign state, even if such assets at stake are not owned by Argentina's diplomatic representation in France.[167] The decisions related to receivables owed by French companies to Argentina, which the holdouts sought to attach.[168] Akin to its first decision on the Argentine bondholder claims, the *Cour de Cassation* examined whether Argentina's contractual waiver in the bond indenture allowed for the attachment of these specific receivables.

The court first clarified that, according to the UNCSI, which broadly reflects customary international law, 'immunity may be waived only expressly and specifically by mentioning the property or class of property for which the waiver is granted.'[169] In the Argentine FAA, however, the waiver was of general nature and did not encompass a list of attachable assets.[170] Given that Argentina's claims against the aforementioned French corporations, which included tax, social, and oil royalties, were not (explicitly) included in the waiver, they could not be attached by NML Capital.[171] Moreover, the *Cour de Cassation* emphasized that the protection of an asset under international law depended on its *use* rather than its origin.[172] As the claims at stake were taxlike debts, they clearly had a sovereign use flowing into Argentina's state budget, and should, thus, be protected under international law.[173]

2.2.1.6. Switzerland

2.2.1.6.1. SWISS FEDERAL SUPREME COURT[174]

Post-restructuring litigation in Switzerland was limited to a single yet critical case that was again initiated by NML Capital and targeted Argentine holdings of currency reserve at the BIS. Specifically, the case related to the attachment of funds held by the BCRA at accounts at the BIS in Basel, an international financial institution owned by 62 central banks that is sometimes referred to as the 'central bank of central banks.'[175] Argentina had, according to NML Capital, transferred a significant chunk of its foreign exchange reserves to the BIS in the wake of its default, allegedly to avoid attachment through creditors.[176] The application to the Swiss courts was based on two payment orders by the SDNY obtained in the wake of the default. The central legal issue was whether assets held at the BIS enjoyed special immunities against creditor seizure.[177]

The case reached the Swiss Federal Supreme Court (SFSC) after Basel's Debt Enforcement Office ordered the freezing of all assets held by Argentina at the BIS upon NML Capital's request.[178] The Swiss Foreign Office had successfully appealed to the Supervisory Committee of Basel's Debt Enforcement Office, insisting that the BIS enjoyed immunity in Switzerland with respect to assets entrusted to it by its members.[179] NML Capital challenged this decision in the SFSC, inter alia asserting that it violated the plaintiff's right of access to court under Article 29a of the Swiss Constitution and Article 6 ECHR.[180]

The SFSC reviewed the arrest order against the backdrop of the immunity guaranteed to the BIS by Article 55(2) of the Statute of the BIS[181] and Article 4 of the BIS Headquarters Agreement.[182] It remarked that according to Article 4(1)(a) of the Headquarters Agreement, the BIS enjoyed immunity from jurisdiction and execution, 'save to the extent that such immunity is formally waived.'[183]

Yet the BIS had expressly denied the existence of such formal waiver.[184] Moreover, the SFSC found that central bank deposits at the BIS were protected from debt enforcement attempts by private creditors under to the Headquarters Agreement[185]: given its functions as a 'central bank for central banks,' an attachment order against funds held by the BCRA at the BIS would undermine the institution's core functions and organizational purpose.[186]

Regarding the question whether the transferral of funds to the BIS by BCRA amid the country's economic crisis constituted an abuse of the institution's immunity,[187] as claimed by the holdout creditor, the SFSC remained silent and granted a wide margin of discretion to the BIS.[188] It emphasized that municipal courts ought not to decide independently which transactions undertaken between an international organization and its members were necessary in line with its mandate or – as asserted by the plaintiff – constituted an abuse of law.[189] The international organization's internal assessment was decisive.[190]

Finally, the SFSC weighed in on Article 6 ECHR,[191] which – according to the plaintiff – was violated by the decision to decline an application for execution against assets deposited at the BIS. While the court agreed that Article 6 ECHR encompassed a right to a fair execution proceeding, it does not restrict the party's free enjoyment of property if this was both legitimate *and* proportionate.

Referring to the ECtHR decision in *Waite and Kennedy v Germany*,[192] the SFSC clarified that the privileges and immunities granted to the BIS pursued a legitimate public interest aim, given its function as international global payments platform (*Zahlungsdrehscheibe*).[193] Regarding proportionality, the court assessed that there was no reasonable alternative to ensure a necessary and adequate level of protection to international organizations in the host state, Switzerland.[194] BIS operations would be severely impaired if Swiss courts were to render judgements regarding the legitimacy of central bank transactions based on monetary policy decisions, such as the transfer of Argentine assets to the BIS.[195]

2.2.2. Holdout Litigation in International Courts and Tribunals

2.2.2.1. International Tribunal for the Law of the Sea

Notwithstanding numerous unconventional asset attachment attempts, the *ARA Libertad* case[196] stood out – it exemplified the vulture holdouts' relentless hunt for assets, which quite literally stretched the entire globe. NML Capital's attempt to seize an Argentine military vessel in an African port prompted irritation among observers and fury among Argentine officials – a result very much to the liking of the plaintiff. As Paul Singer, the hedge fund's founder, shrewdly admitted, he 'did not purchase [Argentinian] debt in order to acquire a ship too large to sail in Long Island Sound.'[197]

The Argentine training navy vessel *ARA Libertad* had arrived at the Ghanaian port of Tema on 1 October 2012 for an official visit.[198] Just a day later, NML Capital filed Statement of Claim in the High Court of Accra, Ghana's capital, with the professed objective of enforcing money judgements rendered by New York courts against Argentina. The Ghanese court subsequently detained the ship and prohibited the crew from leaving the country for as long as Argentina failed to post collateral with a value of at least USD20 million.[199] Argentina challenged the decision in Ghanaian courts, but the country's High Court saw no reason to set the injunction aside.[200]

Argentina, thus, appealed to the ITLOS, where it questioned the legality of the Ghanaian court order under the international law of the seas. Specifically, Argentina argued that Ghana's acts violated the United Nations Convention on the Law of the Sea (UNCLOS),[201] to which both Argentina and Ghana were parties, asserting that Ghana had violated its obligations to respect the immunity of military vessels according to Article 32 of the UNCLOS,[202] Article 3 of the 1926 International Convention for the Unification of Certain Rules Concerning the Immunity of State-Owned Vessels,[203] and customary international law.[204] Ghana did not dispute the fact that warships sailing on the high seas were protected under customary international law but rather posited that the dispute was beyond the jurisdiction of the ITLOS as Argentina had expressly waived its immunity regarding said debt obligations.[205]

In its twentieth case, the ITLOS focused on assessing and defining the immunity of military ships under UNCLOS as well as customary international law. In accordance with Article 290(5) UNCLOS, the tribunal considered Argentina's claim on a prima facie basis, thus without assessing its merits.[206] It held that the *ARA Libertad* fell under the definition of a warship pursuant to Article 29 UNCLOS[207] due to its functions in Argentina's navy. The tribunal further remarked that such warships 'enjoy[ed] immunity under general international law, including in internal waters.'[208] Thus, the Ghanaian court order, which barred the vessel from leaving the country, violated the immunity of warships under the pertinent rules of international law.

The ITLOS tribunal, moreover, found that proceedings for interim measures were appropriate, for the attempt of Ghanaian authorities to board the Libertad 'demonstrated the gravity of the situation and underlined the urgent need for measures pending the constitution of the Annex VII arbitral tribunal.'[209] The urgency of the situation, thus, required the tribunal to act in accordance with Article 290(5) UNCLOS and prescribe that 'Ghana shall forthwith and unconditionally release the frigate ARA Libertad.'[210] Following the ITLOS decision, to avoid further international embarrassment, Ghana immediately revoked the arrest warrant and the *Libertad* left the port of Tema on 19 December 2013.

2.2.2.2. International Court of Justice

Following its defeat before the US Supreme Court in *Argentina v NML*,[211] the Argentine government filed an application to institute proceedings against the US before the International Court of Justice (ICJ).[212] Argentina's challenge faced the almost insurmountable obstacle of the US government consenting to the jurisdiction of the ICJ, which would have amounted to nothing short of a 'miracle.'[213]

Even in the – extremely unlikely – case that the US government would have accepted ICJ jurisdiction, the claim that the US court decisions unduly interfered with Argentina's sovereignty, and thus breached its obligations under international law, had close to no chance of success on the merits. After all, it was the Argentine government that submitted to the jurisdiction of courts in the State of New York for disputes relating to its sovereign bond contracts. The US government was never a party to the contract. It would have had to obstruct, or at least influence, the conduct of its independent federal courts to bring about a different outcome for Argentina. Constitutional obstacles abound, such course of action was never realistic.

In fact, the US government publicly supported Argentina during the trial by issuing a sharply worded amicus brief that criticized the courts' broad reading of sovereign immunity and warned about the implications for US foreign relations and the treatment of US individuals in foreign courts.[214] Moreover, it was far from clear that US courts had breached an obligation under international law or that the ICJ would have taken any issue with the way the court decided.[215] Finally, and perhaps most importantly, the US Supreme Court has taken the view[216] that ICJ decisions are not binding on US courts and do not form part of domestic law.

2.2.3. *Interim Conclusions: Enforcing Sovereign Debt in Foreign Courts*

Sovereign debt enforcement in foreign courts, the ultimate threat in the holdout creditors' repertoire, remains a daunting and uncertain endeavour. The post-Argentine restructuring litigation confirmed old legal principles and doctrines but also nurtured the rise of unconventional holdout strategies, culminating in the seminal *NML* decision in US federal courts. This section seeks to draw the key lessons from the Argentine case law against the backdrop of the aforementioned rulings and orders, focusing on sovereign immunity from suit and enforcement as well as the novel injunction fashioned by the SDNY to compel Argentina to pay the holdouts.

2.2.3.1. Adjudicatory Sovereign Immunity

Sovereign immunity from suit is widely considered a relative concept in the context of state financing activities on private financial markets.[217] There is no need to revisit the substantive case law in this area, which others have done in a comprehensive and compelling manner.[218] Rather, this section focuses on the central point of contention in the Argentine litigation, namely the mixed activity conundrum that complicates the delineation of commercial and non-commercial sovereign acts. It also addresses the issue of recognition of foreign judgements in light of the UK courts' decisions in the *NML* matter, for recognition may allow creditors to circumvent immunity constraints if these have already been dealt with in a foreign court.

2.2.3.1.1. THE COMMERCIAL ACTIVITY EXCEPTION: 'ONCE A TRADER ALWAYS A TRADER' AND THE MIXED ACTIVITY CONUNDRUM

Sticking closely to the first sovereign debt cases in the 1980s, where the restrictive theory of sovereign immunity was honed, US courts flatly rejected Argentina's immunity from suit.[219] Argentina's sovereign immunity waiver in the 1994 FAA as well as the FSIA's clear statutory rules on commercial activities meant that there was little scope for federal courts to deviate from the well-established Supreme Court case law.[220] To this end, the SDNY's opinion in *Lightwater* reflected the archetypical holdout litigation against Argentina in New York.[221] The government's interference with creditors' repayment rights through executive actions and legislative moratoria was irrelevant for the courts' narrow focus on whether contracts governed by New York law had been breached.

Other jurisdictions, however, entertained alternative interpretations of the sovereign immunity doctrine. In contrast to the bulk of decisions rendered by courts in New York, the UK, and Germany, the Italian judiciary in *Borri* considered Argentina immune from suit.[222] Critically, human rights considerations played an important role in the court's assessment and specifically for the qualification of Argentina's emergency legislation as *acta iure imperii*.[223]

Borri also underscored the complicated relationship between the qualification of government debt issuance as commercial activity and the ex post interference with creditor rights through legislation.[224] Undoubtedly, in the course of the 20th century, most municipal courts and international tribunals had moved from qualifying public debt issuances as *acta iure imperii* to considering them commercial legal acts that may be subject to foreign court review.[225] While the Italian Supreme Court acknowledged this development, it also casted doubt on whether this precludes states from employing legislation, and hence a sovereign legal act, to restructure their debts and, thereby, also immunize these restructuring measures from court review. The *Borri* decision suggested they may.

Several scholars have criticized this approach.

Bröhmer,[226] for example, notes that '[i]t makes no sense to treat the issuance of bonds as commercial act only to turn around and qualify the decision not honour these bonds as a sovereign act.'[227] Bonafe[228] essentially agrees with Bröhmer, noting this:

> [while] the Italian courts have recognised that the *issuance* of the global bonds was a commercial activity on the part of Argentina, . . . Italian courts have adopted two different criteria to establish whether Argentina was entitled to claim immunity from jurisdiction.

On the one hand, they have regarded the issuance of global bonds as *acta iure gestionis* according to the *nature* (not purpose) of this financial transaction in line with the UNCSI.[229] On the other hand, the Italian Supreme Court regarded the moratorium of Argentina's public debt and the payment rescheduling as *acta iure imperii* according to the *purpose* of such government activity.[230] Both Bröhmer's and Bonafe's criticisms of the Argentine bondholder case boil down to a conundrum that arises in the context of 'mixed' state activities.[231]

A state engages in a mixed activity if it initially concludes a commercial contract with private bondholders (*acta iure gestionis*) but subsequently breaches the contract through executive or legislative orders (*acta iure imperii*).[232] The same issue has also been discussed under the umbrella of the 'once a trader always a trader' or 'once commercial always commercial' debate.[233]

In light of the restrictive concept of sovereign immunity for state financing activities under customary international law, the question as to whether states can ever again claim immunity *after* they have signed an undoubtedly commercial contract is vital. However, the UNCSI or pertinent international jurisprudence provides little guidance on this issue. Bonafe, thus, notes that 'it is far from clear which state activity should be regarded as determinative – the prior act *iure gestionis* or the subsequent act *iure imperii*.'[234]

So which activity should be decisive: the issuance of a bond or a subsequent debt moratorium or default?[235] The Italian Supreme Court opted for the latter. However, as much as this view bestows a strong level of protection from disruptive holdout litigation upon sovereign debtors, there is insufficient evidence that this legal reasoning finds an anchor in customary international law,[236] especially with regard to instruments governed by laws other than those over which the sovereign debtor has full control.[237] Moreover, the *Borri* decision's stance on adjudicatory immunity clearly deviated from other rulings rendered in the wake of the Argentine debt crisis, including that of the German BGH in 2015. While the BGH elaborated in great lengths on the necessity defence, as discussed later, it shrugged off sovereign immunity concerns given the unequivocal immunity waiver in the bonds as well as the qualification of Argentina's bond issuance as *acta iure gestionis*.[238]

The decision in *Borri* also differed from previous leading cases on mixed state activities, such as the decision in *Trendtex v Nigeria*.[239] In that case, the Court of Appeal of Wales and England essentially ruled that Nigeria had no immunity in respect of commercial transactions. Trendtex sued Nigeria for damages for the non-payment of imported cement as well as the non-acceptance of outstanding shipments after the government ordered the Nigerian Central Bank that no further payment must be made to the international trading company. Siding with the plaintiff, the UK court denied immunity for the government's order, given that the basis that the original legal relationship between Trendtex and the Central Bank of Nigeria was a purely commercial transaction.[240] Neither the purpose (protecting Nigeria from default) nor the nature of the order (*acta iure gestionis*) mattered to the English court; instead, it cemented the 'once a trader always a trader' principle as a matter of English law.[241]

2.2.3.1.2. RECOGNITION OF FOREIGN JUDGEMENTS

Immunity from suit is typically assessed by the court that has jurisdiction pursuant to the choice of forum clause or the pertinent conflict of law rules. However, creditors may also seek to have a foreign court judgment recognized in another jurisdiction without a separate decision on both the procedural (usually immunity) or the merits of the case. This is what the NML Capital did in the UK.

NML v Argentina (UK) made it clear that holdouts could rely on New York court judgements to enforce (foreign) government bonds in the UK and, therefore, seize commercially used sovereign assets on British soil. The judgment, at least theoretically, expanded the scope of attachable assets and strengthened the holdouts' bargaining position vis-à-vis the sovereign debtor. Indeed, as Megliani points out, the 'Queen's Bench, ruling on the enforcement of a debt judgment against Argentina, did not take into consideration the Argentine acts related to debt restructuring,' solely relying on the New York court's view on the substance of NML's claim.[242]

A full trial before an English court, which could take a much stricter view than the SDNY, may therefore not be necessary to enforce the bonds of a foreign sovereign on English soil.[243] As Gyner notes, the principles established by Lord Philipps allow investors to use another route to lift immunity.[244] Since the decision held that the immunity waiver also amounted to a submission to jurisdiction, future holdout litigants now have a considerable advantage with respect to the cross-border enforcement of sovereign debt contracts. Whether the UKSC would also recognize and enforce judgements by other courts (i.e., non-US courts) depends on whether that country's rules are compliant with the ones applicable under English law.[245]

2.2.3.2. *Immunity from Enforcement*

Almost all countries set a relatively higher bar to enforcing judgements against sovereigns than to suing them; the world's two financial centres are no exception.

In the US, §1610 FSIA stipulates that while sovereigns may waive their immunity from execution, which they commonly do when they issue bonds under New York law, the property must still be in the United States *and* used for commercial activities in the US whenever execution is sought on that foreign state property.[246] In the UK, Section 13 of the SIA also requires prior written consent from the state (i.e., a waiver) as well as measures taken in respect of property in use or intended use for commercial purposes.[247] There were few asset attachment attempts into property located in the US following Argentina's default, notably because the government kept a low (commercial) profile.

However, as the cases analysed earlier suggest, the global hunt for Argentine assets resulted in a remarkable amount of case law in other jurisdictions, notably in Europe. Most of the enforcement attempts on the continent were unsuccessful, underlining the difficulties associated with attaching assets owned by a sovereign state or its instrumentalities, even if the sovereign has previously waived its immunity from execution. From the holdouts' perspective, the main obstacle was that there was significant uncertainty as to which Argentine assets were used for commercial purposes and which for sovereign, and hence protected, purposes.

2.2.3.2.1. THE IMMUNITY OF PUBLIC CLAIMS FROM CREDITOR ATTACHMENT

As shown earlier, both the highest French and German courts ruled that holdout creditors may not attach tax or taxlike obligations owed by companies to Argentina. Given that such obligations may amount to significant sums, seizing them could theoretically be a highly lucrative source to satisfy money judgements obtained in courts. The pertinent judicial rulings made clear, however, that these types of financial claims deserve special protection, even if a sovereign waived immunity from enforcement, as Argentina had done. The post-Argentina litigation in Europe also confirmed the stance taken by US courts in earlier cases, such as *LNC v Nicaragua*, where the Second Circuit held that taxes owed by American companies to Nicaragua may not be attached because they were protected under §1610(a) FSIA.[248]

The German BGH focused on its international jurisdiction, positing that taxes and custom obligations owed by German companies to Argentina lay outside Germany's territory and could, thus, not be seized by creditors. It largely relied on a 2005 precedent, in which it held that Russian claims against airlines for overflight fees could not be seized by third-party creditors due to their public law nature.[249] However, that ruling said nothing about the territoriality principle that the BGH invoked in the Argentine litigation, leaving some uncertainty as to the controlling factors to determine the attachability of tax(like) claims.[250]

Similar to the BGH's 2010 decision, in *NML v Argentina II*, the French *Cour de Cassation* held that tax claims owed by French companies to Argentina may not be attached because they were linked to the exercise of state functions and, thus, immune. Since the claims were *used* for sovereign functions, they could not be attached.[251] The ruling also raised some questions, however. Blumenrosen and Malet-Deraedt, for instance, point out that 'state revenue is problematic precisely because it may not have been allocated for any specific purpose, or may be mixed purpose, that is, in part allocated for governmental purposes and in part for commercial activities.'[252] They contend that Article 19(c) UNCSI does leave some room for interpretation by merely stating that measures of constraint are prohibited if 'the property is specifically in use or intended for use by the State for other than government non-commercial purposes.'[253] It, hence, seems that the *Cour de Cassation* subsumed taxlike assets under the category of non-commercial assets as defined in Article 21 UNCSI,[254] effectively adding a new category of immune property to the list under Article 21 UNCSI, namely tax and social claims owed by a company to the foreign state.

In 2016, the French Parliament further strengthened the protection of foreign state assets from holdout creditor enforcement.[255] Article 60 of the French Law Against Breaches of Probity (*Loi De La Lutte Contre Les Manquements À La Probité*)[256] significantly restricts the enforcement of foreign judgements in France by hedge funds, barring (i) the execution against states that are the beneficiaries of development aid and (ii) the execution of judgements relating to bonds that were acquired after default. NML Capital subsequently challenged the law, but the French Constitutional Council concluded that the pertinent provisions did not unduly interfere with the fundamental right to the free enjoyment of property.[257]

2.2.3.2.2. THE IMMUNITY OF CENTRAL BANK RESERVES FROM ATTACHMENT

The most valuable assets that most foreign sovereigns hold in the US, and hence subject to higher risk of seizure by litigious creditors, are foreign exchange reserves deposited at the FRBNY. The FRBNY plays a critical role in the international financial and payments architecture, as it offers banking and financial services to about 250 central banks, governments, and international official institutions on behalf of the Federal Reserve System.[258] The holdouts' contention was that Argentina had moved significant foreign exchange reserves to the FRBNY as well as the BIS to evade asset seizure attempts while continuing to repay exchanging bondholders.

They adopted (at least) two strategies to seize hard currency deposited at the FRBNY: (i) directly exploit the legal loophole in the FSIA, which stems from the fact that central banks are, at least sometimes, engaged in commercial activities and thus not immune from suit and enforcement and (ii) argue that § 1611(b)(1) FSIA does not apply to the central bank since it is the government's alter ego in line with the Supreme Court's *Banec* test. In *EM v BCRA*, discussed earlier, the holdout plaintiff relied on the latter argument and lost.

Given that the FSIA remains silent on the alter ego concept, the court in *EM v BCRA* resorted to international law and federal common law, borrowing heavily from the principle of veil piercing developed under corporate law.[259] *Banec*[260] had set an even higher bar for central banks to be deemed the government's alter ego, reflecting the FSIA's legislative decision to bestow upon foreign central banks additional protection from creditor enforcement action under § 1611 FSIA.[261] Even though some observers criticize *Banec* for its vague language, *EM v BCRA* confirmed the importance that both the courts and the legislator attach to the protection of foreign central bank assets located at the FRBNY.[262]

A glance beyond US-specific obstacles to enforcing judgements against a foreign country's central bank reveals a broadly consistent picture across major jurisdictions, with a few remaining differences.

In Germany, while the immunity of central banks from execution procedures is not enshrined in domestic law,[263] German case law requires an unambiguous and explicit waiver of sovereign immunity for central bank assets, which usually poses significant obstacles to enforcement actions.[264] In Belgium, a vulture fund unsuccessfully tried to attach assets of the central bank of the Democratic Republic of Congo.[265] UK courts have famously protected the Central Bank of Nigeria's assets from private creditors in the *Trendtex* decision from 1977.[266]

By contrast, in Switzerland, courts have loosened the requirements to pierce the veil between the governments and its central bank.[267] However, the BIS, located in Basel but subject to special immunities, marks an exception to that trend. Like foreign states' accounts at the FRBNY, monies stored at the BIS represent an alluring target for holdout creditors in their global 'hunt for assets.'[268] While the FRBNY is exclusively protected by US law, the BIS enjoys the privileges and immunities of an international organization under international law.[269] In the US, international organizations like the BIS would have likely benefitted from §1611(a) FSIA, which exempts properties of international organizations from attachment and execution. In Switzerland, the legal situation was murkier.

While doctrinally different, the SFSC's ruling essentially reflects the same legal policy considerations as the US Second Circuit's judgment in *EM v BCRA*.[270]

By barring debt enforcement into funds held by foreign central banks on BIS accounts, the host state, Switzerland, protected the BIS in order to facilitate smooth payments flows between central banks and to maintain currency reserves for various international transactions.[271] The SFSC had consistently endorsed a broad interpretation of the immunity of international organizations located in Switzerland and its decision in *NML v BIS* aligned with earlier decisions.[272]

In the literature, the Swiss decision was discussed somewhat controversially. For Neumann and Peters, the distinction drawn under international law between state immunity, which is restrictive in nature, and the immunity of international organizations, which remains quasi-absolute, is justified by the fact that the latter do not dispose of any territorial basis.[273] At the same time, to justify this augmented level of immunity, acts by an international organization should, as a general rule, relate closely to the organization's functional character of its legal personality, as, for instance, clarified by the Swiss courts in the *CERN*[274] case. To this end, by focusing on the functional necessity doctrine to narrow down the scope of organizational immunities, Neumann finds that the SFSC in *NML v BIS* 'missed a chance to provide a more substantial argumentative underpinning of, and to explain more thoroughly, its traditional, heavily treaty-oriented absolute immunities concept.'[275]

Neumann and Peters, moreover, contend that the SFSC failed to identify and evaluate the particular interests of the holdout creditor in having the BIS's immunity reviewed under Article 6 of the ECHR.[276] The ECtHR[277] would usually first examine whether an applicant may resort to alternative dispute settlement mechanism, and therefore, enjoyed sufficient protection of its human rights, before addressing the question of immunity.[278] By throwing out the suit without reviewing the merits of the plaintiff's claims, the SFSC, in Neumann's and Peter's views, wrongly applied the ECtHR's jurisprudence.[279]

In response to this critique one may assert that international organizations can only function satisfactorily if its independence and immunity from local court enforcement is absolute for tasks performed in accordance with its mandate. Hence, even if NML Capital had a justifiable interest in the protection of its property through the enforcement of its court orders against Argentina, a contentious claim by many accounts, international organization's immunity defence remains critical to insulate them from private creditor litigation. While this result may at times seem harsh from the perspective of the creditor, most IFIs enjoy immunity of private lawsuits, including the IMF[280] or the ECB,[281] for tasks they conduct within their mandate.[282] At a more conceptual level, the protection of international organizations reflects the international community's preference to resolve disputes pertaining to international organizations at the political rather than the judicial level.[283]

2.2.3.2.3. ARA LIBERTAD AND THE IMMUNITY OF (MILITARY) VESSELS

The *ARA Libertad* case was widely discussed in the literature, with most scholars agreeing to the outcome of the ITLOS case.[284] From a dogmatic point of view, the ITLOS buttressed the immunity of warships and set an important precedent for the rule of international customary law in domestic ports.[285] The decision elucidated that even if states had waived their immunity in their sovereign debt securities, certain cogent rules of international law would, almost always, override the state's contractual consent. Naturally, the ITLOS did not assess whether the warship had actually served a sovereign purpose; rather, reflecting Article 32 UNCLOS, it presumed under customary international law that property of a military character used, or intended for use for military purposes, shall not be considered as property specifically in use or intended for use by the state for other than government non-commercial purposes.[286]

In future sovereign debt crises, the immunity of ships owned by a sovereign but used for commercial purposes will be more important than that of military vessels. While the ITLOS decision in *ARA Libertad* provided more legal certainty with regard to the protection of warships anchored in foreign ports, trade ships may still be arrested for the purpose of debt execution, as they are not covered by the UNCLOS. Venezuela, with its fleet of oil tankers, marks a case in point. Its ships – and especially the precious liquid stored in their hulls – present a far more attractive target to litigious creditors in the wake of a potential future sovereign debt restructuring than an Argentine sailing boat.[287]

2.2.3.3. Third-Party Injunctions: A New Super Remedy to Circumvent the Immunity Defence?

Both the unorthodox interpretation of the pari passu provision and the (injunctive) remedy in *NML v Argentina* have arguably threated, if not upset, the sovereign debt equilibrium.[288] At least in the first few years after the ruling, there was broad agreement in the literature[289] and among policymakers[290] that the decisions created compelling incentives for creditors to delay the restructuring of sovereign debt governed by New York law and hold out for a better deal, including such investors that would traditionally not act as holdouts. And as Weidemaier and Gelpern posit, 'it would be a mistake to dismiss the [*NML*] case as completely sui generis.'[291]

At the same time, as argued further later, the SDNY's subsequent clarifications on the meaning of the pari passu clause and the reach of the injunction have further defused the threat from this specific type of litigation strategy. This does not mean the threat is gone. While money judgements have allowed creditors to attach certain sovereign assets, the pari passu injunction considerably bolsters their ability to exert pressure on a defiant sovereign borrower.[292] It is not a completely novel device, having been endorsed for the first time by a Brussels court in 2000 against Peru.[293] Virtually any payment made by a debtor country to bondholders that passes through New York City could be at risk of being blocked by virtue of the pari passu injunction.[294] Moreover, given its reach, any financial institution involved in the payment and clearing process would risk acting in contempt of the court by not complying. *NML v Argentina* was also an unambiguous expression of US extraterritoriality: any bank or agent, be they licensed in the US or elsewhere, that assisted Argentina in ensuring timely repayment of (non-holdout) creditors was subject to the injunction.[295]

Additionally, it may be argued that *NML v Argentina* neglected important aspects of the sovereign immunity doctrine. While FSIA generally does not preclude injunctions, there remains some uncertainty whether an injunction is an appropriate legal remedy to compel foreign sovereign debt repayment.[296] In effect, holdouts were able to circumvent the obstacles to attaching sovereign assets laid down in the FSIA and the UNCSI, thereby eventually pressing Argentina to settle on their terms.[297] The Second Circuit argued that the §1609 FSIA would not be applicable to injunctions, as they 'do not attach, arrest, or execute upon any property,'[298] the order effectively constrained Argentina from providing *exchanged* bondholders access to funds they were entitled to pursuant to their contracts. The argument thus seems one-dimensional, ostensibly protecting the holdouts' contractual rights while directly interfering with the claims exchanged bondholders were entitled to.

Looking ahead, (at least) two legal questions will determine *NML v Argentina*'s implications for future sovereign restructurings:

- First, could a pari passu injunction again be invoked by holdouts? On the one hand, the ubiquitous use of pari passu clauses in international sovereign bonds means that the New York courts' interpretation matters for many sovereign issuers around the globe. On the other hand, Argentina's pari passu clause was drafted in a particularly ambiguous manner, and more recent sovereign bond prospectuses have explicitly discarded Judge Griesa's understanding of ratable payment. In addition, New York courts have recently clarified that sovereign debtors may, under certain circumstances, pay their creditors selectively.[299] What the pari passu clause clearly prohibited was the subordination of some (holdout) creditors' claims by virtue of law (formal subordination).[300] Indeed, most scholars seem to discard the view that pari passu clause requires ratable payment to holdouts and restructured bondholders alike.[301]
- Second, how does one become a 'uniquely recalcitrant debtor' and, thus, the potential target of a pari passu injunction?[302] In the court's view, Argentina's resistance to paying the holdouts justified the injunction due to considerations of equity. However, it appears difficult to ascertain what kind of behaviour renders a sovereign debtor uniquely recalcitrant. While it is true that few countries had so persistently refused to pay its debts,[303] the concept of unique recalcitrance is defined neither by case law nor by statute(s). Thus, Judge Griesa's concept of unique recalcitrance is a poor yardstick to assess whether equipping holdouts with a pari passu injunction is equitable or not.[304] Most sovereign debt crises are in fact unique, for they can threaten the economic and political stability of a nation and warrant extraordinary action on the government's and often the international community's part.[305]

Overall, the likelihood that pari passu injunctions will eternally haunt sovereign bond restructurings in New York seems less likely in 2023 than in 2014.[306]

For one, the hitherto only case of copycat litigation has been unsuccessful. In 2013, Export-Import Bank of the Republic of China sued Grenada in New York federal courts and argued that Grenada breached the pari passu clause by paying off non-restructured bondholders, seeking to capitalize on the *NML v Argentina* decision.[307] In that judgment, however, the SDNY concluded that there was no pari passu violation, as Grenada had not introduced a law to impede any form of payment to non-bondholders and since the payments in favour of non-exchanging bondholders was conditional on the availability of resources.[308]

For another, as discussed later,[309] following the settlement between holdouts and the new Argentine government in 2016, Judge Griesa arguably defused the threat of the pari passu injunction. Finally, countries have taken active steps to mitigate risks from the clause. For instance, in its 2013 exchange offer, Belize explicitly rejected the ratable payment interpretation.[310] Moreover, upon recommendation by both private and official sector bodies, most sovereign creditors now issue international sovereign bonds with modified pari passu clauses that explicitly discount the payment interpretation advanced by the SDNY.[311] The share of bonds with problematic pari passu language is gradually diminishing, though it may take decades until all securities with potentially vulnerable clauses have matured.

2.3. Holdout Arbitration After Argentina

2.3.1. International Investment Arbitration Before ICSID Tribunals

Holdouts not only litigated against Argentina, but they also filed claims against Argentina under international investment law. This section analyses two seminal holdout arbitration proceedings in the ICSID concerning Argentina's alleged violation of different BITs in the context of its 2001 sovereign default and restructurings: the *Abaclat*[312] and the *Ambiente Ufficio*[313] cases.[314] While the Argentine government reached numerous settlements with ICSID claimants between 2001 and 2013, a significant number of retail holdouts stayed firm and pressed on with their claims. In 2016, however, the new administration relented to a settlement with tens of thousands of Italian bondholders to facilitate its return to international debt markets.[315] The post-default arbitration illustrated that ICSID may serve as (yet another) forum to exert considerable pressure on a sovereign debtor in default, even if direct debt collection attempts based on ICSID awards remain subject to considerable uncertainty.[316]

2.3.1.1. Abaclat and Others v Argentine Republic[317]

The group of claimants in *Abaclat* consisted of 180,000 individual bondholders, most of which were Italian retail investors.[318] It was the hitherto largest ICSID arbitration case measured by the number of claimants. Bondholders had filed their request for arbitration in 2006, shortly after the first Argentine restructuring offer in 2005, which many claimants deemed insufficient and unfair. The ICSID tribunal was constituted in February 2007, and the first sessions were held in 2008.

In essence, the claimants contended that they were deprived of the value of their investment because of Argentina's public debt moratorium.[319] Specifically, they alleged the following: (i) Argentina had repudiated its obligations and pursued a unilateral, punitive exchange offer targeting; (ii) Argentina had enacted legislation to the same effect, thus destroying the value of their investment; and (iii) Argentina had acted as a rogue debtor by breaching its international treaty obligations. Argentina rejected this view, positing that the conditions for ICSID jurisdiction were not fulfilled, as the ICSID Convention[320] did not permit collective claims, the tribunal lacked jurisdiction *ratione personae*, and the claims depended fundamentally on contractual obligations rather than the Argentina-Italy BIT.[321]

Against this backdrop, the tribunal essentially focused on two legal questions:

- First, do sovereign bonds constitute an investment in international investment law?
- Second, are mass claims admissible to arbitration under the rules of the ICSID Convention?

2.3.1.1.1. SOVEREIGN BONDS AS INVESTMENT

In assessing its jurisdiction before reviewing the claims on merit, the tribunal focused on the interpretation of Article 25 ICSID Convention and the Argentina-Italy BIT. According to the prevailing double-barrelled test, for the investment to be protected under international investment law, it ought to fit into both the definition of investment under the applicable BIT and the definition set out in the ICSID (Washington) Convention.[322]

The tribunal first clarified that there was no specific definition of investment in the Convention, which is why several ICSID tribunals have sought to specify the concept of investment over the years, notably in the *Salini* decision.[323] The *Salini* definition of investment focused on its *nature* rather than the rights and values deriving therefrom.[324]

The tribunal in the *Abaclat* case found, however, that applying the *Salini* criteria to Argentina 'would be contradictory to the ICSID Convention's aim, which is to encourage private investment while giving the Parties the tools to further define what kind of investment they want to promote.'[325] Thus, only a reading of the ICSID Convention that subsumed bonds under the concept of contribution to the host state would be in line with the parties' objective of protecting the value generated through the sale of debt instruments.[326]

In a second step, the tribunal held that the investors' rights set out in the Argentine bond contracts were indeed protected by the Argentina-Italy BIT.[327] More specifically, Article 1(1)(c) of the pertinent Treaty, according to which investments in the host state included 'obligations, private or public titles or any other right to performances or services having economic value, including capitalized revenue,' also extended to government bonds and, hence, the investment that bondholders had made in Argentina.[328] This conclusion essentially rested on the argument that lit (c) of Article 1(1) of the Argentina-Italy BIT contained broad language and should, therefore, extend to sovereign bonds: it explicitly mentioned 'financial instruments,' which were any fungible, negotiable instruments representing financial value, as well as 'public titles,' which referred to debt obligations issued by the sovereign.[329]

2.3.1.1.2. JURISDICTION OVER MASS CLAIMS

Regarding its jurisdiction *ratione personae*, the tribunal assessed whether the adjudication of mass claims would be compatible with the spirit of the ICSID framework.[330] Argentina warned that allowing mass claims would 'encourage hold-outs' and 'go against the current efforts to modernise foreign debt restructuring processes.'[331] The tribunal rejected this view, however, opining that the ICSID Convention's silence on the admissibility of mass claim proceedings was a 'gap' rather than a 'qualified [and hence intended] silence.'[332]

According to the tribunal, the high number of claimants rendered it impossible assess the merits of each individual claim. Rather, it deemed their collective review appropriate: the claims were 'sufficiently homogenous,'[333] as (i) the same BIT protected all claimants, (ii) they were subject to the same debt restructuring operation in 2005, and (iii) they were all affected by breach of the investment treaty signed by Argentina and Italy.[334]

Finally, and crucially, the ICSID tribunal found that the policy arguments invoked by Argentina were inapposite for the ICSID: the tribunal could not reject the admissibility of claims based on a controversial and speculative threat to the stability and fairness of sovereign debt restructurings by holdout creditors.[335] Policy reasons ought to be considered at the stage of negotiating and signing a BIT rather than ex post at the review stage.[336]

2.3.1.1.3. THE DISSENTING OPINION BY PROFESSOR ABI-SAAB

In a sweeping dissenting opinion, Professor Georges Abi-Saab rejected the majority opinion, which can be condensed into the following three arguments:[337]

- First, with respect to the definition of investment under the ICSID Convention, Abi-Saab noted that the '[t]he purpose for using the term 'investment' in Article 25(1) was to set objective outer-limits to the types of disputes that can be treated within the ICSID.'[338] Consequently, Article 25 was not 'infinitely elastic' and 'had a hard-core that cannot be waived even by agreement of States parties to a BIT.'[339]
- Second, Abi-Saab held that while portfolio investments were not per se excluded from the definition of 'investment' enshrined in the ICSID Convention, it ought to be decided on a case-by-case basis whether certain instruments issued by a state fell under the type of investment protected by the Convention.[340] To this end, the territorial link or nexus between the alleged investment and the host country was decisive.[341] Here, the alleged investment (namely the security entitlements held by the Italian bondholders) were not

located in Argentina, as they had been sold in international markets outside the country (the situs of the debt) and the forum selection clause conferred jurisdiction upon the courts of New York State rather than Argentina.

- Third, regarding the admissibility of mass claims, Abi-Saab voiced concerns that ICSID tribunals would risk 'producing a monster.'[342] Firstly, it was evidently impossible for the tribunal to evaluate a treaty claim for compensation without knowing for each individual asset when it was acquired, what price was paid for it, and what currency it was denominated in.[343] Secondly, while the 'level of homogeneity' resulting from the circumstances may have been sufficient to aggregate and register all claims for purposes of pre-trial management, it was clearly insufficient to examine them as if they were one claim either in fact or in law.[344] Thirdly, the 'qualified silence' in the ICSID Convention could be intentional due to disagreement between the drafters of the Convention.[345]

2.3.1.2. Ambiente Ufficio v Argentine Republic[346]

The *Ambiente Ufficio* arbitration – like *Abaclat* – concerned the treaty-based rights of Italian nationals who held Argentine bonds. Ninety individuals applied for an award to be compensated for losses incurred in Argentina's debt restructuring.

The tribunal, first elaborated on the application of the double-barrelled test, holding that both the applicable BIT and the Washington Convention had to be consulted for the definition of protected investments.[347] Regarding Article 25 ICSID Convention, it noted that – in application of Article 31 VCLT – the provision was to be given a 'broad meaning, hence with jurisdictional limits arising from this provision only at the outer margins of economic activity.'[348] Against this backdrop, the tribunal found no reason why sovereign bonds should per se not fall under jurisdiction of the ICSID:

> if and to the extent that there is evidence that the States parties, ie Argentina and Italy, considered those to be investments to be protected, in view of which they both gave their advance and irrevocable consent that any dispute [on this basis] may be submitted to arbitration.
>
> (Article 8(3) of the Argentina-Italy BIT)[349]

Delving deeper into the controversy that revolved around the qualification of sovereign bonds as investment, the tribunal pointed to the *Salini*[350] criteria as well as the principles established in the *Fedax*[351] case.[352] Somewhat in deviation from *Abaclat*, the *Ambiente Ufficio* tribunal argued that the *Salini* decision had 'introduced a peculiar and amplified version of the double-barrelled test.'[353] Following Professor Schreuer's approach, the tribunal concluded that the *Salini* test 'must not be perceived as expressing jurisdictional requirements *stricto sensu*' but rather serve as useful guideline that should be applied in conjunction and in a flexible manner.[354]

Hence, relying on a flexible and wide interpretation of the *Salini* criteria, the tribunal found that (i) the bonds issued by Argentina amounted to a 'substantial contribution on the investor's part' given the budgetary support they provided, (ii) the duration of the investment was sufficient, (iii) the claimants assumed a commercial risk by purchasing Argentine bonds, (iv) the investors received regular profits and returns through the coupon payments, and (v) the claimants made a significant contribution to the development of the host country.[355] With regard to the meaning of 'investment' under Article 1(1) of the Argentina-Italy BIT, the tribunal again noted that lit I, which classified 'obligations' as protected investment, also protected the bondholders' interests.[356]

Another issue broached by the *Ambiente Ufficio* tribunal were prima facie treaty claims.[357] Specifically, the tribunal considered it necessary that the facts alleged by the claimants would be capable of constituting a breach of the applicable BIT.[358] In this context, it was of concern whether the acts performed by Argentina in the wake of its default were of sovereign nature. Similar to the *Abaclat* case, the *Ambiente Ufficio* tribunal considered that Argentina's emergency measures to halt debt repayment were based on a legislative act and, thus, an 'expression of State power and not of rights or obligations Argentina had as a debtor under a specific contract.'[359] Bondholders would, therefore, be able to pursue claims on the basis of both their bond contracts as well as invoke treaty claims under the applicable instrument of international investment law.

2.3.2. Interim Conclusions

2.3.2.1. Sovereign Bond Arbitration Against Argentina – Producing a Monster?

In his seminal work on the origins and the evolution of sovereign debt arbitration before international courts and tribunals, Waibel cautioned that '[i]ncreased creditor protection via ICSID could shake up the crisis arsenal of defaulting countries and derail efforts by the international community to resolve debt crises in an orderly manner.'[360] Similarly, in his dissenting opinion in *Abaclat*, Abi-Saab warned of the monster that mass claims arbitration relating to sovereign bonds may produce.[361]

The decisions in *Abaclat* and *Ambiente Ufficio* seem to have confirmed at least some of the fears that investment arbitration could be leveraged by holdouts to pressure governments into favourable settlements. To be sure, both cases only dealt with ICSID *jurisdiction* and have not resulted in awards. This is one reason why the enforceability of ICSID awards, and the likely obstacles associated with it, were not (yet) as relevant for Argentina.[362] Despite not having had their cases reviewed on the merits, however, the Italian claimants were duly compensated in the 2016 settlement with the Argentine government, as discussed later.[363] Therefore, while it took 13 years in some cases to reach settlements, the holdout investors' bargaining position was significantly bolstered by the ICSID tribunals' willingness to exercise jurisdiction over claims related to Argentina's default and debt restructuring measures. Resolving investment arbitration disputes was key to restoring access to international debt markets for Argentina, as it would be for most states.

Against this backdrop, it may be argued that the threat of ICSID arbitration could compel (some) sovereign debtors to avoid restructuring measures that could breach international investment treaties. Sovereigns need to be aware of that threat. As Park and Samples note in this context, '[w]ithout granting deference to sovereigns (in recognizing either opt-outs in bond contracts negotiated ex ante or good faith exceptions to BIT obligations asserted ex post), ISDS will hamper the ability of governments to balance creditor demands and regulatory objectives.'[364] To reconcile the debtor country's interest in restructuring unsustainable debts and investors' protection from inequitable governmental measures, recent BITs have excluded sovereign bonds from the definition of investment, while other international investment treaties only protect investors outside the remit of 'negotiated restructurings.'[365] Moreover, as discussed later,[366] holdout arbitration in the aftermath of the Greek PSI was markedly less successful from the investor perspective, with the ICSID tribunal reversing some of its key holdings on the investment character of sovereign bonds.

2.3.2.2. ICSID Jurisdiction and the Rejection of the Salini Test

ICSID tribunals became more open to the idea of accepting its jurisdiction by subsuming sovereign bonds under the definition of investment under international investment law. Indeed, the *Abaclat* tribunal's rejection of the *Salini* test, which set a high bar for qualifying sovereign bonds as investment under Article 25 of the ICSID Convention, marked a fundamental shift in ICSID practice. Equally, the interpretation of the applicable BITs appeared to have thrown the gates to ICSID arbitration wide open for sovereign creditors in the event of state default.[367]

Given the importance for future sovereign debt arbitration, this section zooms in on the qualification of sovereign bonds as protected investment and how the *Abaclat* and the *Ambiente Ufficio* arbitrations reshaped the *Salini* test. These include the following: (i) significance of an investment for the host state's development, (ii) duration of the investment, (iii) risk-sharing elements, (iv) territorial link, as well as (v) admissibility of mass claims by sovereign investors.[368]

2.3.2.2.1. CONTRIBUTION TO THE DEVELOPMENT OF THE HOST STATE

The requirement that an investment must contribute to the economic development of the host state flowed from the *Salini* decision and was further refined in subsequent decisions.[369] In the case of financial instruments, such as government bonds or notes, proving the existence of such contribution remains challenging.[370] Prior to *Salini*, the *Fedax* tribunal opined that investors made a substantial contribution to Venezuela's development by acquiring promissory notes. According to the tribunal, 'the transactions involved in this case were not ordinary commercial transactions and indeed involved a fundamental public interest.'[371] The notes were not merely short-term, occasional financial arrangements (hence, volatile capital) but rather long investments in the public sector of Venezuela's economy.[372] *Salini* narrowed down the scope of 'contributions' as defined by the *Fedax* decision.

The *Abaclat* tribunal again reversed course by noting that private bondholders' contributions can take different forms and shall not be limited by the criteria set out in *Salini*.[373] In *Abaclat*, the tribunal argued that a strict application of *Salini* would not give the claimants the procedural protection afforded by the ICSID Convention.[374] Thus, instead of contributing to a specific project, the investment had to merely create a certain value for the host state.[375]

This approach was criticized as too wide. Garcia-Bolivar, for instance, contends that '[the ICSID] has a mission that needs to be consistent with the multilateral entities with which it is associated – and that purpose cannot be detached from the promotion of the economic development of host states.'[376] Along similar lines, Dolzer and Schreuer stress that '[i]n case of an investment lawfully admitted and implemented, the very consistency of the project with the legal order of the host state should indicate the contribution to the development of the host state'[377]

Some argue that the post-Argentina arbitration cases have undermined the symmetric treatment of host state and investor under the ICSID framework.[378] Giving up the contribution requirement leads to a convergence between the meaning of 'investment' under the ICSID and its meaning according to the financial law taxonomy. Such alignment is not desirable. It fosters a system in which any creditor can claim to have invested in the host state and avail himself of the strong level of protection granted by international investment law. Moreover, it arguably contradicts the ICSID Convention's stated purpose of protecting development. Indeed, as convincingly stated by Abi-Saab in his dissenting opinion in the *Abaclat* case, 'funds [raised through bond issuance] can be used to finance wars, even wars of aggression, or oppressive measures against restive populations, or even be diverted through corruption to private ends.'[379]

2.3.2.2.2. DURATION

According to the ICSID Convention, an investment must entail the *long-term* transfer of financial resources.[380] The debate, hence, revolves around the criteria that render an investment long term. The *Abaclat* tribunal refrained elaborating on this issue, merely holding that the claimant's (bond) investment was of 'certain duration.'[381] In a similarly cryptic manner, the *Fedax* decision noted that the ICSID Convention did *not* capture investments that 'come in for quick gains and leave immediately thereafter.'[382] The first draft of the ICSID Convention was stricter, requiring an investment to have a duration of 'not less than five years.'[383] In *Salini*, 32 months were deemed as sufficiently long term.[384]

The emergence of securities as the most commonly used commercial sovereign debt instruments posed new problems, as this asset class could easily be traded in the blink of an eye with someone at the other side of the globe. Since the state has already received the funds (i.e., the investment) at the time of issuance, post-issuance trading renders it tricky to determine whether the duration requirement was met. It is unlikely that the founders of the ICSID framework foresaw this development. The new standard shaped by the *Abaclat* tribunal resolved this uncertainty through the requirement of a certain investment duration, thus integrating the increased liquidity of sovereign bonds into the definition of investment.[385]

While introducing a minimum duration requirement would unduly constrain the ICSID's ability to respond flexibly to the evolution of (debt and equity) markets, abandoning the duration criteria, as *Abaclat* suggested, would equally go too far. Indeed, as a matter of legal policy, tribunals should require bondholders to prove that ownership was maintained for a certain amount of time before default, as suggested by Waibel.[386] This would deter speculative secondary market purchases by prospective holdouts that hope to capitalize on the ICSID dispute settlement mechanism as an additional avenue for debt enforcement. For example, in the context of holdout arbitration against Greece discussed later,[387] the ICSID tribunal accepted the investors' assertion that he had not speculated in Greek bonds since instruments were bought as part of the claimants' long-term commitment portfolio.[388]

2.3.2.2.3. RISK-SHARING

The third important element of the *Salini* test related to the (type of) risk assumed by the investor. This risk, according to *Salini*, should not merely reflect the likelihood that the sovereign may no longer repay its debts but the risk of success or failure of a *specific* commercial undertaking.[389] In *Fedax*, promissory notes issued by Venezuela were deemed to inherit more than just a 'commercial [default] risk,' notably since the notes were issued under Venezuela's Public Credit Law.[390] By contrast, in *Abaclat* and *Ambiente Ufficio*, the risk-sharing requirement appeared irrelevant. The tribunals rejected the view that the investment made by Italian creditors had to be linked with a definable project or economic activity.

This shift was grounded on a misguided legal opinion. After all, the ICSID Convention seeks to strengthen partnership between countries in the cause of *economic development*.[391] Public debt, while being essential for the host state's economic development, represents a generic asset class that can finance various state activities – commercial undertakings for economic development but also any other type of public expenditure.[392]

Others were also critical of the shift in arbitration practice. Ostransky forcefully rejected the abandoning of the risk-sharing element as an 'erroneous public interest test' that is 'manifestly absurd and unreasonable, as it makes every commercial dealing with a government an investment.'[393] Finally, Professor Torres Bernandez, who wrote the dissenting opinion in *Ambiente Ufficio*, argued that Argentina was acting as a commercial actor and did, thus, not 'host' any investment but merely sold a financial product.[394]

Summarizing the difference between a commercial or sovereign risk and risks associated with an investment, the PCA, in *Romak*, held this:

> [a]n 'investment risk' entails a different kind of *alea*, a situation in which the investor cannot be sure of a return on his investment, and may not know the amount he will end up spending, even if all relevant counterparties discharge their contractual obligations.[395]

Lastly, as discussed later,[396] the *Poštová banka* tribunal that adjudicated holdout claims against Greece after its restructuring rejected the wide understanding of risk recognized in *Abaclat*. Against this backdrop, the purchase of sovereign bonds to support the issuer's budget appears remote from the type of specific investment risk that the Washington Convention seemingly aims to protect.

2.3.2.2.4. TERRITORIAL LINK

The Argentine arbitration cases also discussed the requirement of a territorial link between the alleged investment and the host country.[397] The requirement of a territorial link is understood to emanate from Article 25(1) of the ICSID Convention, which states that disputes must arise 'directly out of an investment.'[398] In the context of sovereign debt, the territorial link requirement is of particular relevance since bonds are tradable financial instruments where the investor's personality may change from one moment to another. Therefore, whenever a contractual right is a protected investment, it must be legally located in the host state.[399]

The *Abaclat* and the *Ambiente Ufficio* tribunals applied different tests to establish a territorial link, essentially arguing that the place of performance was decisive rather than the situs of the debt.[400] Following the situs approach, which the majority view in the literature seems to support,[401] would have meant that there was no territorial link between the Italian investors and the Argentine issuer; after all the bonds were governed by New York law.[402]

By giving up on the territorial requirement, the ICSID arguably blurred the lines between treaty claims and contractual claims in the realm of sovereign bonds. This development could have undesirable policy implications: bestowing upon holdouts the full protection of international investment law is unequitable at best and dangerous at worst. Indeed, when states issue sovereign debt, they confer jurisdiction to (foreign) municipal courts rather than to the ICSID in Washington.[403]

2.3.2.2.5. THE ADMISSIBILITY OF MASS CLAIMS

Mass claim sovereign bond arbitration becomes particularly relevant in the context of the retail holdout problem,[404] where a large number of small investors may leverage their power and create cost synergies by launching collective ICSID proceedings.[405] While most domestic civil law frameworks provide for class action, international investment arbitration was traditionally designed as a two-party rather than a multiparty process.[406] The *Abaclat* tribunal expanded ICSID jurisdiction over mass claims by affirming that the ICSID Convention accommodated mass arbitration proceedings.

While one may argue that mass claim arbitration is not outruled by the letter of the Convention, the legal framework ICSID rests upon lacks specific rules to accommodate this type of proceedings, leaving considerable discretion to individual tribunals. Taking this freedom too far may create adverse policy implications, including opening up ICSID for retail holdout action.[407] Notably, even less than ordinary courts do tribunals have effective legal or political authority to broker a deal between the holdouts and the host state; their role is to identify whether the actions of the host state breached the BIT and not substitute market-based or official mechanisms for creditor coordination. Moreover, navigating (hundreds of) thousands of bondholders through an ICSID procedure may alter the essence of arbitration, potentially casting doubt on whether the signatories of the Convention or the BIT would have accepted it in the first place.[408]

Other views exist, however; Sushama, for instance, notes that the *Abaclat* majority view rightly realized that 'the rejection of the rights of the bondholders would be an unacceptable denial of justice to the claimants.'[409] Similarly, Feichenfeld argues that '[g]iven that all 60,000 claims concerned similar bonds, it is not evident that the arbitral tribunal would have come to a more accurate decision, had it taken 60,000 separate decisions on jurisdiction.'[410]

These views ignore that each investor may well apply to the ICSID for an award against the host country individually. Mass claim arbitration would simply aggregate the rights of individual investors rather than create them. The potential negative effects of enabling hundreds of thousands of retail holdouts to challenge a debt restructuring before an ICSID tribunal arguably outweigh the benefits of providing them with easier access to legal remedies.[411]

2.4. Settling a Decade of Holdout Lawsuits Against Argentina

2.4.1. The 2016 Election and Argentina's Return to International Financial Markets

One crucial step on Argentina's path towards re-accessing international capital markets was to settle with holdout creditors. To that end, the newly elected President Macri signalled a 180-degree turn in Argentina's international economic policy and initiated what the IMF referred to as a 'necessary and unavoidable transition.'[412] The relationship between the Fund and the Kirchner government had soured, just like the one between Argentina and Wall Street financiers. In September 2016, an IMF team set foot in Buenos Aires for the first time after a 11-year hiatus to conduct its mandatory annual health check on the Argentine economy.

In late 2016, negotiations with most holdouts were completed, and Argentina was ready for a fulminant return to the capital markets. The international financial community was cheering the new administration on: new bonds with a total volume of more than USD30 billion were four times oversubscribed, and Argentina even issued a 'century bond' (with the principal repayment due in 2117).[413]

2.4.2. Settling with the Vulture Holdouts

The injunction granted by the SDNY to the NML Capital[414] in its global litigation campaign was by far the most powerful tool holdout investors had obtained to coerce Argentina into paying them. Yet for the 18 months during which she still held power, President Kirchner refused to budge, trying to initiate proceedings against the US in the ICJ and upping PR efforts against holdout creditors. It was not until the new government took over did settlement talks with the holdouts commence.

Political change also brought about judicial reconciliation. A year after President Mauricio Macri took power in December 2015 and roughly five years after Judge Griesa had unsettled sovereign debt markets with his unconventional pari passu interpretation, the same judge reversed course. In *White Hawthorne, LLC v Republic of Argentina*,[415] he clarified the nature of Argentina's breach of the 1994 FAA pari passu provisions, which had puzzled so many experts.[416] Griesa held that '[n]onpayment on defaulted debt alone [was] insufficient to show are breach of the pari passu clause.'[417] Rather, the pari passu clause ought to be understood as a protection against domestic *laws* that discriminate against certain creditors, an understanding that echoed the conventional view on the clause.[418] In his view, Argentina's Lock Law served as a case in point, for it prohibited the country's executive branch to pay holdout investors who had declined its restructuring offers.[419] Since Argentina's Parliament had repealed the Lock Law and settled with the (majority of) holdout creditors, the plaintiffs in *White Hawthorne* no longer had sufficient legal grounds to establish a breach of the pari passu clause.[420]

Perhaps the end of the pari passu saga had to be as emblematic as its beginnings.

New York courts went full circle from unsettling global sovereign bond markets in 2011 to reeling behind the new Argentine government's endeavour to return to international credit markets as swiftly as possible. It also seemed as if Judge Griesa eventually responded to the concerns voiced by policymakers and scholars, who harshly condemned his decision to entertain an unconventional, potentially even unworkable, interpretation of the infamous clause. For Lockman and Blakemore, who served as Argentina's counsel in US courts, point out, '*White Hawthorne* sensibly rejected an application of the pari passu clause that would unravel the clause itself.'[421]

However, the story was more complicated. Judge Griesa made clear that his more benevolent interpretation of the pari passu clause was motivated by the government's compliance with the holdouts' demand.[422] Given that so much hinged on the Argentine government's ultimate acquiescence, the SDNY's precedent, and the potential dangers it may hold for future sovereign debt restructurings, has not fully disappeared. Moreover, by settling with judgment holders, the Argentine government demonstrated to the vulture holdouts that their stamina did in fact pay off. It rewarded the brave and relentless group of small, distressed fund managers at the expense of those bondholders who accepted Argentina's debt swap offers in 2005 and 2010.

Finally, and perhaps most importantly, *White Hawthorne* left the concept of 'unique recalcitrance' undefined.[423] This meant, in particular, that the relationship between a sovereign's conduct during debt restructuring negotiations and associated risk of violating the pari passu clause. The problems and ambiguities cultivated by Judge Griesa will, therefore, persist until the Second Circuit adjudicates a similar case and follows the *White Hawthorne* reasoning by the SDNY.[424]

Table 2.1 shows the evolution of sovereign debt's trial of the century, from the controversial SDNY ruling in 2011 to the settlement in 2016 on the back of the new path the Macri administration had chosen.

Table 2.1 Timeline of sovereign debt's trial of the century[425]

NML Case					*White Hawthorne Case*
Dec 2011	*Feb 2012*	*Oct 2012*	*Nov 2012*	*Aug 2013*	*Dec 2016*
District Court finds breach of pari passu clause	District Court orders injunctions: Argentina cannot service restructured debt unless it also pays holdouts	Second Circuit affirms breach and injunction	District Court makes a number of technical amendments to injunctions	Second Circuit affirms amended injunction relying on extraordinary behaviour of Argentina	District Court rules in White Hawthorne
Payment of some creditors but not others is a breach of pari passu	Unprecedented finding – chaos in the sovereign debt market	Arguably broad interpretation becomes federal law in New York	Narrowed scope of injunctions	Payment of some creditors but not others continues to be a violation of pari passu but ruling premised on extraordinary behaviour of debtor	Payment of some creditors but not others is not a pari passu violation (unless the debtor is recalcitrant

2.4.3. Settling with the Retail Holdouts

Despite holdout creditors' seeming success in *Abaclat*, *Ambiente Ufficio*, and other decisions, the numerous ICSID cases have not resulted in meaningful asset seizures under the New York Convention,[426] in Argentina or abroad.[427] For those cases where investors obtained awards,[428] Argentina argued that they had to go through Argentina's federal courts to enforce their awards; for several reasons, this remained an unattractive prospect.[429] Indeed, local courts considered the enforcement of ICSID awards for the first time in 2016, suggesting that Argentina had to recognize such awards and could not subject them to exequatur proceedings, diverging from the Argentine Supreme Court's position that exequatur proceedings required an assessment as to whether a foreign trial was fair and in compliance with Argentina's public order.[430]

This said, holdout arbitration was not a failure from the bond investors' perspective. Gradually shifting from a confrontational to a more pragmatic approach, the Argentine government had settled with many ICSID claimants, notably to regain access to World Bank funding and to benefit from trade benefits extended under the US Generalized System of Preferences.[431] But Argentina also continued to vehemently fight the *Abaclat* claimants, and the antipathy was undoubtedly mutual.[432] For the new Macri administration, re-accessing international capital markets required settling with *all* creditors, including the *Abaclat* retail holdouts.

The Argentine Senate approved a deal with the Italian bondholders in March 2016, according to which they received 150% of the value of the bonds.[433] Following the deal, the *Abaclat* tribunal decided on 15 December 2016 that the Settlement Agreement signed by the TFA and the Argentine Republic would be an enforceable award on the agreed terms.[434]

Notes

1 Pola Oloixarac, 'Argentina vs. the Vultures' *The New York Times* (New York, 19 September 2014).

2 The country declared a moratorium on approximately USD95 billion of outstanding financial obligations in December 2001. This was roughly three times the amount that Russia defaulted on in 1998. See Rodrigo Olivares-Caminal, 'Sovereign Bonds: A Critical Analysis of Argentina's Debt Exchange Offer' (2008) 10(1) Journal of Banking Regulation 28–29.

3 Ibid. At the time of the default, Argentina had 152 different series of local and foreign law bonds outstanding that were governed by 8 different laws (51% of the debt was subject to New York, 18% to English law, 17% to German law, 11% to Argentine law, 2% to Japanese law, and the remainder to Italian, Spanish, and Swiss law). As discussed later (Chapter 2.3. 'Holdout Arbitration After Argentina'), the ICSID Tribunal in *Abaclat v Argentina* noted that '[i]n total, from 1991 through 2001, Argentina placed over USD186.7 billion in sovereign bonds across both domestic and international capital markets' and that '[o]ut of the 179 bonds issued by Argentina, 173 were denominated in foreign currencies; six were denominated in Argentine Pesos. Claimants allegedly purchased 83 of the 173 foreign currency bonds.' See *Abaclat and ors v Argentina*, Decision on jurisdiction and admissibility, ICSID Case No ARB/07/5, IIC 504 (2011), despatched 4 August 2011, World Bank; International Centre for Settlement of Investment Disputes [ICSID] [50].

4 Compare, for example, Steven Schwarcz, 'Sovereign Debt Restructuring: A Bankruptcy Reorganization Approach' (2000) 85 Cornell Law Review 956, 960, noting this:

> the difficulty [of restructuring sovereign debt] is exacerbated by the collective action problem of reaching agreement *among* creditors – a problem that has worsened significantly in recent years as States have shifted their borrowing source from banks to bond investors in the lower cost capital markets.

5 See Rodrigo Olivares-Caminal, 'Sovereign Bonds: A Critical Analysis of Argentina's Debt Exchange Offer' (2008) 10(1) Journal of Banking Regulation 28 and Rodrigo Olivares-Caminal, *Legal Aspects of Sovereign Debt Restructuring* (London: Sweet & Maxwell, 2009) 6–003.

6 Bondholders were given three different options: (i) a par bond with no face value reduction that had low but increasing coupons and a 35-year maturity; (ii) a quasi-par bond, with a 30% face value reduction, a 3.31% coupon, and a 42-year maturity; and (iii) a discount bond with a 66.3% face value reduction, an increasing coupon, as well as a 30-year maturity. See Aitor Erce, Enrico Malluci, and Mattia Picarelli, 'A Journey in the History of Sovereign Defaults on Domestic Law Public Debt – Sovereign Histories' (2021) Universidad Publica de Navarra Working Paper D.T. 2108, 24–30 <https://www2.unavarra.es/gesadj/CyD5/depEconomia/documentos-trabajo/2021/WP2108.pdf> accessed 2 November 2021; Frederico Sturzenegger and Jeromin Zettelmeyer, *Debt Defaults and Lessons from a Decade of Crises* (Cambridge: MIT Press, 2007) 182–190. For a financial analysis of the offer, see Christian Engelen and Johann Graf Lambsdorff, 'Hares and Stags in Argentinean Debt Restructuring' (2009) 78 Journal of International Economics 141.

7 John Hornbeck, 'Argentina's Defaulted Sovereign Debt: Dealing with the "Holdouts"' (6 January 2013) Congressional Research Service 5. Prima facie, the percentage of holdouts may appear low. However, as IMF data shows, the acceptance rate of 76% was driven by the acquiescence of domestic creditors, most of which were banks and pension funds. See IMF, 'Ex Post Assessment of Longer-Term Program Engagement and Ex Post Evaluation of Exceptional Access Sovereign' (12 July 2006) 15 (also cited in Laura Alfaro, Noel Maurer and, Faisal Ahmed, 'Gunboats and Vultures: Market Reaction to the "Enforcement" of Sovereign Debt' (2010) 73 Law and Contemporary Problems 39).

8 See Chapter 2.2.1.1. 'United States.'

9 United States Securities and Exchange Commission, 'Annual Report of the Republic of Argentina' (2009) 153 <www.sec.gov/Archives/edgar/data/914021/000090342310000550/roa-18k_0927.htm> accessed 2 November 2021. In broad terms, this law prohibited the Argentine executive branch from reopening the 2005 debt exchange without Congressional approval and any type of settlement involving untendered security that were eligible to participate in the debt swap. In addition to the Lock Law, the swapped bonds also featured a so-called Rights Upon Future Offers (RUFO) clause, which set out that Argentina could not voluntarily make an offer to the holdouts that was better than what the restructured creditors had received. See Benjamin Hébert and Jesse Schreger, 'The Costs of Sovereign Default: Evidence from Argentina' (2017) 107(10) American Economic Review 3119.

10 Ibid 54.

11 Sebastian Horn, Carmen Reinhart, and Christoph Trebesch, 'China's Overseas Lending' (July 2019) NBER Working Paper 26050, 5 <www.nber.org/papers/w26050> accessed 2 November 2021. Between 2005 and 2010, Argentina repaid debt owed to the Paris Club countries (i.e., official sector creditors) as well as IMF loans but continued to pursue a tough stance vis-à-vis private holdout creditors.

12 Alfaro et al (n 7) 56.

13 See Chapter 2.2. 'Holdout Litigation After Argentina.'

14 See Hébert and Schreger (n 9).

15 See Chapter 2.4. 'Settling a Decade of Holdout Lawsuits Against Argentina.'

16 Argentina heavily relied on New York law but also issued bonds governed by German, Italian, and Japanese law.

17 Schumacher et al identify 182 litigation disputes lawsuits in the SDNY alone; see Julian Schumacher, Christoph Trebesch, and Henrik Enderlein, 'Sovereign Defaults in Court' (2018) ECB Working Paper No 2135 <www.ecb.europa.eu/pub/pdf/scpwps/ecb.wp2135.en.pdf> accessed 2 November 2021.

18 To recall, roughly 50% of international sovereign bonds issued are governed by the laws of New York, underscoring the importance it plays in the world of external government finance; see IMF, 'Progress Report on Inclusion of Enhanced Contractual Provisions in International Sovereign Bond Contracts' (March 2015) IMF Staff Report <www.imf.org/external/np/pp/eng/2015/091715.pdf> accessed 2 November 2021.

19 *Lightwater Corporation Limited v Argentina,* No 02 Civ 3804 (TPG), No 02 Civ 3808 (TPG), No 02 Civ 5932 (TPG), 14 April 2003, United States; New York; District Court for the Southern District of New York [SDNY].

20 See Chapter 5.2.1. 'Vulture Funds' (for a discussion of this type of holdout investor).

21 Ibid. They had acquired roughly USD7 million in Argentine bonds only days before the default in December 2001. Upon 1 May 2002, Lightwater and Old Castle, two hedge funds, gave notice of default and declared the acceleration of principal.

22 *Pravin Banker Associates Limited v Banco Popular del Peru and Peru*, Docket No 96–7183, 109 F 3d 850 (2d Cir 1997), 65 USLW 2640, 25 March 1997, United States; Court of Appeals (2nd Circuit) [2d Cir].

23 *Lightwater v Argentina* (n 19). Since 'there [was] no assurance about the success timing of such [debt restructuring] negotiations,' presiding Judge Griesa considered that there was no legitimate reason to impose a judicial standstill and, thereby, bar the plaintiff's actions against the defaulted sovereign.

24 The champerty provision prohibited investors under New York law from buying a bond 'with the intent and for the purpose of bringing an action of proceeding thereon.'

25 The court referred, in particular, See *Elliott Associates LP v Banco de la Nación and Peru*, 194 FRD 116 (SDNY 2000), 2000, United States; New York; District Court for the Southern District of New York [SDNY].

26 *Lightwater v Argentina* (n 19).

27 *Allied Bank International v Banco Credito Agricola de Cartago*, 733 F 2d 23 (2d Cir 1984), 1984, United States; Court of Appeals (2nd Circuit) [2d Cir]; *Allied Bank International v Banco Credito Agricola de Cartago and ors*, Case No 225, Docket 83–7714, 757, 758 F 2d 516 (2d Cir 1985), 77 ALR Fed 281, (1985) 24 ILM 762, 18 March 1985, United States; Court of Appeals (2nd Circuit) [2d Cir].

28 *Lightwater v Argentina* (n 19). The court also shrugged of Argentina's claims that the investors had abused their rights by suing their bonds at a time when the issuer is having a severe economic crisis.

29 Ibid.

30 Ibid.

31 *EM Limited and NML Capital Limited v Banco Central De La República Argentina and Argentina,* Appeal judgment, ILDC 2495 (US 2015), 800 F 3d 78 (2nd Cir 2015), 31st August 2015, United States; Court of Appeals (2nd Circuit) [2d Cir].

32 See *EM Limited and NML Capital Limited v Argentina,* No 05–1525-cv, 131 Fed Appx 745 (2d Cir 2005), 13 May 2005, United States; Court of Appeals (2nd Circuit) [2d Cir]. For a discussion, see Jonathan Blackman, Carmine Boccuzzi, William Lawrence, Jarrett Perlow, Fahad Habib, Jeffrey Robins, Karen Woody, Heather Van Slooten Walsh, Phillip Dye Jr, Justin Marlles, Dawna Gardner, Vitali S Rosenfeld, Rahul Mukhi, and Alida Lasker, 'International Litigation' (2007) 42 The International Lawyer 415. Also compare *EM Limited and NML Capital Limited v Argentina,*

No 11–4065-cv (L), 695 F 3d 201 (2d Cir 2012), 20 August 2012, United States; Court of Appeals (2nd Circuit) [2d Cir].

33 *EM Limited and NML Capital Limited v Banco Central De La República Argentina and Argentina*, Opinion, 720 F Supp 273 (SDNY 2010), 7 April 2010, United States; New York; District Court for the Southern District of New York [SDNY].

34 *EM Limited and NML Capital Limited v Banco Central De La República Argentina*, 652 F 3d 172 (2d Cir 2011), 5 July 2011, United States; Court of Appeals (2nd Circuit) [2d Cir].

35 *EM v BCRA* (n 31).

36 Ibid 8.

37 Ibid 12–13.

38 Ibid 25.

39 *First National City Bank v Banco Para el Comercio Exterior de Cuba,* No 81–984, 462 US 611 (1983), 103 S Ct 2591 (1983), (1983) 22 ILM 840, 17 June 1983, United States; Supreme Court [US]. According to the Supreme Court [626]:

> [f]reely ignoring the separate status of government instrumentalities would result in substantial uncertainty over whether an instrumentality's assets would be diverted to satisfy a claim against the sovereign, and might thereby cause third parties to hesitate before extending credit to a government instrumentality without the government's guarantee. As a result, the efforts of sovereign nations to structure their governmental activities in a manner deemed necessary to promote economic development and efficient administration would surely be frustrated.

40 For an instrumentality to become an alter ego, the *Banec* test required this of the government: (i) used central bank assets like its own, (ii) ignored the central bank's separate status, (iii) obtained approvals for ordinary business decisions from a political actor, and (iv) issued policies or directives that cause the bank to act directly on behalf of the sovereign state. See *EM v BCRA* (n 31) [26]

41 Ibid 27–29. Moreover, BCRA appeared to be a typical government instrumentality entitled to separate legal status.

42 Ibid 33.

43 Ibid 37 ('[p]laintiffs' factual allegations simply do not show that Argentina has used BCRA to frustrate the collection efforts of its creditors, or that Argentina treated BCRA as a "sham" entity to hide its own assets').

44 Ibid 38–42.

45 Ibid 42.

46 Ibid 41. The court added that if it were to follow the plaintiffs' theory, it would 'dramatically expand the scope of the commercial-activity exception to sovereign immunity.'

47 *NML Capital Limited v Argentina,* No 08 Civ 6978 (TPG), No 09 Civ 1707 (TPG), No 09 Civ 1708 (TPG), 7 December 2011, United States; New York; District Court for the Southern District of New York [SDNY] [2].

48 Joseph Cotterill, 'Choose Your Own Adventure, Sovereign Debt Trial of the century edition' *Financial Times Alphaville* (London, 8 February 2013) <https://ftalphaville.ft.com/2013/02/08/1379162/choose-your-own-adventure-sovereign-debt-trial-of-the-century-edition/> accessed 2 November 2021.

49 See IMF, 'Sovereign Debt Restructuring – Recent Developments and Implications for the Fund's Legal and Policy Framework' (26 April 2013) 12 <www.imf.org/external/np/pp/eng/2013/042613.pdf> accessed 2 November 2021.

50 See *Elliott Associates LP v Panama,* No 96 Civ 5514(DC), 975 F Supp 332 (SDNY 1997), 10 September 1997, United States; New York; District Court for the Southern District of New York [SDNY].

51 Compare, for example, Anna Gelpern, 'Contract Hope and Sovereign Redemption' (2013) 8(2) Capital Markets Law Journal 132, 135.

52 While much has been written about the trial, this book attempts to covers it from the beginnings to the aftermath, including the settlement in 2016 with holdout creditors.

53 To be precise, NML sought to sue for the bonds' full face value plus outstanding interests. See, for example, 'At Last' *The Economist* (London, 5 May 2016).

54 See, for example, *NML Capital Limited v Argentina I,* Opinion, Nos 02 Civ 3804, 02 Civ 3808, 02 Civ 4124, 02 Civ 5432, 02 Civ 2507, 02 Civ 8528, 02 Civ 8845 (TPG), 29 March 2005, United States; New York; District Court for the Southern District of New York [SDNY].

55 Ibid.

56 *NML Capital Limited v Argentina II,* 12 September 2008, United States; New York; District Court for the Southern District of New York [SDNY].

57 For example, the hedge fund convinced a court in Ghana to prevent an Argentine navy ship from leaving the country for more than two months; see David Smith, 'Seized Argentinian Sailing Ship Leaves Ghana' *The Guardian* (London, 20 December 2012) and Chapter 2.2.2.1. 'International Tribunal for the Law of the Sea' for a review of the ensuing case before ITLOS.

58 See Michael Hiltzik, 'Argentina Is Cautionary Tale as US Debates Debt Limit' *Los Angeles Times* (Los Angeles, 15 January 2013). However, most of these cases had symbolic character and failed to yield the desired monetary satisfaction on the holdout's side.

59 See Chapter 2.2.1.3. 'Italy,' Chapter 2.2.1.4. 'United Kingdom,' Chapter 2.2.1.5. 'France,' and Chapter 2.2.1.6. 'Switzerland.'

60 Even if Argentina would have been able to attach the Argentine navy vessel, the presidential airplane, or the central bank assets, the proceeds would never have been enough to cover the outstanding debt of over USD1 billion. See, for the background story, Andrea Fontevecchia, 'The Real Story of How a Hedge Fund Detained a Vessel in Ghana and Even Went for Argentina's "Air Force One"' *Forbes Markets* (New York, 10 May 2012) <www.forbes.com/sites/afontevecchia/2012/10/05/the-real-story-behind-the-argentine-vessel-in-ghana-and-how-hedge-funds-tried-to-seize-the-presidential-plane/> accessed 2 November 2021.

61 Specifically, the pari passu clause used in Paragraph 1(c) of Argentina's 1994 Fiscal Agency Agreement (FAA) read as follows:

> [t]he Securities will constitute . . . direct, unconditional, unsecured and unsubordinated obligations of the Republic and shall at all times rank pari passu without any preference among themselves. The payment obligations of the Republic under the Securities shall at all times rank at least equally with all its other present and future unsecured and unsubordinated External Indebtedness.

See *NML Capital Limited v Argentina I* (n 54).

62 *NML Capital Limited v Argentina III,* No 08 Civ 6978 (TPG), No 09 Civ 1707 (TPG), No 09 Civ 1708 (TPG), 7 December 2011, United States; New York; District Court for the Southern District of New York [SDNY].

63 Ibid 5.

64 Rule 65(d) of the US Federal Rules of Civil Procedure outlines the contents of an order granting and injunction. Such injunction must, inter alia, (a) state the reasons why it is issued, (b) state its terms specifically, and (c) describe in reasonable detail the acts or acts restrained or required. For an online version of the Federal Rules of Civil Procedure see, for example, Cornell University Law School, 'Federal Rules of Civil Procedure' (as of 1 December 2015) <www.law.cornell.edu/rules/frcp> accessed 2 November 2021.

65 *NML Capital Limited v Argentina III* (n 62).

66 Specifically, the SDNY held that 'all parties involved in advising upon, preparing, processing, or facilitating any payment on the Exchange Bonds . . . shall be bound by the terms of this order.' *NML Capital Limited v Argentina VI,* Docket No 08 Civ 6978, 21st November 2012, United States; New York; District Court for the Southern District of New York [SDNY] [2(e)]. The list of third parties included all indenture trustees, registered owners, clearing systems, trustees, paying agents, and others.

67 In modern financial markets, sovereigns issue a single global certificate to the securities custodian, which keeps track of how many securities each bondholder has. Only larger financial institutions are, however, participants in securities depository systems, such as that of the Depository Trust Corporation (DTC) in the US and Euroclear and Clearstream in Europe. See Pierre-Hughes Verdier, *Global Banks on Trial: U.S. Prosecutions and the Remaking of International Finance* (Oxford: Oxford University Press, 2020) 168–169.

68 To ensure that Argentina would not simply change its fiscal agents or clearing houses to continue making payments to restructured bondholders, Judge Griesa also enjoyed it from effecting any alterations to the payment transfer mechanism, which relied heavily on agents located in New York City. See *NML Capital Limited v Argentina IV*, No 08 Civ 6978 (TPG), 23 February 2012, United States; New York; District Court for the Southern District of New York [SDNY].

69 Ibid 18.

70 *NML Capital Limited v Argentina VIII*, Opinion affirming orders of the district court, 727 F 3d 230 (2d Cir 2013), 23 August 2013, United States; Court of Appeals (2nd Circuit) [2d Cir] [21].

71 Ibid 22.

72 Ibid.

73 Ibid 24. The Second Circuit further noted that the SDNY did not, as alleged by the defendant, abuse its discretionary powers by prescribing actions that could – as a matter of fact – not be complied with. In fact, Argentina had in the meantime accumulated over USD40 billion in foreign currency reserves – several times the amount claimed by the plaintiffs.

74 Ibid.

75 Ibid 27.

76 Ibid.

77 *NML Capital Limited v Argentina VI* (n 66).

78 *NML Capital Limited v Argentina VIII* (n 70).

79 *Argentina v NML Capital Limited,* Appeal judgment, Docket No 12–842, 573 US ___ (2014), ILDC 2201 (US 2014), 134 S Ct 2250 (2014), 189 L Ed 2d 234 (2014), 16 June 2014, United States; Supreme Court [US].

80 See, for example, Adam Liptak, 'Argentina's Debt Appeal Is Rejected by Supreme Court' *The New York Times* (New York, 16 June 2014) <http://dealbook.nytimes.com/2014/06/16/supreme-court-denies-appeal-by-argentina/?_r=0> accessed 2 November 2021; Larry Elliott, 'Argentina Debt Crisis Fears Grow After US Supreme Court Ruling' *The Guardian* (London, 16 June 2014); Katy Watson, 'Argentina Defaults for Second Time' *BBC News* (London, 31 July 2014) <www.bbc.com/news/business-28578179> accessed 2 November 2021. Given that Argentina signalled its refusal to comply with the injunction, one of the world's leading ratings agency, Standard & Poor's, downgraded Argentina to default status a few weeks after the Supreme Court's decision.

81 Karen Halverson Cross, 'The Extraterritorial Reach of Sovereign Debt Enforcement' (2015) 12 Berkeley Business Law Journal 111.

82 *Argentina v NML* (n 79).

83 Ibid 3.

84 Ibid 2.

85 Halverson Cross (n 81) 127.
86 *Argentina v NML* (n 79) [8].
87 Schumacher (n 21).
88 Argentine Necessity Case, *K and ors v Argentina* (represented by President Néstor Kirchner), Order of the Second Senate, 2 BvM 1/03, 2 BvM 2/03, 2 BvM 3/03, 2 BvM 4/03, 2 BvM 5/03, 2 BvM 1/06, 2 BvM 2/06, BVerfGE 118, 124, ILDC 952 (DE 2007), NJW 2007, 2610, (2010) 138 ILR 1, (2007) 4 AJIL 857, 8 May 2007, Germany; Constitutional Court [BVerfG].
89 The plaintiffs held Argentine Global Bonds governed by German law and a choice of forum clause conveying jurisdiction upon German courts.
90 Draft Articles on Responsibility of States for Internationally Wrongful Acts, adopted by the Commission at its 53rd session in 2001 (Final Outcome) (International Law Commission [ILC]) UN Doc A/56/10, para.76, UN Doc A/RES/56/83, Annex [2001] II(2) UNYBILC 26, UN Doc A/CN.4/L.602/Rev.1, GAOR 56th Session Supp 10, 26 ['ILC Draft Articles']. Given that Article 25 of the *Grundgesetz* transposes the general rules of international law into German law, the BVerfG, as the court of last resort, was to adjudicate whether economic necessity, as enshrined in (customary) international law was a valid ground to deny the holdouts claims for repayment of a financial obligation governed by private law.
91 The necessity defence is enshrined in Article 25(1) of the ILC Draft Articles (n 90). The Article states that necessity can be invoked to preclude the wrongfulness of an act if it (i) is the only way to safeguard an essential interest against a grave and imminent peril and (ii) does not seriously impair an essential interest of the state towards which the obligation exists or the international community as a whole. Moreover, Article 25(2) of the Draft Articles stipulates that a state cannot invoke necessity if it has contributed to the emergence of the peril.
92 Ibid 18. In a press release, Argentina asserted that the acts it had adopted during the 2001/2002 crisis had the 'public purpose . . . of protecting the primary need of economic survival of the population in a historical context of very serious national emergency.' See Beatrice Bonafè, 'State Immunity and the Protection of Private Investors: The Argentine Bonds Case Before Italian Courts' (2006) 16(1) The Italian Yearbook of International Law 165–166.
93 Ibid 15.
94 Ibid.
95 Ibid.
96 Ibid 29.
97 Ibid 32.
98 Ibid 33. The BVerfG noted that the *opinio iuris sive necessitatis* for such a rule to become legally binding under customary international law is absent.
99 *K and ors v Argentina* (n 88) [52]. CMS Gas Transmission Company v Argentina, Application for annulment and request for stay of enforcement of arbitral award, ICSID Case No ARB/01/8, IIC 66 (2005), 8 September 2005, World Bank; International Centre for Settlement of Investment Disputes [ICSID]. In *CMS v Argentina,* the ICSID tribunal assessed the necessity defence with regard to international obligations arising from the US-Argentina BIT rather than a private bond contract. The BVerfG reached the same conclusion after reviewing the arbitration in *LG&E Energy Corporation and ors v Argentina,* Award, ICSID Case No ARB/02/1, IIC 295 (2007), despatched 25 July 2007, World Bank; International Centre for Settlement of Investment Disputes [ICSID]. Similarly, in two seminal international law cases, the *Serbian Loans* case and the *French Company of Venezuelan Railroads*, the tribunals had to assess whether necessity could be applied in intra-state relationships rather than a private creditor and a sovereign, though there was no final decision on the question. See Payment of Various Serbian Loans Issued in France, *France v Kingdom of the Serbs, Croats, and Slovenes*, Judgment, Judgment No 14, PCIJ Series A No 20, ICGJ 260

(PCIJ 1929), 12 July 1929, League of Nations (historical) [LoN]; Permanent Court of International Justice (historical) [PCIJ; French Company of Venezuelan Railroads Case, *France v Venezuela*, (1962) X RIAA 285, 31st July 1905, Mixed Claims Commission (France-Venezuela). Also see, for a background analysis in Beate Rudolf and Nina Hüfken, 'Joined Case Nos. 2 BvM 1–5/03 & BvM 1–2/06' (2007) 101(4) The American Journal of International Law 857.

100 *K and ors v Argentina* (n 88) [50].

101 See, for example, Rudolf Dolzer, 'Staatliche Zahlungsunfähigkeit: Zum Begriff und zu den Rechtsfolgen im Völkerrecht' in Jürgen Jekewitz (ed), *Des Menschen Recht zwischen Freiheit und Verantwortung: Festschrift für Karl Josef Partsch zum 75. Geburtstag* (Berlin: Duncker & Humblot, 1989) 550.

102 *K and ors v Argentina* (n 88) [62].

103 Ibid.

104 Ibid 79–94. To substantiate her arguments, she cited several decisions by international courts and tribunals. For example, in the *Russian Indemnity Case*, the PCIJ held that 'however little the responsibility may imperil the existence of the state; it would constitute a case of *force majeure* which could be pleaded in public international law as well as by a private debtor.' Russian Claim for Interest on Indemnities (Damages Claimed by Russia for Delay in Payment of Compensation Owed to Russians Injured During the War of 1877–1878), *Russia v Turkey*, Award, (1961) XI RIAA 421, ICGJ 399 (PCA 1912), (1912) 1 HCR 547, 11 November 1912, Permanent Court of Arbitration [PCA]. She also argued that, in cases where there was no explicit reference to private legal relationships, such as the *French Company of Venezuelan Railroads* (n 99), the necessity defence had in her view always been recognized as a general principle of law and was not per se limited to inter-state disputes. In Judge Lübbe-Wolff's opinion, the aforementioned decisions by international tribunals confirmed that the 'object and purpose of necessity would not support that a debtor State would be less protected against its foreign private creditors as against another State.' Also see Stephan Schill, 'Der völkerrechtliche Staatsnotstand in der Entscheidung des BVerfG zu Argentinischen Staatsanleihen – Anachronismus oder Avantgarde?' (2008) 68 ZaöRV 45.

105 For instance, *Société Commerciale de Belgique, Belgium v Greece*, Judgment, PCIJ Series A/B No 78, ICGJ 331 (PCIJ 1939), 15 June 1939, League of Nations (historical) [LoN]; Permanent Court of International Justice (historical) [PCIJ].

106 *K and ors v Argentina* (n 88) [83–84].

107 Ibid 86. In her view, the majority decision's understanding of necessity, namely that states were less protected vis-à-vis private foreign creditors than vis-à-vis other states, would undermine both objective and purpose of the defence.

108 Ibid 93 (referencing for instance *Pravin Banker Associates Limited v Banco Popular del Peru and Peru*, 895 F Supp 660 (SDNY 1995), 24 August 1995, United States; New York; District Court for the Southern District of New York [SDNY]).

109 See, for example, *Lightwater v Argentina* (n 19).

110 BGH, Beschluss vom 25 November 2010 – VII ZB 120/09, 25 November 2010, Germany; Federal Court of Justice [BGH].

111 Ibid 8–9. See earlier *K and ors v Argentina* (n 88).

112 BGH (n 110).

113 Ibid 17–19 (further noting that claims that are located in the sovereign debtor's territory are not subject to German jurisdiction).

114 Ibid 20.

115 BGH, Urteil vom 24.02.2015 – XI ZR 193/14, XI ZR 193/14, NJW 2015, 2328, 24 February 2015, Germany; Federal Court of Justice [BGH].

116 The fact that litigation had started in the early 2000s and had still not concluded in 2015 accentuates the difficulties in obtaining and enforcement judicial orders against a sovereign nation, especially one that is willing to challenge each and every claim.

117 Ibid 13.
118 *K and ors v Argentina* (n 88).
119 BGH (n 115) [17–18].
120 Ibid 21.
121 Ibid.
122 Ibid 25. The same applies to the UNCTAD Principles (Principles on Promoting Responsible Sovereign Lending and Borrowing (United Nations Conference on Trade and Development [UNCTAD]). Article 7 of these Principles states that '[i]n circumstances where a sovereign is manifestly unable to service its debts, all lenders have a duty to behave in good faith and with cooperative spirit to reach a consensual rearrangement of those obligations.' However, it is undisputed that these Principles have soft law character. Hence, they bind neither sovereigns nor their creditors.
123 BGH (n 115) [27–39]. For a discussion of the *Abaclat v Argentina* (n 3) decision, see Chapter 2.3.1.1. 'Abaclat and Others v Argentine Republic.' The BGH also reviewed Professor Goldmann's expert opinion in support of Argentina's appeal but concluded that he had misconstrued the development of international law in the realm of sovereign debt: sovereign borrowers and lenders have so far favoured the market-oriented approach by including CACs in their sovereign debt instruments rather than establishing a bankruptcy system for states. The Argentine bonds held by the plaintiff had no CACs, which meant that there were no legal means to bind bondholders to a majority-approved restructuring. Their enforcement rights were thus left untouched.
124 Ibid 28.
125 See BVerfG, Urteil vom 3.7.2019–2 BvR 824/15, 2 BvR 825/15, Second Senate, 3 July 2019, Germany; Constitutional Court [BVerfG].
126 Ibid 39.
127 Ibid 41.
128 Ibid 43.
129 See Chapter 5.2.4. 'Retail Investors' for a discussion of this type of holdout investor.
130 Schumacher (n 21) 68.
131 *Borri v Argentina*, Request for a ruling on jurisdiction, Case No 11225, Order No 6532/2005, ILDC 296 (IT 2005), (2005) 88 Riv Dir Int 856, 27 May 2005, Italy; Supreme Court of Cassation.
132 Ibid.
133 Ibid.
134 For a discussion of the debt moratorium, see Chapter 2.1. 'Argentina's Sovereign Debt Restructurings (2001–2010).'
135 *Borri v Argentina* (n 131) [F2]. Additionally, Argentina posited that the specific contractual provisions in the bond documentation conferred jurisdiction exclusively upon the courts of New York and Argentina, rather than those in Italy.
136 Ibid.
137 Ibid D2.
138 Moreover, the Supreme Court remarked that Art 2(2) of the UN Convention on Jurisdictional Immunities of States and Their Property of 2 December 2004 makes clear that – for the purpose of ascertaining the commercial or sovereign nature of a legal act – 'reference should be made primarily to the nature of the transaction, but its purpose should be taken into account.' See Convention on Jurisdictional Immunities of States and their Property (United Nations [UN]) UN Doc A/RES/59/38, Annex, UN Doc A/59/508.
139 *Borri v Argentina* (n 131) [D2].
140 The *Corte di Cassazione* also investigated possible violations of human rights by the Argentine government. Applying a rather unconventional reasoning, the court observed that foreign state jurisdictional immunity could, in principle, be denied

when a defendant state was accused of international crimes and gross violations of human rights. Argentina could not have invoked its immunity if the legislation would have interfered with 'universal values of respect for human dignity that transcend the interests of individual state communities.' The *Borri* court found, however, that no such violation of human dignity occurred in Argentina, and it was, thus, immune from private creditor suits. See ibid [D2] and [D4.3]. In this regard, the *Borri v Argentina* decision referenced the famous *Ferrini* case (*Ferrini v Germany*, Appeal decision, Decision No 5044/2004, ILDC 19 (IT 2004), (2004) 87 Riv Dir Intern 539, (2005) 99 AJIL 242, (2006) 128 ILR 658, 11 March 2004, Italy; Supreme Court of Cassation. In this decision, the Italian Supreme Court held that 'while customary law prescribes immunity from jurisdiction of a foreign state for acts, which are the expression of its sovereign authority, such immunity should be lifted when such acts amount to international crimes.'

141 *Borri v Argentina* (n 131) [D4.2]. Ultimately, while the Italian courts were reluctant to delve into the intricacies of the issue, the question whether a hierarchy exists under international law between the opposing interests of investors and citizens has been subject to comprehensive discussions in pertinent scholarship.

142 Ibid D4.3.

143 Ibid.

144 *NML Capital Limited v Argentina*, Appeal judgment, [2011] UKSC 31, [2011] 2 AC 495, [2011] 3 WLR 273, ILDC 1805 (UK 2011), (2011) 147 ILR 575, 6 July 2011, United Kingdom; Supreme Court [SC].

145 See Chapter 2.2.1.1. 'United States.' The overall sum Argentina was due to pay to NML according to the SDNY judgment exceeded USD280 million.

146 Immunity from suit played a lesser role in UK jurisprudence pertaining to the Argentine default. Indeed, UK courts, based on pertinent legislature, had long established that the issuance of sovereign debt qualifies as a commercial transaction; see, for example, *AIC Ltd v Federal Government of* Nigeria [2003] EWHC 1357 (QB).

147 A possible advantage of having the judgment recognized is that UK courts have been more restrictive than US courts when it comes to the enforcement of sovereign debt claims. See, for an overview, for example, Stephen Schwarcz, 'Sovereign Debt Restructuring and English Governing Law' (2017) 12 Brooklyn Journal of Corporate, Financial & Commercial Law 73.

148 The leading decision under English law with respect to the state immunity from suit was *Trendtex Trading Corporation v Central Bank of Nigeria*, Appeal decision, ILDC 1735 (UK 1977), [1977] 1 QB 529, [1977] 1 All ER 881, [1977] 2 WLR 356, (1979) 64 ILR 111, 13 January 1977, United Kingdom; England and Wales; Court of Appeal [CA]; Civil Division [EWCA Civ].

149 According to Section 3(1) of the SIA, '[a] state is not immune as respects proceedings relating to – (a) a commercial transaction entered into by the state.' Section 3(3)(b) defines 'commercial transaction' as including 'any loan or other transaction for the provision of finance.'

150 Ibid 34. It simply stipulated that the states lack immunity for proceedings 'relating to commercial transactions' rather than extending this principle to foreign judgements that related to commercial transactions.

151 Ibid 44. Section 31 of the 1982 Act reads as follows:

> (1) A judgment given by a court of an overseas country against a state other than the United Kingdom or the state to which that court belongs shall be recognised and enforced in the United Kingdom if and only if . . . (a) it would be so recognised and enforced if it had not been given against a state; and (b) that court would have had jurisdiction in the matter if it had applied rules corresponding to those applicable to such matters in the United Kingdom in accordance with sections 2 to 11 of the State Immunity Act 1978.

152 Ibid 49. He specified this:

> state immunity cannot be raised as a bar to the recognition and enforcement of a foreign judgment if, under the principles of international law recognised in this jurisdiction, the state against whom the judgment was given was not entitled to immunity in respect of the claim.

Lord Walker added that what mattered to the enforcement of the New York judgment in the UK was whether 'the foreign State would not have been immune if the foreign proceedings had been brought in the United Kingdom'; see ibid 118.

153 Ibid 85.

154 Ibid.

155 See, for example, Hazel Fox and Philippa Webb, *The Law of State Immunity* (Oxford: Oxford University Press, 2013) 219 (also remarking that the minority view was in fact endorsed by the ICJ as the correct position in international law, according to which a third-party national court must ask itself whether it would have reached the same conclusion as the deciding court in regard to the merits of the case).

156 Ibid.

157 See Chapter 2.2.2.1. 'International Tribunal for the Law of the Sea.' Also see Craig Allen, 'Law of the Sea tribunal Resoundingly Affirms the Sovereign Immunity of Warships and Orders Ghana to Release Argentine Tall Ship ARA Libertad' (*Opinio Juris*, 15 December 2012) <http://opiniojuris.org/2012/12/15/law-of-the-sea-tribunal-resoundingly-affirms-the-sovereign-immunity-of-warships-and-orders-ghana-to-release-argentine-tall-ship-ara-libertad/> accessed 2 November 2021.

158 The waiver reads as follows:

> [t]o the extent that the Republic or any of its . . . assets . . . shall be entitled . . . to any immunity from . . . jurisdiction . . . from attachment prior judgment, from attachment in aid of execution of judgment, *from execution of a judgment* . . . the Republic has irrevocably agreed not to claim and has irrevocably waived such immunity to the fullest extent permitted by the laws of such jurisdiction.
>
> (emphasis added)

See Elie Kleiman and Julie Spinelli, 'NML v Argentina: Supreme Court Tightens Waiver of Sovereign Immunity Test' (July 2013) Freshfields Bruckhaus Deringer Client Briefing <www.lexology.com/commentary/litigation/france/freshfields-bruckhaus-deringer-llp/nml-v-argentina-supreme-court-tightens-waiver-of-sovereign-immunity-test> accessed 2 November 2021.

159 See, for example, *NML Capital Limited v Argentina*, Appeal judgment, Case No 09–72 057, 867, (2012) 139 JDI 668, 28 September 2011, France; Court of Cassation [Cass]; Civil Division [1(4°)].

160 Vienna Convention on Diplomatic Relations (United Nations [UN]) 500 UNTS 95, (1972) 23 UST 3227, TIAS No 7502, UN Reg No we-7310 ['Vienna Convention on Diplomatic Relations'].

161 *NML Capital Limited v Argentina* (n 159) [1(1°)]. This principle applied even if such waiver was of general nature and did not explicitly mention certain assets targeted by the creditor.

162 Ibid 3. Article 32 of the Vienna Convention on Diplomatic Relations (n 160) states the following:

> 1. The immunity from jurisdiction of diplomatic agents and of persons enjoying immunity under article 37 may be waived by the sending State.
> 2. Waiver must always be express.
> 3. The initiation of proceedings by a diplomatic agent or by a person enjoying immunity from jurisdiction under article 37 shall preclude him from invoking

immunity from jurisdiction in respect of any counterclaim directly connected with the principal claim.

4. Waiver of immunity from jurisdiction in respect of civil or administrative proceedings shall not be held to imply waiver of immunity in respect of the execution of the judgement, for which a separate waiver shall be necessary.

163 *NML Capital Limited v Argentina* (n 159). The court also referred to the French law on execution procedures (Loi n° 91–650 du 9 juillet 1991 portant réforme des procédures civiles d'exécution), according to which enforcement measures cannot be undertaken against legal or natural persons that enjoy immunity.

164 Ibid 2.

165 Ibid 3.

166 Ibid. The court added that '[e]ven if a certain amount of the monies deposited in the bank accounts were not directly used for the day-to-day running of the embassy, a presumption of public utility existed for such assets.'

167 *Société NML Capital Limited v Argentina and Air France*, No 11–13–323, 28 March 2013, France; Court of Cassation [Cass]; Civil Division. See, for an English translation, Kleiman and Spinelli (n 158).

168 Specifically, the assets NML sought to attach pecuniary claims of the Argentine government vis-à-vis BNP Paribas (a French bank), Air France (the state-owned carrier), and Total Austral (an oil company) stemming from tax obligations and social security companies owed by these companies.

169 *Société NML Capital Limited v Argentina and Air France* (n 167). The court also cited cases by the ECtHR, such as *Al-Adsani v United Kingdom*, Merits, App No 35763/97, ECHR 2001-XI, IHRL 2981 (ECHR 2001), [2001] ECHR 761, (2002) 34 EHRR 11, (1987) 12 BHRC 88, (2003) 123 ILR 24, 21st November 2001, European Court of Human Rights [ECHR]; Grand Chamber [ECHR]. See Convention on Jurisdictional Immunities of States and their Property (United Nations [UN]) UN Doc A/RES/59/38, Annex, UN Doc A/59/508 (hereinafter 'UNCSI').

170 The waiver reads as follows:

> Argentina will irrevocably waive and agree not to plead any immunity from the jurisdiction of any such court to which it might otherwise be entitled (including sovereign immunity and immunity from pre-judgment attachment, post-judgment attachment and execution) in any action based upon the Securities.

See *Société NML Capital Limited v Argentina and Air France* (n 167).

171 The Belgian Supreme Court reached the same conclusion when NML sought to attach Argentine bank accounts used for diplomatic purposes, stating that an express waiver that specifies the assets that are not immune is required. See *République d'Argentine v NML Capital*, n C.11.0688.F, 22 November 2012, Belgium, Cour de cassation [Cass].

172 *Société NML Capital Limited v Argentina and Air France* (n 167).

173 Ibid.

174 BGer, Urteil vom 12.07.2010–5A.360/2010, *NML Capital Limited and EM Limited v Bank for International Settlements and Debt Enforcement Office Basel-Stadt*, Final appeal judgment, 5A.360/2010, BGE 136 III 379, ATF 136 III 379, ILDC 1547 (CH 2010), 12 July 2010, Switzerland; Federal Supreme Court [BGer].

175 Sixty central banks from countries that make up about 95% of world GDP are members of the BIS. See BIS, 'About the BIS – Overview' <www.bis.org/about/index.htm?m=1%7C1> accessed 2 November 2021.

176 Most members only store about 10%–15% of their foreign exchange reserves with the BIS; see Anne Peters, 'Die funktionale Immunität internationaler Organisationen und die Rechtsweggarantie; zugleich Anmerkung zur Entscheidung des schweizerischen Bundesgerichts zur Immunität der Bank für Internationalen Zahlungsausgleich (BIZ)

vom 12 Juli 2010 (BGE 136 III 379, 5A 360/2010)' (2011) 21 Revue Suisse de Droit International et Européen 397, 425.

177 See, for example, August Reinisch (ed), *The Privileges and Immunities of International Organisations in Domestic Courts* (Oxford: Oxford University Press, 2011) 20.

178 The order was based on Article 271(1)(4) of the Swiss Code 281.1 of 11 April 1889 on Debt Enforcement and Bankruptcy (*Bundesgesetz über Schuldbetreibung und Konkurs*) (Switzerland) [ch]), which allows for an asset freeze if a sufficient connection between the claim and Switzerland exists. Here, the connection was established through the deposition of Argentine funds at the BIS in Basel. The Basel's Debt Enforcement Office held that the Argentine government had illegally transferred large sums to the BIS in the wake of its 2001 debt crisis with the objective of evading debt enforcement measures, thereby abusing the BIS's immunity. See August Reinisch, 'European Court Practice Concerning State Immunity from Enforcement Measures' (2006) 17(4) European Journal of International Law 803.

179 BGer (n 174) [381].

180 For a discussion of the decision, see Dimitij Euler, 'Switzerland's Department of Foreign Affairs Endorsed BGH Decision (BGE 136 III 379) Not to Lift Bank of International Settlement's (BIS) Immunity Due to an Attempt of NML Capital to Freeze USD300m (£186m) on Argentina's Bank Accounts' (*Young ICCA Blog*, 3 December 2012) <www.youngicca-blog.com/switzerlands-department-of-foreign-affairs-endorsed-federal-supreme-court-decision-bge-136-iii-379-not-to-lift-bank-of-international-settlements-bis-immunity-due-to-an-attempt-of/#_ftn9> accessed 2 November 2021.

181 See Convention respecting the Bank for International Settlements 104 LNTS 441 ('Statute of the BIS'). Article 55 BIS Statutes reads as follows:

> (1) The Bank shall enjoy immunity from jurisdiction, save:
> (a) to the extent that such immunity is formally waived in individual cases by the Chairman of the Board, the General Manager, the Deputy General Manager, or their duly authorised representatives; or
> (b) in civil or commercial suits, arising from banking or financial transactions, initiated by contractual counterparties of the Bank, except in those cases in which provision for arbitration has been or shall have been made.
> (2) *Property and assets of the Bank shall, wherever located and by whomsoever held, be immune from any measure of execution* (including seizure, attachment, freeze or any other measure of execution, enforcement or sequestration), except if that measure of execution is sought pursuant to a final judgment rendered against the Bank by any court of competent jurisdiction pursuant to sub-paragraph 1(a) or (b) above.
>
> (emphasis added)

182 Agreement between the Swiss Federal Council and the Bank for International Settlements to determine the Bank's legal status in Switzerland of 10 February 1987 (text as amended effective 1 January 2003 by the exchange of letters of 18 December 2002/13 January 2003) ('Headquarters Agreement'). Article 4 stipulates the following:

> 1. The Bank shall enjoy immunity from jurisdiction, save:
> (a) to the extent that such immunity is formally waived in individual cases by the President, 2 the General Manager of the Bank, or their duly authorised representatives;
> (b) in civil or commercial suits, arising from banking or financial transactions, initiated by contractual counterparties of the Bank, except in those cases in which provision for arbitration has been or shall have been made;
> (c) in the case of any civil action against the Bank for damage caused by any vehicle belonging to or operated on behalf of the Bank.

183 BGer (n 174) [384–385].
184 Ibid.
185 Ibid.
186 Ibid 387–388. The immunity of international organizations is deemed vital to safeguard their independent operation in the host state. However, for such immunity to be justified, all actions must be closely linked to its organisational purpose. See Sam Muller, *International Organizations and Their Host States: Aspects of Their Legal Relationship* (Amsterdam: Martinus Nijhoff, 1995) 151.
187 BGer (n 174) [388].
188 See, for a discussion in Thore Neumann and Anne Peters, 'Switzerland' in Reinisch (n 178) 250.
189 BGer (n 174) [387].
190 Ibid 388.
191 Article 6(1) ECHR reads as follows:

> [i]n the determination of his civil rights and obligations or of any criminal charge against him, everyone is entitled to a fair and public hearing within a reasonable time by an independent and impartial tribunal established by law. Judgment shall be pronounced publicly but the press and public may be excluded from all or part of the trial in the interests of morals, public order or national security in a democratic society, where the interests of juveniles or the protection of the private life of the parties so require, or to the extent strictly necessary in the opinion of the court in special circumstances where publicity would prejudice the interests of justice.

192 *Waite and Kennedy v Germany,* Merits, App No 26083/94, ECHR 1999-we, IHRL 3200 (ECHR 1999), OXIO 272, [1999] ECHR 13, (1999) 30 EHRR 261, (1999) 118 ILR 121, [1999] 6 BHRC 499, 18 February 1999, European Court of Human Rights [ECHR]; Grand Chamber [ECHR].
193 BGer (n 174) [390].
194 Ibid.
195 Ibid 391 (further arguing that granting attachment orders to private market participants would, too, not be in the interest of international financial stability).
196 'ARA Libertad' Case, *Argentina v Ghana,* Order, request for the prescription of provisional measures, ITLOS Case No 20 [2012] ITLOS Rep 21, ICGJ 454 (ITLOS 2012), 15 December 2012, International Tribunal for the Law of the Sea [ITLOS].
197 Michelle Celarier, 'Singer Takes Victory Lap in Debt Feud' *New York Post* (New York, 30 October 2012).
198 'ARA Libertad' Case, *Argentina v Ghana,* Order, request for the prescription of provisional measures, ITLOS Case No 20, [2012] ITLOS Rep 21, ICGJ 454 (ITLOS 2012), 15 December 2012, International Tribunal for the Law of the Sea [ITLOS] [7].
199 Ibid 8.
200 Ibid.
201 Convention on the Law of the Sea (United Nations [UN]) 1833 UNTS 3, UKTS 81 (1999), UN Doc A/Conf.62/122, UN Reg No I-31363 ('UNCLOS').
202 Article 32 UNCLOS states that 'nothing in this Convention affects the immunities of warships.'
203 International Convention for the Unification of Certain Rules of Law relating to Bills of Lading (as amended) 120 LNTS 155, Reg No LoN-2764.
204 'ARA Libertad' Case, *Argentina v Ghana,* Order, request for the prescription of provisional measures, ITLOS Case No 20, [2012] ITLOS Rep 21, ICGJ 454 (ITLOS 2012), 15 December 2012, International Tribunal for the Law of the Sea [ITLOS] [31].
205 Moreover, Ghana argued that the dispute was one of general international law and, thus, not justiciable under the UNCLOS, which exclusively related to the law of

the sea; see *ARA Libertad*, Written Statement of the Republic of Ghana, app. 3 (28 November 2012). This is Ghana's view:

> Article 32 of the [UNCLOS] Convention refers to the immunity of warships in the territorial sea and *does not refer to any such immunity when in internal waters* and that it was understood that the regime of ports and internal waters was excluded from the 1982 Convention.
>
> (emphasis added)

206 On this basis, the ITLOS may grant provisional (interim) measures in order to protect sovereign assets and minimize the losses to the respective party before a final order on merits was rendered. More specifically, Article 290(5) UNCLOS (n 201) allows for prima facie jurisdiction if 'the urgency of the situation so requires in the sense that action prejudicial to the rights of either party is likely to be taken before constitution of the Annex VII arbitral tribunal.'

207 According to Article 29 UNCLOS (n 201), ' "warship" means a ship belonging to the armed forces of a State bearing the external marks distinguishing such ships of its nationality, under the command of an officer duly commissioned by the government of the State and whose name appears in the appropriate service list or its equivalent, and manned by a crew which is under regular armed forces discipline.'

208 'ARA Libertad' Case, *Argentina v Ghana,* Order, request for the prescription of provisional measures, ITLOS Case No 20, [2012] ITLOS Rep 21, ICGJ 454 (ITLOS 2012), 15 December 2012, International Tribunal for the Law of the Sea [ITLOS] [93].

209 Ibid 99.

210 Ibid 108.

211 *Argentina v NML* (n 79). See Chapter 2.2.1.1.3. 'NML Capital v Argentina.'

212 Jake Rylatt, 'Sitting, Waiting, Wishing: Argentina Initiates Sovereign Default Claim Before the ICJ' (*Cambridge International Law Journal Blog*, 10 August 2014) <http://cilj.co.uk/2014/08/10/sitting-waiting-wishing-argentina-initiates-sovereign-default-claim-international-court-justice-requesting-usa-consent-jurisdiction/> accessed 2 November 2021.

213 Ibid. Some commentators even labelled Argentina's attempt to bring in the ICJ 'frivolous.' Julian Ku, 'Here Comes That Frivolous Argentina ICJ Claim! Oh, and They Have No Jurisdiction Either!' (7 August 2014) <http://opiniojuris.org/2014/08/07/comes-frivolous-argentina-icj-claim-oh-jurisdiction-either/> accessed 2 November 2021 (noting that one should '[e]xpect more grandstanding from the Argentine government as it tries to use the ICJ as an international public relations platform').

214 For critical opinion on the US government's amicus brief, see Ellen Ginsberg Simon and Q Monty Crawford, 'The Impact of Republic of Argentina v NML Capital, Ltd.: Why the Supreme Court's Ruling Against Argentina Avoided a Host of Unintended, Negative Consequences' (2015) 30(1) Maryland Journal of International Law 55, 60 (noting that the US governments comity argument promoted a 'distorted reading of the FSIA, disregarded its legislative history and amendments to the statue that support Justice Scalia's understanding and endorsed a changed understanding of the statute that would have resulted in more realistic and ultimately destructive policy implications').

215 For instance, the ICJ considered in *France v Norway* that the question of non-discrimination between different creditors was to be decided under national law rather than international law. See Certain Norwegian Loans, *France v Norway*, Judgment, jurisdiction; separate opinion of Judge Lauterpacht, ICJ GL No 29, [1957] ICJ Rep 9, [1957] ICJ Rep 34, ICGJ 175 (ICJ 1957), 6 July 1957, United Nations [UN]; International Court of Justice [ICJ].

216 *Medellin v Texas*, Docket No 06–984, 552 US 491 (2008), 25 March 2008, United States; Supreme Court [US].

217 See Mauro Megliani, *Sovereign Debt: Genesis, Restructuring, Litigation* (Berlin: Springer, 2015); Rodrigo Olivares-Caminal, *Legal Aspects of Sovereign Debt Restructuring* (London: Sweet & Maxwell, 2009); Ernest Bankas, *State Immunity Controversy in International Law* (Berlin: Springer, 2005); Mark Weidemaier, 'Sovereign Immunity and Sovereign Debt' (2014) 1 University of Illinois Law Review 68.

218 For example, Megliani (n 217) 395 et seq.

219 In particular, *Argentina and Banco Central de la República Argentina v Weltover Incorporated and ors,* Final appeal, Docket No 91–763, 504 US 607 (1992), ILDC 1924 (US 1992), 112 S Ct 2160 (1992), 119 L Ed 2d 394 (1992), (1995) 100 ILR 510, 12 June 1992, United States; Supreme Court [US] and *Allied Bank* (n 27).

220 Most notably, ibid.

221 See Chapter 2.2.1.1.1. 'Lightwater v Argentina.'

222 See Chapter 2.2.1.3.1. 'Italian Supreme Court (Corte Suprema di Cassazione).' Some argue that the decision unnecessarily dove into the sovereign immunity debate, for the Italian judges could have simply thrown out the lawsuit on the basis of the forum selection clause, which did not confer jurisdiction onto courts in Italy. See Megliani (n 217) 396.

223 It should be noted that Italy had long been considered a special case when compared to other jurisdictions, given that no statutory basis for sovereign immunity exists under Italian law. See Andrea Atteritano, 'Immunity of States and Their Organs: The Contribution of Italian Jurisprudence Over the Past Ten Years' (2008) Contribution to the Annual Conference of the Italian Association of Law and Economics <www.sidi-isil.org/wp-content/uploads/2010/12/1_02_atteritano1.pdf> accessed 2 November 2021.

224 See Hayk Kupelyants, *Sovereign Defaults Before Domestic Courts* (Oxford: Oxford University Press, 2018) 284 et seq.

225 In the leading decision by the US Supreme Court, *Argentina v Weltover* (n 219), it was established that the issuance of sovereign bonds on foreign debt markets amounts to an *actus iure gestonis*. Also compare § 1603(d) FSIA which reads as follows: '[t]he commercial character of an activity shall be determined by reference to the nature of the course of conduct or particular transaction, rather than by reference to its purpose.'

226 Jürgen Bröhmer, 'Immunity and Sovereign Bonds' in Anne Peters, Evelyne Lagrange, Stefan Oeter, and Christian Tomuschat (eds), *Immunities in the Age of Global Constitutionalism* (The Hague: Brill Nijhoff, 2014) 190.

227 Ibid 191. This, as he argues, is just a 'poorly disguised attempt [by the Italian court] to revive the purpose test' since the only distinction between the decision to issue public debts and the decision not to pay them lies in the potential public purpose of the former.

228 Bonafè (n 92) 167.

229 Ibid 169.

230 Ibid. Bonafe argues that following this approach 'would ultimately reverse the development of the state immunity rule that has taken place under customary law, thus restoring the old rule of absolute state immunity.'

231 See, for a discussion, a different assessment of the mixed activity conundrum seems warranted in cases where the sovereign debtor remains the 'master' of the law governing the debt instrument, as discussed in Chapter 4.4. 'Sovereign Immunity Revisited.'

232 See Bankas (n 217).

233 See Kupeylants (n 224) 284 (quoting Lord Wilberforce in the *I Congreso del Partido* case, who observed that 'the "restrictive theory" [of sovereign immunity] does not and could not deny capability of a state to resort to sovereign or governmental action it merely asserts that acts done within the trading or commercial activity are not immune').

234 Bonafè (n 92) 172.

235 In this context, Atteritano, for instance, notes that '[i]n *Borri*, the Court did not consider the nature of the contract for the sale of bonds, but the nature of the measure taken by Argentina in order to face its financial crisis'; compare Atteritano (n 223) 42.

236 Moreover, as Reinisch and Binder point out, the Italian Supreme Court's decision not only disregarded the fact that the initial bond issuance was a commercial activity, but it also ignored the express waivers of immunity in the bond issuance conditions; see August Reinisch and Christina Binder, 'Debts and State of Necessity' in Juan Pablo Bohoslavsky and Jemej Letnar Cernic (eds), *Making Sovereign Financing and Human Rights Work* (London: Bloomsbury, 2014) 118.

237 See, for example, Kupeylants (n 224) 284–286 (stipulating that 'since the bonds [in the Argentine case] were often governed by some foreign law, the Argentine declaration of moratorium was inapplicable and the creditor did not need to challenge it separately.').

238 See Chapter 2.2.1.2.1. 'BVerfG Decision of 8 May 2007.' Though the judgment creditors did not manage to locate attachable assets, their fortunes turned to the better when Argentina's administration changed in 2016. According to newspaper reports, the new Macri government agreed to pay the German creditors who obtained a money judgment in Germany 150% of the face value of their bonds while the haircut for the restructured creditors amounted to 70%. See Carolina Millan, 'Argentina Haunted by Default Legacy as German Suit' *Bloomberg* (New York, 27 September 2016) <www.bloomberg.com/news/articles/2016-09-27/argentina-still-haunted-by-default-legacy-as-german-suit-looms> accessed 2 November 2021 (highlighting that some German investors were still not satisfied, arguing that based on the German court rulings, they should receive a payment that is around 250% of the bond's face value).

239 *Trendtex v Nigeria* (n 148).

240 Bonafè (n 92) 173.

241 *Trendtex v Nigeria* (n 148).

242 Megliani (n 217) 395.

243 See *NML v Argentina (UK)* (n 114) [62]. Lord Philipps noted the following in this context:

> [t]he reality is that Argentina agreed that the bonds should bear words that provided for the widest possible submission to jurisdiction for the purposes of enforcement, short of conferring jurisdiction on any country whose domestic laws would not, absent any question of immunity, permit an action to enforce a New York judgment.

244 Oliver Gayner, 'Case Comment: NML Capital Limited v Republic of Argentina [2011] UKSC 31' (*UKSC Blog*, 22 July 2011) <http://ukscblog.com/new-judgment-nml-capital-ltd-v-republic-of-argentina-2011-uksc-31/> accessed 2 November 2021; Clifford Chance, 'Sovereign Immunity: Don't Cry for Me' (2011) Client Briefing <www.cliffordchance.com/content/dam/cliffordchance/briefings/2011/07/sovereign-immunity-dont-cry-for-me.pdf> accessed 2 November 2021 (noting that 'Argentina has no sovereign immunity in respect of proceedings in England to enforce a New York judgment on a bond issue').

245 Kupelyants (n 224) 295.

246 See *FG Hemisphere Assocs. v Republique du Congo*, 455 F 3d 575 (5th Cir 2006), 10 July 2006, United States; Court of Appeals (5th Circuit) [5th Cir].

247 Though, in contrast to the FSIA, the SIA does not require the property to be *in commercial use* at the time of the attachment attempt. See Kupeylants (n 224) 287.

248 Though, in contrast to the FSIA, the SIA does not require the property to be *in commercial use* at the time of the attachment attempt. See Kupeylants (n 224) 287.

249 VII ZB 9/05, 4 October 2005, Germany; Federal Court of Justice [BGH].

250 German courts have, however, made clear that creditors may not attach assets used for diplomatic purposes without a specific waiver, that is, one that goes beyond the

standard immunity waiver in international debt contracts; see BVerfG, Beschluss vom 06.12.2006–2 BvM 9/03, 6 December 2006, Germany; Constitutional Court [BverfG].

251 To that end, the French decision seemed to echo the US Fifth Circuit's decision in *Walker v Republic of Congo*, which held that property of a state cannot be attached if there is no evidence how it was used. See *Walker International Holdings v Republic of Congo*, 395 F3d 229 (5th Cir 2004), 22 December 2004, United States; Court of Appeals (5th Circuit) [5th Cir].

252 Alexander Blumrosen and Fleur Maelt-Deraedt, 'NML Capital Ltd. V Republic of Argentina' (2013) 107(3) The American Journal of International Law 638, 642.

253 Ibid.

254 Article 21 UNCSI further specifies Article 19 UNCSI. It includes a non-exhaustive list on property, which is deemed non-commercial and thus protected from execution.

255 See Victor Grandaubert, 'France Legislates on State Immunity from Execution: How to Kill Two Birds with One Stone?' (*EJIL: Talk*, 23 January 2017) <www.ejiltalk.org/france-legislates-on-state-immunity-from-execution-how-to-kill-two-birds-with-one-stone/> accessed 2 November 2021.

256 Act No 2016–1691 of 9 December 2016 on the Fight Against Missing Morality (*Loi De La Lutte Contre Les Manquements À La Probité*) (France [fr]).

257 Decision No 2016–741 DC of 8 December 2016, French Constitutional Council (*Le Conseil Constitutionnel*).

258 See FRBNY, 'Services for Central Banks and International Institutions' (October 2015) <www.newyorkfed.org/aboutthefed/fedpoint/fed20> accessed 2 November 2021.

259 Essentially, the veil of a corporate entity is pierced if the corporation was 'so heavily controlled by its owner that a relationship of principal and agent is created.' See *EM v BCRA* (n 31). The alter ego doctrine was also invoked in the context of Venezuela's default and subsequent enforcement attempts by creditors, who tried to attach shares of the state-owned oil company. For an analysis of that case, see Kevin D Benish, 'Crystallex Int'l Corp. v Bolivarian Rep. Venez. (3D Cir.)' (2021) 60(2) International Legal Materials 147.

260 *First National Bank v Cuba* (n 39).

261 See George Foster, 'When Commercial Meets Sovereign: A New Paradigm for Applying the Foreign Sovereign Immunities Act in Crossover Cases' (2014) 52(1) Houston Law Review 361, 402. In the special case of central banks, Foster also stresses this of the FSIA's legislative history:

> indicates that Congress conferred special protection on such property to encourage foreign governments to maintain foreign currency reserves in the US, as well as to avoid tension with other countries that could result from large seizures of central bank assets.

262 Joshua Aizenman, 'Foreign Exchange Reserve Management' in Steven Durlauf and Lawrence Blime (eds), *The New Palgrave Dictionary Of Economics* (London: Palgrave Macmillan, 2009) (arguing that 'providing a secure immunity regime is necessary to the global financial system's stability').

263 See Alexander Szodruch, *Staateninsolvenz und private Gläubiger: Rechtsprobleme des Private Sector Involvement bei staatlichen Finanzkrisen im 21. Jahrhundert* (Berlin: Berliner Wissenschaftsverlag, 2010) 378–379.

264 See, for example, Matthias J Müller, *Staatsbankrott und private Gläubiger* (Baden-Baden: Nomos, 2015) 205.

265 Patrick Wautelet, 'Vulture Funds, Creditors and Sovereign Debtors: How to Find a Balance?' in Matthias Audit (ed), *Insolvabilité des États et Dettes Souveraines* (Paris: LDGJ, 2011) 67 et seq.

266 *Trendtex v Nigeria* (n 148).

267 Wautelet (n 265) 38 (noting that 'the Swiss Federal Tribunal ruled in the famous *Noga* saga that the creditor could seize tolls collected on behalf of the Russian authority for

air control, held by IATA (International Air Transport Association)'). Though they have barred enforcement against the BIS; see Chapter 2.2.1.6. 'Switzerland.'

268 With a balance sheet of roughly SDR356.2 billion (USD500 billion), of which SDR288 billion make up deposits by its members, the BIS administers a considerable amount of foreign sovereign reserves. See BIS, 'Financial Statements' (31 March 2021) <www.bis.org/banking/balsheet.htm> accessed 2 November 2021.

269 US law is by no means exceptional: Most central bank laws provide some form of legal protection from lawsuits to ensure their independence and limit their liability. See Ashraf Khan, 'Legal Protection: Liability and Immunity Arrangements of Central Banks and Financial Supervisors' (2018) IMF Working Paper WP/18/176 <www.imf.org/en/Publications/WP/Issues/2018/08/02/Legal-Protection-Liability-and-Immunity-Arrangements-of-Central-Banks-and-Financial-46086> accessed 2 November 2021.

270 *EM v BCRA* (n 31); for a discussion, see Chapter 2.2.1.1.2. 'EM v Banco Central de la República Argentina.'

271 This understanding of the BIS's role reflects Article 3 of the BIS Statutes, which states this:

> [t]he objects of the Bank are: To promote the co-operation of central banks and to provide additional facilities for international financial operations; and to act as trustee or agent in regard to international financial settlements entrusted to it under agreements with the parties concerned.

272 Most notably, *Groupement d'Entreprises Fougerolle v European Organization for Nuclear Research (CERN)*, BGE 118 Ib 562, 21 December 1992, Switzerland; Federal Supreme Court [BGer].

273 Neumann and Peters (n 188) 246.

274 BGer (n 272) [1(a)].

275 Thore Neumann, 'NML Capital Ltd and EM Limited v Bank for International Settlements and Debt Enforcement Office Basel-Stadt' (2010) Oxford Reports on International Law in Domestic Courts (ILDC) 1547. Also see for a similar view, Sandrine Giroud, 'Enforcement Against State Assets and Execution of ICSID Awards in Switzerland: How Swiss Courts Deal with Immunity Defences' (2012) 30 ASA Bulletin 4/2012, 758 (adding that '[another] lesson is that foreign affairs remain an area largely withdrawn from legal action and it falls within the discretionary powers of a State to intervene or not in relation to possible abuses of immunity privileges.').

276 Neumann and Peters (n 188) 246.

277 For instance, in *Waite and Kennedy v Germany,* Merits, App No 26083/94, ECHR 1999-we, IHRL 3200 (ECHR 1999), OXIO 272, [1999] ECHR 13, (1999) 30 EHRR 261, (1999) 118 ILR 121, [1999] 6 BHRC 499, 18 February 1999, European Court of Human Rights [ECHR]; Grand Chamber [ECHR].

278 Peters (n 176) 422.

279 In regard to the potential abuse of BIS immunity by Argentina, Peters notes that the SFSC should have assessed whether private parties have standing to invoke abuse of law by a sovereign actor rather than dismissing the claim on the grounds of absolute immunity. See ibid.

280 See Article XI Section 3 of the IMF's AoA, which states this:

> [t]he Fund, its property and its assets, wherever located and by whomsoever held, shall enjoy immunity from every from of judicial process except to the extent that it expressly waives its immunity for the purpose of any proceedings or by the terms of any contract.

See Articles of Agreement of the International Monetary Fund (as amended) (International Monetary Fund [IMF]) 2 UNTS 39, UN Reg No I-20, TIAS 1501, 60 Stat 1401, 3 Bevans 1351 [henceforth 'IMF AoA'].

281 Article 39 of the ESCB Statute, which states this:

> [t]he ECB shall enjoy in the territories of the Member States such privileges and immunities as are necessary for the performance of its tasks, under the conditions laid down in the Protocol on the privileges and immunities of the European Union.

The CJEU, for instance, held that documents connected to the performance of the tasks of the ESCB and of the Eurosystem are subject to immunity and may not be unilaterally seized by (local) law enforcement authorities. See *ECB v Slovenia*, Judgment, reference for a preliminary ruling, Case C-316/19, ECLI:EU:C:2020:1030, [2020] OJ C187/59, 17 December 2020, Court of Justice of the European Union [CJEU]; European Court of Justice [ECJ].

282 The World Bank's immunity is more nuanced. On the one hand, the World Bank Group's AoA are narrower than the IMF's and allow for judicial procedures against the World Bank under certain circumstances. On the other hand, the World Bank's AoA stipulate in Article VII that '[t]he property and assets of the Bank shall, wheresoever located and by whomsoever held, be immune from all forms of seizure, attachment or execution before the delivery of final judgment against the Bank.' Thus, the World Bank enjoys absolute immunity from enforcement. See Articles of Agreement of the International Bank for Reconstruction and Development (International Bank for Reconstruction and Development [IBRD]) 2 UNTS 134, UN Reg No I-20, TIAS 1502, 60 Stat 1440, 3 Bevans 1390. In this context, the SCOTUS decided in *Jam v International Finance Corporation (IFC)* that the IFC, which is part of the World Bank Group, did not enjoy absolute immunity from suit, as suggested by the US International Organizations Immunity Act, but that it only affords the same immunity that is also afforded to sovereign states. See *Jam et al v International Finance Corporation,* 27 February 2019 (No 17–1011, 139 S. Ct. 759 (2019)), OXIO 474, Supreme Court [US]; United Nations [UN]; International Finance Corporation [IFC].

283 That said, there is probably no customary rule of international law that grants immunity to international organizations, see Michael Wood, 'Do International Organizations Enjoy Immunity under Customary International Law' (2014) (10)(2) International Organizations Law Review 287, 317–318.

284 See, for example, Thomas E Robinson, 'The Peculiar Case of the ARA Libertad: Provisional Measures and Prejudice to the Arbitral Tribunal's Final Result' (2015) 20 Harvard Negotiation Law Review 265; James Kraska, 'The "ARA Libertad" (*Argentina v Ghana*). ITLOS Case No 20 Provisional Measures' (2013) 107 The American Journal of International Law 1; Ted L McDorman, 'Sovereign Immune Vessels: Immunities' in Henrik Ringbom (ed), *Jurisdiction Over Ships: Post-UNCLOS Developments in the Law of the Sea* (Amsterdam: Brill, 2015) 82; B M Dimri, 'The Arrest of Argentine Warship "ARA Libertad": Revisiting International Law Governing Warships, Sovereign Immunity, and Naval Diplomatic Roles' (2013) 7(3) Journal of Defence Studies 97; Martin Cabrera Mirassou, 'ARA Libertad, The' in Rüdiger Wolfrum (ed), *Max Planck Encyclopaedia of Public International Law* (Heidelberg: Oxford University Press, 2019, online version). Luke Peterson, 'Argentina and Ghana Announce Settlement of Arbitration Over Detained Warship' (*Kluwer Arbitration Blog*, 28 September 2013) <http://kluwerarbitrationblog.com/2013/09/28/argentina-and-ghana-announce-settlement-of-arbitration-over-detained-warship-ara-libertad/> accessed 2 November 2021.

285 Kraska (n 284) 7. As Robinson, for instance, notes, the ITLOS tribunal endorsed in *ARA Libertad* the principle of sovereign immunity of military assets from judgment: 'a nearly inviolate concept in international law.' Robinson (n 284) 287.

286 As the ILC states in its commentary to the UNCSI, the word 'military' includes the navy, air force and army. See Commentaries to Draft Articles on Jurisdictional

Immunities of States and Their Property adopted by the International Law Commission at its forty-third session in 1991 [[1991] II(2) UNYBILC 13] 59.

287 See Robert Kahn, 'Venezuela on the Edge' (*Council of Foreign Relations Blog*, 23 February 2013) <www.cfr.org/blog/venezuela-edge> accessed 2 November 2021. One problem that remains from a creditor's perspective is that Venezuela's oil tankers are owned by PDVSA, the state's oil company. Creditors would probably have to prove that PDVSA acts as Venezuela's alter ego if they were to successfully seize an oil tanker. For a discussion of this specific issue, see Mark Weidemaier, 'Venezuela is Like . . . PDVSA's Alter Ego, and Vice Versa?' (*Credit Slips*, 17 August 2017) <www.creditslips.org/creditslips/2017/08/venezuela-is-like-any-other-shareholder.html#more> accessed 2 November 2021.

288 See, for example, Mark Weidemaier, 'Sovereign Debt After NML v Argentina' (2013) 8(2) Capital Markets Law Journal 123; Jesse Kaplan, 'Collective Action and the Competence of Courts: The Lessons from *NML v Argentina*' (2014) 1 Stanford Journal of Business and Finance Law 3; Lee C Buchheit and G Mitu Gulati, 'Restructuring Sovereign Debt After *NML v Argentina*' (2017) 12(2) Capital Markets Law Journal 224; See Mark Weidemaier and Anna Gelpern, 'Injunctions in Sovereign Debt Litigation' (2014) 31(1) Yale Journal on Regulation 189.

289 Buchheit and Gulati (n 288) (arguing that *NML v Argentina* upset the strategic balance between sovereign debtors and creditors that has encouraged both to negotiate rather than litigate); Jamison Joiner, 'Past Due: An Introduction to Sovereign Debt, the Ongoing Dispute Between NML Capital and Argentina, and Possible Ramifications of the Dispute's Outcome' (2015) 21(1) Law and Business Review of the Americas 85, 97 (noting that 'the precedent set by the result of the NML v Argentina saga could set the path for many future conflicts between sovereign debtors and holdout creditors, especially with regard to the interpretation of *pari passu* clauses.'); Anna Gelpern, '*NML Capital, Ltd. V Republic of Argentina* and the Changing Roles of the *Pari Passu* and Collective Action Clauses in Sovereign Debt Agreements' (2015) 53 Columbia Journal of Transnational Law 396, 422 (noting that the injunction upended the balance at the foundation of sovereign debt restructuring); Anna Gelpern, 'Sovereign Damage Control' (2013) Peterson Institute of International Economics Policy Brief 13–12 <https://piie.com/publications/pb/pb13-12.pdf> accessed 2 November 2021. Other scholars consider *NML* less of a threat, or even a positive development; see Monteleone, Theresa, 'A Vulture's Gamble: High-Stakes Interpretation of Sovereign Debt Contracts in NML Capital Ltd v Republic of Argentina' (2014) 8(2) Capital Markets Law Journal 159, 161 (observing that '[w]hether or not putting more power in the hands of holdouts should be considered a bad thing may depend on whether opportunistic sovereigns or holdout creditors pose a bigger threat to sovereign debt markets.'); Julian G Ku, 'Don't Cry for Sovereign Debtors: Why Argentina's Defeat in US Courts Does Not Justify a Sovereign Debt Treaty' (2014) 36 University of Pennsylvania Journal of International Law 433, 456; Müller (n 264) 317 (contending that New York courts have found a 'pragmatic' and 'flexible' way to balance the interests of litigious creditors and a sovereign in financial distress.).

290 The IMF noted that '[i]f future courts interpret the New York Court Decisions broadly, there is a significant risk that the sovereign debt restructuring process will become more complicated.' See IMF (n 118) 13. Similarly, in its amicus brief, the US Ministry of Justice warned that the ruling in *NML v Argentina* 'undermined a system of cooperative resolution of sovereign debt crises' and rendered future voluntary debt restructurings even more difficult; see *NML Capital Limited v Argentina VII*, Order, Docket No 12–105, 1st March 2013, United States; Court of Appeals (2nd Circuit) [2d Cir].

291 Weidemaier and Gelpern (n 288) 192.

292 Tim R Samples, 'Rogue Trends in Sovereign Debt: Argentina, Vulture Funds, and Pari Passu Under New York Law' (2014) 35(1) Northwestern Journal of International Law & Business 49.

293 *Elliott Associates, L.P.*, General Docket No. 2000/QR/92 (Cour d'Appel [CA] [Court of Appeal] Bruxelles, 8ème ch. 26 September 2000). See, for background, Rodrigo Olivares-Caminal, 'The Pari Passu Interpretation in the Elliott Case: A Brilliant Strategy but an Awful (Mid-Long Term) Outcome?' (2011) 40(1) Hofstra Law Review 39, 62 (noting that '[t]he problem was that in the *Elliott* case there was no actual breach of the pari passu clause, just a misinterpretation of its meaning and scope'). This said, the pari passu injunction had never been issued by US courts whose jurisdiction over international bonds stretches much farther than that of other states, such as Belgium.

294 Buchheit and Gulati (n 288). Moreover, a careful reading of the SDNY's order suggests that all payments extended to restructured bondholders (coupon and principal) by Argentina would trigger payment of all amounts due to bonds held by holdouts (coupon *and* principal).

295 Verdier (n 67) 169 (noting that 'Judge Griesa's intentions were perfectly clear: He was ordering dozens of central participants in the international financial architecture to cut off Argentina's ability to make payments on the new bonds until it paid the holdouts').

296 See, for a discussion, Weidemaier and Gelpern (n 288) 199–209.

297 This said, neither the ILC Draft Articles ILC Draft Articles nor the UNCSI clarify the scope of injunctions in the context of sovereign debt enforcement.

298 *NML Capital Limited v Argentina V*, 699 F3d 246, 26 October 2012, United States; Court of Appeals (2nd Circuit) [2d Cir].

299 *White Hawthorne LLC v Argentina,* 2016 US Dist LEXIS 177895, 2016, United States; New York; District Court for the Southern District of New York [SDNY].

300 Cohen (n 153).

301 For an overview, see Bratton (n 121). Buchheit and Pam even argue that – if this interpretation was true – 'changes the patterns of international finance.' See Lee C Buchheit and Jeremiah S Pam, 'The Pari Passu Clause in Sovereign Debt Instruments' (2004) 53 Emory Law Review 870. Along similar lines, the Financial Markets Law Committee Financial Markets Law Committee (FMLC) comprising renowned English lawyers and academics) deems the payment interpretation of pari passu both 'uncommercial and unworkable.' See FMLC, 'Pari Passu Clauses – Analysis of the Role, Use and Meaning of Pari Passu Clauses in Sovereign Debt Obligations as a matter of English Law' (April 2015) 8 <www.fmlc.org/uploads/2/6/5/8/26584807/fmlc_paper_analysing_the_role,_use_and_meaning_of_pari_passu_clauses_in_sovereign_debt_obligations_as_a_matter_of_english_law.pdf> accessed 2 November 2021. Even ICMA, the largest private association representing sovereign debt traders, suggested that the Second Circuit got it wrong by requiring issuers to make ratable payments to restructured creditors and holdouts. See International Capital Markets Association (ICMA), 'ICMA Sovereign Bond Consultation Paper', December 2013 <https://www.icmagroup.org/assets/documents/Maket-Practice/Regulatory-Policy/Sovereign-Debt-Information/ICMA-Sovereign-Bond-Consultation-Paper-79801-5-863-v1-8-161213.pdf> (accessed 2 November 2021).

302 Halverson Cross (n 81) 131.

303 Enderlein et al similarly argue this:

> the well-known case of Argentina from 2001 to 2005 displays an exceptional degree of coerciveness, as the government officially declares default, sticks to the proclaimed moratorium by stopping all payments to its bondholders for four years, freezes foreign assets, and rejects any meaningful negotiations.

Henrik Enderlein, Christoph Trebesch, and Laura von Daniels, 'Sovereign Debt Disputes: A Database on Government Coerciveness During Debt Crises' (2012) 31(2) Journal of International Money and Finance 250, 261. Tran notes that 'Argentina was a unique example of a sovereign debtor pursuing a unilateral and coercive approach to debt restructuring, wilfully ignoring its own obligations to official creditors and international financial institutions'; see Hung Tran, 'The Role of Markets in Sovereign Debt Crisis Detection, Prevention and Resolution' (2013) BIS Papers

No 72 – Sovereign Risk: A World Without Risk-Free Assets? Proceedings of a Seminar on Sovereign Risk Including Contributions by Central Bank Governors and Other Policy-Makers, Market Practitioners and Academics, Basel, 8–9 January, 95.

304 Would any sovereign debtor insisting on not paying holdout investors be considered recalcitrant? What makes certain behaviours unique? Would, for instance, Greece's emergency measures of retroactively introducing CACs to cram down holdouts and implement a debt restructuring against the will of a significant chunk of bondholders have fallen under this category?

305 Most notably, neither the SDNY nor the Second Circuit presented a benchmark against which the legitimacy of debt adjustment programs under New York law could be ascertained. The court ignored the fact that a government might become unable to repay all its creditors in full. In fact, by reasoning that the uniqueness of the Argentine case demanded a unique response from the US judiciary, the judges exposed the arbitrariness they seemed to apply to instances of holdout litigation.

306 This said, as Weidemaier and Gelpern (n 288) 192 point out, '[a]s long as creditors have trouble satisfying money judgments, we expect courts to hear requests for injunctive relief in sovereign debt cases and in other lawsuits against foreign sovereigns.'

307 *The Export-Import Bank of the Republic of China v Grenada*, 2013 US Dist LEXIS 117740, 19 August 2013, United States; New York; District Court for the Southern District of New York [SDNY].

308 Ibid. For a discussion, see Megliani (n 217) 480; Asonuma et al (n 140) 20.

309 See Chapter 2.4.2. 'Settling with the Vulture Holdouts.'

310 Megliani (n 217) 535.

311 See IMF, 'Fourth Progress Report on the Inclusion of Enhanced Contractual Provisions in International Sovereign Bonds' (March 2019) <www.elibrary.imf.org/view/journals/007/2019/008/article-A001-en.xml> accessed 2 November 2021.

312 *Abaclat v Argentina* (n 3).

313 *Ambiente Ufficio SpA v Argentina*, Decision on jurisdiction and admissibility, ICSID Case No ARB/08/9, IIC 576 (2013), 8 February 2013, World Bank; International Centre for Settlement of Investment Disputes [ICSID].

314 As of 2012, ICSID tribunals had rendered 33 decisions on jurisdiction, 17 awards on the merits, 7 decisions on annulment, and 7 decisions on stay of enforcement. See Jose E Alvarez and Gustavo Topalian, 'The Paradoxical Argentina Cases' (2012) 6(3) World Arbitration & Mediation Review 491, 496.

315 See, for a discussion of the settlement, Chapter 2.4.3. 'Settling with the Retail Holdouts.'

316 For the seminal work on sovereign debt and investment arbitration, see Michael Waibel, *Sovereign Debt Before International Courts and Tribunals* (Cambridge: Cambridge University Press, 2011) 99–102.

317 *Abaclat v Argentina* (n 3).

318 Ibid 1–4.

319 Ibid 238–243.

320 Convention on the Settlement of Investment Disputes Between States and Nationals of Other States (International Centre for Settlement of Investment Disputes [ICSID]) 575 UNTS 159, UN Reg No I-8359, 17 USTS 1270, TIAS 6090, UKTS 25 (1967) Cmnd 3255 ['ICSID Convention'].

321 *Abaclat v Argentina* (n 3) [234].

322 See Christoph Schreuer, Loretta Malintoppi, August Reinisch, and Anthony Sinclair, *The ICSID Convention* (Cambridge: Cambridge University Press, 2010, 2nd ed) 71 et seq.

323 *Salini Costruttori SpA and Italstrade SpA v Morocco*, Decision on jurisdiction, ICSID Case No ARB/00/4, IIC 206 (2001), (2004) 6 ICSID Rep 398, (2004) 6 ICSID Rep 400, (2003) 42 ILM 609, (2002) 129 Clunet 196, 16 July 2001, despatched 23 July 2001, United Nations [UN]; World Bank; International Centre for Settlement of Investment Disputes [ICSID]. According to the *Salini* test, a specific economic

transaction or operation must include (a) a substantial contribution of the investor, (b) a certain duration, (c) the existence of an operational risk, (d) a certain regularity of profit, and (e) a contribution to the economic development of the host state.

324 Ibid 348.

325 Ibid 364.

326 Ibid.

327 Ibid 355–360.

328 Ibid 355.

329 Ibid.

330 Ibid 507.

331 Ibid 512 (claimants contented that 'the present mass proceedings are within the jurisdictional limits of ICSID, the question of its management being a question of mere procedure covered by Article 44 ICSID Convention and thereby within the power of the tribunal').

332 Ibid 521–526. Thus, the tribunal had the power under Article 44 of the Convention to fill such gap, albeit only to the extent necessary to deal with specific problems arising in the respective proceedings. Article 44 ICSID Convention reads as follows:

> [a]ny arbitration proceeding shall be conducted in accordance with the provisions of this Section and, except as the parties otherwise agree, in accordance with the Arbitration Rules in effect on the date on which the parties consented to arbitration. If any question of procedure arises which is not covered by this Section or the Arbitration Rules or any rules agreed by the parties, the Tribunal shall decide the question.

333 Ibid 540.

334 Ibid.

335 Ibid 549.

336 Ibid 550. The tribunal, thus, declined its competence to 'repair an inappropriately negotiated or drafted BIT.'

337 *Abaclat and ors v Argentina*, Dissenting Opinion of Professor Georges Abi-Saab, ICSID Case No ARB/07/5, 28 October 2011, World Bank; International Centre for Settlement of Investment Disputes [ICSID].

338 Ibid 45.

339 Ibid 46. To that end, Article 25 ICSID Convention (n 320) ought to be seen in light of the Convention's key objective, namely as follows:

> to encourage investment that contributes to the economic development of the host country, ie to the expansion of its productive capacity, a contribution that presupposes a commitment to this task not only of economic resources, but also in terms of duration in time and the taking of risk, with the expectation of reaping profits and/or revenue in return.

340 Ibid 60–61.

341 Ibid 74.

342 Ibid 130.

343 Ibid 143.

344 Ibid 144.

345 Ibid 161.

346 *Ambiente Ufficio v Argentina* (n 313).

347 Ibid 437.

348 Ibid 470. The Convention's *Travaux Preperatoires* were considered inconclusive in this regard, which is why the 'object and purpose' approach in Article 31 VCLT was to be employed.

349 Ibid 472.

350 *Salini v Morocco* (n 323).

351 *Fedax NV v Venezuela*, Award, ICSID Case No ARB/96/3, IIC 102 (1998), (2002) 5 ICSID Rep 200, (1998) 37 ILM 1391, (1999) XXIVa YB Com Arb 39, 9 March 1998, World Bank; International Centre for Settlement of Investment Disputes [ICSID].

352 Ibid 43. In *Fedax v Venezuela* the main question was whether promissory notes would qualify as investment under the ICSID Convention (n 492), which the ICSID tribunal ultimately affirmed on due to the public law nature of the promissory notes at stake.

353 *Ambiente Ufficio v Argentina* (n 313) [478].

354 Ibid 481. According to the tribunal *Fedax v Venezuela* (n 351), '[t]he important question is whether the funds made available are utilized by the beneficiary of the credit, as in the case of the Republic of Venezuela, so as to finance its various governmental needs.' It further noted that '[i]t is not disputed in this case that the Republic of Venezuela, by means of the promissory notes, received an amount of credit that was put to work during a period of time for its financial needs.' Overall, thus, the tribunal found that '[t]here is clearly a significant relationship between the transaction and the development of the host State, as specifically required under the Law for issuing the pertinent financial instrument.' While Schreuer initially proposed the test, which the *Salini v Morocco* (n 323) tribunal employed, he later criticized the tribunal for transforming the legal character of these criteria from a descriptive to a normative one.

355 *Ambiente Ufficio v Argentina* (n 313) [482–487].

356 Ibid 488–495.

357 Ibid 535.

358 Ibid 541.

359 Ibid 544.

360 Ibid 317.

361 See *Abaclat v Argentina* (n 337) [130].

362 For an overview of the enforcement of ICSID claims against sovereigns, see Schreuer et al (n 322) 1115–1150.

363 See Chapter 2.4.3. 'Settling with the Retail Holdouts.'

364 Stephen K Park and Tim R Samples, 'Tribunalizing Sovereign Debt: Argentina's Experience with Investor-State Dispute Settlement' (2017) 50 Vanderbilt Journal of Transnational Law 1033, 1062.

365 See Giuseppe Bianco, 'European Union's Investment Agreements and Public Debt' (2017) 2 European Business Law Review 119 (citing Annex 8-B of the Comprehensive Economic and Trade Agreement (CETA) between the EU and Canada, which states the following:

> 1. For the purposes of this Annex: *Negotiated restructuring* means the restructuring or rescheduling of debt of a Party that has been effected through (a) a modification or amendment of debt instruments, as provided for under their terms, including their governing law, or (b) a debt exchange or other similar process in which the holders of no less than 75 per cent of the aggregate principal amount of the outstanding debt subject to restructuring have consented to such debt exchange or other process; and governing law of a debt instrument means a jurisdiction's laws applicable to that debt instrument.
>
> 2. *No claim that a restructuring of debt of a Party breaches an obligation* under Sections C [Non-discriminatory treatment] and D [Investment protection] *may be submitted*, or if already submitted continue, under Section F [Resolution of investment disputes between investors and states] *if the restructuring is a negotiated restructuring at the time of submission, or becomes a negotiated restructuring after such submission*, except for a claim that the restructuring violates Article 8.6 [National treatment] or 8.7 [Most-favoured-nation treatment].
>
> (emphasis added)

366 See Chapter 3.6.2. 'Interim Conclusions: Closing Pandora's Box?.'

367 See Park and Samples (n 364) 1060 (noting that 'ISDS may needlessly hamper the restructuring and recovery process by increasing creditor fragmentation and

undermining the flexibility for sovereigns attempting to negotiate settlements in good faith.').

368 Michael Waibel, 'Opening Pandora's Box: Sovereign Bonds in International Arbitration' (2007) 101 American Journal of International Law 711.

369 *Salini v Morocco* (n 323).

370 Ibid (in *Salini v Morocco* the investors' contribution was unambiguous, for the Italian investors had constructed a specific building in Morocco).

371 *Fedax v Venezuela* (n 351) [42].

372 See Waibel (n 368) for an overview.

373 *Abaclat v Argentina* (n 3) [364–365]. Although ICSID tribunals are generally not bound by precedents, they take into account previous arbitral awards and justify deviations in their reasoning.

374 Ibid 364. Other decisions followed the approach taken by the *Abaclat* tribunal; see *Alemanni and 74 others v Argentina*, Decision on jurisdiction and admissibility, ICSID Case No ARB/07/8, IIC 666 (2014), despatched 17 November 2014, World Bank; International Centre for Settlement of Investment Disputes [ICSID] [100], noting this:

> as to the '*Salini* test' itself and the five conditions which the respondent derives from it, the Counter-Memorial submits that some tribunals have attached undue weight to them, citing in particular the more flexible approach taken by the *CSOB, MCI v Ecuador, and Biwater Gauff* tribunals.

See *Salini v Morocco* (n 323).

375 As, for instance, required by the tribunal in *Československa obchodní banka AS v Slovakia,* Decision on objections to jurisdiction, ICSID Case No ARB/97/4, (1999) 14 ICSID Rev-FILJ 251, IIC 49 (1999), (2002) 5 ICSID Rep 330, 24 May 1999, World Bank; International Centre for Settlement of Investment Disputes [ICSID].

376 Omar Garcia-Bolivar, 'Defining an ICSID Investment: Why Economic Development Should Be the Core Element' (*Investment Treaty News*, 13 April 2012) <www.iisd.org/itn/2012/04/13/defining-an-icsid-investment-why-economic-development-should-be-the-core-element/> accessed 2 November 2021.

377 Rudolf Dolzer and Christoph Schreuer, *Principles of International Investment Law* (Oxford: Oxford University Press, 2012) 69.

378 See Waibel (n 368) 724:

> [t]o avoid asymmetrical treatment of host state and investor, the actual, present impact in the host country arguably needs to be given equal weight, reflecting the twofold objective of the ICSID Convention: First, to increase investor protection, and second, to ensure that investments perform an essential economic and social service in developing countries.

379 *Abaclat v Argentina* (n 3) [113], further noting this:

> [t]his is why, for such loans to constitute investments under the ICSID Convention, they have to be concretely traced, even at several removes, to a particular productive project or activity in the territory of the host country; and not merely by postulating a stop-gap abstract assumption that does not hold its ground.

380 Waibel (n 368) 726.

381 *Abaclat v Argentina* (n 3) [342].

382 *Fedax v Venezuela* (n 351) [43] (coining the term 'volatile capital').

383 Waibel (n 368) 235.

384 *Salini v Morocco* (n 323) [54].

385 In *Deutsche Bank v Sri Lanka*, the ICSID tribunal held that the duration element is governed by the terms of the contract, rather than by how long the investors owned the bonds. In that case, the pertinent commitment between the parties was for 12 months and, therefore, considered sufficient to satisfy the duration element. See *Deutsche*

Bank AG v Sri Lanka, Final award, ICSID Case No ARB/09/02, IIC 578 (2012), despatched 31st October 2012, United Nations [UN]; World Bank; International Centre for Settlement of Investment Disputes [ICSID] [303–304] (also noting that '[t]he fact that [the agreement] was terminated after 125 days is irrelevant').

386 Waibel (n 368) 726.

387 See Chapter 3.6. 'Holdout Arbitration After Greece.'

388 *Poštová banka as and Istrokapital SE v Greece*, Award, ICSID Case No ARB/13/8, IIC 679 (2015), despatched 9 April 2015, World Bank; International Centre for Settlement of Investment Disputes [ICSID] [147, 366]. However, the ICSID tribunal still rejected its jurisdiction on other grounds.

389 See Josef Ostransky, 'Sovereign Default Disputes in International Treaty Arbitration: Jurisdictional Considerations and Policy Implications' (2015) 3(1) Groningen Journal of International Law 27, 48; Waibel (n 368) 726 (there must thus be a certain degree of risk sharing between the investor and the host state: The default risks as such 'does not in itself indicate the presence of risk-sharing,' for the 'mere presence of such [default] risk is not enough').

390 *Fedax v Venezuela* (n 351) [43].

391 See Preamble to the ICSID Convention (n 320).

392 For a critical assessment of recent trends in the realm of international investment law, see Julian David Mortenson, 'The Meaning of "Investment": ICSID's Travaux and the Domain of International Investment Law' (2010) 51(1) Harvard International Law Journal 257.

393 Ostransky (n 389) 48.

394 *Ambiente Ufficio SpA v Argentina*, Decision on jurisdiction and admissibility; dissenting opinion of Santiago Torres Bernárdez, ICSID Case No ARB/08/9, 2 May 2013, World Bank; International Centre for Settlement of Investment Disputes [ICSID].

395 See *Romak v Uzbekistan*; see *Romak SA (Switzerland) v Uzbekistan*, Final Award, ICGJ 462 (PCA 2009), PCA Case No AA280, 26 November 2009, Permanent Court of Arbitration [PCA] [230].

396 See *Poštová banka v Greece* (n 388). For a discussion, see 3.6.2. Interim Conclusions: Closing Pandora's Box?

397 *Abaclat v Argentina* (n 3) [74–76].

398 Ostransky (n 389) 45; Waibel (n 316) 218.

399 Ostransky (n 389) 45; Zachary Douglas, 'Property, Investment and the Scope of Investment Protection Obligations' in Zachary Douglas (ed), *The Foundations of International Investment Law: Bringing Theory into Practice* (Oxford: Oxford University Press, 2014) 23.

400 *Abaclat v Argentina* (n 3) [397] (opining that 'forum selection clauses are clauses of a procedural nature aiming to determine the place of settlement of a dispute . . . [t]hey have nothing to do with the place where a party is supposed to perform its obligations').

401 For a discussion, see Waibel (n 316) 239; Zachary Douglas, *The International Law of Investment Claims* (Cambridge: Cambridge University Press, 2009) 171.

402 Given the fact that the Argentine bonds were governed by New York law, the debt's situs would have no doubt been outside the territory of Argentina: the choice-of-law and forum clauses subjected these instruments to a foreign legal system and judiciary. Also see, for a similar argument, *Abaclat v Argentina* (n 3) [87].

403 Waibel (n 316) 733–734. Umbrella clauses are the exception to the rule since they elevate all contractual to treaty clams.

404 See, for example, Nicolas Costabile, 'Argentina: From International Market Isolation to Promising Opportunities for Investors' (*Commercial Dispute Resolution News*, 27 September 2016) <www.cdr-news.com/categories/arbitration/6733-argentina-from-international-market-isolation-to-promising-opportunities-for-investors> accessed 2 November 2021.

405 For a detailed analysis, see Stacie Strong, *Class, Mass, and Collective Arbitration in National and International Law* (Oxford: Oxford University Press, 2013).

406 See, for example, Katarzyna Barbara Szczudlik, 'Mass Claims Under ICSID' (2015) 4(2) Wroclaw Review of Law, Administration & Economics 70. Also see, for example, Jessica Beess und Chrostin, 'Sovereign Debt Restructuring and Mass Claim Arbitration Before the ICSID, The Abaclat Case' (2012) 53(2) Harvard International Law Journal 505.

407 Waibel, for instance, warns that admitting mass claims to ICSID arbitration 'could imperil the host state's or the investor's due process rights.' See Michael Waibel, 'Coordinating Adjudication Processes' (January 2014) Cambridge University Legal Studies Research Paper Series, Paper No 6/2014, 15.

408 To this end, in a domestic arbitration case, the SCOTUS held that 'class-action arbitration changes the nature of arbitration to such a degree that it cannot be presumed the parties consented to it by simply agreeing to submit their disputes to an arbitrator.' See *Stolt-Nielsen S A v AnimalFeeds Int'l Corp,* 559 US 662, 683 [2010] 9 December 2009, United States; Supreme Court [US].

409 Deepu Jojo Sushama, 'Mass Claims in Investment Arbitration – The Need of the Hour' (*Kluwer Arbitration Blog*, 4 March 2015) <http://kluwerarbitrationblog.com/2015/03/04/mass-claims-in-investment-arbitration-the-need-of-the-hour/> accessed 2 November 2021.

410 Friedrich Rosenfeld, 'Mass Claims in International Law' (2013) 4(1) Journal of International Dispute Settlement 159, 174.

411 Some ICSID tribunals seem to have taken seriously some of the concerns heeded by experts in the wake of the Argentine bondholder arbitration when adjudicating claims of Greek bondholders; see Chapter 3.6.1. 'Poštová banka v Hellenic Republic.'

412 IMF, 'Argentina: 2016 Article IV Consultation-Press Release; Staff Report; and Statement by the Executive Director for Argentina' (October 2016) IMF Country Report No 16/346, 40 <www.imf.org/en/Publications/CR/Issues/2016/12/31/Argentina-2016-Article-IV-Consultation-Press-Release-Staff-Report-and-Statement-by-the-44386> accessed 2 November 2021.

413 See Julie Wernau and Taos Turner, 'Argentina Sells $2.75 Billion of 100-Year Bonds' *Wall Street Journal* (New York, 19 June 2017) (noting that the sale was 'the latest sign of investor hunger for yield as the country joined a small group to sell so-called century bonds'). However, Argentine financial history has always set a fast pace, and only three years after, the century bond was issued Argentina restructured it in 2020 following the ninth sovereign default over a 100-year time horizon. For a discussion of the 2020 Argentine debt restructuring, see De La Cruz and Lagos (n 83).

414 See, for a discussion of vulture holdouts, Chapter 5.2.1. 'Vulture Funds.'

415 *White Hawthorne v Argentina* (n 299).

416 See James Blakemore and Michael Lockman, 'Pari Passu Undone: Game-Changing Decisions for Sovereigns in Distress' (2017) 3 Emerging Markets Restructuring Journal <www.clearygottlieb.com/~/media/cgsh/files/2017/publications/emrj-spring-2017/pari-passu-undone-gamechanging-decisions-for-sovereigns-in-distress.pdf> accessed 2 November 2021.

417 *White Hawthorne v Argentina* (n 299) [7]. The District Court made a reference to the Court of Appeals' judgment in *NML Capital Limited v Argentina VIII* (n 70), which said that a sovereign does not necessarily breach the pari passu provision when it pays creditors selectively. However, the Court of Appeals' decision left considerable ambiguity in this respect, which Judge Griesa sought to resolve.

418 See, for example, Rodrigo Olivares-Caminal, 'Understanding the *Pari Passu* Clause in Sovereign Debt Instruments: A Complex Quest' (2009) 43(3) The International Lawyer 1217, 1227:

> the only possible interpretation of the clause was the narrow or ranking interpretation, and that it was included to avoid the creation of preferences either by the sovereign (paying one or some creditors in detriment of others) or by creditors.

419 *White Hawthorne v Argentina* (n 299) [8].

420 Ibid 8.
421 Blakemore and Lockman (n 416) (further noting that '*White Hawthorne* takes seriously the Second Circuit's view that NML was an exceptional case').
422 *White Hawthorne v Argentina* (n 299).
423 See ibid for a discussion.
424 See Buchheit and Gulati (n 288).
425 Blakemore and Lockman (n 416).
426 Convention on the Recognition and Enforcement of Foreign Arbitral Awards (United Nations [UN]) 330 UNTS 3, 21 UST 2517 ('New York Convention').
427 See Park and Samples (n 364).
428 As noted earlier, the *Abaclat* and *Ambiente Ufficio* decisions only concerned ICSID tribunals' jurisdiction and did not result in awards. See Chapter 2.3.2. 'Interim Conclusions' and Chapter 2.3.2.1. 'Sovereign Bond Arbitration Against Argentina – Producing a Monster?.'
429 Park and Samples (n 364) 1057–1058.
430 Leandro Javier Caputo and Ignacio J Minorini Lima, 'First Argentine Court Judgment on the Recognition of an ICSID Award' (*Kluwer Arbitration Blog*, 15 March 2016) <http://arbitrationblog.kluwerarbitration.com/2016/03/15/first-argentine-court-judgment-on-the-recognition-of-an-icsid-award/> accessed 2 November 2021. For a discussion of the decision of the Argentine Supreme Court in *Claren Corporation*, see Alejandro Gabriel Manzo, 'Enforceability of Judgments Against Sovereign States: Critical Analysis of the NML vs. Argentina Injunction' (2018) 14(2) Revista Direito GV 682, 698. However, the Argentine court left open whether a screening of an ICSID award on public policy reasons could bar enforcement.
431 See, for example, Emmanuel Gaillard and Ilija Mitrev Penushliski, 'State Compliance with Investment Awards' (2020) 35(3) ICSID Review 540, 553. By 2007, according to newspaper reports, at least 17 ICSID cases had been settled or suspended, though not all were directly linked to the 2001 sovereign default. See Jason Mitchell, 'Argentina Settles Majority of Claims Filed with ICSID' *Euromoney* (New York, 6 July 2007) <www.euromoney.com/article/b132237ncc2ync/argentina-settles-majority-of-claims-filed-with-icsid> accessed 2 November 2021. In 2013, five more cases, with a total volume of USD450 million, were settled, including the aforementioned *CMS v Argentina* case. See Allen & Overy, 'Argentina Settles Five Investment Treaty Awards' (7 November 2013) <https://perma.cc/NW3Q-VLRZ> accessed 2 November 2021.
432 In 2013, Argentina even briefly considered exiting the ICSID Convention, an ultima ratio measure that a few Latin American countries had taken in the past in response to unfavourable decisions. See Park and Samples (n 364) 1058. For example, Venezuela exited the ICSID Convention (n 320) in 2012. See ICSID, 'Venezuela Submits a Notice Under Article 71 of the ICSID Convention' (January 26, 2012) News Releases <https://icsid.worldbank.org/news-and-events/news-releases/venezuela-submits-notice-under-article-71-icsid-convention> accessed 2 November 2021. Ecuador returned to the ICSID Convention in 2021 after exiting in 2009 in the wake of its sovereign debt crisis; see Gustavo Prieto, 'Ecuador Returns to the ICSID Convention: A Brief Assessment of Its Decade-Long International Investment Law "Exit Strategy"' (*EJIL: Talk*, 19 July, 2021) <www.ejiltalk.org/ecuador-returns-to-the-icsid-convention-a-brief-assessment-of-its-decade-long-international-investment-law-exit-strategy/> accessed 2 November 2021.
433 Vinod Sreeharsha, 'Argentina's Senate Allows Payment to Bondholders' *The New York Times* (New York, 31 March 2016). For an in-depth analysis of the settlements, Cruces and Samples show that the average size of sovereign debt haircuts stood at 37% between 1970 and 2010, underscoring the exceptionality of Argentina's tender. See Juan Cruces and Tim Samples, 'Settling Sovereign Debt's Trial of the Century'

(2016) 31 Emory International Law Review 5. Of course, the retail holdouts' payout was paled by NML's astronomic returns, underscoring the various factors that determine the profitability of holdout behaviour, ranging from the purchase date of the debt instrument to the type of legal strategy that is employed.

434 *Abaclat and ors v Argentina*, Consent award, ICSID Case No ARB/07/5, IIC 905 (2016), despatched 29 December 2016, World Bank; International Centre for Settlement of Investment Disputes [ICSID].

3 Holdout Creditor Problems and Domestic Law Debt

The Greek Debt Restructuring in Courts and Tribunals (2012–2020)[1]

3.1. Introduction

Greece was the first country in the euro area to restructure its public debt since the currency union's inception in 1998 and one of the first advanced economies in modern economic history to do so. At roughly EUR106 billion in debt relief, the Greek PSI also marked the biggest sovereign debt restructuring in history, almost twice the size of Argentina's two debt swaps in the 2000s.[2] The goal of the PSI, which was part of a large macroeconomic adjustment program,[3] was to restore Greek debt sustainability and facilitate the country's return to international capital markets.[4]

The historic debt swap raised numerous questions – old and new – relating to both the economic trade-offs inherent to sovereign debt restructuring[5] as well as the legal principles underpinning them.[6] The holdout creditor problem manifested itself in two different forms during the Greek debt crisis. On the one hand, holders of Greek securities governed by English law held out from the restructuring and were royally rewarded, with the government seeking to avoid drawn-out legal battles in London courts at all costs. On the other hand, a certain percentage of holders of domestic law bonds challenged the government's retroactive introduction of majority restructuring provisions in local and foreign courts as well as before international investment arbitration tribunals.

Both types of holdout inefficiencies will be dissected in the subsequent sections, with a focus on the challenges to the restructuring of domestic law instruments.

3.2. The Greek Sovereign Debt Crisis: 2009–2015

The economic crisis in Greece, a member of both the EU and the euro area, had been exceptionally severe, even compared to the crisis in Argentina. Greece's drop in output was deeper and more persistent than in almost any crisis on record.[7]

The crisis took its course when Greece's budget deficit surpassed 12% in 2009.[8] This stark deviation from the previously anticipated debt deficit of roughly 3%, broadly in line with the limits for new deficits set out in the pertinent European legislation, raised red flags among market participants and EU policymakers.[9] While markets had previously taken a benign view on individual sovereign risk

DOI: 10.4324/9781003361879-3

following the introduction of the common currency in 1998, investors feared that the solidarity between euro area governments might dwindle in a full-blown crisis.[10] A sudden stop of capital flows dramatically heightened the rollover risk, hence the danger that Greece might no longer be able to issue new debt to repay the principals of maturing bonds.[11]

In mid-2010, fellow euro area governments, supported by the IMF, the European Commission, and the ECB – dubbed Troika – finally reacted to the looming threat of a full-blown sovereign debt crisis in Europe by passing its first rescue package to Greece.[12] Despite an unprecedently large financial assistance program, however, financing conditions for the country further deteriorated in the course of the following months.[13] Additional financial rescue measures became inevitable to avert the imminent financial collapse.

At the same time, some Heads of State in the euro area were slowly waking up to the option of debt restructuring, even involving haircuts. During the Deauville Euro Summit in October 2010, the French President and the German Chancellor considered that PSI – sharing the burden of restructuring with private bondholders – was the best of many bad options.[14] Notwithstanding the agreement in principle on private sector participation at the highest level of European policy-making, however, financial stability risks were still perceived as too great a threat in the euro area for a swift implementation of this option.[15] Fears stemmed, in particular, from potential disruptions in the banking sector through the sovereign-bank nexus or 'doom loop,'[16] given that major European financial institutions held sizeable amounts of Greek sovereign debt.

Possible holdout problems, including legal challenges, were certainly another compelling argument against a Greek PSI.[17] The imperative was that a voluntary solution had to be found. The official sector was appalled by the idea of a unilateral debt repudiation à la Argentina. Long nights in office buildings along Brussel's *Rue de La Loi*, the boulevard where several EU institutions are located, ensued.

3.3. The Greek Debt Restructuring of 2012

3.3.1. Debt Restructuring Negotiations: The Role of the Troika and the IIF

The Greek debt restructuring of 2012 was the result of a lengthy and intricate process of negotiation at the highest level between the Greek government, EU Institutions, EU Member States, the IMF, and the private sector. In May 2010, the IMF Executive Board approved a stand-by arrangement (SBA) to provide exceptional access financing to Greece given that debt was sustainable but not with high probability.[18] The EU institutions that were part of the Troika – the European Commission and the ECB – were openly opposed to any restructuring of government debt within the euro area.[19]

On the private sector side, the IIF played an important – though controversial – role in negotiating the PSI.[20] The IIF demanded from Greece to tender a range of options for private investors to choose from, allowing the latter to select a write-down option that would be most preferable in terms of their investment strategy.[21] This is not per se an unusual request, but it undoubtedly prolonged the negotiations. While most economists now agree that a Greek debt restructuring should have come earlier, the ECB's reluctance to jeopardize financial stability in the euro area, the IIF's resistance against any cuts to bonds held by banks, and the IMF's willingness to proceed with the SBA in the face of unsustainable debt and macro-economic uncertainties, in hindsight, delayed the inevitable by several months.

The restructuring took place in March 2012, shortly before a large principal payment was due. The terms and conditions of the tender offer were outlined in the 'Invitation Memorandum,'[22] with the government proposing to restructure 96.9% of the EUR205.5 billion face amount of outstanding government bonds.[23]

In exchange for their debt instruments and in line with debt restructuring practice, creditors were offered three different categories of new bonds with a reduced face value as well as different maturities and rates of interest.[24] Bondholders who accepted the offer incurred losses of approximately 59% measured against the instruments' face value.[25]

Greece employed (at least) three restructuring methods to allay holdout problems:

- First, it clarified that Greece would not repay any of its debts to creditors who refused to participate in the restructuring.[26] The threat of unilaterally swapping bonds was the stick element[27] in the Greek PSI and clearly designed to discourage potential holdouts.
- Second, reinforcing the first stick, the offer contained a minimum participation threshold, according to which the exchange would only go forward if 90% of total outstanding debt (i.e., foreign and domestic law bonds) would participate.[28] The threshold was, thus, higher than the 66 2/3% voting requirement under the statutory restructuring mechanism discussed later.[29]
- Third, the Invitation Memorandum announced that the Greek Parliament would pass a statutory collective action mechanism in the Greek Bondholder Act 4050/2012 (henceforth, GBA)[30] that made the bond exchange conditional upon the consent of a qualified (two thirds) majority of holders.[31] The mechanism, which resembled a CAC, was crucial to cram down any holdouts that would oppose the restructuring, provided that a sufficient super majority of bondholders would opt in. But it also had a second function, namely, to provide Greece with a robust defence in court against litigious holdouts.[32]

3.3.2. Restructuring Greek Law Bonds

Greek law bonds made up roughly 93% of all bonds issued by Greece – English law governed most of the remaining 7% of bonds.[33] These domestic papers lacked most of the traditional creditor protection clauses used in Eurobond issuances, such as the negative pledge clause or cross-default provisions. As mentioned earlier, the collective action mechanism introduced by the GBA and referred to as 'class action voting mechanism' by its architects,[34] enabled the government and the central bank to invite creditors to cast a vote on the offer across all outstanding bond series and subsequently exchange the old for new bonds.[35]

The restructuring of Greek law bonds was a success: approximately 91.5% of the eligible Greek law government bonds participated, and approximately 94.23% of the participating bondholders voted in favour of the exchange.[36] This majority easily met the required voting threshold of 66 2/3% of outstanding principal amount to cram down the remainder of holdouts. The 'local law advantage' was critical, allowing Greece to retroactively amend the bond terms and retrofit the collective voting mechanism.[37] While other cases exist in which states used legislation to suspend debt repayment obligations,[38] the Greek PSI was the first time in history that a sovereign nation rewrote local law to restructure almost the entire stock of its (privately held) government debt.

There were still thousands of individual holdouts that refused to consent to the debt reduction, arguing that the procedure chosen by Greece amounted to 'consent by coercion.'[39] In scholarly circles, an intense debate emerged as to whether the legislative technique applied by the Greek Parliament to facilitate was in fact 'coercive'[40] and 'arbitrary'[41] or rather a 'legitimate exercise of sovereign power'[42] to resolve its debt crisis. As discussed later in detail,[43] after almost a decade of litigation, courts and international tribunals ultimately rejected the holdouts' arguments and broadly endorsed the Greek approach to restructuring its domestic law debt.[44]

3.3.3. Restructuring Foreign Law Bonds

Approximately 7% of all outstanding Greek government bonds (36 bond series) were governed by foreign law, most of them by English law.[45] All these instruments included CACs, albeit the series-by-series voting mechanism common in English law sovereign bonds at the time was more prone to holdout risk than the collective action mechanism Greece had fitted onto domestic law bonds, which allowed for a single vote binding all participating series.[46] Only 17 of the 36 outstanding English law bonds was restructured successfully, resulting in holdout claims amounting to roughly EUR6.4 billion.[47]

Other than most Greek law bonds, English law securities additionally contained several additional clauses to protect bondholders' rights.[48] For instance, English law bonds contained cross default clauses, making it easier for creditors to 'exit a crisis situation (where Greece is beginning to default on some of its bonds) at much earlier stage than the holders of the Greek-law bonds.'[49] Dreading litigation that could delay the closing of the restructuring deal or hamper the country's return to international credit markets for a prolonged period of time, the Greek government decided to pay holdouts with foreign law instruments in full.[50]

In economic terms, the preferential treatment of English law bonds revealed the relevance of law in sovereign debt[51]: while the owners of local law bonds accepted or forced to accept a 50% haircut, holders of foreign law bonds received full face value payments.[52] Strikingly, a single US-based hedge fund realized a profit of roughly USD200 million by purchasing English law debt at a discount and successfully insisting on full debt repayment during the restructuring.[53]

3.4. Holdout Creditor Litigation After Greece in Foreign Courts

Given that Greece used a retrofitted class action voting mechanism in its restructuring, holdouts' target was the underlying legislative act: the GBA. After all, there was no evident breach of contract. Greek bonds were amended by an affirmative majority vote of investors under the retroactively introduced mechanism in accordance with the new Greek law. As a result, the nature of the litigation in Greece and Argentina differed with respect to both procedural and substantive law aspects:

- First, holdouts with Greek law bonds could not hold out in the strict sense (i.e., block the restructuring). Only *after* the PSI was implemented did bondholders show their opposition openly by filing suit: there was no default or moratorium before the restructuring operation like in the case of Argentina.
- Second, and related to the first point, in contrast to Argentina, courts were asked to assess the legality of a law rather than the sovereign's compliance with a contract. The sequence of measures taken by the Greek government that led to the bondholders' losses complicated this legal review: Greece had first passed a law, then executed a majority vote, and, on that basis, swapped the old bonds for new bonds by changing the record in the Greek central bank's registry. The interference with bondholders' property rights was thus indirect and more difficult to claim than in Argentina.
- Third, Greek bonds had no choice-of-forum clauses, which raised complex questions of international jurisdiction. Indeed, as litigation in German and Austrian municipal courts showed, the pertinent EU and domestic rules for jurisdiction are anything but straightforward when they must be applied in the sovereign debt restructuring context.

The next two sections analyse holdout litigation in Germany and Austria, before reviewing holdout suits in EU courts and the ECtHR, as well as arbitration proceedings filed at the ICSID. Both Austria and Germany saw numerous legal challenges filed by their nationals who had purchased Greek debt securities and claimed damages after having been subjected to the haircut.[54] The final decisions were rendered as recently as 2020, more than eight years after the Greek PSI was closed. Most courts, and notably both countries' highest judicial bodies, ultimately threw out holdout challenges.

3.4.1. *Germany*[55]

3.4.1.1. *BGH Judgment of 8 March 2016*[56]

The plaintiffs in this case, three German retail holdouts, holding Greek domestic law securities with a face value of roughly EUR 170,000, had rejected the exchange offer in March 2012 but were forced to accept the reduction of their claims given that required voting threshold for a valid modification of payment terms was reached.[57] They filed suit in German federal civil courts applying for damages resulting from the involuntary debt swap as a result of which losses were imposed on their securities.[58]

The two lower courts, District Court of Frankfurt and the OLG Frankfurt, held that Greece enjoyed sovereign immunity from trial, given the GBA's nature as a sovereign act (*acta iure imperii*).[59] The German Federal Supreme Court (*Bundesgerichtshof* or BGH) essentially followed their legal reasoning.

According to the BGH, the distinction between public and non-public legal acts was to be assessed against the backdrop of the *nature* of the GBA.[60] In other words, the classification of a sovereign act as public or private depended on whether the state had acted with the unique powers of a sovereign state or like any other participant in the market.[61] The German Supreme Court conceded that the issuance of government bonds was considered a non-public legal act (*acta iure gestionis*) under customary international law and may, thus, be subject to a lawsuit before the courts of another state.[62]

However, since the retail holdouts had challenged the involuntary withdrawal and exchange of their securities, they invoked an unlawful interference with their rights vested *in* the sovereign debt papers rather than the violation of the contractual right to repayment.[63] The exchange of their papers, and hence the alleged damages stemming from the non-performance of the contractual obligation, was the consequence of Greek legislation.

Thus, given the *iure imperii* nature of the GBA, it may not be subject to judicial review by German courts. States were always masters of their domestic law, which means that the retroactive insertion of a collective voting mechanism by law ought *not* to be deemed a 'pure fiscal activity.'[64] While a number of German courts followed the BGH's assessment,[65] several lower courts articulated conflicting legal opinions.[66]

3.4.1.2. BGH Judgment of 19 December 2017[67]

In response to the 2016 BGH decisions, which focused on damages in rem, plaintiffs invoked their contractual right to repayment due to Greece's non-performance.[68] During the appeals, several lower courts rendered inconsistent judgements. The Court of Appeals of Oldenburg (*Oberlandesgericht* or *OLG*) denied sovereign immunity, noting that 'a legal relationship that was once considered private cannot lose this character as a consequence of subsequent public acts'[69] Plaintiffs had invoked *contractual* right to repayment under the Greek debt securities while, in the previous BGH case, they had claimed damages stemming from the interference with the bondholders rights in the debt papers.[70] In a decision a few weeks later, the OLG Köln came to the same conclusion as the OLG Oldenburg.[71] The OLG Schleswig, by contrast, held that the plaintiff's claims for contractual performance was extinguished by the Greek legislator and may therefore not be entertained.[72]

Plaintiffs appealed to the previously mentioned judgements by the appeal courts in Oldenburg[73] and Köln.[74] The BGH reiterated that while the issuance of sovereign debt indeed fell under the category of *acta iure gestionis*, the Greek Retrofit was based on a legislative action and could, therefore, not be subject to review on merits.[75] The fact that plaintiffs now invoked their contractual right to repayment that was allegedly disturbed by the GBA did not alter this assessment since awarding compensation for non-performance or damages ex contractu would inevitably require the court to assess the illegality of the Greek law.[76] Such assessment of *acta iure imperii* would not be reconcilable with the principle that states may not exercise jurisdiction over each other.[77]

The court further noted that its view did not contradict the CJEU's decision in *Fahnenbrock*[78] in which the CJEU clarified that, in the context of the service of judicial and extrajudicial documents, the issuance of sovereign bonds was to be considered a commercial activity. In the BGH's view, this decision should be interpreted narrowly, given that it only pertained to the delivery of documents and sought to enable the general assessment of the case based on a successful delivery and not the nature of bond issuance activities as such.[79] Finally, the BGH considered that it had no duty to determine whether German courts had international jurisdiction under the Brussels I Regulation, which the OLG Schleswig had already denied.[80]

3.4.1.3. BVerfG Judgment of 6 May 2020[81]

Holdouts responded to the 2016 BGH decision by bringing a constitutional complaint at the BVerfG, claiming that the BGH should have referred the case to the BVerfG and, therefore, violated their right of due process and impartiality of the judge under Article 101(2) German Basic Law.[82] The constitutional question that the plaintiffs sought clarification on was whether state immunity was to be denied once a country had entered debt markets and issued bonds. And following from this, whether the principle once a trader always a trader[83] was, thus, not a general principle of international law that German civil courts had to obey.[84]

The BVerfG rejected the complaint and concluded that it was unfounded, for the BGH applied a 'sufficiently clarified rule of international law.'[85] The GBA, as sovereign act, was immune from foreign court review. Even if a state becomes trader by issuing bonds in private markets, legislative measures affecting the issued instruments would retain their *iure imperii* character.[86]

The court justified this holding by pointing to a garden variety of judgements on holdout lawsuits from different jurisdictions in relation to different crises. These included the 2016 *Mamatas* ruling by the EctHR,[87] the Italian Supreme Court's decision in *Borri* from 2005,[88] the Austrian OGH's case law on the Greek PSI,[89] as well as the US Supreme Court's *Weltover* decision[90] dating back to 1992.[91] In particular, notwithstanding the US courts' standing endorsement of the once a trader always a trader principle, the BVerfG concluded that there was no general principle of international law that would deny states from retroactively interfering with private contracts.[92] Greece had acted fully in line with the pertinent rules of international law and enjoyed sovereign immunity with respect to challenges to the GBA.[93]

3.4.2. Austria[94]

Akin to the German bondholder cases, holdout litigation before the Austrian Supreme Court (*Oberster Gerichtshof* or OGH) revolved around two key themes: (i) whether Greece enjoyed immunity sovereign immunity for both the issuance of government bonds and the subsequent legislation to amend the initial contractual terms, and (ii) whether Austrian courts had international jurisdiction over the claims. In contrast to the German BGH, however, the Austrian court referred the case for a preliminary ruling to the CJEU to clarify foreign municipal courts' jurisdiction over holdout claims pursuant to the Brussel I Regulation.[95]

3.4.2.1. OGH Judgment of 20 May 2014[96]

The plaintiffs in this case had acquired Greek sovereign bonds through an Austrian retail bank and claimed that the Greek government failed to pay its debts in full at the point of maturity following the (involuntary) write-down of the claims in March 2012.[97] The lower courts had rejected the holdouts' claims, noting that Greece was immune from suit. As a preliminary matter, the OGH agreed with the lower courts' assessment that the GBA was as public act (*iure imperii*), which may not be reviewed by a foreign court.[98] At the same time, since Greece acted like a private corporation in a contractual context (hence *iure gestionis*) when it issued public debt securities. Provided that holdout creditors claimed performance under the commercial obligations that Greece had entered, the immunity defence was to be rejected.[99] The case was thus remanded to the trial court for reassessment under the assumption that Greece was not immune.[100]

3.4.2.2. OGH Judgment of 27 January 2016[101]

In a second judgment, rendered in January 2016, the Austrian Supreme Court focused solely on the issue of international jurisdiction *ratione materiae*.[102] The central legal question was whether the litigation related to a civil and commercial matters pursuant to Article 1(1) Brussels I Regulation, which would render the Regulation applicable. The OGH answered the question to the affirmative, given the private law nature of bond issuance activities and the irrelevance of retroactive legislative changes for the purpose of determining jurisdiction over the claims.[103]

As a next step, the defendant, Greece, had to prove that the application of the Brussels I Regulation did not confer jurisdiction upon Austrian courts.[104] An assessment of the factual circumstances henceforth provided by the Greek government suggested that no venue under said Regulation could be established:

- First, referring to the decision by the OGH in a parallel case,[105] the plaintiffs did not qualify as consumers in the sense of Article 15(2) of the Brussels I Regulation (Article 17(2) of the Brussels I Regulation (recast)), in which case courts in the consumers' domicile (i.e., Austria) could establish

international jurisdiction.[106] Plaintiffs had acquired their claims through an intermediary bank rather than directly from the sovereign, which is why the necessary contractual link between the sovereign and the consumer under Article 15 of the Brussels I Regulation was not established.
- Second, the conditions set out in Article 5(3) Brussel I Regulation, which define the place of jurisdiction for claims pertaining to *non*-contractual liability, were also not met.[107] The subject matter of the dispute did not relate to tort, delict, or quasi-delict – rather, it concerned a (quasi-)contractual relationship between Greece as debtor and the bondholder as creditor.[108]

However, the OGH considered obiter that Article 5(1) of the Brussels I Regulation (Article 7(1) of Brussels I Regulation (recast)) may provide the necessary legal basis to establish Austrian courts' jurisdiction.[109] The case was dismissed, for holdouts had not invoked that venue. However, the same jurisdictional issue would be tested by creditors in the second set of OGH decisions discussed in the next section.[110]

3.4.2.3. OGH Judgements of 25 April 2017[111] *and 22 January 2019*[112]

These two cases relied on the same fact pattern as the previous OGH judgements, the legal dispute again focused on international jurisdiction. Invoking Article 7(1)(a) of the Brussels I Regulation (recast) (formerly Article 5(1) of the Brussels I Regulations),[113] the holdouts claimed that the place of performance of the Greek bonds was situated in Austria and that, therefore, Austrian courts had jurisdiction over their subject matter. This was because the Greek government paid interest and principal to Austrian bank accounts owned by the plaintiffs.[114]

The OGH followed the plaintiffs' argumentation, citing Article 321 of the Greek Civil Code, according to which a monetary claim had to be paid at the place where the creditor was *domiciled* when the claim fell due.[115] However, given the primacy of application of Union law in the context of cross-border civil and commercial litigation, the OGH decided to request a preliminary ruling by the CJEU in regard to the interpretation of the Brussels I Regulation (recast), and specifically its Article 7(1)(a).[116]

As discussed later,[117] rejecting the OGH's previous judgements, the CJEU concluded that legal challenges to the GBA would fall outside the scope of the Brussel I Regulation, as a result of which the Regulation was not applicable to holdout challenges against Greece.[118] In its judgment, the OGH echoed Luxembourg's preliminary ruling, adding that 'exceptional circumstances' of the Greek debt crisis warranted an 'exceptional [statutory] solution.'[119]

3.4.2.4. OGH Judgment of 21 February 2020[120]

While the OGH judgment of 22 January 2019 and the CJEU's *Kuhn* decision[121] effectively closed the door to Austrian courts, a holdout lawsuit preceding these decisions reached the OGH in early 2020. In the that last case, the lower courts had established Austrian courts' jurisdiction and denied Greece's immunity, a finding that the OGH was bound by under Austrian civil procedure rules.[122]

The OGH, thus, for the first time, reviewed the bondholders' claims on the merits. Put differently, it assessed whether the GBA and the haircut on bonds held by the plaintiffs unduly interfered with their property rights, breaching the ECHR and the GRC. Referring the ECtHR's *Mamatas* decision,[123] the OGH concluded that the interference with bondholders' property rights was based on a legislative act, pursued a public interest objective, did not destroy the fair balance between the general interest and the protection of property rights, and did not put a special and excessive burden on investors.[124] Importantly, it noted it could not be inferred from the ECtHR decision that guarantees (of property rights) enshrined in the ECHR were to be interpreted differently in relation to Greek and Austrian citizens.[125] Finally, the OGH noted that the same considerations also applied to an assessment of the holdouts' claims under Article 17 of the GRC (the equivalent to Article 1 of Protocol No 1 ECHR, which the *Mamatas* court addressed).[126]

The plaintiffs additionally asserted that the Greek GBA, and the allegedly lawless and unjustified expropriation of investors to the benefit of a foreign state, violated the Austrian *ordre public*.[127] According to the OGH, however, the plaintiff failed to demonstrate how the Greek restructuring measures violated the Austrian legal order or upset the domestic sense of justice to an intolerable extent.[128] The claim was thus thrown out, and no new holdouts suit has since reached the Austrian Supreme Court.

3.4.3. *Interim Conclusions*

3.4.3.1. *Sovereign Immunity in Domestic Law Restructurings*

The question whether the GBA was to be characterized as *acta iure gestionis* or *imperii* ran like a red thread through the post-PSI litigation in Germany and Austria. It is also intractably linked to EU courts' review of the Greek PSI and specifically whether challenges against the restructuring constituted civil and commercial matters, which are discussed later.[129]

In a much-anticipated decision, the Austrian OGH rejected Greece's sovereign immunity defence in 2014, adopting a narrower immunity concept than the German BGH. In assessing the GBA, the OGH reflected the majority view in the pertinent literature[130] as well as the restrictive reading of sovereign immunity developed by US courts in the early days of sovereign debt litigation[131] and endorsed in the Argentine context. By contrast, the German BGH and the BVerfG made clear that a sovereign remained the master of its own laws and that foreign courts must not exercise jurisdiction over challenges to legislative (*iure imperii*) measures, even if they altered a private legal relationship between the state and the bondholder.[132] The once a trader always a trader controversy, which was central to the post-Argentina litigation,[133] had again gained centre stage.[134]

By 2020, however, the OGH had reversed its stance on Greece's immunity. Referring to the CJEU's decision in *Kuhn*, which held that the GBA was a sovereign act at least for the purposes of the Brussels I Regulation, the OGH shut all doors for holdout litigation.[135] *Kuhn*, however, did not address the question of sovereign immunity, as the CJEU had no formal jurisdiction. Without explaining the reasons, Austrian court seemed to suggest that EU court's assessment of the GBA for the purposes of the Brussels I Regulation also unfolded binding legal effects on the immunity defence.[136]

Another concerning issue was that neither the Austrian nor German courts pointed to the most obvious difference between immunity for state measures relating to instruments governed by the issuer's own laws and such relating to foreign law debt.[137] While no excuse for vague and incomplete rulings, it should be noted that useful precedents in other jurisdictions almost always pertained to *foreign* law debt, which meant that there was little guidance for the Austrian and German courts. This scarcity of case law meant that the judges had two options. First, they could seek to protect the Greek PSI from creditor interference by arguing that the measures were exercises of sovereign power. Or second, they could emulate the well-established once a trader always a trader principle, which had so far been applied in a foreign law debt context, to a restructuring of domestic law bonds. The BGH essentially opted for the former while the OGH chose the latter, though both courts' opinions failed to sufficiently explain why they reached these (opposing) conclusions.

Similarly, while the German Constitutional Court concluded that *acta iure imperii* remained immune to challenges in foreign courts, it equally failed to distinguish between foreign law and domestic law instruments, sweeping them into one jumbled bucket. Indeed, by commingling the decisions by US courts in the Argentine debt context with rulings by Austrian courts in the aftermath of the Greek PSI, the BVerfG patently ignored that Argentina restructured bonds beyond its legislative purview while Greece did the same as the master of the instruments' governing statute. As a practical matter, however, this questionable assessment of Greece's adjudicatory immunity did not matter all that much: as discussed later, German and Austrian courts' jurisdiction over holdout claims was curtailed by the CJEU's decision on the applicability of the Brussels I Regulation.[138]

3.4.3.2. (Some) Hypothetical Problems with Enforcing Greek Sovereign Debt in Germany and Austria

If bondholders had obtained enforceable judgment against Greece, as the holdouts had against Argentina in Germany in 2015,[139] sovereign debt enforcement would have been far from guaranteed.[140] Even if the issue remains hypothetical, it seems warranted to make a few observations should future sovereign debt defaults in the euro area yield other judicial outcomes.

The first issue relates to the Greek government's response to a defeat in court. Would Greece have paid off the few bondholders at the risk of copycat litigation? Or would it have assumed a defiant posture like Argentina and refused to comply with the decisions?

In the case of the latter, the government may have considered challenging the respective attachment orders, provided that creditors had been able to identify and locate adequate targets. For instance, Article 34 of the Brussels I Regulation provides that judgements shall not be recognized if this would be manifestly contrary to the public policy in the Member State in which recognition is sought. This provision could have complicated the attachment of Greek assets located in Austria or Germany.[141] European courts considered that the GBA and the Retrofit had not violated any property rights guarantees and the OGH in 2020 similarly found that no *ordre public* concerns were raised. This said, refusing enforcement on substantial public policy grounds remains very rare.[142]

But even if enforcement prospects remain unclear, the financial and political fallout from adjudicating claims in the holdouts' favour could have been grave.[143] A standoff akin to that between Argentina and its bondholders was seen as a non-option for most policymakers. Not only has Greece enjoyed constant access to international debt markets for decades, it is also a member of the world's wealthiest economic and monetary union. Asset seizure attempts by creditors against Greek state property in other euro area countries would have clashed with domestic and European political realities, culminating in a constitutional quandary of epic proportions.[144]

3.5. Holdout Litigation After Greece in European Courts

This section provides an overview of litigation in the EU and European courts related to the Greek debt restructuring, focusing on three cases adjudicated by the CJEU and one by the ECtHR.[145] While the sovereign debt instruments restructured by Greece did not explicitly confer jurisdiction upon European courts, the primacy of EU law as well as the CJEU's and the ECtHR's respective monopolies in interpreting the EU Treaties and the ECHR meant that some cases inevitably reached the benches in Luxembourg and Strasbourg.[146]

3.5.1. Court of Justice of the EU (CJEU)

3.5.1.1. Accorinti v ECB

In *Accorinti*,[147] the EGC reviewed the carve-out of Greek debt securities held by the ECB in the context of the 2012 restructuring.[148] As mentioned earlier, the 19 Eurosystem central banks, represented by the ECB, entered into an exclusive arrangement with the Greek government, pursuant to which their holdings were not subject to the haircut imposed on Greek debt securities.[149] The decision was controversial, as the various responses from journalists,[150] private sector market participants,[151] and sovereign debt experts[152] illustrated.

The applicants in *Accorinti* advanced several arguments as to why the agreement between the ECB and the Greek government that excluded Eurosystem claims from the PSI entitled them to compensation and damages. They posited that the carve-out (i) breached the principle of protection of legitimate interests[153]; (ii) breached the principle of equal treatment of private creditors[154]; (iii) constituted a misuse of powers and breached the principles of proportionality, coherence, and rationality[155]; and (iv) infringed upon Articles 123 and 127 TFEU as well as Article 21 of the ESCB and ECB Statute.[156] Even though the Greek bonds lacked a contractual pari passu clause, they argued that the ECB was bound by a general principle of non-discrimination enshrined in Article 10 TFEU and Articles 20 and 21 of the CFR.[157]

The EGC rejected the applicants' claims in their entirety. The ECB had not violated the investors' legitimate expectations:

> 'public statements of the members of the ECB on which the applicants rely do not constitute precise, unconditional and consistent tending to preclude any restructuring of the Greek public debt, nor do they originate from authorised and reliable sources within the meaning of the case-law.'[158]

Moreover, creditors had no right to equal treatment under EU law since they had purchased Greek bonds 'solely in their private pecuniary interest' while the Eurosystem's purchases were 'exclusively guided by objectives in the public interest.'[159]

The EGC could also not determine any misuses of power or breaches of the proportionality principle since the carve-out was 'specifically intended to preserve the central banks' scope for manoeuvre and to ensure the continuity of the smooth functioning of the Eurosystem' and, thus, not 'manifestly or seriously exceeding the limits of [the ECB's] discretion or powers in monetary policy matters.'[160] Finally, the Eurosystem's involvement in the PSI could have resulted in a violation of Article 123 TFEU, which prohibits monetary financing in the EU, and was, therefore, justified from a monetary policy perspective.[161]

3.5.1.2. Fahnenbrock v Hellenic Republic

In *Fahnenbrock*,[162] the CJEU responded to a request for preliminary ruling according to Article 267 TFEU by the German District Court in Kiel regarding the interpretation of Article 1(1) of Regulation (EC) No 1393/2007 (Service of Documents Regulation), which regulates the cross-border service of judicial and extrajudicial documents in civil or commercial matters.[163] *Fahnenbrock* addressed the delivery of documents to institute proceedings by German holdout creditors against Greece via diplomatic channels.[164] But the importance of the case went beyond procedural considerations, as the CJEU had to take a stance on the nature of the GBA, which ultimately resulted in write-down of bondholder claims, as either a 'commercial and civil matter' or 'an action in the exercise of State authority.'[165]

The CJEU considered that actions against the Greek restructuring measures concerned 'civil and commercial matters' pursuant to Article 1(1) of the Service of Documents Regulation. Specifically, it held that 'the issue of bonds does not necessarily presuppose the exercise of powers falling outside the scope of the ordinary legal rules applicable to relationships between individuals, hence the rules of private law.'[166] Moreover, it was not obvious that the 'adoption of the GBA led directly and immediately to changes to the financial conditions of the securities in question and therefore caused the damage alleged by the applicants.'[167] Rather, those changes were adopted by a majority of bondholders in the context of the retrofitted class action voting mechanism, whose introduction by the Greek state implied that the government wanted to 'keep the management of the bonds within a regulatory framework of a civil nature.'[168]

In sum, legal proceedings against Greece in relation to the 2012 PSI 'fall within the scope of that regulation in so far as it does not appear that they are manifestly outside the concept of civil or commercial matters.'[169] Notably, the EGC's ruling contradicted Advocate General Bot, whose opinion posited that challenges to the Greek GBA may not be qualified as civil and commercial matters, and would, therefore, fall outside the scope of the Service of Documents Regulation.[170]

3.5.1.3. Hellenic Republic v Kuhn[171]

The *Kuhn* decision followed the Austrian OGH's request for preliminary ruling of 25 April 2017, discussed earlier.[172] The CJEU was requested to determine whether the Brussels I Regulation (recast) questions was applicable to Greek bondholder claims; following the *Fahnenbrock* ruling,[173] the OGH had assumed that actions were indeed commercial and civil matters, but it harboured doubts as to whether any of the Brussels I Regulation's venues would confer jurisdiction upon Austrian courts.[174]

Advocate General Bot challenged the OGH's holding regarding the commercial and civil nature of the (bondholder) actions.[175] He further noted that even if the Court found the Brussels I Regulation (recast) to be applicable, the place of performance was located in Greece under the Brussels I Regulation (recast), for the paying agent was located in Greece and all decisions on the modalities of payment were regulated by Greek law (both the Greek Act No 2198/1994 and subsequently the GBA).[176] In the Advocate General's view, neither the assignment of the claim nor the actual payment to a foreign bank account could alter the contractually defined place of performance.[177]

In a very brief opinion, the CJEU echoed the Advocate General's position that 'the substantive origin of the dispute in the main proceedings is an act of public authority'[178] and that, therefore, the Brussels I Regulation (recast) was not applicable.[179] It refrained from assessing whether Austrian courts' jurisdiction may be established under the Brussels I Regulation (recast), as it had been asked to do by the Austrian court.[180] The Court also clarified that the qualification of a measure as relating to 'civil and commercial matters' in the sense of the Brussels I Regulation did not define 'the content and scope of that notion.'[181]

More specifically, the court noted that 'although certain actions between a public authority and a person governed by private law may come within the scope of that regulation, it is otherwise where the public authority is acting in the exercise of its public powers.'[182] The exercise of sovereign power by the Greek legislature manifested itself in 'both the nature and the modalities of the changes to the contractual relationship between the Greek State and the holders of the securities at issue in the main proceedings and the exceptional context in which those changes took place.'[183]

The CJEU went as far as stating that the Retrofit was 'dictated by the necessity, within the framework of an intergovernmental assistance mechanism, to restructure the Greek State's public debt and to prevent the failure of the restructuring plan,' which it did through the exercise of public authority rather than a civil or commercial measure.[184]

3.5.2. European Court of Human Rights (ECtHR)

3.5.2.1. Mamatas v Greece[185]

The *Mamatas* case decided by the European Court of Human Rights (ECtHR) in 2016 was the crucial missing piece in the juridical workup of the Greek crisis. Leaving aside the Austrian Supreme Court's February 2020 judgment,[186] which relied to a significant degree on *Mamatas*, the ECtHR's ruling was the only one that addressed actual the *merits* of the bondholders' claims and, hence, whether the Greek PSI was lawful.[187] It originated from three applications by roughly 6,000 Greek bondholders who had acquired bonds with a face value between EUR 10,000 and EUR 1,510,000 and had challenged the lawfulness of the debt exchange in local courts. Most of them were retail holdouts,[188] though, in comparison to plaintiffs in Austrian and German courts, they were mostly Greek citizens. As Europe's highest human rights court and the ultimate authority to interpret the ECHR, the ECtHR had to weigh in after the applicants appealed to a judgment passed by the Greek Council of State in 2014 in *Symvoulio tis Epikrateias*.[189] The highest administrative court in the country had previously rejected their claims for compensation.[190]

In the local court cases, plaintiffs claimed that the PSI violated the Greek Constitution, with bondholders alleging a breach of the rule of law (Article 5 of the Greek Constitution), the principle of equality (Article 4 of the Greek Constitution), and property rights more generally (Article 17 of the Greek Constitution).[191] The Greek Council of the State reached the following conclusions:

- First, an investment in government bonds was not exempt from the risk of losses, especially if the issuer's capacity to repay its debt becomes severely constrained because of an unprecedented financial crisis.[192]
- Second, the measures taken by the Greek government and Parliament to resolve the crisis were of preeminent public interest, for they served the substantial national public interest as well as the common interest of the euro area.[193]
- Third, the GBA was adequate and necessary to forestall a Greek default, which, in any case, would have further deteriorated the state's capacity to honour its financial obligations.[194]
- Fourth, the haircut followed from a voluntary decision taken by a qualified majority of the bondholders rather than a sovereign act by the Greek legislature.[195]

In their submissions to the EctHR,[196] the applicants asserted an infringement of their legitimate expectations to be repaid under Article 1 of Protocol No 1 ECHR.[197] They argued that both Greek and European authorities maintained in their official communication before the restructuring that natural persons would not be affected by a possible debt cut and that the burden of the debt adjustment would be shared between institutional investors and the government debtor.[198] They essentially argued that the Parliament's decision to Retrofit CACs to the entirety of Greek bonds without involving retail bondholders in prior negotiations wrongfully interfered with their legitimate expectations, thus infringing upon their property rights protected by the ECHR.[199]

First, the ECtHR assessed whether the GBA had in fact interfered with bondholders' property rights protected under the Convention.[200] It noted that investors in Greek debt could legitimately expect to have their claims met in accordance with the (budgetary) law specifying the contractual arrangements between bondholders and issuer. More specifically, by rewriting local law, Greece '[had] altered the conditions governing the bonds, binding all bondholders to a cut in the nominal value of their claims.'[201] This, the ECtHR opined, 'amounted to an interference with [the applicants'] right to the enjoyment of their property.'[202]

Second, however, such interference may still be lawful under Article 1 Protocol No 1 ECHR if it pursued a legitimate public interest aim and was, in pursuing this aim, proportionate.[203] As to the public interest aim, it found that Greece had faced a serious political, social, and economic crisis in early 2012 when it implemented the expropriatory measures. To that end, the GBA's main objective was to reduce the Greek debt burden and, thereby, avert imminent financial collapse – a legitimate aim that aligned with the public's interests.[204]

Reviewing the criterion of proportionality, the ECtHR looked at extent to which investors could rely on the original (i.e., unmodified) payment terms for Greek government bonds.[205] Since the legislative changes to the repayment terms were necessary to avert imminent insolvency and as the debt cut did not equate to a '[total] extinguishment' of their rights,[206] the Retrofit was an 'appropriate and necessary means of reducing Greek public debt and saving the respondent state from bankruptcy.'[207] Taking all these considerations into account, the Greek state had, in the courts' view, neither upset the fair balance between the public interest and the protection of the applicants' property nor inflicted an 'individual and excessive burden on them.'[208] The GBA was, thus, compliant with Article 1 Protocol No 1 ECHR and the holdouts' applications were dismissed.

3.5.3. Interim Conclusions

3.5.3.1. Sovereign Debt Restructurings in European Courts: Novel Judicial Challenges

A closer look at the post-PSI case law reveals a sense of discomfort among judges to address holdouts' claims. At least three factors contributed to the divergent and, at times, inconclusive opinions on vital legal issues:

- First, there were few judicial precedents to draw upon: many existing rulings on sovereign defaults were rendered by US or British courts and did not relate to the restructuring of domestic but foreign law instruments – this made them politically far less contentious, with the forum located thousands of miles away from the place where decision's effects reverberated the most.

- Second, the post-Greek PSI lawsuits, much like the Argentine litigation a few years prior, brought to the fore the glaring gaps in the existing substantive norms to reconcile creditor rights with the sovereign's decision to restructure. Aside from the OGH's final judgment in 2020 and the ECtHR's *Mamatas* decision, most courts managed to navigate around the delicate question as to whether the Greek restructuring measures had sufficiently respected creditors' property rights, essentially by buckling down in the thicket of international, European, and domestic procedural rules pertaining to immunity and jurisdiction.
- Third, the division of labour between European and domestic courts that reviewed the Greek PSI on the basis of different legal regimes and norms (international, domestic, and EU law) added a layer of complexity that remains difficult to entangle.

3.5.3.2. The (Tenuous) Link Between Sovereign Immunity and Jurisdiction Under EU Law

Though European courts only addressed sovereign immunity *indirectly*, their preliminary rulings were crucial for the resolution of holdout litigation in the wake of the Greek PSI. From a formalistic viewpoint, the interpretation of what is a 'commercial and civil matter' according to the Brussels I Regulation and the Service Document Regulation had no prejudicial effect on the decision whether the debtor state enjoyed sovereign immunity protection for a CAC Retrofit. However, it may be argued that the seeming discrepancy across EU courts in qualifying mixed activities, where the issuance of bonds is understood as *acta iure gestionis* while retroactive legislative measures concerning the securities are deemed *acta iure imperii*, has fostered legal uncertainty.

The CJEU's decision in *Fahnenbrock*[209] implied that lawsuits challenging the GBA, despite the Act's legislative nature, were civil and commercial matters. According to the *Fahnenbrock* decision, because Greece chose to insert a CAC in the contracts to facilitate a vote on the restructuring plan instead of using its legislative powers to unilaterally impose a debt suspension or debt cut, the Greek government sought to retain the civil (*iure gestionis*) nature of its relationship with the creditors.[210] By contrast, in *Kuhn*, the CJEU unequivocally emphasized the exercise of sovereign power that the Greek law reflected. It justified this obvious divergence by noting that the concept of 'civil and commercial matters' was independent from the content and the scope of that notion under national legal systems.[211] Hence, while *Fahnenbrock* essentially opened the floodgates in 2015 to holdout litigation in foreign municipal courts, *Kuhn* resealed them three years later.[212]

While it is true that – strictly speaking – *Fahnenbrock* exclusively concerned the Service of Documents Regulation, and may, therefore, not bind the qualification of an act as *iure imperii* for the purpose of the Brussels I Regulation or the assessment of the immunity defence in domestic courts, the inherent inconsistency in determining when an act is commercial or public risk seems unjustified.

The Service of Documents Regulation, the Brussels I Regulation, as well as the doctrine of sovereign immunity all embody very similar concepts to distinguish between public and private acts by a sovereign.[213] Notably, both Article 1 of the Brussels I Regulation and Article 1 of the Service of Documents Regulation are identical, stating that '[the Regulations] shall not extend, in particular, to revenue, customs or administrative matters or to the liability of the State for acts and omissions in the exercise of State authority (*acta iure imperii*),' implying that a commercial and civil matter is an act *iure gestionis*. Similarly, the ESCI in Article 12(1) refers to the concept of 'civil or commercial matter' to delineate cases in which sovereigns may not invoke immunity.[214] Indeed, several decisions by Austrian and German courts seemed to suggest that the same standard was to be applied across these legal instruments for the purpose of ascertaining the nature of a public measure. For instance, the Courts of Appeals in Köln and Oldenburg both cited *Fahnenbrock* to support their holding that Greece may *not* invoke its immunity for the legislative Retrofit given the *iure gestionis* nature of sovereign debt issuances and states may not ex post transform it into an act *iure imperii*.[215]

There are different approaches to resolve the resulting Gordian knot. One may, for instance, argue that the assessment depends on the way that the claim is advanced by the applicant.[216] Another suggestion was made by Advocate General Bot in the *Kuhn* case as well as the German BGH in its 2016 decision, both of which contended that the assessment undertaken at the *stage* of the request for service was of specific nature and, thus, not necessarily relevant in the subsequent adversarial proceedings.[217] However, while currently not supported by the CJEU, a third approach that integrates and aligns the respective definitions of acts *iure gestionis* and *iure imperii* seems conceivable, too.

For decades, the CJEU standard to determine whether a matter was civil and commercial under the Brussels regime was whether there has been an 'exercise of public power.' In the *Rina* case, the Advocate General noted that one could argue that 'the concept of "civil and commercial matters" should coincide with the negative scope of jurisdictional immunity.'[218] While the CJEU did not fully endorse this proposition, it conceded that may be a link between the distinction of private and public acts under international law for immunity purposes and under EU law for jurisdictional questions.[219] Indeed, the CJEU's apparent desire to distinguish between the definition of 'public powers' under public international law and under EU law seems to foster an unnecessary degree of legal ambiguity, even if these assessments are made separately from each other as a matter of procedural law.[220]

It remains to be seen whether the Court will further move away from the autonomous assessment of public powers under the Brussels I Regulation.[221] It is regrettable that the *Kuhn* decision did not review the important argument made in *Fahnenbrock* that the Retrofit 'confirms the intention of the Greek State to keep the management of the bonds within a regulatory framework of a civil nature.'[222] What is clear is that the post-Greek PSI holdout litigation has reinvigorated the debate and laid bare the difficulties facing domestic courts in reconciling the diverse notions of *acta iure gestionis* and *acta iure imperii* both across different legal orders and at different stages of a trial.

Finally, as Mankowski rightly notes, the CJEU's conclusion on the inapplicability of the Brussels I Regulation only means that 'Greece as the defendant is left to the possibly tender mercy of the *national* jurisdiction rules of her EU partner States once one is prepared to proceed to the realm of international jurisdiction,' which, in turn, means that 'it all boils down to the question whether Greece enjoys immunity for her haircut administered.'[223] And on the latter issue, as discussed earlier, national courts had fairly divergent views.[224]

3.5.3.3. Jurisdiction Under the Brussels I Regulation

If the Brussels I (recast) Regulation were to be applicable to retroactive legislative measures by a EU government, as some courts in Germany and Austria suggested pre-*Kuhn*, it would still require one of the venues in the Regulation to be established in foreign municipal court's jurisdiction.[225] As mentioned earlier, the Austrian OGH had asked the CJEU to clarify where the 'place of performance' of euro area sovereign bonds lay pursuant to Article 7(1) Brussels I (recast) Regulation.[226] The Advocate General in *Kuhn* noted in response that regardless of the nationality of the bondholder or secondary market trading of the instrument, the place of performance always remained the same: the location of issuance under Article 7(1) of said Regulation on special jurisdiction for contractual obligations.[227] In the case of Greece, the location of issuance was Greece.

Even though the Advocate General's opinion is non-binding for future precedents, his analysis appears correct. The Greek state had no intention to submit disputes to foreign courts, and there are few factual circumstances that would support the view that contractual performance was to occur outside of Greece; the forum was, therefore, 'highly predictable.'[228] Crucially, the *lex causae* was unambiguously Greek law, further supporting the Advocate General's view in *Kuhn*.[229] However, the issue is not straightforward, and case law on this specific question of jurisdiction with regard to securities litigation remains relatively scarce.[230] Thus, both sovereign issuers and investors are likely to benefit from unambiguous choice-of-forum clauses, with regard not only to foreign but also to domestic law bonds.[231]

3.5.3.4. Property Right Guarantees for Sovereign Bondholders in Unilateral European Sovereign Bond Restructurings

The perhaps most important legal question for those designing and implementing the PSI concerned its compliance with human rights obligations enshrined in domestic constitutional law as well as EU and international law. Prior to the ECtHR's *Mamatas* decision, and to some extent the *Poštová banka* arbitration at the ICSID discussed later,[232] it was uncertain whether any court, domestic or foreign, European or international, would approve of the (legal) methods Greece employed.[233] *Mamatas* has become and will remain the main legal yardstick for governments seeking to restructure their debts in Europe.[234] It clarified a government's scope for interference with private bondholders' property rights in the context of an economic crisis, endorsing the Greek government's legal strategy of interfering with creditor claims, though only as ultima ratio and due to the supposedly market-friendly retrofitting of CACs. Overall, the ECtHR granted a wide margin of discretion to a sovereign issuer amending its contractual framework during economic emergencies, which arguably echoes the court's general stance on the (limited) protection of property rights.[235]

Specifically, three important observations help to put the *Mamatas* case into perspective:

- First, the ECtHR clarified that sovereign bonds fell under the scope of possessions, as stipulated in Article 1 of Protocol No 1 of the ECHR. The court has traditionally relied on a very broad interpretation of what constitutes a possession, subsuming under the term all types of rights ex contractu and rights in rem.[236]
- Second, the ECtHR concluded that the insertion of CACs was what saved Greece from defaulting on its sovereign debt. Crucially, the CACs empowered the bondholders to decide whether the government's restructuring offer was fair and proportionate. They had the last say, not the government.[237]
- Third, the GBA and the subsequent investor vote only reduced investors' claims but did not eliminate them.[238]
- Last, and most critically the *Mamatas* judgment introduced a risk-based approach to the proportionality assessment. The court mirrored the element of sovereign credit risk in its legal assessment, arguing that the reduced market value also implied a reduced level of property right protection.[239] This approach markedly deviated from comparable cases, as courts have so far not taken account of the difference between the face value and the market value of a bond. Given that the vulture holdouts' business model relies on the arbitrage effects stemming from the difference between the securities' face value and their actual value, Europe's human rights courts took a clear stance against speculative practices in the context of sovereign financial distress.

Some academics discussed *Mamatas* critically, with one commentator even referring to the decision as the 'nail in the investors' coffin,'[240] while others noting that the ECtHR did not consider all relevant circumstances of the bondholders' case.[241] Some of the other courts involved seemed relieved that the ECtHR clarified the legality of the PSI. The formal endorsement of *Mamatas* by the Austrian OGH and the informal one by the German BVerfG (both in 2020), as discussed earlier,[242] solidified the benevolent judicial assessment of the Greek haircut's legality.

This said, while the ECtHR retains the monopoly of interpreting the ECHR, national constitutional laws may offer additional protections of private property, such as the Austrian Organic Law of 1867 (*Staatsgrundgesetz*).[243] The main reason why property guarantees were not invoked by bondholders was that the highest courts in both Austria and Germany rejected their claims on jurisdictional or sovereign immunity grounds.[244]

3.5.3.5. *The (Preferential) Treatment of Eurosystem Claims in Euro Area Sovereign Debt Restructurings*

The *Accorinti* ruling by the EGC clarified that sovereigns may grant preferential treatment to central banks in sovereign debt restructurings by excluding them from the restructuring perimeter. In economic and financial terms, this usually means that other creditors must bear a larger share of the overall debt adjustment burden, especially when the central bank holds a significant share of the country's public debt.[245]

The *Accorinti* case, thus, bears significant relevance for any treatment of Eurosystem central banks' claims held against a euro area government future debt restructuring. Given that the ECB and the other 19 euro area central banks have become the major creditor to governments in the currency zone, the issue is of vital political and economic concern, and will remain relevant for the years to come.[246] Following the private sector's outcry over the preferred treatment of the Eurosystem, the ECB clarified that it would accept a pari passu treatment in future debt restructuring operations.[247] What remains less clear is whether investors may successfully challenge any future carve-outs of central bank holdings in a restructuring in court à la Greece, should the a central bank again opt for that strategy.[248]

One may argue that *Accorinti*, which was later confirmed by the EGC in *Nausicaa*,[249] conveyed a wide margin of discretion to the Eurosystem regarding the participation in a restructuring of euro area government claims it holds, provided that the respective central banks act in the exercise of their basic duties under the Treaties. Since all public asset purchase programmes conducted by the Eurosystem since 2015 were deemed compliant with the pertinent rules of EU law, notably by the CJEU in *Weiss*,[250] a repetition of the Greek carve-out would likely meet the *Accorinti* standard. For private sector holdouts that seek to bring a similar claim against the Eurosystem in a potential future euro area debt restructuring, the legal remedies in EU courts will likely remain limited.[251]

3.6. Holdout Arbitration After Greece

This section reviews the role of holdout arbitration before ICSID tribunals in the aftermath of the Greek PSI. Almost a decade after the Greek PSI, only two applications[252] by investors were submitted to ICSID: one under the 1992 Cyprus-Greece BIT and the other one under the Greece-Slovakia BIT.[253] Greece has, however, not entered BITs with the US or the UK, which may explain why holdouts that are often based in the US (or tax havens in the US orbit) have not initiated investment arbitration proceedings against Greece.[254]

Since most BITs[255] signed by Greece appeared to include sovereign debt in the definition of protected investment. Against the backdrop of the Argentine holdout arbitration cases,[256] and the creditor-friendly interpretation of the ICSID

Convention in the wake of Argentina's default, it was to be expected that holdouts would also have recourse to the ICSID following the Greek PSI.

3.6.1. Poštová banka v Hellenic Republic[257]

The main claimant in this case was a Slovak bank (Poštová banka).[258] It asserted that Greece's retroactive implementation of CACs had resulted in a significant erosion of the value of their investment in Greek government bonds.[259] The claims were based on breaches of the Greece-Slovakia BIT, the Cyprus-Greece BIT, as well as the ICSID Convention, respectively.[260] The request for arbitration reached Washington, DC, in May 2013, and the ICSID tribunal was constituted on 21 October 2013.[261] The tribunal rendered its (negative) decision on jurisdiction and admissibility on 9 April 2015.[262]

To establish jurisdiction *ratione materiae* under Article 25 of the ICSID Convention, claimants argued that Greek government bonds were a protected investment.[263] In a second step, they posited that the rights under that investment were taken away by Greece's 'forced surrender of the bonds.'[264] Greece rejected such broad reading of the BIT and posited that neither the Greece-Slovakia BIT nor the Cyprus-Greece BIT expressly included sovereign debt instruments.[265]

The tribunal concluded that the bonds did not fall under definition of investment in the pertinent BITs on the following grounds:

- First, specific examples of investment provided by the text of Greece-Slovakia BIT[266] must be interpreted narrowly since, otherwise, the list of protected investments laid down in Article 1 of the BIT would become 'unnecessary, redundant or useless.'[267]
- Second, the pertinent BITs did not include debt securities in the definition of 'investment.'[268] They were not 'claims to money or to any performance under contract having financial value,' which was a protected investment under Article 1(1)(c) of the Greece-Slovakia BIT, as this required the existence of a contractual relationship.[269] Greece merely had a contractual relationship with the participants in the Bank of Greece's Securities System and the primary dealers.[270] By contrast, '[Poštová banka's] contractual relationship under the Greek Government Bonds (GGBs) was exclusively with the Participants through Clearstream.' The government bonds equally did not qualify as loans under the BIT, given the absence of contractual privity between the claimants and the respondent.[271]

Upon declining its jurisdiction *ratione materiae* under the BITs pursuant to the 'subjective approach,' the tribunal refrained from assessing whether the investment would fall under Article 25 of the ICSID Convention in line with the 'objective approach.'[272] However, it noted obiter that it would also reach the same conclusion under both approaches. This was because the claimant's interest in the government bonds did not contribute to an economic venture that implied an operational risk,[273] as required by the *Salini* test (and thus, Article 25 ICSID Convention).[274]

In September 2016, the tribunal rejected an annulment procedure, initiated by the claimant under Article 52(3) of the ICSID Convention.[275] The high threshold for annulment under Article 52(1)(e) of the ICSID Convention was not satisfied, especially because the legal reasoning of the tribunal was 'not fundamentally contradictory.'[276]

3.6.2. Interim Conclusions: Closing Pandora's Box?

Similar to the *Abaclat*[277] and *Ambiente Ufficio*[278] decisions, the *Poštová banka*[279] arbitration circled around the definition of 'investment' under the applicable sources of international law and, specifically, whether that definition extended to bonds that a sovereign issued and later defaulted on or restructured. While the post-Argentina arbitration ultimately resulted in a victory for the holdouts, with ICSID tribunals supporting a broad reading of the pertinent BIT, *Poštová banka* marked a return to a more restrictive interpretation of international investment law, essentially rejecting the notion that the ICSID Convention protects 'sovereign risk.'[280]

With regard to the subjective approach, the *Poštová banka* tribunal advanced a narrower reading of the applicable BIT language than the Argentine tribunals. As Nakajima observed, while the *Ambiente Ufficio* tribunal understood the language of the Italy-Argentina BIT to include a 'catch-all clause,'[281] *Poštová banka* emphasized that there was no such broad provision in the Greece-Slovakia BIT.[282] While this argument certainly goes beyond pure semantics, it seemed somewhat formalistic against the backdrop of the Argentine arbitration.

In particular, while Article 1(1)(c) of the Greece-Slovakia BIT protected 'claims to money or to any performance under contract having financial value,' the tribunal understood this provision not to cover government bonds:

- First, the tribunal seemed to imply that 'claims to money' and 'any performance under contract having financial value' are inextricably connected so that 'claims to money' are only protected if based on a contractual relationship between investor and host state.[283] One may, however, also reach the conclusion that 'claims to money' constitutes a genuine type of protected investment that does not depend on whether the parties have concluded a contract. This seems justified when looking at other BITs. For instance, the Germany–Sri Lanka BIT or the Switzerland-Uzbekistan BIT, both of which the *Poštová banka* cites, include 'claims to money' as a sui generis type of protected investment – they make no reference to a contractual relationship.[284]
- Second, even if one were to assume that the BIT only protected contractual relationships, the tribunal's argument that the bondholders had no contract with the sovereign issuer is not entirely persuasive.[285] Indeed, municipal courts[286] as well as the pertinent literature[287] seem to assume that bondholders and the sovereign are bound together by a contract, even if bonds were acquired on the secondary market. The tribunal, in fact, concedes that the claimant had 'certain rights against the Greek Government under the terms of the Greek Government Bonds,' while at the same time insisting that these

rights did not indicate a contractual relationship between issuer and bondholder.[288] Moreover, the structure of the Bank of Greece's Securities System, in which the bondholders were not participants, is by no means unique –in fact, the securities clearing and settlement arrangements used by Argentina were functionally very similar.[289] And the ICSID tribunals adjudicating the claims against Argentina clearly assumed that there was a contractual relationship between the bondholders and the host state (issuer).[290]

Regarding the objective approach, the tribunals definition of 'investment' under Article 25 ICSID Convention, too, digressed from the Argentine arbitration cases. In this regard, Montanaro states, '[t]his conception of the 'substantial contribution' requirement differs radically from that in *Ambiente Ufficio*, where the majority decision did not link the contribution to a productive activity.'[291] The *Poštová banka* tribunal seemed intent to revive the *Salini* test that revolved around the requirement to 'make a substantial contribution to a specific project in the host state' and which the *Abaclat* and *Ambiente Ufficio* decision had rejected.[292] As discussed earlier,[293] the contribution requirement had long been subject to ambiguity in ICSID cases,[294] and *Poštová banka* confirmed the divergent opinions that different tribunals offered when adjudicating sovereign defaults.

In sum, the post-Greek PSI arbitration clearly limited investors' rights under international investment law related to sovereign bond default, insulating Greece from the same pressure that Argentina felt to settle with holdouts.[295] However, the renunciation of the legal arguments established in the Argentine arbitration cases puzzled some commentators.[296] The *Poštová banka* award would have benefited from a comprehensive discussion why the legal view, especially on Article 25 of the Washington Convention, differed so starkly from that in *Abaclat*[297] and *Ambiente Ufficio*.[298]

Moreover, the ostensibly formal distinction between the categories of investment protected by the respective BITs means that bad drafting may result in accidents.[299] Going forward, ICSID tribunals should consistently promote the *Salini* criteria when it comes to sovereign bond investments, thereby reducing incentives to hold out while at the same time reinforcing the ICSID's role in promoting development. Indeed, a heterogenous body of ICSID jurisprudence concerning debt restructurings has the potential to further increase the level of legal uncertainty in future crises, ultimately harming both sovereign debtors *and* the investor community.[300] From a policy perspective, thus, *Poštová banka*'s return to *Salini* should be welcomed as a closed Pandora's box that could have severely complicated future debt workouts at the international level. From a legal perspective, however, the ruling left much to be desired on clarity and consistency.

Notes

1 Certain parts of this chapter were published by the author in journals; see, notably, Sebastian Grund, 'Restructuring Government Debt Under Local Law: The Greek Case and Implications for Investor Protection in Europe' (2017) 12(2) Capital Markets Law Journal 253.

2 See IMF, 'Greece – Ex-Post Evaluation of Exceptional Access Under the 2012 Extended Arrangement – Press Release; Staff Report; and Statement by the Executive Director for Greece' (February 2017) IMF Country Report No 17/44 <www.imf.org/en/Publications/CR/Issues/2017/02/07/Greece-Ex-Post-Evaluation-of-Exceptional-Access-Under-the-2012-Extended-Arrangement-Press-44636> accessed 2 November 2021.

3 See, for an ex post assessment of the program, European Commission, 'Compliance Report ESM Stability Support Programme for Greece' (July 2018) Fourth Review <https://ec.europa.eu/info/sites/default/files/economy-finance/compliance_report_4r_2018.06.20.docx.pdf> accessed 2 November 2021. For a critical analysis of the reform measures, see George Pagoulatos, 'Greece After the Bailouts: Assessment of a Qualified Failure' (2018) Hellenic Observatory Discussion Papers on Greece and Southeast Europe Paper No 130 <www.lse.ac.uk/Hellenic-Observatory/Assets/Documents/Publications/GreeSE-Papers/GreeSE-No130.pdf> accessed 2 November 2021.

4 In retrospect, the IMF concluded that the macroeconomic adjustment program, including the mega debt restructuring, failed to restore debt sustainability and growth. IMF (n 2) 34.

5 According to the IMF (n 2), the potential adverse impact of the restructuring on Greece's banking sector was a particularly important issue. The Fund noted that, on the one hand, '[t]he Greek debt restructuring of March 2012, the largest in history, was calibrated to bring Greece's public debt down to 120 percent by 2020.' On the other hand, the Fund acknowledged that 'the PSI further weakened a system that was already impaired by heavy deposit outflows' and that 'to contain the fallout on the financial sector . . . EUR50 billion from the program was set aside for bank recapitalization with the capital requirements to be gradually phased in.'

6 See Grund (n 1).

7 Pierre-Oliver Gourinchas, Thomas Philippon, and Dimitri Vayanos, 'The Analytics of the Greek Crisis' (2016) 31(1) NBER Macroeconomics Annual 1. Real GDP per capita declined from EUR 22,600 in 2008 to EUR 17,000 by 2014, and the unemployment rate rose from 7.8% to 26.6% over the same period. Greece was, however, not the only EU country in trouble: when economic activity snapped in the wake of the global financial crisis, confidence in government finance eroded, and advanced European economies, such as Ireland, Greece, Iceland, and Portugal, suddenly lost access to international capital markets. See, generally, Adam Tooze, *Crashed: How a Decade of Financial Crises Changes the World* (New York: Penguin Random House, 2018).

8 This led to an upward revision of the deficit projection by Eurostat from 3.7% to 12.5%; compare Eurostat, 'Provision of Deficit and Debt Data for 2008 – Second Notification' (*Newsrelease Euroindicators*, October 2009) <https://ec.europa.eu/eurostat/documents/2995521/5074630/2-22102009-ap-en.pdf/490aa296-ccc7-4714-91c5-b5c8ddb73948?version=1.0> accessed 2 November 2021.

9 As it turned out, the US investment bank Goldman Sachs played a key role in assisting Greece to mask its real level of debt for a long period. See Beat Balzli, 'How Goldman Sachs Helped Greece to Mask Its True Debt' *Spiegel Online* (Hamburg, 8 February 2010) <www.spiegel.de/international/europe/greek-debt-crisis-how-goldman-sachs-helped-greece-to-mask-its-true-debt-a-676634.html> accessed 2 November 2021; Louise Story, Landon Thomas and Nelson Schwartz, 'Wall St. Helped to Mask Debt Fuelling Europe's Crisis' *New York Times* (New York, 13 February 2010).

10 Ample evidence exists with regard to the underappreciation of sovereign risk in the euro area in the run-up to the crisis as well as excessive pricing in times of distress; see, for example, Hans Dewachter, Leonardo Iania, Marco Lyrio, and Maite de Sola Perera, 'A Macro-Financial Analysis of the Euro Area Sovereign Bond Market' (2015) 50 Journal of Banking & Finance 308 (finding that shocks unrelated to the fundamental component of the spread have played an important role in the dynamics of bond spreads since the intensification of the sovereign debt crisis in the summer of 2011).

11 See, for example, Philip Lane and Gian Maria Milesi-Ferretti, 'International Financial Integration in the Aftermath of the Global Financial Crisis' (2017) IMF Working Paper WP/17/115 <www.imf.org/en/Publications/WP/Issues/2017/05/10/International-Financial-Integration-in-the-Aftermath-of-the-Global-Financial-Crisis-44906> accessed 2 November 2021.

12 See IMF, 'Europe and IMF Agree €110 bn Financing Plan With Greece' (*IMF Survey Online*, 2 May 2010) <www.imf.org/external/pubs/ft/survey/so/2010/car050210a.htm> accessed 2 November 2021. For more details on the Eurogroup's First Economic Adjustment Programme for Greece, which totalled EUR80 billion to be disbursed over a period of three years, see The European Commission, 'The Economic Adjustment Programme for Greece' (2010) Occasional Papers 61 <http://ec.europa.eu/economy_finance/publications/occasional_paper/2010/pdf/ocp61_en.pdf> accessed 2 November 2021.

13 Greek sovereign bonds spreads vis-à-vis German government bonds (*Bunds*), used to measure the tightness of financing conditions for states, rose to unprecedented levels. Compare Roberto A De Santis, 'The Euro Area Sovereign Debt Crisis – Safe Haven, Credit Rating Agencies and the Spread of the Fever From Greece, Ireland and Portugal' (2012) ECB Working Paper Series No 1419 <www.ecb.europa.eu/pub/pdf/scpwps/ecbwp1419.pdf?20b5463a06e46d4321d81b1f8fb1990f> accessed 2 November 2021.

14 The rationale was that financial assistance provided by the public sector to a euro area country should be linked to a parallel reduction in the value of the debt held by private creditors – the burden should be shared. It may be useful to note at this stage that Germany and France had very different views as to how a crisis within a monetary union may be resolved. While German policymakers emphasize the importance of enforcing discipline through market mechanisms, the French approach preferred filling liquidity gaps to avoid multiple equilibria that would inevitably transform liquidity into solvency problems. See Markus Brunnermaier, Harold James, and Jean-Pierre Landau, *The Euro and the Battle of Ideas* (Princeton: Princeton University Press, 2016). B Lorenzo Bini Smaghi, 'The European Debt Crisis' (17 October 2011) Speech by Mr Lorenzo Bini Smaghi, Member of the Executive Board of the European Central Bank, at the Atlantik-Brücke event, meeting of Regional Group Frankfurt, Frankfurt am Main <www.bis.org/review/r111026c.pdf> accessed 2 November 2021. In his view, outstanding liabilities to official sector creditor, such as the European Commission, the ECB, or the IMF, should not become subject to a haircut since they enjoyed a de facto PCS.

15 'Contagion' became a buzzword in the policy debate, and serious financial stability risks as corollary to the so-called sovereign-bank doom loop, which refers to the close interlinkages between banks' and sovereigns' solvency, loomed large. See Brunnermaier et al (n 14).

16 Just months before the PSI, the Greek Prime Minister Lucas Papademos noted this:

> The effects of a sovereign default on confidence, the liquidity of the Greek banking system – which already faces serious funding problems – and the real economy, are difficult to predict and quantify, but they are likely to be substantial and should not be underestimated.

And he feared that '[s]uch effects would also undermine the fiscal consolidation process, especially if the debt restructuring causes a credit crunch and adversely affects economic activity.' See Lucas Papademos, 'The Pitfalls of EZ Sovereign Debt Restructuring' (*VoxEU*, 26 October 2011) <https://voxeu.org/article/greek-debt-restructuring-perils-and-promises> accessed 2 November 2021.

17 The risk of holdout investors undermining the success of a PSI was voiced from the very beginning of the crisis. See, for example, Mitu Gulati and Jeromin Zettelmeyer, 'Making a Voluntary Greek Debt Exchange Work' (2012) 7(2) Capital Markets Law Journal 169.

18 For an in-depth review of the application of the exceptional access policy in Greece, see Katherine Christopherson and Wolfgang Bergthaler, 'The IMF's Financing Role in Europe During the Global Financial Crisis' in Fabian Amtenbrink, Christoph Herrmann, and Rene Repasi (eds), *The EU Law of the Economic and Monetary Union* (Oxford: Oxford University Press, 2020) 956–958. Also see Susan Schadler, 'Living with Rules: The IMF's Exceptional Access Framework and the 2010 Stand-By Arrangement with Greece' (8 July 2016) IEO Report <www.ieo-imf.org/ieo/files/completedevaluations/EAC__BP_16-02_08__Living_with_Rules_-_The_IMF_s_Exceptional_Framework_and_the_2010_SBA_with_Greece.pdf> accessed 2 November 2021 (elaborating on the basis for the decision to amend the criteria [for the Greek programme], the procedural aspects of seeking Board approval of the amendment, the quality of the assessment of compliance with the four criteria as amended, and the follow-up on those assessments through program reviews in 2010–2011). To accommodate an IMF arrangement, the Fund invoked the systemic exemption, which allowed members exceptional access to IMF financing even in cases when debt was not sustainable with a high probability. See IMF, 'The Fund's Lending Framework and Sovereign Debt – Further Considerations' (April 2015) 12 <www.imf.org/~/media/Websites/IMF/Imported/external/np/pp/eng/2015/_040915pdf.ashx> accessed 2 November 2021 (noting that '[s]taff is of the view that [the systemic] exemption does not achieve the objective of limiting contagion and risks increasing costs for the sovereign debtor and its creditors'). However, both the IMF and its IEO conceded later that the systemic exemption, which allowed access without a debt restructuring, failed to achieve this objective. The IEO took issues with the strategy to wait with PSI, noting this:

> the decision not to seek pre-emptive debt restructuring fundamentally left debt sustainability concerns unaddressed, magnified the required fiscal adjustment, and thereby – at least in part – contributed to a large contraction of output and a subsequent loss of Greek public support for the program.

See IEO, 'The IMF's Role in Greece in the Context of the 2010 Stand-By Arrangement' (2016) Background Paper BP/16-02/11 <www.ieo-imf.org/ieo/files/completedevaluations/EAC__BP_16-02_11__The_IMFs_Role_in_Greece_in_the_Context_of_the_2010_SBA.pdf> accessed 2 November 2021 and IEO, 'The IMF and the Crises in Greece, Ireland, and Portugal: An Evaluation by the Independent Evaluation Office' (8 July 2016) IEO Report <www.ieo-imf.org/ieo/pages/CompletedEvaluation267.aspx> accessed 2 November 2021.

19 In a speech given in 2011, Lorenzo Bini Smaghi, former Member of the Executive Board of the ECB, noted that 'the problem emerges when debt restructuring is carried out not as the last resort but as a preventive tool.' Lorenzo Bini Smaghi, 'Private sector involvement: From (good) theory to (bad) practice' (6 June 2011) Speech by Mr Lorenzo Bini Smaghi, Member of the Executive Board of the European Central Bank at the Reinventing Bretton Woods Committee, Berlin <www.ecb.europa.eu/press/key/date/2011/html/sp110606.en.html> accessed 2 November 2021. According to reports, the former ECB President Jean-Claude Trichet shouted at a French delegation the Deauville agreement between France and Germany: he was certain that a PSI inside the euro area 'would destroy the euro.' See Tooze (n 7). In the same vein, a Monthly Bulletin article of October 2011, ECB staff argued that previous PSI experiences are not a reliable guidance for sovereign debt restructurings in the euro area and took a highly critical stance. See ECB, 'Private Sector Involvement and Its Financial Stability Implications' (October 2011) ECB Monthly Bulletin 43–44 <www.ecb.europa.eu/pub/pdf/other/mb201110_focus05.en.pdf?b5d740db72355e4b15f3302e8ca5a42a> accessed 2 November 2021.

20 See, for an overview of the IIF's role, for example, Giuseppe Bianco, *Restructuring Sovereign Debt: Private Creditors and International Law* (PhD thesis, University of Oslo, Oslo, 2017) (on file with author).

21 Manolis Kalaitzake, 'The Political Power of Finance: The Institute of International Finance in the Greek Debt Crisis' (2017) 45(3) Politics & Society 389, 400. The IIF also managed to convince euro area authorities to utilize large amounts of public money (primarily through the EFSF notes that were offered as sweeteners) while the larger private creditors progressively migrated out of Greek government bonds. Moreover, the terms of its proposal were apparently so soft that they may have led to an *increase* in the net present value of Greece's debt; see IMF (n 2) 40.

22 For the original text of the Invitation Memorandum see Hellenic Republic, 'Invitation Memorandum' (24 February 2012) <http://ftalphaville.ft.com/files/2012/02/Reg_S_Invitation_Memorandum.pdf> accessed 2 November 2021.

23 Aturo C Porzecanski, 'Behind the Greek Default and Restructuring of 2012' (2014) MPRA Paper No 44166, 9 <https://mpra.ub.uni-muenchen.de/44166/1/Behind_the_Greek_Default_and_Restructuring_of_2012.pdf> accessed 2 November 2021. Notably, the ECB, as Greece's single largest bondholder, did not participate in the PSI, arguing that this would violate the EU Treaties. See *Gauweiler and ors v Deutscher Bundestag*, Judgment, reference for a preliminary ruling, Case C-62/14, ECLI:EU:C:2015:400, 16 June 2015, Court of Justice of the European Union [CJEU]; European Court of Justice [ECJ]; European Court of Justice (Grand Chamber). For an analysis, see, for example, Paul Craig and Menelaos Markakis, 'Gauweiler and the Legality of Outright Monetary Transactions' (2016) 41(1) European Law Review 241. This – allegedly unequal – treatment of official and private sector creditors was later challenged in EU courts, without success from the applicants' perspective; see *Accorinti v European Central Bank*, Judgment, Case T-79/13, [2015] Court of Justice of the European Union [CJEU]; GC of the European Union [EGC].

24 Greece offered the following: (i) new Greek sovereign bonds with a face value equal to 31.5% of the exchanged bonds' original value, (ii) highly rated ESFS notes with a maturity date of two years or less from the PSI settlement date, as well as (iii) detachable GDP-linked securities with notional amount equal to the face value of each holder's new bonds. See Hellenic Republic (n 22).

25 Jeromin Zettelmeyer, Christoph Trebesch, and Mitu Gulati, 'The Greek Debt Restructuring: An Autopsy' (2013) 28(75) Economic Policy 513, 531 (noting that 'the yield curve approach produces an average haircut that is notably lower; at around 59% (sensitivity analysis suggests a range from about 55% to 61%').

26 Otto Sandrock, 'The Case for More Arbitration When Sovereign Debt Is to Be Restructured: Greece as an Example' (2012) 23 The American Review of International Arbitration 507, 513.

27 See Lee Buchheit and Elena Daly, 'Minimising Holdout Creditors: Sticks' in Rosa Lastra and Lee Buchheit (eds), *Sovereign Debt Management* (Oxford: Oxford University Press, 2014). For a discussion of sovereign debt restructuring techniques, see Chapter 1.2.3.2.2. 'Debt Restructuring Techniques: Sticks and Carrots.'

28 Zettelmeyer et al (n 25) 526 note the following:

> [the minimum participation threshold] implied, in particular, that if Greece succeeded with its attempt to amend its domestic law sovereign bonds within the framework set out by the February 23 law, the exchange would likely go forward, since the Greek-law sovereign bonds alone amounted to about 86% of the total eligible debt.

29 The minimum participation threshold served three specific purposes. First, it signalled to the creditor group that unless most of them accept the offer, none of them will be taken out, and the status quo will remain in place. Second, it assured participating creditors that they would not be left with illiquid bonds if only a small number of holders joined the exchange. Third, it indicated that, for the issuer, a partial solution, even approved by a significant majority, was worse than no solution. For a discussion, see, for example, Ran Bi, Marcos Chamon, and Jeromin Zettelmeyer, 'The Problem That Wasn't: Coordination Failures in Sovereign Debt Restructurings' (2011) IMF

Working Paper No 11/265 <www.imf.org/external/pubs/ft/wp/2011/wp11265.pdf> accessed 2 November 2021. See, for the collective action mechanism, Chapter 3.3.2. 'Restructuring Greek Law Bonds.'

30 For the bill, compare Andreas Koutras, 'A Better Translation of Bondholders Act 4050' (*Andreas Koutras Blog*, March 2012) <http://andreaskoutras.blogspot.com.au/2012/03/better-tarnslation-of-bondholders-act.html> accessed 2 November 2021.

31 This mechanism was proposed in a paper by Buchheit and Gulati in 2010, at the onset of the crisis, entitled 'Restructuring a Nation's Debt.' See Lee Buchheit and Mitu Gulati, 'Restructuring a Nation's Debt' (2010) 29 International Financial Law Review 46.

32 If Greece had simply repudiated (part of its) debts by unilateral statutory measures, the chances of creditors successfully claiming compensation for expropriation would have been considerably higher. This was essentially confirmed by courts and international tribunals; see Chapter 3.4. 'Holdout Creditor Litigation After Greece in Foreign Courts,' Chapter 3.5. 'Holdout Litigation After Greece in European Courts,' and Chapter 3.6. 'Holdout Arbitration After Greece.'

33 Miranda Xafa, 'Lessons from the 2012 Greek Debt Restructuring' (*VoxEU*, 25 June 2014) <http://voxeu.org/article/greek-debt-restructuring-lessons-learned> accessed 2 November 2021.

34 See Lee Buchheit and Mitu Gulati, 'Sovereign Debt Restructuring in Europe' (2018) 9(1) Global Policy 65.

35 Article 1(9) of the GBA stipulated this:

> the decision adopted by the bondholders to accept or refuse the restructuring offer made by the Greek State is to apply erga omnes, is binding on all the bondholders concerned, and overrides any general or specific law, any administrative decisions, and any contracts which conflict with it.

See *Hellenic Republic v Kuhn,* Judgment, Case C-308/17, ECLI:EU:C:2018:911, 15 November 2018, Court of Justice of the European Union [CJEU]; European Court of Justice [ECJ]; European Court of Justice (1st Chamber) [14].

36 See *Poštová banka as and Istrokapital SE v Greece*, Award, ICSID Case No ARB/13/8, IIC 679 (2015), despatched 9 April 2015, World Bank; International Centre for Settlement of Investment Disputes [ICSID] [74].

37 Grund (n 1). To be sure, Greece was not the first country to exploit the advantages of domestic law debt, as documented by, for example, Aitor Erce, Enrico Malluci, and Mattia Picarelli, 'A Journey in the History of Sovereign Defaults on Domestic Law Public Debt – Sovereign Histories' (2021) Universidad Publica de Navarra Working Paper D.T. 2108, 24–30 <https://www2.unavarra.es/gesadj/CyD5/depEconomia/documentos-trabajo/2021/WP2108.pdf> accessed 2 November 2021 (identifying 132 events of restructuring of domestic law debt instruments in 50 countries from 1980 to 2018).

38 For example, Argentina's debt moratorium on roughly USD155 billion of public foreign-currency debt, declared on 23 December 2021. See The Economist, 'Argentina's Default – Foreign Creditors Join the Pyre' *The Economist* (London, 3 January 2002).

39 Ibid. Similarly, the retroactive implementation of CACs was characterized as a clear violation of the sanctity of contracts; see Porzecanski (n 23) 8. *The Economist* newspaper described it as a tool that 'forced investors holding out for a better deal to swallow the loss'; see The Economist, 'An Illusory Haven – What Lessons Should Investors Learn from the Argentine and Greek Restructurings? *The Economist* (London, 20 April 2013).

40 This view is supported inter alia by Sandrock (n 26); Porzecanski (n 23) and Andreas Witte, 'Private International Law and European Law Limits to Unilateral Sovereign Debt Restructuring' (2012) 9(3) Manchester Journal of International Law 307.

41 Martin Guzman, José Antonio Ocampo and Joseph E Stiglitz (eds), *Too Little, Too Late: The Quest to Resolve Sovereign Debt Crises* (New York: Columbia University Press, 2016) 164.

42 Marcus Miller and Dania Thomas, 'Eurozone Sovereign Debt Restructuring: Keeping the Vultures at Bay' (2013) 29(4) Oxford Review of Economic Policy 745,753.
43 See Chapter 3.4. 'Holdout Creditor Litigation After Greece in Foreign Courts.'
44 For an overview of the cases before Greek courts, see, for example, Dimitris Tsibanoulis and Iakovos Anagnostopoulos, 'The Greek PSI and the Litigation Surrounding It' (2014) 2 International Review of Financial Services 18. Litigation before Greek courts will not be separately analysed in this study for the following reasons: first, language barriers render it difficult to review primary sources of law; second, holdouts were generally unsuccessful before Greek courts; third, the ECtHR analysed the constitutionality of the Greek Bondholder Act in light of the ECHR (this judgment will be discussed in Chapter 3.5.2.1. 'Mamatas v Greece').
45 Miller and Dania (n 42) 747.
46 While they were rarely included before the Greek PSI, aggregation features have become the gold standard in both international sovereign bonds as well as local law securities issued by euro area governments following concerted efforts by both the private and official sector.
47 See Zettelmeyer et al (n 25) for details.
48 See Lee Buchheit and Mitu Gulati, 'Greek Debt: The Endgame Scenarios' (April 2011) unpublished manuscript <http://scholarship.law.duke.edu/faculty_scholarship/2380/> accessed 2 November 2021.
49 Stephen J Choi, Mitu Gulati, and Eric A Posner, 'Pricing Terms in Sovereign Debt Contracts: A Greek Case Study with Implications for the European Crisis Resolution' (2011) 6(2) Capital Markets Law Journal 163, 175.
50 Ibid.
51 See, for example, Mark Weidemaier and Mitu Gulati, 'The Relevance of Law to Sovereign Debt' (2015) 11 Annual Review of Law and Social Science 395 (arguing that 'law plays a central, and constantly evolving, role in structuring sovereign debt markets').
52 According to *Reuters*, private creditors who accepted the haircut were furious, calling the decision to pay the holdouts 'scandalous'; see Renee Matezou, 'In About-Face, Greece Pays Bond Swap Holdouts' *Reuters* (London, 15 May 2012) <www.reuters.com/article/us-greece-bond-idUSBRE84E0MY20120515> accessed 2 November 2021. Especially, the smaller retail investors that held Greek law debt and were not part of the negotiations between the official sector and the IIF lamented that the decision to pay holders of English law instruments undermined intercreditor equity; it also encouraged them to challenge the Retrofit, as discussed in Chapter 3.4. 'Holdout Creditor Litigation After Greece in Foreign Courts.'
53 See Thomas Landon, 'Bet on Greek Bonds Paid Off for "Vulture Fund"' *New York Times* (New York, 15 May 2012).
54 To the authors' best knowledge, litigation in foreign courts was limited to these two jurisdictions.
55 See, for an extensive analysis of the litigation in German courts, Sebastian Grund, 'The legal Consequences of Sovereign Insolvency – a Review of Creditor Litigation in Germany Following the Greek Debt Restructuring' (2017) 24(3) Maastricht Journal of European and Comparative Law 399.
56 BGH, Urteil vom 08.03.2016 – VI ZR 516/14, VI ZR 516/14, NJW 2016, 1659, 8 March 2016, Germany; Federal Court of Justice [BGH].
57 Ibid 5–6.
58 Ibid 10.
59 Ibid 12. See, for the judgment of the Court of Appeals in OLG (Frankfurt), Urteil vom 18.09.2014–16 U 41/14, 18 September 2014, Germany; Hesse; Frankfurt am Main; Higher Regional Court [OLG].
60 Ibid 18.
61 Ibid.

62 Ibid. This assessment aligns with case law in the US and the UK, compare, for example, Mark Weidemaier, 'Sovereign Immunity and Sovereign Debt' (2014) 1 University of Illinois Law Review 68.

63 BGH (n 56) [22].

64 Ibid 29. The BGH, however, noticed that many voices in literature assume that the principle of sovereign immunity does not apply to legislative measures that disturb the contractual relationship between a state and its counterparty. See, for example, Alexander Szodruch, *Staateninsolvenz und private Gläubiger: Rechtsprobleme des Private Sector Involvement bei staatlichen Finanzkrisen im 21. Jahrhundert* (Berlin: Berliner Wissenschaftsverlag, 2010) 379. It also pointed out that the CJEU had taken a different view in *Fahnenbrock* but that this judgment concerned the service of documents and was not prejudicial for the assessment of Greece's immunity. See *Fahnenbrock v Hellenic Republic*, Judgment, reference for a preliminary ruling, Case C-226/13, Case C-245/13, Case C-247/13, Case C-578/13, ECLI:EU:C:2015:383, [2015] OJ C270/2, 11 June 2015, Court of Justice of the European Union [CJEU]; CJEU [ECJ]; CJEU (1st Chamber). For a review of that judgment, see Chapter 3.5.1.2. 'Fahnenbrock v Hellenic Republic.'

65 See, for example, OLG (Schleswig), Urteil vom 07.07.2016–5 U 84/15, 7 July 2016, Germany; Schleswig-Holstein; Higher Regional Court [OLG].

66 See, for example, LG (Frankfurt), Urteile vom 30.03.2015–2–1 S 108/14, 204/14, 280/14, 30 March 2015; Germany; Frankfurt am Main; District Court [LG].

67 BGH, Urteil vom 19.12.2017 – XI ZR 796/16, 19 December 2017, Germany; Federal Court of Justice [BGH].

68 The BGH (n 56) had indeed suggested that a distinction needs to be made between rights in rem and rights ex contractu; see Chapter 3.4.1.1. 'BGH Judgment of 8 March 2016.'

69 OLG (Oldenburg), Urteil vom 18.04.2016–13 U 43/15, 18 April 2016; Germany; Lower Saxony; Oldenburg; Higher Regional Court [OLG] [21]. In other words, a government may not immunize what was once a commercial legal act by introducing legislation that alters the nature of the creditor-sovereign relationship. Instead, Greece was to be treated akin to a private legal actor that refused to repay its debts on grounds that they have been revoked by virtue of legislation.

70 OLG (Oldenburg) (n 69) [22].

71 OLG (Köln), Urteil vom 12.05.2016–8 U 44/15, 8 U 44/15, ZIP 2016, 40, WM 2016, 1590, 12 May 2016, Germany; North Rhine-Westphalia; Cologne; Higher Regional Court [OLG].

72 OLG (Schleswig), Urteil vom 07.07.2016–5 U 84/15, 7 July 2016, Germany; Schleswig-Holstein; Higher Regional Court [OLG] [53]. The OLG Schleswig also cited the Italian Supreme Court's decision on the Argentine holdout suits from 2005 (*Borri v Argentina*, Request for a ruling on jurisdiction, Case No 11225, Order No 6532/2005, ILDC 296 (IT 2005), (2005) 88 Riv Dir Int 856, 27 May 2005, Italy; Supreme Court of Cassation). However, the OLG Schleswig rejected the plaintiffs' claims due to lack of international jurisdiction under Articles 5 (domicile jurisdiction) as well as 15 and 16 (jurisdiction over consumer contracts) of the Brussels I Regulation (Council Regulation on jurisdiction and the recognition and enforcement of judgements in civil and commercial matters (Council of the European Union) 44/2001/EC, [2001] OJ L12/1 ['Brussels I Regulation']). For an analysis of the ruling by the OLG Schleswig, see Grund (n 55). See for a similar conclusion, OLG (Oldenburg) (n 69) [31].

73 OLG (Oldenburg) (n 69).

74 OLG (Köln) (n 71).

75 BGH (n 67) [17–18].

76 Ibid 25.

77 Ibid 26.
78 See *Fahnenbrock v Hellenic Republic* (n 64).
79 BGH (n 67) [30].
80 Ibid 33.
81 BVerfG, Urteil vom 6.5.2020–2 BvR 331/18, Second Senate, 6 May 2020, Germany; Constitutional Court [BVerfG].
82 Ibid 14 et seq.
83 For a discussion of the once a trader always a trader doctrine, see, for example, Michael Singer, 'Abandoning Restrictive Sovereign Immunity: An Analysis in Terms of Jurisdiction to Prescribe' (1985) 26 Harvard International Law Journal 1, noting this:

> '[o]nce a trader, always a trader' would be a rule appropriate for a model of the restrictive doctrine of sovereign immunity based upon Lauterpacht's analysis, in which increased state trading, challenges to the sovereign prerogative, and recognition of human freedoms are held out as the forces leading to adoption of the restrictive view.

84 Ibid 13.
85 Ibid 17.
86 Ibid. According to the BVerfG, sovereign acts 'also include the unilateral imposition of taxes and levies on those subject to a state's sovereignty for the purpose of generating revenue without providing anything in return.'
87 *Mamatas v Greece*, App No 63066/14, App No 64297/14, App No 66106/14, 21st July 2016, European Court of Human Rights [ECHR].
88 *Borri v Argentina*, Request for a ruling on jurisdiction, Case No 11225, Order No 6532/2005, ILDC 296 (IT 2005), (2005) 88 Riv Dir Int 856, 27 May 2005, Italy; Supreme Court of Cassation.
89 See Chapter 3.4.2. 'Austria.'
90 *Argentina and Banco Central de la República Argentina v Weltover Incorporated and ors*, Final appeal, Docket No 91–763, 504 US 607 (1992), ILDC 1924 (US 1992), 112 S Ct 2160 (1992), 119 L Ed 2d 394 (1992), (1995) 100 ILR 510, 12 June 1992, United States; Supreme Court [US].
91 BVerfG (n 81) [23–30].
92 Ibid 30.
93 The BVerfG added that its opinion did not contradict Article 10 of the UNCSI and the Convention's restrictive approach to sovereign immunity since the UNCSI had not been ratified by Germany or Greece and because it does not regulate the retroactive sovereign interference in obligations rooted in private law. See ibid 31.
94 See, for an earlier analysis of litigation before Austrian courts, which does not include the most recent cases, Sebastian Grund, 'The Greek Debt Crisis and Sovereign Debt Litigation in Austrian Courts' (2018) 21(1) Austrian Review of International and European Law Online 131.
95 The CJEU decision is discussed in Chapter 3.5.1.3. 'Hellenic Republic v Kuhn.'
96 *RB and TB v Hellenic Republic*, Interlocutory appeal judgment, 4Ob227/13f, ILDC 2214 (AT 2014), 20 May 2014, Austria; Supreme Court of Justice [OGH].
97 Ibid.
98 Ibid 5.
99 Ibid.
100 The OGH left the issue of international jurisdiction untouched for now.
101 *RB and GB v Hellenic Republic*, Appeal judgment, 4 Ob 163/15x, 27 January 2016, Austria; Supreme Court of Justice [OGH].
102 *RB and GB v Hellenic Republic* (n 101).
103 Ibid 6. This was also the view taken by the CJEU in *Fahnenbrock v Hellenic Republic* (n 64).

104 Ibid. More specifically, it noted that the jurisdiction of Austrian Courts in the present case may be based on Article 15(1) in conjunction with Article 16(1) of Brussels I Regulation (n 72). This, however, means that the plaintiff has to prove that it is a consumer in the sense of EU law in its contractual relationship with Greece. This, as German case law indicates, may prove difficult if the bondholder has acquired his debt instrument through a third party. See OLG (Oldenburg), Urteil vom 15.04.2016–13 U 43/15, 15 April 2016, Germany; Lower Saxony; Oldenburg; Higher Regional Court [OLG].

105 See *TW v Hellenic Republic*, Appeal judgment, 8 Ob67/15h, 30 July 2015, Austria; Supreme Court of Justice [OGH].

106 See ibid. Article 15(2) of the Brussels I Regulation (n 72) states the following:

> 2. Where a consumer enters into a contract with a party who is not domiciled in the Member State but has a branch, agency or other establishment in one of the Member States, *that party shall*, in disputes arising out of the operations of the branch, agency or establishment, *be deemed to be domiciled in that State*.
>
> (emphasis added)

107 *RE v Hellenic Republic* [5–7]. Also see, for a very similar conclusion, *RE v Hellenic Republic*, Appeal judgment, 8 Ob125/15p, 25 November 2015, Austria; Supreme Court of Justice [OGH].

108 *RB and TB v Hellenic Republic IV* (n 106) [6].

109 Ibid 10. Article 5(1) of the Brussels I Regulation (n 72) stipulates that 'a person (herein the Hellenic Republic) may be sued in another Member State in matters relating to a contract, in the Courts for the *place of the performance* of the obligation.' The plaintiff's reluctance to argue in favour of Art 5(1) Brussels Regulation stemmed from the difficulty of proving that Austria rather than Greece was the place of performance for principal and interest payments on Greek government bonds. Essentially, the failure to rebut Greece's claim that such payments are to be made by the Greek National Bank, and therefore in Greece, also led to the rejection of the claims made by bondholders in German Courts.

110 See Chapter 3.4.2.3. 'OGH Judgments of 25 April 2017 and 22 January 2019.'

111 *L v Hellenic Republic I*, Appeal judgment, 10 Ob34/16x, 25 April 2017, Austria; Supreme Court of Justice [OGH].

112 *L v Hellenic Republic II*, Appeal judgment, 10 Ob103/18x, 22 January 2019, Austria; Supreme Court of Justice [OGH].

113 Regulation of the European Parliament and of the Council on jurisdiction and the recognition and enforcement of judgments in civil and commercial matters (European Parliament) (Council of the European Union) 1215/2012/EU, [2012] OJ L351/1 ['Brussels I Regulation (recast)']. The new Brussels I Regulation (recast) entered into force on 20 December 2012 and was, thus, applicable to some of the later holdout suits against Greece, including the present case.

114 *L v Hellenic Republic I* (n 112). Article 7(1)(a) of the Brussels I Regulation (recast) (n 113) establishes special jurisdiction for persons outside the defendant's home state (here, Greece), provided that contract at stake has to be performed in another Member State.

115 Given that the creditor was a retail investor domiciled in Austria, this reading of the Greek law would have given rise to the jurisdiction of Austrian courts, opening the path for a review of the holdouts' claims on the merits. The application of Greek law was beyond question by the Austrian court (under the principle *iura novit curia*), for the contracts at stake were governed by Greek law. *RB and TB v Hellenic Republic V* (n 111) [9].

116 The OGH in *L v Hellenic Republic I* (n 111) posed three questions concerning its jurisdiction under the Brussels I Regulation to the CJEU:

> 1. Do multiple assignments of a sovereign bond alter its place of performance?

2. Do coupon payments rather than principal payments suffice to establish a factual place of performance under Article 7 Brussels I Regulation?

3. If the underlying contract sets out a place of performance, could another place of performance be established in the country where the contract is actually performed?

117 See 3.5.1.3. Hellenic Republic v Kuhn.

118 *Hellenic Republic v Kuhn* (n 35).

119 Ibid 8. This exceptional measure was the adoption of a Greek law that retroactively amended the debt contracts to facilitate a majority vote on the government's restructuring plan. This meant that Austria's jurisdiction was to be decided as a matter of Austrian law; plaintiffs had, however, not advanced that claim, which is why the OGH rules in the defendant's favour. Moreover, in an obiter dictum, the OGH reversed its position on the sovereign immunity defence, referring to the CJEU's qualification of the GBA as *iure imperii* measure. *L v Hellenic Republic* (n 112) [6–7] (also citing the German BGH's (n 67) decision that granted Greece immunity against holdout litigation). It should be noted, however, that *Kuhn* only assessed the nature of the GBA in the context of international jurisdiction and not in that of sovereign immunity (which was to be decided by the national court).

120 *GS v Hellenic Republic*, Appeal judgment, 4 Ob 233/19x, 21st February 2020, Austria; Supreme Court of Justice [OGH].

121 See *Hellenic Republic v Kuhn* (n 35).

122 *GS v Hellenic Republic* (n 120) [6–7]. The OGH was bound to the holding by virtue of §42(3) of the Austrian Law on Jurisdiction (*Jurisdiktionsnorm*) in conjunction with §528(2) no. 2 of the Austrian Code of Civil Procedure (*Zivilprozessordnung*).

123 See *Mamatas v Greece* (n 87); discussed in detail in Chapter 3.5.2.1. 'Mamatas v Greece.'

124 *GS v Hellenic Republic* (n 120) [7].

125 Ibid 8.

126 See Chapter 3.5.2.1. 'Mamatas v Greece.'

127 *GS v Hellenic Republic* (n 120) [8].

128 Ibid.

129 See Chapter 3.5.3.2.

130 See Sigrid Lorz, *Auslandische Staaten vor Deutschen Zivilgerichten: Zum Spannungsverhaltnis Von Staatenimmunitat Und Recht Auf Zugang Zu Gericht* (Tuebingen: Mohr Siebeck, 2017) 84 et seq. and Matthias J Müller, *Staatsbankrott und private Gläubiger* (Baden-Baden: Nomos, 2015).

131 See, in particular, *Allied Bank International v Banco Credito Agricola de Cartago and ors*, Case No 225, Docket 83–7714, 757, 758 F 2d 516 (2d Cir 1985), 77 ALR Fed 281, (1985) 24 ILM 762, 18 March 1985, United States; Court of Appeals (2nd Circuit) [2d Cir] and *Argentina v Weltover* (n 90).

132 *Borri v Argentina* (n 88).

133 See Chapter 2.2.3.1.1. 'The Commercial Activity Exception: 'Once A Trader Always A Trader' and the Mixed Activity Conundrum.'

134 For a discussion of the mixed activity conundrum from a German civil procedural law perspective, see Lorz (n 130).

135 There was some surprise in the literature that the OGH relied on the CJEU's assessment of the GBA for the purpose of its own immunity review. Stephan Walter, 'The Aftermath of the CJEU's Kuhn Judgment – Hellas Triumphans in Vienna, Really' (*ConflictofLaws*, 12 February 2019) <https://conflictoflaws.net/2019/the-aftermath-of-the-cjeus-kuhn-judgment-hellas-triumphans-in-vienna-really/> accessed 2 November 2021.

136 While one may advocate that a more integrated view on the issue of sovereign and commercial and civil actions, respectively, the OGH should have still justified how

Kuhn altered its assessment of the immunity defence; see, for a discussion, Chapter 3.5.3.2. 'The (Tenuous) Link Between Sovereign Immunity and Jurisdiction Under EU Law.'

137 The BGH's conclusion that 'Greece was the master of the law governing the debt contracts' may have been the clearest expression of the unique situation that states enjoy when they restructure domestic law instruments. See Chapter 3.4.1.1. 'BGH Judgment of 8 March 2016.'

138 See Chapter 3.5.3.3. 'Jurisdiction Under the Brussels I Regulation.'

139 See Chapter 2.2.1.2.3. 'BGH Decision of 24 February 2015.'

140 Relatedly, the question whether courts engaged in 'judicial self-censoring' to prevent these ramifications by constraining the Greek government's ability to respond to respond to the debt crisis remains academically compelling but practically irrelevant. See Georg Vanberg and Mitu Gulati, 'Financial Crises and Constitutional Compromise' in Tom Ginsburg, Mark D Rosen, and Georg Vanberg, *Constitutions in Times of Financial Crises* (Cambridge: Cambridge University Press, 2019).

141 See Tolek Petch, *Legal Implications of the Euro Zone Crisis* (Amsterdam: Kluwer, 2014) 135.

142 Dorothee Schramm, 'Enforcement and the Abolition of Exaquatur Under the 2012 Brussels I Regulation' (2013/14) 15 Yearbook of Private International Law 143, 164, noting this:

> [t]he European Parliament and Council finally sided with those concerned about giving up a tool that could still be needed in some rare and extreme situations and that could act as an 'emergency brake for cases in which something went terribly wrong.'

143 Mankowski posits as follows:

> [t]he underlying ratio [of the CJEU's case law] is evident: Greece must not fall for otherwise the Eurozone in its entirety is feared to break down. The individual creditors' particular interests are sacrificed for the common good of Greece, the Eurozone and the EU.

See Peter Mankowski, 'The Saga of the Greek State Bonds and Their Haircut: Hellas Triumphans in Luxemburg, Really?' (*Conflict of Laws.net*, 22 November 2018) <https://conflictoflaws.net/2018/the-saga-of-the-greek-state-bonds-and-their-haircut-hellas-triumphans-in-luxemburg-really/> accessed 2 November 2021.

144 See, for the seminal work on constitutional problems in financial crises, Ginsburg et al (n 140).

145 For an in-depth analysis, see Sebastian Grund, 'Enforcing Sovereign Debt in Court – A Comparative Analysis of Litigation and Arbitration Following the Greek Debt Restructuring of 2012' (2017) 1 University of Vienna Law Review 34.

146 Some of the decisions concern preliminary rulings upon requests by the Austrian and German courts, which are reviewed in the previous sections.

147 *Accorinti v ECB* (n 23).

148 The EGC is a constituent court of the CJEU and hears actions taken by individuals and Member States against the EU. However, certain matters are reserved for the ECJ. For background, see Francis G Jacobs, 'European Court, Court of Justice and General Court' in Rüdiger Wolfrum (ed), *Max Planck Encyclopaedia of Public International Law* (Heidelberg: Oxford University Press, 2019, online version).

149 See Chapter 3.3.1. 'Debt Restructuring Negotiations: The Role of the Troika and the IIF.'

150 For example, Ralph Atkins, 'ECB Avoids Forced Losses on Greek Bonds' *Financial Times* (London, 16 February 2012).

151 Paul Dobson and Abigail Moses, 'ECB Greek Plan May Hurt Bondholders While Triggering Debt Swaps' *Bloomberg* (London, 17 February 2012) <www.bloomberg.

com/news/articles/2012-02-17/ecb-plan-to-shield-its-greek-bonds-may-subordinate-some-holders-ubs-says> accessed 2 November 2021 (quoting several banks that vowed to challenge the ECB's seniority status).

152 Witte (n 40) 335.

153 *Accorinti v ECB* (n 23) [73–84].

154 Ibid 85–94. In their view, the ECB had illegally assigned itself the status of a preferred creditor to the detriment of the private sector.

155 Ibid 104–111.

156 Additionally, the applicants asserted that 'they were entitled to compensation even in the absence of an unlawful act on the part of the ECB,' as 'they suffered disproportionate and intolerable interference with the very essence' of their right to property as holders of Greek bonds, in that the nominal value of those bonds was reduced in a disproportionate manner.' Ibid 117.

157 Ibid 85.

158 Ibid 81.

159 Ibid 91.

160 Ibid 107.

161 Ibid.

162 *Fahnenbrock v Hellenic Republic* (n 64).

163 Regulation of the European Parliament and of the Council on the service in the Member States of judicial and extrajudicial documents in civil or commercial matters (service of documents), and repealing Council Regulation (EC) No 1348/2000 (European Parliament) (Council of the European Union) 1393/2007/EC, [2007] OJ L324/79 ['Service of Documents Regulation'].

164 Specifically, the German Federal Justice Office expressed doubts whether it could deliver the documents to Greece, given that it was not clear if the plaintiffs' actions concerned a civil or commercial matter. It, therefore, asked for a preliminary ruling by the CJEU to interpret the Service of Documents Regulation. See *Fahnenbrock v Hellenic Republic* (n 64) [15–16].

165 Ibid 15. As discussed later, the determination whether the GBA amounted to *acta iure imperii* was, at least indirectly, relevant for the assessment of Greece's state immunity, and the jurisdiction of municipal courts under the Brussel I Regulation, the CJEU's ruling was of wider importance. Crucially, *Fahnenbrock* seemingly deviated from several other pertinent decisions by EU as well as municipal courts; see Chapter 3.5.3.2. 'The (Tenuous) Link Between Sovereign Immunity and Jurisdiction Under EU Law.'

166 *Fahnenbrock v Hellenic Republic* (n 64) [53–56]. The EGC further noted that 'the fact that that possibility was introduced by a law is not, in itself, decisive in order to conclude that the State acted in the exercise of State authority.'

167 Ibid 57.

168 Ibid.

169 Ibid 59.

170 *Fahnenbrock v Hellenic Republic*, Opinion of the Advocate General, Joined Cases C-226/13, C-245/13, C-247/13 and C-578/13, [2014], 9 December 2014, Court of Justice of the European Union [CJEU]; European Court of Justice [ECJ] [3].

171 *Hellenic Republic v Kuhn* (n 35).

172 See Chapter 3.4.2.3. 'OGH Judgements of 25 April 2017 and 22 January 2019.'

173 See Chapter 3.5.1.2. 'Fahnenbrock v Hellenic Republic.'

174 The Austrian OGH referred the following questions for a preliminary ruling:

> Must Article 7(1)(a) of Regulation [No 1215/2012] be interpreted as meaning that:
> – even in the case – as in the present proceedings – of the repeated contractual transfer of a claim, the place of performance within the meaning of that provision is determined by the first contractual agreement;

> – in the case of the assertion of a claim seeking compliance with the terms of a government bond – such as that issued by the Hellenic Republic in the present case – or seeking compensation for non-fulfilment of that claim, the actual place of performance is established immediately upon the payment of interest from that government bond into an account of a person holding a domestic securities portfolio;
>
> – the fact that the first contractual agreement established a legal place of performance within the meaning of [that agreement], precludes the assumption that the subsequent actual performance of a contract establishes a – further – place of performance within the meaning of [that] provision?

See *Hellenic Republic v Kuhn* (n 35) [26].

175 *Hellenic Republic v Kuhn*, Opinion of the Advocate General, Case C-308/17, ECLI:EU:C:2018:528, [2018], 4 July 2018, Court of Justice of the European Union [CJEU]; European Court of Justice [ECJ] [76]:

> I propose that the Court should answer the questions referred for a preliminary ruling to the effect that an action brought by a natural person who has purchased bonds issued by a Member State, against that Member State, seeking to enforce the initial borrowing terms or seeking damages for the non-fulfilment of those terms, on account of those bonds having been exchanged for bonds of a lesser value, that exchange having been imposed on that natural person by a law, adopted by the national legislature in exceptional circumstances, unilaterally and retrospectively amending the conditions applicable to the bonds by inserting a CAC enabling the majority of the bondholders to impose such an exchange on the minority, does not fall within the scope of 'civil and commercial matters' within the meaning of Article 1(1) of Regulation No 1215/2012.

176 Ibid 78–104.
177 Ibid 110.
178 Ibid 75.
179 *Hellenic Republic v Kuhn* (n 35) [30] (noting that '[the Brussels I Regulation (recast)] Regulation No 1215/2012 is not to extend, in particular, to 'the liability of the State for acts and omissions in the exercise of State authority (*acta iure imperii*)').
180 There was, hence, no need to ascertain whether the place of performance under Article 7 of the Brussels I Regulation (recast) lay in Greece or in Austria and engage with the Advocate General's views on that matter.
181 *Hellenic Republic v Kuhn* (n 35) [32], further noting this:

> the Court has held that that notion is to be regarded as an independent concept to be interpreted by referring, first, to the objectives and scheme of those regulations and, second, to the general principles which stem from the corpus of the national legal systems.

182 Ibid 34.
183 Ibid 37.
184 Ibid.
185 *Mamatas v Greece* (n 87).
186 *GS v Hellenic Republic* (n 120).
187 The other cases reviewed earlier mainly concerned jurisdictional questions.
188 See Chapter 5.2.4. 'Retail Investors.'
189 See Ioannis Glinavos, 'Casenote: Decision 1116–1117/2014 (21.3.14) of the Greek Council of State (Συμβούλιο της Επικρατείας)' SSRN, unpublished manuscript <https://papers.ssrn.com/sol3/papers.cfm?abstract_id=2445568> accessed 2 November 2021.
190 Also see, for an overview of the local case, Hayk Kupelyants, *Sovereign Defaults Before Domestic Courts* (Oxford: Oxford University Press, 2018) 164–165.

191 Ibid. The authors note that two challenges against the PSI had been filed at the ECtHR, both of which had been rejected as inadmissible.
192 Tsibanoulis and Anagnostopoulos (n 44) 10–12. Also see Kupeylants (n 190) 164 et seq.
193 See *Mamatas v Greece* (n 87) [26–36].
194 Ibid. To recall, Greece never technically defaulted but rather implemented a voluntary exchange of debt securities in accordance with the GBA.
195 See Glinavos (n 189) (noting that '[i]t is a fallacy therefore to see the introduction of the CACs and the bondholder votes as distinct phenomena').
196 Following the holdouts' defeat in Greek courts, the only remaining remedy was an appeal to the ECtHR, which has the power to review national courts' decisions and bind the Member States of the Council of Europe, to which Greek belongs, to its decisions.
197 *Mamatas v Greece* (n 87).
198 Ibid 36 (noting that about 1% of Greece's overall debt was held by such natural persons).
199 Ibid.
200 The protection of peaceful enjoyment of possessions in the European human rights framework requires courts to conduct a two-step test: first, did the state interfere with the individual's property rights? Second, did the interference pursue a legitimate (public interest) aim and was it appropriate?
201 *Mamatas v Greece* (n 87) [90–95].
202 Ibid.
203 With regard to the limitation of the protection of property, Article 1 of Protocol No 1 ECHR sets out the following:

> The preceding provisions shall not, however, in any way impair the right of a State to enforce such laws as it deems necessary to control the use of property in accordance with the general interest or to secure the payment of taxes or other contributions or penalties.

See Convention for the Protection of Human Rights and Fundamental Freedoms, as amended by Protocol No 11 (Council of Europe) 213 UNTS 222, ETS No 5, UN Reg No I-2889.
204 Ibid.
205 Ibid 106–120.
206 The securities' real value had been diminishing through the markets' anticipation of a Greek default, thereby reflecting the Greek government's inability to honour its obligations under the original repayment terms.
207 *Mamatas v Greece* (n 87) [118]. Crucially, the ECtHR found that the 'nominal value of a bond was the actual market value at the time of enactment of the impugned legislation [rather than the face value].'
208 Ibid 141–142.
209 See *Fahnenbrock v Hellenic Republic* (n 64).
210 Ibid and Chapter 3.5.1.2. 'Fahnenbrock v Hellenic Republic.'
211 See *Hellenic Republic v Kuhn* (n 35) [32].
212 German courts took a much more critical approach to *Fahnenbrock* than the Austrian OGH, with the BGH or the BVerfG stressing that rules pertaining to the service of documents were irrelevant for the assessment of Greece's immunity while the Austrian court relied on the *Fahnenbrock* ruling for the purpose of assessing Greek immunity.
213 See, for the seminal CJEU judgment on the exercise of public power in the context of the Brussels I Regulation: *LTU v Eurocontrol*, Judgment, reference for a preliminary ruling, Case C-29/76, ECLI:EU:C:1976:137, [1976], 14 October 1976, Court of Justice of the European Union [CJEU]; European Court of Justice [ECJ].

214 See European Convention on State Immunity (Council of Europe) ETS No 74, 1495 UNTS 181, UN Reg No I-25699.
215 See Chapter 3.4.1.2. 'BGH Judgment of 19 December 2017.'
216 See Kupelyants (n 190) 65 (arguing that the distinction between civil and public acts ought to be based on whether governmental measures pertain to foreign law– and domestic law–governed contracts, respectively, which was, however, not the argument made in *Fahnenbrock* and *Kuhn*).
217 *Hellenic Republic v Kuhn*, Opinion of the Advocate General (n 175) [53–54] (further noting that '[the *Fahnenbrock* court] took the view that the return of the request for service by the receiving agency should have been reserved to disputes which, clearly, fall outside the scope definition of civil and commercial matters'). For the BGH decision, see BGH (n 67). This approach also seems to be endorsed by the CJEU in other decisions; see, for example, *Supreme Site Services GmbH and Others v Supreme Headquarters Allied Powers Europe*, Case C-29/76, ECLI:EU:C:2020:638 [2020], 3 September 2020, Court of Justice of the European Union [CJEU]; European Court of Justice [ECJ] [62] ('the privilege of immunity relied on by an international organisation under international law does not automatically preclude the application of Regulation No 1215/2012').
218 *Rina SpA v Ente Registro Italiano Navale*, Opinion of Advocate General, Case C-641/18, ECLI:EU:C:2020:3, [2020], 14 January 2020, Court of Justice of the European Union [CJEU]; European Court of Justice [ECJ]. Also see Gilles Cuniberti, 'Sovereign Immunities and the Scope of the Brussels Ibis Regulation after Rina and SHAPE' (*The European Association of Private International Law*, 9 February 2021) <https://eapil.org/2021/02/09/sovereign-immunities-and-the-scope-of-the-brussels-ibis-regulation-after-rina-and-shape/> accessed 2 November 2021.
219 *Rina SpA v Ente Registro Italiano Navale*, Judgment, Case C-641/18, ECLI:EU:C:2020:349, [2020], 7 May 2020, Court of Justice of the European Union [CJEU]; European Court of Justice [ECJ].
220 As Power notes in his commentary on *Rina*, '[the decision] begs the question could there be a difference between the "public international law" and "EU law" concepts of a sovereign act; it is submitted that there ought to be no difference.' See Vincent Power, 'Ships, Sovereign Immunity and the Subtleties of the Brussels I Regulation: Case C-641/18 LG and Others v Rina SpA, Ente Registro Italiano Navale: Ships, Sovereign Immunity and the Subtleties of Brussels I: Rina Case Note' (2021) 28(3) Maastricht Journal of European and Comparative Law 419, 426.
221 See Cuniberti (n 218).
222 *Fahnenbrock v Hellenic Republic* (n 64) [57].
223 Mankowski (n 143).
224 See Chapter 3.4.3.1. Sovereign Immunity in Domestic Law Restructurings.
225 Recall that, in contrast to most international sovereign debt instruments but like most euro area sovereign debt securities, Greek local law bonds contained *no* contractual choice-of-forum clause.
226 See Chapter 3.4.2.3. OGH Judgements of 25 April 2017 and 22 January 2019.
227 See *Hellenic Republic v Kuhn,* Opinion of the Advocate General (n 175).
228 As required by Recitals (15) and (16) of Brussels I Regulation (recast) (n 113).
229 Moreover, as Poon suggests, linking the place of performance to the governing law would reinforce the 'commercial centre of gravity of the contract' and, thereby, enhance the 'conceptual unity underlying choice-of-law and jurisdiction rules regarding contractual disputes.' Arthur Poon, 'Place of Performance under Article 7(1) Brussels I Recast' (2021) 70(3) International and Comparative Law Quarterly 635, 646–647.
230 For the seminal case, see *Harald Kolassa v Barclays Bank plc*, Case C-375, ECLI:EU:C:2015:37, [2015] 28 January 2015, Court of Justice of the European Union [CJEU]; European Court of Justice [ECJ].

231 It should also be mentioned that the inapplicability of the Brussels I Regulation does not mean that foreign courts may not establish international jurisdiction pursuant to the rules of their domestic civil procedure rules.

232 See *Poštová banka v Greece* (n 36) and Chapter 3.6.1. 'Poštová banka v Hellenic Republic.'

233 See for an overview, Witte (n 40) 337, concluding the following:

> [u]nder substantive European law, the measure was probably lawful; under public international law, it was probably not, but the procedural remedies are limited: Even where a judgment against Greece may be achieved – for which ICSID is the most likely forum – the enforcement of such an award will be problematic.

234 See Astrid Iversen, 'The Future of Involuntary Sovereign Debt Restructurings: *Mamatas and Others v Greece* and the Protection of Holdings of Sovereign Debt Instruments Under the ECHR' (2019) 14(1) Capital Markets Law Journal 34; Yannis Manuelides, 'Using the Local Law Advantage in Today's Eurozone (with Some References to the Republic of Arcadia and the *Mamatas* Judgment)' (2019) 14(4) Capital Markets Law Journal 469, 483–484 (noting that *Mamatas* introduced four different arguments why proportionality was ensured: (i) the GBA did not lead to a total extinction of the claim, (ii) the applicants could have sold their claims, (iii) major international investors demanded the retrofitting of CACs, (iv) Greece struck a fair balance between the public interest and the applicants' individual rights).

235 An interference with property rights is generally deemed lawful if it was 'appropriate for achieving its aim and not disproportionate thereto.' See, for example, *James and ors v United Kingdom*, Merits, App No 8793/79, Case No 3/1984/75/119, A/98, IHRL 55 (ECHR 1986), [1986] ECHR 2, (1986) 8 EHRR 123, [1986] RVR 139, (1987) 75 ILR 396, 21st February 1986, European Court of Human Rights [ECHR]. For a general overview of the ECtHR's standard of review regarding property rights, see Aida Grgir, Zvonimir Mataga, Matija Longar, and Ana Vilfan, 'The Right to Property Under the European Convention on Human Rights' (2007) Human Rights Handbooks of the European Council No 10 <https://rm.coe.int/168007ff55> accessed 2 November 2021.

236 See, for example, *Bramelid and Malmström v Sweden*, Admissibility, App No 8588/79, App No 8589/79, (1982) 29 DR 76, [1982] ECHR 16, (1983) 5 EHRR 249, (1983) 5 EHRR CD278, (1986) 8 EHRR 116, 12 October 1982, European Commission on Human Rights (historical) [ECHR].

237 As Manuelides (n 234) 484 points out, '*Mamatas* notes that without collective action rules, the willingness of stakeholders to participate in the resolution of the crisis diminishes, generating a vicious circle of increased costs for participants, itself acting as a disincentive for participation.'

238 The ECtHR held that Russia had deprived the bondholders of their rights during the debt restructuring of 1998 in *Malysh and ors v Russian Federation*, Admissibility, App No 30280/03, 11 February 2010, European Court of Human Rights [ECHR].

239 A similar logic is, for instance, behind recent legislative initiatives to curb vulture holdout litigation, which limit the amount recoverable from the insolvent debtor state to the price paid by the claimant for the bond on the secondary market. See Chapter 5.2.1. 'Vulture Funds.'

240 See Markus Kerber, 'Sargnägel auf dem Anlegerschutz? – Anmerkungen zur Legalisierung der Zwangsumschuldung der Gläubiger griechischer Staatsanleihen durch die Urteile des EGMR vom 21.7.2016 und des EuGH vom 15.11.2018' (2019) 29 Wirtschafts & Bankrecht 395.

241 Luca Boggio, 'Investors and Sovereign Debt Restructurings: The Protection of Financial Property Before International Courts and Arbitrators' (2018) 15(2) Manchester Journal of International Economic Law 143, 156–157. For a different view, see Belle, who argues that *Mamatas* can be seen as a judicial endorsement of the UNCTAD and

UNGA principles on sovereign debt restructuring; see Alexandre Belle, 'Mamatas and Others v Greece: How the European Court of Human Rights Could Change Sovereign Debt Restructuration' in John D Haskell and Akbar Rasulov (eds), *New Voices and Perspectives in International Economic Law* (Berlin: Springer, 2020) 153–171.

242 See Chapter 3.4.2.4. 'OGH Judgment of 21 February 2020' and Chapter 3.4.1.3. 'BVerfG Judgment of 6 May 2020,' respectively.

243 See, in particular, Article 5 of the Organic Law, which stipulates that '[t]he property is inviolable. An expropriation against the owner's will may only be justified in circumstances and conditions stipulated by law.' See Austrian Organic Law on the General Rights of Citizens of 21 December 1867 (*Staatsgrundgesetz über die allgemeinen Rechte der Staatsbürger*) (Austria [at]).

244 It should be mentioned that the Austrian OGH, in addition to rejecting the holdouts' suits on the basis of the ECHR (endorsing *Mamatas*) and the GRC, held that the Greek measures did not violate Austria's *ordre public*. See Chapter 3.4.2.4. 'OGH Judgment of 21 February 2020.'

245 The judgment, of course, raises intricate questions that go beyond the scope of this book pertaining to the relationship between the prohibition of monetary financing under Article 123 TFEU and the Eurosystem's financial independence and discretion to incur losses from its monetary policy operations. See, for an overview of the debate, Sebastian Grund and Filip Grle, 'The European Central Bank's Public Sector Purchase Programme (PSPP), the Prohibition of Monetary Financing and Sovereign Debt Restructuring Scenarios' (2016) 41(6) European Law Review 781.

246 See Buchheit and Gulati (n 34).

247 See ECB, 'ECB Announces Expanded Asset Purchase Programme' (22 January 2015) <www.ecb.europa.eu/press/pr/date/2015/html/pr150122_1.en.html> accessed 2 November 2021.

248 At least with regard to the ECB's Outright Monetary Transactions (OMT), the ECB programme behind former ECB President Draghi's famous 'whatever it takes' speech, *Accorinti* underscored that the ECB's pari passu pledge may not be invoked by Greek bondholders because it was both made ex post facto and since the situations were not comparable. See *Accorinti v ECB* (n 23) [102].

249 See *Nausicaa Anadyomène and Banque d'escompte v ECB*, Judgment, Case T-749/15, [2017], 24 January 2017, Court of Justice of the European Union [CJEU]; European General Court [EGC] (reiterating that 'by purchasing Greek debt instruments, the ECB and the national central banks acted in the exercise of their basic duties, with the aim of safeguarding price stability and the sound administration of monetary policy').

250 *Weiss and ors*, Judgment, Case C-493/17, ECLI:EU:C:2018:1000, 11 December 2018, Court of Justice of the European Union [CJEU]; European Court of Justice [ECJ].

251 To this end, Buchheit and Gulati (n 34) 66 warn that 'investors will begin demanding higher coupons to compensate for their increasingly subordinated position in bonds that ostensibly benefit from inclusion in an ECB bond buying program' and that '[o]nce the market concludes that a debt restructuring is likely, therefore, an attempt by the ECB to depress coupon levels through bond purchases may end up increasing coupon levels.'

252 *Marfin Investment Group Holdings SA, Alexandros Bakatselos and others v Republic of Cyprus*, ICSID Case No ARB/13/27, Notice of Dispute (23 January 2013) (not publicly available); *Poštová banka v Greece* (n 36).

253 In sum, Greece signed 38 BITs, including BITs with Cyprus and Germany but excluding some important advanced economies. See Sandrock (n 26) 526.

254 Another explanation may be that specialized investors targeted English law–governed bonds, under which they received full pay out. See Chapter 3.3.3. 'Restructuring Foreign Law Bonds.'

255 Compare, for example, 'Article 1(1) Greek-Slovak BIT of 1991' <https://investmentpolicy.unctad.org/international-investment-agreements/treaties/otheriia/1815/

greece–slovakia-bit-1991-> accessed 2 November 2021, which states that 'investment' means every kind of asset and in particular, c) loans, claims to money, or to any performance under contract having a financial value. The Chinese-Greek BIT, for instance, uses exactly the same definition of 'investment'; see Chinese-Greek BIT of 1992 <https://edit.wti.org/document/show/59648dac-d963-4e94-92a2-dcfadbeb86c5?textBlockId=50709ec6-3dce-4619-aaae-e45899706555&page=1> accessed 2 November 2021.

256 See Michael Waibel, *Sovereign Debt Before International Courts and Tribunals* (Cambridge: Cambridge University Press, 2011).

257 *Poštová banka v Greece* (n 36).

258 Ibid 20. The bank had acquired five different series of Greek government bonds with a face value of roughly EUR500 million between January and April 2010, all of which were governed by Greek law and had no CACs at the time of issuance.

259 Ibid.

260 Ibid 1–4.

261 Ibid 17.

262 Ibid.

263 Claimants noted that 'every ICSID tribunal that has considered the issue has held that government debt instruments purchased in the secondary market constitute an "investment" under the ICSID Convention'; see ibid 144.

264 *Poštová banka v Greece* (n 36) [127]. It was also disputed between the parties whether or not the purchase on the secondary market had an impact on the tribunal's jurisdiction due to the lack of a direct contractual relationship. Moreover, the respondent asserted that the tribunal lacks jurisdiction *ratione personae*. See ibid 134. Also compare, for an overview of all Greece's arguments against the jurisdiction, Jonathan Chevry, '*Poštová banka, a.s. and ISTROKAPITAL SE v Hellenic Republic*, ICSID Case No ARB/13/8 (Poštová banka v Greece)' (2016) 15 World Trade Review 169, 171.

265 *Poštová banka v Greece* (n 36) [127].

266 Article 1 of the Slovakia-Greece BIT comprised a (non-exhaustive) list of what rights are to be considered an 'investment': 'the definition of "investment" contained "every kind of asset and in particular, though not exclusively, . . . (c) loans, claims to money or to any performance under contract having a financial value."' See ibid.

267 Ibid 276.

268 Ibid 301, 308. To this end, the applicable BIT clearly differed from the Italy-Argentina BIT that the *Abaclat* tribunal relied on, which had included 'obligations, private or public titles' as investments. See earlier *Abaclat and ors v Argentina*, Decision on jurisdiction and admissibility, ICSID Case No ARB/07/5, IIC 504 (2011), despatched 4 August 2011, World Bank; International Centre for Settlement of Investment Disputes [ICSID].

269 *Poštová banka v Greece* (n 36) 341–343.

270 Ibid 265.

271 Ibid 339–340. The tribunal stated this:

> the specific use of the term 'debentures' only for debt issued by companies in Article 1(1)(b) of the Slovakia-Greece BIT and the specific use of the term 'loans' in another section of the Slovakia-Greece BIT, Article 1(1)(c), together with the lack of reference to any sort of public indebtedness, leads the Tribunal to consider that the Parties to the treaty did not intend to treat government securities, such as the GGBs, as investments for purposes of the BIT.

272 Ibid 357.

273 Ibid 371.

274 Ibid 359, 369. According to the tribunal, 'under an "objective" approach, an investment risk would be an operational risk and not a . . . sovereign risk,' which 'includes

the risk of interference of the Government in a contract or any other relationship, which risk is not specific to public bonds.'

275 *Poštová Banka AS and Istrokapital SE v The Hellenic Republic,* Decision on Poštová Banka's application for partial annulment of the award, ICSID Case no ARB/13/8, IIC 854 (2016), despatched 29 September 2016, United Nations [UN]; World Bank; International Centre for Settlement of Investment Disputes [ICSID].

276 Ibid 160.

277 *Abaclat v Argentina* (n 268).

278 *Ambiente Ufficio SpA v Argentina,* Decision on jurisdiction and admissibility, ICSID Case No ARB/08/9, IIC 576 (2013), 8 February 2013, World Bank; International Centre for Settlement of Investment Disputes [ICSID].

279 *Poštová banka v Greece* (n 36).

280 Perhaps more revealingly, the *Poštová banka* tribunal concluded that '[r]isk is inherent in life and cannot per se qualify what is an investment.' See ibid 367. In that finding, it borrowed heavily from the PCA award in *Romak v Uzbekistan*; see *Romak SA (Switzerland) v Uzbekistan,* Final Award, ICGJ 462 (PCA 2009), PCA Case No AA280, 26 November 2009, Permanent Court of Arbitration [PCA]. For a discussion of the risk-sharing criterion of the *Salini* test, see Chapter 2.3.2.2.3. 'Risk-Sharing.'

281 The pertinent BIT included the term 'obligations.' Thus, the tribunal in *Ambiente Ufficio v Argentina* (n 278) [491] held that 'the Parties sought to actually exclude [certain] instruments from the scope of the application of the BIT, they would have had to say so explicitly.'

282 *Poštová banka v Greece* (n 36) [314]. See Kei Nakajima, 'Parallel Universes of Investment Protection? A Divergent Finding on the Definition of Investment in the ICSID Arbitration on Greek Sovereign Debts' (2017) 15(3) The Law & Practice of International Courts and Tribunals 472, 482.

283 *Poštová banka v Greece* (n 36) [343].

284 Ibid 291.

285 Ibid 348 (noting that 'Poštová banka holds a right in a title – a right in rem – against the Participants, and would have rights against Greece, not arising from a contract with Respondent, but from the title and the consequences provided therein').

286 See Chapter 3.4. 'Holdout Creditor Litigation After Greece in Foreign Courts.'

287 See, for example, Edwin Borchard and Justus S Hotchkiss, *State Insolvency and Foreign Bondholders: General Principles* (New Haven: Yale University Press, 1951) 23 (noting that '[t]he principal document containing the terms of the contractual relationship between the debtor government and the individual lender is the bond'); Marcel Kahan, 'Rethinking Corporate Bonds: The Trade-Off Between Individual and Collective Rights' (2002) 77 New York University Law Review 1040, 1045 ('[b]eyond their contractual rights, bondholders-as creditors and security holders-have rights that arise under statutory and common law').

288 *Poštová banka v Greece* (n 36) [345].

289 See *Argentina v NML Capital Limited,* Brief of Amicus Curiae Euroclear Bank SA/NV in Support of Petitioner, Docket No 13–990, 24 March 2014, United States; Supreme Court [US].

290 See *Abaclat v Argentina* (n 268) [319] (stating that '[i]t is undisputed that Claimants, as owners of security entitlements, have a potential contract claim against Argentina for payment of the principal amount and interest of such security entitlement' and that '[t]his relationship is of a private and contractual nature, subject to the terms and conditions of the bonds, which vary depending on the bond series').

291 Francesco Montanaro, 'Case Comment *Poštová Banka SA and Istrokapital SE v Hellenic Republic* – Sovereign Bonds and the Puzzling Definition of "Investment" in International Investment Law' (2015) 30(3) ICSID Review 549, 554.

292 *Salini Costruttori SpA and Italstrade SpA v Morocco,* Decision on jurisdiction, ICSID Case No ARB/00/4, IIC 206 (2001), (2004) 6 ICSID Rep 398, (2004) 6 ICSID

Rep 400, (2003) 42 ILM 609, (2002) 129 Clunet 196, 16 July 2001, despatched 23 July 2001, United Nations [UN]; World Bank; International Centre for Settlement of Investment Disputes [ICSID].

293 See Chapter 2.3.2.2.1. 'Contribution to the Development of the Host State.'

294 Emmanuel Gaillard, 'Identify or Define? Reflections on the Evolution of the Concept of Investment in ICSID Practice' in Christina Binder, Ursula Kriebaum, August Reinisch, and Stephan Wittich (eds), *International Investment Law for the 21st Century: Essays in Honour of Christoph Schreuer* (Oxford: Oxford University Press, 2009) 403.

295 The fact that Argentina ultimately settled with Italian bondholders who obtained ICSID awards showed that arbitration can serve as a powerful avenue for indirect sovereign debt enforcement.

296 See, for example, Nakajima (n 282) and Montanaro (n 291).

297 *Abaclat v Argentina* (n 36) [50].

298 *Ambiente Ufficio SpA v Argentina*, Decision on jurisdiction and admissibility, ICSID Case No ARB/08/9, IIC 576 (2013), 8 February 2013, World Bank; International Centre for Settlement of Investment Disputes [ICSID].

299 To this end, a more profound analysis of Article 25 ICSID Convention in the sovereign debt context could have contributed to establishing a bright line rule.

300 In that vein, Reinisch notes that '[the] rapid increase in investment arbitration has led to a situation where inconsistent outcomes are no longer a merely theoretical threat.' See Reinisch, 'The Future of Investment Arbitration' in Binder et al (n 294) 906.

4 Holdouts in Foreign Versus Domestic Law Debt Restructurings

Walking Back from Argentina and Greece

4.1. Introduction

As the previous chapters showed, the two largest sovereign defaults in history led to a copious amount of decisions by domestic courts and international tribunals, many of which will shape the resolution of holdout problems in sovereign debt restructurings in the years to come. Since almost all legal disputes connected to Argentina and Greece have now been settled, this chapter zooms in on some of the fundamental legal doctrines and principles, and compares how they have been addressed across jurisdictions. Specifically, it discusses the following: (i) the role of governing law in debt restructurings; (ii) the legal basis for sovereign debt agreements, distinguishing between statute and contract-based instruments; (iii) the current state of sovereign immunity in debt matters; and (iv) the protection of sovereign creditors' (property) rights.[1]

4.2. The Role of Governing Law in Sovereign Debt Restructurings

The vast majority of bonds issued today by sovereigns across all income levels are governed by the issuer's own laws. While the market for *international* (foreign law) sovereign debt securities has a volume of roughly USD1 trillion, the total outstanding volume of domestic securities is about 40 times as large.[2] At the same time, since domestic debt problems may be resolved by the debtor through a host of economic, financial, and legal means, holdout problems tend to be significantly more prominent in the restructuring of foreign law debt.[3]

As the analysis of holdout litigation in the previous chapters suggests, governing law became the decisive issue for holdouts' chances of success. Like many emerging economies, Argentina had sought to reap the full benefits of financial globalization: the government went on international roadshows, waived its immunity from suit and enforcement, and agreed to have disputes settled in foreign courts. And indeed, most foreign courts ruled against Argentina, denying the legality of its restructuring measures as a matter of the lex fori.[4] While some courts accepted public policy defences[5] or constrained the attachment of Argentine assets in their respective jurisdictions,[6] the majority of courts ruled in the creditors' favour. By

DOI: 10.4324/9781003361879-4

contrast, Argentina's local courts, notably the Supreme Court in the *Galli* case, endorsed the restructuring measures taken by the legislative and executive branch as a matter of domestic law.[7]

For Greece, the role of governing law became particularly obvious with regard to the divergent treatment of local and foreign law bonds. To be sure, Greece opted for an approach that ended up being more effective in curbing potential confrontations with creditors than Argentina. Yet it faced the same conundrum: the threat that foreign courts, or investment arbitration tribunals for that matter, would issue orders in the holdouts' favour, possibly resulting in asset seizure motions and Greece's exclusion from international credit markets for a sustained period of time. With respect to its domestic law bonds, Greece treaded less carefully and fully capitalized on the local law advantage when it retrofitted the collective action mechanism.[8]

In the post-Greek PSI litigation, many courts were for the first time enmeshed in sovereign debt litigation, which resulted in inconsistencies and, at times, warped legal opinions.[9] After years of judicial crisscross, a consensus seemed to emerge that as the masters of its own laws and statutes, Greece ought to be immune. Those courts that did delve into the substantive law aspects of bondholder protection granted a considerable margin of discretion. Perhaps unsurprisingly, investors henceforth demanded that Greece no longer use its own laws to issue public debt.[10]

As discussed in the subsequent sections, the foreign/domestic law dichotomy has additional legal implications, affecting, in particular, the application of the sovereign immunity doctrine[11] as well as the protection of substantive creditor rights.[12]

4.3. The Legal Basis for Sovereign Debt Instruments: Contracts Versus Statutes

Another important structural legal issue, which is usually linked to governing law but mostly overlooked in the sovereign debt literature, is the basis for public debt: sovereigns may rely on either a contract *or* a law, decree, or order as the legal vehicle for their debt issuance.[13] For instance, while the terms and conditions of Greek (local law) government bonds were enshrined in a Greek statute, those applicable to Argentine (foreign) instruments were stipulated in a contract.[14]

Much of the international sovereign bond market (i.e., foreign law governed bonds) has a contractual scaffolding.[15] However, there are two categories of issuers that predominantly use public law rather than private law to regulate the terms and conditions of their sovereign debt instruments:[16]

- First, the most advanced economies (elite issuers) are so creditworthy that the legal terms under which they issue their securities are largely irrelevant for investors. They can rely on rudimentary domestic statutes as the legal basis for their sovereign bonds. While even then, the legal relationship between the issuer and its creditors has private law aspects, these are often not spelt out in the legal documentation, which tends to be either non-existent or very cursory.[17] However, there is no strict rule, and sovereigns are free to choose whatever combination of different legal variables (statute/contract/governing law/listing location).[18]

- Second, lower-rated sovereigns issuing local currency bonds may, too, rely on laws and regulations rather than contracts.[19] The pertinent budgetary laws may authorize the finance ministries or debt management units to issue government bonds, without necessarily prescribing the holders' rights and remedies in the event of a default.

As mentioned earlier, Greece, at least until the implementation of the PSI, mostly relied on statutory rules to finance its budgetary activities: it issued its sovereign bonds based on a statute, Greek law 2198/1994.[20] This meant that the Greek local law bonds subject to the 2012 PSI did not feature any of the standard contract provisions used in international sovereign bonds, ranging from negative pledge clauses, sovereign immunity waivers, choice-of-forum provisions to definitions of default, acceleration clauses, and – most notably – CACs.[21]

It also meant that court had no contract to review when holdouts challenged the debt restructuring, instead relying on the interpretation of *general* principles of public and private law applicable to financial obligations.[22] Of course, this does not mean that statute-based (or public law-based) instruments may not incorporate contractual or considerations of contract law. Rather, the private law obligations in the debtor-creditor relationship are created by an act of public law, as a consequence of which, public law plays a much greater role in the court's review.[23]

Against this backdrop, it may be argued that the legal structure of public indebtedness is relevant for the design and success of a restructuring operation. Indeed, in none of the post-Greek PSI cases could holdout creditors successfully invoke *contractual* provisions. Rather, their claim was that their right to be repaid in full and on time, and thus, their legitimate expectations under general law were violated by the CAC Retrofit. Moreover, the GBA with which the clauses were retrofitted filled a legal void, as Greek government bonds were essentially based on a simple IOU that lacked any details on the rights and obligations of the respective parties. By refraining from ex ante committing to treating bondholders in a certain way (eg, by providing them with certain guarantees), the issuer retains maximum flexibility should a debt restructuring become necessary.[24] This is because from a civil procedure law perspective, at least in the jurisdictions reviewed in this book, the assessment whether the state has exercised public powers, and may, thus, be protected by adjudicatory immunity, comes *before* any review on the merits.[25]

Conversely, in foreign law sovereign debt restructurings, the contract versus statute distinction remains of lesser relevance. Like the securities of most emerging market issuers, Argentina's bonds were contract-based and foreign law governed. Courts in New York City, and to some extent those in England, made their commitment to enforcing contractual provisions – letter by letter, word by word – very clear.[26] Arguably, the existence of a contractual commitment to the bondholders meant that a lex specialis existed in the form of the contract provisions that courts could turn to. Other than in the post-Greek litigation, the general rules of private and private law were only applicable as lex generalis to fill gaps in the contracts.[27]

4.4. Sovereign Immunity Revisited

The principle of sovereign immunity remains the central legal doctrine in the context of sovereign debt restructuring and litigation.[28] As Viterbo notes, '[o]nly state immunity still remains at the core of every sovereign debt restructuring process.'[29] Argentina and Greece were no different.

A closer look at the judgements in the wake of the two debt workouts reveals the continuous change that the immunity doctrine has been subject to over the past few decades. With some notable exceptions, the judicial review of Argentina's approach to resolving its debt crisis furthered the erosion of state immunity in the sovereign debt context, while the judicial reluctance to review the Greek Retrofit on immunity grounds reinvigorated the doctrine.[30]

The emerging dichotomy between state immunity in the foreign (Argentine) versus a domestic law (Greek) context warrants further explanation.

The first crucial difference between securities issued by Argentina and Greece, respectively, was that the latter lacked immunity waivers.[31] Thus, when adjudicating holdout disputes, German and Austrian courts, and at least indirectly European courts, had to assess state immunity against the backdrop of public international law and its transposition into the respective national legal frameworks.[32] In contrast to the US and the UK, where a number of seminal judgements in the 1980s and 1990s delineated the scope of state immunity,[33] judges in the European courts had little to no experience with legal challenges to government debt restructuring measures and especially such pertaining to securities governed by the issuer's own laws.[34]

The second and related key issue was the mixed activity conundrum or the once a trader always a trader principle, which I touched upon in a previous chapter.[35] Litigation after Argentina and Greece showed that the level of judicial cross-fertilization remains relatively low in this contentious area of law:

- With respect to public debt governed by New York or English law, courts in both jurisdictions typically prohibit states from ex post immunizing sovereign bond issuance activities (i.e., *acta iure gestionis*) through sovereign measures, such as legislation or executive order. Similarly, when the German BGH had weighed in on Argentina's moratorium on repayment obligations to bondholders that were governed by German law, it stuck closely to the strand of US jurisprudence on sovereign immunity and essentially endorsed the once a trader always a trader doctrine promulgated by US and English courts. This view arguably reflects Article 10 of the UNCSI, a Treaty that is widely considered customary law since the ICJ's ruling *Germany v Italy* case in 2012.[36] At the same time, the French *Cour de Cassation*[37] (on execution immunity) as well as the Italian *Corte Suprema di Cassazione*[38] (on adjudicatory immunity) deviated from the text – and arguably the spirit – of the UNCSI with regard to mixed activities in the sovereign debt context.

- For domestic government debt restructurings, the Greek PSI suggested that the scope of the immunity defence was even more ill-defined. Several lower German courts and the highest Austrian court followed the Anglo-Saxon view on adjudicatory immunity, holding that states' commercial activities, such as bond issuances, may not ex post become protected from suit by virtue of sovereign intervention. Thus, they made no distinction between the restructuring of foreign and domestic law instruments.[39] However, the German Federal Court of Justice and, in later decision, also the Austrian OGH refuted the plaintiffs' case on the grounds of sovereign immunity in Greece.[40] What role the CJEU's recent jurisprudence played remains ambiguous, as discussed earlier.[41] It is evident, however, that retroactive legislative changes to local law debt instruments attacked in Europe are most likely not subject to review on the merits in foreign courts.[42]

In policymaking circles, the sovereign immunity doctrine, too, remains the subject of much debate. For instance, the UN General Assembly's 2015 Resolution on the Basic Principles on Sovereign Debt Restructuring Processes (in Principle 6) called for exceptions to sovereign immunity to be interpreted restrictively.[43] Whether and how the Resolution and its Principles may be transposed into hard law remains to be seen; yet the lack of G7 support for the Basic Principles meant that the process has stalled. What the Resolution, which was supported by 136 states, certainly rendered evident was that immunity will continue to be a subject of great interest to debtors, creditors, and the international community more widely.

Going forward, policy efforts should be directed towards the codification of the sovereign immunity doctrine with a view at reconciling the interests of actors involved in debt restructurings. Crucially, in drawing the lessons from the two restructurings, policy and lawmakers ought to take into proper account the growing dichotomy in the sovereign immunity doctrine between foreign and domestic law debt restructurings, including clarifying international treaties, such as the UNCSI as well as European and national laws on state immunity. While both a reversal or a reinforcement of the recent trends on sovereign immunity and sovereign debt may be justified as a matter of international law, only a transparent and honest dialogue at the local and international level will contribute to a more predictable sovereign debt resolution framework.

4.5. The Protection of Sovereign Creditors' Property Rights

If creditors clear the immunity (from suit) hurdle, the final yet pivotal legal question is whether the sovereign debtor's interference with the creditors' right to repayment was lawful or gives rise to compensatory claims.[44] As so often in the realm of international financial law, the short answer is that it depends.

As discussed in Chapter 1, restructurings may occur with (voluntary) or without (involuntary) the consent of all contracting parties – it is the latter that usually results in a plethora of legal consequences, including holdout litigation.[45] An involuntary restructuring usually includes changes to the payment terms of the respective debt instruments. In most jurisdictions, the unilateral suspension or modification of government borrowing agreements is confined to exceptional circumstances.[46] For instance, the US Supreme Court, in one of its famous Gold Clause cases, provided that Congress may not 'alter or repudiate the substance of its own engagements when it has borrowed money under its constitutional authority.'[47] Similar protections against the interference with pecuniary rights of private individuals by state action are ubiquitous across the globe.[48] Different procedural and substantive law defences against challenges to restructuring measures have been tried and tested over the years, increasingly without success.[49]

The analysis of case law in the aftermath of Argentina and Greece suggests that no right to restructure exists. States may, nevertheless, execute restructurings, and courts may approve of or not interfere with them; but there are neither customary nor codified norms that provide countries with protection from legal action. US courts, under whose roofs much of the litigation has taken place, have long done away with the act of state doctrine,[50] which protects certain state actions from foreign court review, or the comity defence, according to which courts can defer to the executive branch to assess whether it accepts foreign restructuring measures.[51] Pacta sunt servanda reigns supreme in New York, but also in London, shoring up the world financial centres' position as safe havens for investors.

The contemporary view on the legality of interfering with private creditor claims seems to be most accurately captured by the German Federal Constitutional Court, which concluded in 2019 that international law still lacks a framework for sovereign insolvency that would bind domestic courts.[52] Neither the initiatives by UNCTAD[53] and the UN[54] nor the widespread use of CACs are, as a matter of (German) law, considered sufficient proof of a rule in customary international law or under the general principles of law that would constrain domestic courts from upholding the sovereign's repayment promise. Accordingly, leaving aside the complexities relating to state immunity, the suspension or repudiation of government debt obligations continues to be qualified as breach of the underlying agreement, even if the government's actions were deemed financially and economically necessary by the international community.[55]

Many legal scholars have been concerned with judges' reluctance to protect states from holdout litigation and sketched out pathways to better accommodate human rights and related concerns in national court decisions on sovereign debt matters.[56] Goldmann notably argues that respecting human rights in sovereign debt workouts does not amount to denying the validity of contractual commitments.[57] Similarly, the necessity defence has been discussed extensively in scholarship as a legal means to curb creditor litigation and again gained centre stage in the context of the COVID-19 pandemic.[58] Numerous proposals exist on the integration of the odious debt doctrine into national court practice.[59] Most scholarly proposals were all but ignored by courts.

The *Mamatas* case before the ECtHR marked a cesura, however. It defined a new standard regarding the protection of investors' property rights, adopting a risk-based approach that balances the need for a restructuring with the creditors' individual rights.[60] The precedent will guide national courts in all the 46 member countries of the Council of Europe should they be confronted with sovereign bondholder claims in the future. It may even have repercussions beyond Europe's borders, especially given the scarcity of judgements on the legitimacy of government interference with creditor rights.[61]

One caveat should be made: *Mamatas* concerned a local law restructuring. In a foreign law–related debt workout, it is usually not the legislature or executive of the state that has jurisdiction (eg, England) which also enacts the pertinent debt restructuring measures but that of the debtor country (eg, Greece).[62] Whether, in this scenario, the ECtHR would have reached a different conclusion as a matter of substantive law remains speculative. The Greek government's decision not to take a chance with creditors holding its English law instruments appears wise even after *Mamatas*, for English court judgements relating to restructuring measures by foreign sovereigns have never been successfully challenged in the ECtHR.[63]

Yet another perennial challenge for (quasi-)constitutional courts that adjudicate fundamental right disputes, such as the ECtHR, is to maintain their reputation as independent and legitimate arbiters when they become entrenched in politically loaded and delicate issues like sovereign default. Put in a slightly exaggerated way, what if the repercussions of reaching a certain judicial result would be so vast and grave that they endanger the economic survival of a nation? What if the ECtHR would have required Greece to compensate tens of thousands of bondholders, first those who sued, and later copycat litigants, effectively resulting in another judicially-sanctioned sovereign default?

To claim that judges, even if they reside far away from the nation's capital over whose fate they decide, render decisions entirely outside the political, economic, and societal perimeter would likely go too far. As Vanberg and Gulati note with respect to the *Mamatas* case, '[e]ven if the judges believed that the government had blatantly violated the rule of law, they could not expect that a decision to declare the restructuring invalid would be honoured.'[64] Indeed, a court's strength and effectiveness as a dispute settlement authority for holdout litigation ought to be judged by its ability to render both positive and *negative* decisions. As noted earlier, however, a ruling the holdouts' favour would have brought devastating political and economic implications for Greece and EU policymakers, perhaps even the country's exit from the currency union.[65]

Against this backdrop, the SDNY's and other US federal courts' fortitude in supporting Argentine bondholders' quest for financial satisfaction, which did in fact culminate in Argentina's default in 2014, seems to have supported a contentious understanding of the law. Compared to the blunt instrument of contract enforcement at all costs and by all means, the approach taken by the ECtHR provides a considerably more compelling blueprint for the resolution of future holdout disputes. This is not to say that cases like *NML* or *Mamatas* should always be decided in favour of the restructuring state. What matters is that the legal framework employed to adjudicate such complex and potentially far-reaching disputes is both robust and intelligent.[66]

Notes

1 Another legal issue that remains critical in sovereign debt litigation is that of jurisdiction. However, most of the questions relating to the jurisdiction of US and English courts have been answered by courts before Argentina in the wake of the Latin American debt crises of the 1980s. See William Harvey Reeves, 'The Foreign Sovereign Before United States Courts' (1970) 38(3) Fordham Law Review 455. Complicated jurisdictional issues in the domestic law context are discussed earlier in the chapter on the Greek PSI; see notably Chapter 3.5.3.3. 'Jurisdiction Under the Brussels I Regulation.'

2 According to 2020 data by the BIS, the size of the global market for central government *domestic* currency debt amounted to USD43.8 trillion while that for *foreign* currency instruments, USD1.2 trillion. See BIS, 'Central and Government Debt Securities Markets' (2020) <www.bis.org/statistics/c4.pdf> accessed 2 November 2021.

3 For different methods to reduce domestic currency debt, see Carmen Reinhart and Kenneth Rogoff, 'The Forgotten History of Domestic Debt' (2011) 121(552) The Economic Journal 319.

4 See Chapter 2.2. 'Holdout Litigation After Argentina.'

5 See, for example, *Borri v Argentina*, Request for a ruling on jurisdiction, Case No 11225, Order No 6532/2005, ILDC 296 (IT 2005), (2005) 88 Riv Dir Int 856, 27 May 2005, Italy; Supreme Court of Cassation, discussed earlier in Chapter 2.2.3. 'Interim Conclusions: Enforcing Sovereign Debt in Foreign Courts.'

6 See, for example, the French courts' broad interpretation of enforcement immunity earlier in Chapter 2.2.3.2.1. 'The Immunity of Public Claims from Creditor Attachment.'

7 See *Galli, Hugo Gabriel y otro c. Poder Ejecutivo Nacional s/amparo*, Judgment, G 2181 XXXIX, 5 April 2005, Argentina; National Supreme Court of Justice [CSJN]. Also see Gabriel Manzo, 'Enforceability of Judgments Against Sovereign States: Critical Analysis of the NML vs. Argentina Injunction' (2018) 14(2) Revista Direito GV 682, 699 (noting that '[in *Galli*] the CSJN . . . considered constitutional the faculties of the State with respect to its power to suspend payments of its sovereign debt and to restructure it in contexts of extreme economic crisis').

8 Mitu Gulati and Lee Buchheit, 'Use of the Local Law Advantage in the Restructuring of European Sovereign Bonds' (2018) 3(2) University of Bologna Law Review 172.

9 See Chapter 3.4. 'Holdout Creditor Litigation After Greece in Foreign Courts.'

10 Similarly, in its 2019 restructuring, Barbados exchanged its local law bonds for new bonds governed by English law; see Barbados, 'Barbados-Law Bonds Invitation Memorandum' (5 November 2019) <www.oblible.com/Prospectus/www.oblible.com__USP48864AQ80.pdf> accessed 2 November 2021.

11 See Chapter 4.4. 'Sovereign Immunity Revisited.'

12 See Chapter 4.5. 'The Protection of Sovereign Borrowers' Property Rights.'

13 See Matthias Audit, 'Sovereign Bonds by Law: Can a State Debt be Non-Contractual?' (Presentation at the Interdisciplinary Sovereign Debt Research and Management Conference, Geneva, 5–6 October 2017) <www.dropbox.com/s/5wv34c4cxz0u8sj/3C_Matthias%20Audit_Debtcon2%20-%20Non%20contractual%20state%20debt%20%206%20oct%202017.%20V3%20pptx.pdf?dl=0> accessed 2 November 2021. A similar study was carried out by Gulati and Triantis; see Mitu Gulati and George Triantis, 'Contracts Without Law: Sovereign Versus Corporate Debt' (2007) 75 University of Cincinnati Law Review 977.

14 See Chapter 4.3. 'The Legal Basis for Sovereign Debt Instruments: Contracts Versus Statutes.' Bossu and Awadzi posit that securities often rely on a combination between public and private law, though the boundaries are often fluid. See Wouter Bossu and Elsie Addo Awadzi, 'Private Law Underpinnings of Public Debt Securities Markets' (2014) 18 Uniform Law Review 564.

15 Following is under the IMF's own policies:

> international sovereign bonds comprise bonds issued or guaranteed by the government or the central bank, and which are either (i) governed by a law other than the law of the sovereign issues, or (ii) subject to the jurisdiction of a court outside the territory of the issuer.

See IMF, 'Sovereign Debt Restructuring – Recent Developments and Implications for the Fund's Legal and Policy Framework' (26 April 2013) 13 <www.imf.org/external/np/pp/eng/2013/042613.pdf> accessed 2 November 2021.

16 As Bossu and Awadzi note, some issuers 'grant their contractual terms and conditions an explicit public law underpinning' and that 'in France, the characteristics of public debt securities, including the terms of the securities and payment of coupons, are defined by a (public law) decree issued by the Minister of Finance.' Bossu and Awadzi, (n 14), 571.

17 See Wouter Bossu, Cory Hillier, and Wolfgang Bergthaler, 'Local Currency Bond Markets Law Reform: A Methodology for Emerging Markets and Developing Economies' (2020) IMF Working Paper Series WP/20/258, 22–23 <www.imf.org/en/Publications/WP/Issues/2020/11/20/Local-Currency-Bond-Markets-Law-Reform-A-Methodology-for-Emerging-Markets-and-Developing-49905> accessed 2 November 2021 (noting that '[i]n many countries, local currency government bonds are not subject to a specific and well-calibrated contractual framework').

18 For example, Italy and Austria, two elite issuers, use contract-based bonds governed by domestic law bonds in addition to their statute-based bonds. See for Italy: The Republic of Italy, 'USD 2,000,000,000, 5.375% Notes due 2017' (2007) Prospectus Supplement to Prospectus dated 18 January 2006 <www.bourse.lu/security/US465410BS63/115975> accessed 2 November 2021. For Austria, see, for example, The Republic of Austria, 'EUR 30,000,000 Medium Term Note Programme for the issue of Notes from 7 Days to 70 Years from the Date of Issue' (*Offering Circular*, 19 December 2012) <www.bourse.lu/security/US052591AT11/83620> accessed 2 November 2021.

19 See Bossu et al (n 17).

20 See, for example, *Mamatas v Greece,* App No 63066/14, App No 64297/14, App No 66106/14, 21st July 2016, European Court of Human Rights [ECHR] [8].

21 The Greek bonds governed by English law very well did contain these provisions, reflecting a different market standard for international bonds. See Chapter 3.3.3. 'Restructuring Foreign Law Bonds.'

22 For instance, the fact that legislation governing Greek government bonds did not explicitly stipulate which forum had jurisdiction over bondholder challenges allowed foreign courts to speculate, ultimately fostering a considerable degree of uncertainty that lasted for several years after the PSI. See Chapter 3.5.3.2. 'The (Tenuous) Link Between Sovereign Immunity and Jurisdiction Under EU Law.'

23 See Bossu and Awadzi (n 14) 571 (noting that 'while State borrowing agreements and the resulting credit claims may have public law features, they are also, at least to a certain extent, governed by private contract law').

24 In this regard, Weidemaier discusses whether CACs in euro area sovereign bonds, which became mandatory under the ESM Treaty in 2013, have narrowed the options for a sovereign to restructure its local law debt stock. He concludes that even if this were the case, the risk of debtor opportunism, that is, that the sovereign abuses its local law advantage, remains low. See Mark Weidemaier, 'Restructuring Euro Area Sovereign Debt: Have the Options Narrowed?' (2020) 6(1) Journal of Financial Regulation 125.

25 As we have seen time again in the cases discussed in Chapter 2 and Chapter 3, substantive law questions concerning bondholders' substantive claims are only dealt with

after all procedural issues have been addressed and, therefore, in many instances, not at all.

26 As Chapter 2 showed, holdout creditors banked on and leveraged these provisions against Argentina in courts around the world. Moreover, fearing that holders of English law securities issued by Greece would do the same, the Greek government refrained from suspending or otherwise interfering with creditors' contractual rights and instead paid them back in full.

27 One example for such gap filling rules is civil procedure law, which in the *NML* case, for instance, allowed US courts to grant an injunction as enforcement remedy, even if such tool was not provided for in the contracts. See Chapter 2.2.1.1.3. 'NML Capital v Argentina.'

28 See Chapter 1.4. for an analysis of the law of sovereign immunity in the context of sovereign finance.

29 Annamaria Viterbo, *Sovereign Debt Restructuring: The Role and Limits of Public International Law* (Turin: Giappichelli, 2020) 226.

30 See Chapter 3.4.3.1. 'Sovereign Immunity in Domestic Law Restructurings.'

31 Again, this was largely the result of divergent drafting and documentation practice between domestic and foreign law debt instruments; see Bossu et al (n 17).

32 As noted earlier, the UNCSI has only been signed by 28 states and ratified by 22 (Austria is among them, while Germany is not).

33 Notably, *Argentina and Banco Central de la República Argentina v Weltover Incorporated and ors,* Final appeal, Docket No 91–763, 504 US 607 (1992), ILDC 1924 (US 1992), 112 S Ct 2160 (1992), 119 L Ed 2d 394 (1992), (1995) 100 ILR 510, 12 June 1992, United States; Supreme Court [US].

34 Argentina bondholder challenges had, for most, been the first such cases, and typically, the governing law was also the lex fori.

35 For a description, see Chapter 2.2.3.1.1. 'The Commercial Activity Exception: "Once A Trader Always A Trader" and the Mixed Activity Conundrum.'

36 Jurisdictional Immunities of the State, *Germany v Italy*, Judgment, ICGJ 434 (ICJ 2012), 3 February 2012, United Nations [UN]; International Court of Justice [ICJ].

37 See Chapter 2.2.1.5.1. 'French Supreme Court (Cour de Cassation).' As Audit notes in this context, the solution found by the French Supreme Court is 'unworkable' going forward, as it has 'tried to shut the doors to vulture holdouts regardless of their obligation to engage in proper legal reasoning.' See Matthias Audit, 'Sovereign Bonds and National Relativism: Can New York Law Contracts Safely Cross the Atlantic?' (2014) 9(2) Capital Markets Law Journal 177, 188.

38 See Chapter 2.2.1.3.1. 'Italian Supreme Court (Corte Suprema di Cassazione).'

39 For an in-depth discussion, see Chapter 3.4.3.1. 'Sovereign Immunity in Domestic Law Restructurings' and Chapter 3.5.3.1. 'Sovereign Debt Restructurings in European Courts: Novel Judicial Challenges.'

40 Stating that Greece was the 'master of its own laws' and may, therefore, exercise its sovereign prerogatives (*acta iure imperii*) over its financial obligations. At the same time, German decisions were inconsistent. For instance, the German Court of Appeals in Schleswig invoked *Borri* as an authority regarding states' immunity for interference with bondholders' contractual rights, even though the Italian judgment related to foreign law debt instruments. See OLG (Schleswig), Urteil vom 07.07.2016–5 U 84/15, 7 July 2016, Germany; Schleswig-Holstein; Higher Regional Court [OLG].

41 See Chapter 3.5.3.2. 'The (Tenuous) Link Between Sovereign Immunity and Jurisdiction Under EU Law.'

42 To be sure, given that the ECtHR has the monopoly of interpreting the ECHR, which may offer protection to sovereign creditors, even cases launched in domestic courts may end up in foreign courts, as the *Mamatas* case showed. See, for discussion on the

merits of bondholders' claims, Chapter 4.5. 'The Protection of Sovereign Borrowers' Property Rights.'

43 United Nations General Assembly Resolution 69/319: Basic Principles on Sovereign Debt Restructuring Processes (United Nations General Assembly [UNGA]) UN Doc A/RES/69/319. See critically, Vassilis Paliouras, 'The Right to Restructure Sovereign Debt' (2017) 20 Journal of International Economic Law 115, 120 (noting that 'UN GA Resolutions, however, can only be of a declaratory nature as far as state rights and duties contained therein are concerned,' and therefore, 'the formal source of a right to restructure sovereign debt should be sought somewhere else.').

44 As Reeves (n 1) 495 observes, the question dates back hundreds of years. In treaties from the late 17th century, this was claimed:

> [a]lthough no king in his senses will refuse to pay his honest obligations, if he considers that his security and honor rest upon his standing by his agreements, and that it is unworthy of him who is given his position in order to mete out justice, deliberately to trample it underfoot.

45 See Chapter 1.2.3. 'Legal and Transactional Aspects of Sovereign Debt Restructurings' for a general overview.

46 However, some scholars go as far as positing that states have a unilateral right to denounce not only debt that is odious, illegal, or illegitimate but also such debt that is unsustainable. See Ilias Bantekas, 'The Right to Unilateral Repudiation of Odious, Illegal, and Illegitimate Sovereign Debt as a Human Rights Defence' in Ilias Bantekas and Cephas Lumina (eds), *Sovereign Debt and Human Rights* (Oxford: Oxford Scholarship Online, 2019) 554. While the doctrine of odious debt has gained much more traction in both scholarship and practice, a right to restructure when debt is *unsustainable* remains very contentious. See, for example, Paliouras (n 43) for an attempt to delineate this right.

47 *Perry v United States*, 294 US 330, [1935] 18 February 1935, United States; Supreme Court [US] [12]. The US government still won since no damages were awarded. See, for a historical account, Sebastian Edwards, *American Default: The Untold Story of FDR, the Supreme Court, and the Battle Over Gold* (Princeton: Princeton University Press, 2018).

48 However, exceptions exist. As Hayk Kupelyants, *Sovereign Defaults Before Domestic Courts* (Oxford: Oxford University Press, 2018) 162 points out, in a 1962 ruling, the German Federal Constitutional Court approved the cancellation of Third Reich government, which was previously approved by the German Parliament, debt without compensation.

49 The necessity defence under international law, for instance, allows countries to abrogate their responsibility for norm violations under certain circumstances, though its applicability to state default has rarely been endorsed. Indeed, domestic courts have usually denied the necessity defence in the sovereign default context; see, for example, Chapter 2.2.1.2.1. 'BVerfG Decision of 8 May 2007.' Mauro Megliani, *Sovereign Debt: Genesis, Restructuring, Litigation* (Berlin: Springer, 2015) 390–459 reviews the following defences sovereign debtors may invoke against enforcement attempts: sovereign immunity, act of state doctrine, comity doctrine, forum non conveniens, necessity, force majeure, unjustified enrichment, inequality of obligations, estoppel, abuse of rights, corruption, exchange control, odious debt doctrine, and peremptory norms. However, most of them were not accepted by courts in the context of the Argentine and Greek litigation.

50 See *Allied Bank International v Banco Credito Agricola de Cartago*, 733 F 2d 23 (2d Cir 1984), 1984, United States; Court of Appeals (2nd Circuit) [2d Cir] (holding that the Act of State doctrine is not applicable to the enforcement of Costa Rican (quasi-)sovereign debt obligations). Other substantive law defences by the sovereign

debtor against debt enforcement in the US have, too, been eroded over time. See Jonathan I Blackman and Rahul Mukhi, 'The Evolution of Modern Sovereign Debt Litigation: Vultures, Alter Egos, and Other Legal Fauna' (2010) 73(4) Law and Contemporary Problems 47.

51 See, for background, Megliani (n 49) 424–425.

52 See earlier in Chapter 2.2.1.2.4. 'BVerfG Decision of 3 July 2019.'

53 See, for background, Carlos Esposito, Yuefen Li, and Juan Pablo Bohovslavsky (eds), *Sovereign Financing and International Law – The UNCTAD Principles on Responsible Lending and Borrowing* (Oxford: Oxford University Press, 2013).

54 In particular, the UN Basic Principles mentioned earlier, see United Nations General Assembly Resolution 69/319: Basic Principles on Sovereign Debt Restructuring Processes (United Nations General Assembly [UNGA]) UN Doc A/RES/69/319.

55 For instance, a debt restructuring, or rescheduling, may become necessary as part of a macroeconomic adjustment programme the debtor country has committed to, including to unlock financial resources by IFIs. Yet courts could still find that the debt workout violated the creditors' rights and allow them to collect on the judgment.

56 See, for many, Bantekas and Lumina (n 46).

57 Matthias Goldmann, 'Human Rights and Sovereign Debt Workouts' (April 2014) unpublished manuscript <www.academia.edu/5561607/Human_Rights_and_Sovereign_Debt_Workouts> accessed 2 November 2021. Rather, he asserts, it would make sovereign debt restructurings fairer and prevent cases of excessive hardship. The legal basis for courts to show regard for human rights would be the UN Covenant on Economic, Social and Cultural Rights (ICESCR), which, in Article 22, lays down the entitlement of everyone to 'realization . . . of the economic, social and cultural rights indispensable for his dignity and the free development of his personality.'

58 See Mark Weidemaier and Mitu Gulati, 'Necessity and the Covid-19 Pandemic' (2020) 15(3) Capital Markets Law Journal 277, 283 (also noting, however, that '[the necessity] defence cannot fill the gaps created by the lack of a bankruptcy regime for sovereign nations').

59 For an overview of the debate, see Jeff King, *The Doctrine of Odious Debt in International Law – A Restatement* (Cambridge: Cambridge University Press, 2016).

60 See, for details, Chapter 3.3.3.4. 'Property Right Guarantees for Sovereign Bondholders in Unilateral European Sovereign Bond Restructurings.'

61 Of course, the ECtHR's decisions are not binding to countries that are not members of the ECHR, such as the US. However, just like courts in Europe referred to US precedents, courts in New York may well consider the evolution of sovereign debt litigation as a guidepost, even if an informal, non-binding one.

62 For example, if the domestic court reviews a domestic law restructuring, the judicial branch may defer to the legislator in deciding whether an interference with rights and expectations can be justified. For instance, as Hayk Kupelyants (n 48) 150 suggest in the context of domestic restructurings under English law, 'the orthodox view in English domestic law is that the UK Parliament has absolute supremacy and any legitimate expectations can be overcome by a properly worded statute.'

63 Ibid 171–207 (covering defences to sovereign debt repayment with a focus on English law).

64 See Mitu Gulati and George Vanberg, 'Paper Tigers (or How Much Will Courts Protect Rights in a Financial Crisis?)' in Franklin Allen, Elena Carletti, and Mitu Gulati (eds), *Institutions and the Crisis* (Florence: European University Institute, 2018) 111–132 (the authors note that '[a]s an international court, staffed by foreign judges, the ECHR enjoyed little public support in Greece' and that '[i]t is unlikely that a decision by the Greek government not to comply with an adverse judicial decision would have imposed domestic political costs on the government').

65 See Chapter 3.5.3.1. 'Sovereign Debt Restructurings in European Courts: Novel Judicial Challenges.'

66 Many European courts, in particular the CJEU, had to render difficult decisions in the wake of the euro area sovereign debt crisis. While most judgements supported the actions taken by EU institutions and national governments, the Court also asserted its prerogatives, for instance, with respect to government bond purchases by the ECB or the reviewability of Memoranda of Understandings between EU bodies and governments in the context of financial assistance programmes; see Alicia Hinarejos, 'The Legality of Responses to the Crisis' in Fabian Amtenbrink, Christoph Herrmann, and Rene Repasi (eds), *The EU Law of the Economic and Monetary Union* (Oxford: Oxford University Press, 2020) 1364–1399.

5 A Genealogy of Holdout Creditors

The Future of Sovereign Debt Restructuring

5.1. The Proliferation of Holdout Creditors

This final chapter shifts focus from the review of sovereign debt litigation and arbitration in the previous chapters to mapping the *types* of creditors that may undertake to challenge a government debt restructuring. As discussed earlier,[1] holdout creditors remain a key concern for nations restructuring their debt obligations. As noted by Buchheit et al, while holdouts have long been seen as 'benign spurs to sovereign debtors from demanding excessive amounts of debt relief,' in the wake of an increasing amount of litigation against poor countries in the 1990s and 2000s,[2] as well as Argentina's litigation saga, their suppression has become 'an imperative not only for sovereign debtors but also for the vast majority of other lenders.'[3]

Expanding the pertinent literature, this chapter presents a new and comprehensive genealogy of holdout creditors. The goal is to provide a better understanding of *who* may disrupt a debt workout on the international plane, what incentives they have, and how a nuanced view on holdout creditors can enhance policymakers' response. While two types of holdout creditor problems were responsible for the vast majority of lawsuits in Argentina and Greece (specialized hedge funds and retail investors), new types of actual and potential holdouts have since emerged. As noted earlier,[4] the influence of the London and the Paris Club over debt restructurings has been increasingly compromised by the availability of new sources of financing for sovereigns and especially poorer countries.[5] New and old players will feature in future sovereign debt restructurings, and appreciating their interests and strategies will be critical to resolving holdout issues effectively.

Against this backdrop, I apply a multi-level approach to categorize holdouts that focuses on creditor categories rather than instruments (see Table 5.1).[6] Generally, holdouts can be divided into private and official sector creditors. Among private creditors, one may distinguish between vulture funds,[7] real money investors, retail investors, and commodity traders that provide financing to sovereigns. Official sector holdouts could include non–Paris Club bilateral lenders as well as instrumentalities of states, such as central banks (in the context of currency unions) or SOEs.

Since international debt markets are evolving at a rapid pace and given the unpredictable medium- to long-term effects the COVID-19 pandemic will have on them, the genealogy of holdouts presented herein may not anticipate all

DOI: 10.4324/9781003361879-5

Table 5.1 A genealogy of holdout creditors

Type of Holdout	*Subcategory*	*Examples*
Private sector creditors	Vulture funds	• Specialized hedge funds, such as Elliot Management, which litigate against governments in domestic courts (eg, Peru, 1998; Argentina, 2005/2010) with an objective to maximize returns
	Real money investors	• Even though real money investors, such as asset managers, pension funds, mutual funds, and exchange-traded funds, are unlikely to act as holdouts, the demarcation between aggressive negotiation tactics and (disruptive) holdout behaviour has become increasingly blurred in recent restructurings (notably, Argentina's 2020 debt exchange)
	Retail investors	• 50,000 Italian retail investors in Argentine global bonds (represented by the Task Force Argentina) who pursued claims before the ICSID and ultimately settled with the government in 2016 • 6,400 Greek retail (domestic law) bondholders, which (unsuccessfully) litigated in Greek and European courts following the 2012 Greek PSI
	Commodity traders	• International commodity traders that provide financing to sovereigns in exchange for access to commodities, such as oil, and may refuse to participate in restructuring negotiations with other creditors (eg, Chad, 2020)
Official sector creditors	Bilateral lenders (Paris Club or non–Paris Club)	• Russia's refusal to participate in Ukraine's 2015 debt exchange as the holder of an English law-governed bond
	Instrumentalities of borrower governments	• State-owned policy banks (eg, the reluctance of Chinese state-owned banks to provide deep debt relief)[8] • Central banks (eg, the Eurosystem's preferred treatment during the Greek PSI of 2012)

developments. Collective action problems among creditors are certain to remain a central aspect of government debt restructurings – whether they will arise between or will be caused by the same actors is an altogether different question.

5.2. Private Sector Holdouts

5.2.1. Vulture Funds

Vulture holdouts, as they are colloquially referred to, have attained great prominence in recent sovereign debt crises. However, they are not a new phenomenon.[9]

For instance, in the 19th century, newly independent Latin American states were targeted by speculators, who acquired debt in distress to make a significant profit when decades later these were restructured.[10] In modern times, vulture funds are usually US-based hedge funds that have targeted bonded debt instruments governed by foreign law.[11]

Various definitions of vulture funds exist.[12] In essence, these creditors purchase distressed debt instrument on the secondary market when most (risk-averse) investors have left. In their investment decisions, they are guided by economic motives and the quest for arbitrage opportunities stemming from low debt prices and higher (expected) recovery values. To that end, such funds speculate that the timing of their investment decision will reap financial rewards, either through increasing debt prices after the restructuring, a favourable settlement with the sovereign debtor, or successful litigation or international arbitration.[13] Empirical studies suggest that for some countries, vulture fund litigation can be a serious financial burden, undermining their ability to use those funds for essential public purposes.[14]

Most investors lack the stamina, specialization, and capital to aggressively pursue the sovereign through litigation.[15] Perhaps paradoxically, vulture funds benefit from this dynamic. They want to be the only holdout or part of a small group of holdouts, as the debtor state will be more inclined to paying off a few aggressive vultures rather than risk jeopardizing the success of its entire debt operation.[16] Thus, the larger the number of holdouts, the lower the prospects for vulture funds to be paid more or in full, given the finite nature of the (insolvent) debtor's funds.[17]

Definitions of vulture funds are often coloured by certain political and moral notions; vultures' strategies tend to evoke strong emotional responses by those they target, given that they achieve high returns on their investment in a country that is rattled by a serious economic crisis.

For example, in a speech before the UN General Assembly in 2014, Cristina Kirchner, former Argentine President, claimed that 'vulture funds . . . threaten and hold the economy of our country hostage' and that 'those who destabilize the economy of a country and create poverty, misery and hunger through the sin of speculation are economic terrorists.'[18] Politicians from other countries have also weighed in: former British Prime Minister Gordon Brown describes '[v]ulture funds are companies which buy up the debt of poor nations cheaply when it is about to be written off, then sue for the full value of the debt plus interest.'[19] Even judges have associated vulture funds with a certain amoral behaviour. For instance, Lord Philipps of the UK Supreme Court notes that '[vulture funds] feed on the debts of sovereign states that are in acute financial difficulty by purchasing sovereign debt at a discount to face value and then seeking to enforce it.'[20]

Definitions can also be found in statues and other legal instruments. Most notably, in 2015, the Belgium Parliament passed a law that expressly defines 'vulture funds' and restricts their right to debt recovery through court enforcement measures.[21] The new legislation considers a sovereign creditor a 'vulture funds' if its negotiations with the debtor country are characterized by an 'immoral' strategy.[22] The rationale behind the Belgian Act is to help the judiciary in the determination of circumstances where actions against the debtor amount to 'insane and dangerous speculation.'[23] It focuses on the 'manifest disproportion' between the amount claimed and the nominal or face value of the debt, introducing objective criteria to consider under what circumstances an investor is a vulture.[24] In addition, the law provides a set of indicative criteria that may help courts to identify vulture funds.[25]

Parliaments in other jurisdictions have, too, adopted laws to curb sovereign debt enforcement by vulture holdouts.[26] The UK Debt Relief (Developing Countries) Act 2010 seeks to tackle the problem of a small minority of creditors taking HIPC-eligible members to court and try to get back the full value of their debts, including interest and penalties for arrears.[27] However, in contrast to the Belgian law, whose scope covers all countries, the UK Act only constrains the enforcement of distressed debt issued by HIPCs. Moreover, the UK Debt Relief Act does not expressly define 'vulture holdouts' but rather approaches the issue by curtailing enforcement rights of any creditor to a HIPC country that has received debt relief under the HIPC initiative by the IMF and the World Bank.[28]

Similar to the legislators in the UK and in Belgium, the UN Human Rights Council[29] sought to define vulture funds by describing their modus operandi.[30] The definitions in domestic statutes and the Human Rights Council seemingly target the types of firms that took Argentina to court over its 2001 default. All the three holdouts with the largest claims against Argentina, NML Capital,[31] Gramercy,[32] and Aurelius Capital,[33] were US-based hedge funds and notorious recidivists, all of which are also registered in tax havens.[34]

Vulture funds, as their name implies, belong to the most contentious actors in financial markets; they push the rule of law and the logic of financial markets to the limits, exploiting loopholes in the architecture and employing aggressive, though usually lawful, tactics to achieve their goals. But are they as disruptive as much of the literature claims or are they rather a necessary evil to ensure the proper functioning of sovereign credit markets?

A financial crisis inevitably presents some opportunities for arbitrage for some market actors, given the variety of risk profiles. That is true in both a corporate and a sovereign context.[35] Complex and arduous procedures for enforcement as well as the lack of a predictable bankruptcy procedure deter most sovereign investors from seriously considering litigation and arbitration an alternative to sovereign debt restructurings.[36] With the emergence of a secondary market for sovereign bonds, Wall Street's scavengers seized an opportunity for arbitrage that they had successfully applied during the 1980s in the private debt market:[37]

- First, as long as the borrower country continues to service its debt, the returns (i.e., coupon or interest payments calculated on the basis of the principal of the respective debt instrument) are typically very high.[38] Given the high yield on distressed-debt instruments, vulture holdouts can reap significant profits in the run-up to a sovereign default.[39]
- Second, if a sovereign borrower subsequently defaults, vulture funds have several options to proceed. For instance, the country may recover from its economic tragedy, the bonds will be upgraded, and the vultures make a

considerable profit by selling these papers for a premium.[40] Similarly, they could 'gamble for redemption,' hoping that official sector creditors, such as central banks or the IMF, would intervene to drive up prices before default materializes.[41] The phenomenon of private sector participants relying on official sector bailouts is referred to as 'creditor moral hazard' in the sovereign debt literature.[42]

- Third, vulture holdouts may hold positions in credit default swaps (CDS).[43] With such derivate financial instruments, vultures can bet on a credit event (notably a sovereign default), to the likelihood of which they themselves may contribute by engaging in a highly uncooperative manner during a sovereign debt workout.[44] Some may even launch legal action against a sovereign with the goal of forcing the country into default and, thereby, triggering a credit event. According to the Argentine government's own representation, the vulture fund Elliott Management (parent company of the litigant NML Capital Ltd in the *NML* case[45]) also engineered the country's default before US courts to profit from CDS, albeit hard evidence is missing to support this claim.[46]

Sovereign debt restructuring is, in essence, a zero-sum game. If one creditor, however, makes an extraordinarily high return on his or her investment, someone must bear equally high losses. On the one hand, the sovereign may need to carry these losses when it fails to reach a mutually acceptable restructuring solution. On the other, the fellow creditors, who must share a smaller amount among each other, will lose out as a collective.[47] To summarize, while exploiting financially attractive investment opportunities is not per se malignant, successful holdout behaviour can have three main negative effects:

- First, it may distort intercreditor equity by allowing a small minority of litigious creditors to extract more from a bankrupt sovereign than the rest of creditors.
- Second, it can hamper the quick and orderly restructuring of sovereign debt, thereby prolonging the negative effects of sovereign debt crises, such as deadweight losses and debt overhang effects.
- Third, it may encourage creditors who would have otherwise settled under mutually acceptable conditions with a sovereign debtor to press for a deal similar to the one struck by the holdouts (referred to as the 'free-rider problem').

Thus, states will experience more difficulties in reducing unsustainable debt levels if the creditors have a leveraged bargaining position due to legal enforcement options. Vulture fund litigation may exacerbate chances for a quick economic recovery in both advanced and emerging market economies since they complicate the quick and orderly resolution of debt crises.[48] Overall, and Chapter 4 on the Argentine debt workout supports this conclusion, the costs of dealing with and fending off vultures outweigh the benefits of a more liquid secondary market that they sometimes create – and that is true not only from the perspective of the sovereign borrower but also from that of an international policymaker.[49]

5.2.2. Banks

Commercial banks were active players in the international foreign loan market between the 1970s and 1990s. They usually provided funds to sovereigns through New York or English law–governed syndicated loans, which allowed larger loans while ensuring individual members in the syndicate from bearing the entire default risk.[50] As explained earlier, the restructuring of external syndicated loans was usually organized under the umbrella of the London Club, and debt operations, notwithstanding intense and lengthy negotiations, were mostly successful.[51] There are differing accounts as to the degree to which banks posed holdout problems.

On the one hand, Stumpf considers that the structure of the syndicated loan market did harbour holdout risks and describes the circumstances during the 1980s London Club restructurings as follows:

> Holdout creditors were a major headache, leading to delays in finalizing the restructuring. But given that commercial bank agreements are by their nature registered arrangements, the identity of the holdouts was instantly known. Various *ad hoc* techniques were used to deal with them. Peer pressure was one. Threat of exclusion from future syndications played a part. Jawboning by regulators helped. And when all else failed, the creditor was bought out.[52]

On the other hand, the literature also suggests that holdout issues were not a major concern for sovereign loan restructurings. MacMillan, for instance, argues that banks were no serious threat to smooth government debt workouts, noting that only few bank holdouts pursued lawsuits in the 1980s.[53] While, in principle, courts in financial centres[54] had already signalled their willingness to entertain lawsuits against sovereign debt, larger banks often faced serious political consequences for suing and breaking with the creditor community.[55] Smaller institutions were afraid of reputational consequences since litigation could threaten their status in the international banking community, albeit the empirical evidence is still limited.

Finally, the sharing clause in restructuring agreements concerning international syndicated loans meant that the proceeds from holdout litigation had to be distributed among banks in the syndicate, rendering go-alone litigation relatively unattractive endeavour for the holdout.[56] As a result, Buchheit notes, 'lawsuits brought against LDC borrowers since 1982 have sought recovery of short-term interbank lines, a debt category for which the protection of the sharing clause is not available.'[57] However, the clause was never transferred to bond documentation, leaving these instruments significantly more vulnerable to go-alone litigation.[58]

Moreover, banks became a smaller player in the course of the 1990s. Burnt by the sovereign defaults in Latin American nations and other EMEs, most bigger banks withdrew from directly lending to sovereigns via loans. The Brady Plan did its part in accelerating the growth of a secondary market.[59] Countries with access to international capital markets – the number of which is increasing – tend to prefer bond over loan financing, given deeper markets and better funding conditions.

However, banks have not completely withdrawn from the lending to sovereign debtors and entities controlled by them. In 2020, the IMF noted in the context of debt vulnerabilities in LICs that '[s]yndicated [bank] loans continue to play an important, if declining, role in the financing mix.'[60] While syndicated lending is usually considered a stable source of funding, it is less transparent and costly to the borrower.[61] Potential holdout risks from banks stem, in particular, from two features of this market:

- First, syndicated loans lack the kind of majority restructuring provisions that have become ubiquitous in international sovereign bonds, potentially resulting in collective action problems and undesirable costs, delays, and compromises to intercreditor equity.[62]
- Second, modern syndicates may be more global than in the 1980s, comprising not only US banks subject to regulation by US authorities but institutions from various jurisdictions. Tools of moral suasion and regulatory pressure that helped to cajole banking syndicates into collectively accepting a restructuring during the past century may not be readily available today.[63]

5.2.3. Asset Management Funds (Real Money Investors)

With the shift from syndicated bank loans to debt securities, asset management funds, usually structured as investment funds, have become increasingly important creditors to sovereign borrowers. While the term 'asset managers' is fairly broad and encompasses different types of institutional investors, such as hedge funds, the present analysis is limited to real money managers, which are often mutual funds.[64] Real money investors – in contrast to hedge funds (though not distressed debt funds) – are usually not leveraged, which means that they do not borrow to finance their investments.[65]

Data shows that mutual fund flows to emerging markets account for one-third of total portfolio flows and that assets of mutual funds in emerging market bonds have increased seven-fold since 2008.[66] Asset managers have traditionally avoided getting caught up in sovereign debt restructurings,[67] though exceptions exist.[68] Their investors range from risk-averse pension funds to unsophisticated retail investors, many of which do not expect their agents to be mired in lengthy litigation battles that draw negative scrutiny from the press or policymakers.[69] Indeed, many real money investors have traditionally pulled their investments out when the risk sentiment about a given sovereign debtor deteriorated with a view at capping any losses.

However, this does not mean that asset managers will never act as holdout investors in government debt operations:

- First, real money investors tend to acquire sovereign bond instruments at par value or at least close to the price at issuance.[70] As a consequence, they may be less willing to accept steep losses than creditors that came in after prices collapsed – a haircut of, say, 50% will have very different financial implications for real money investors that bought the instrument at face value (100%) shortly after issuance or hedge funds that swept up bonds in the secondary market at a 60% discount. All else equal, the former will incur a significant loss, and the latter will reap a 10% profit.

- Second, unleveraged investment funds, in contrast to banks, for example, have less pressure from external creditors to swiftly conclude a restructuring deal. In other words, leaving aside reputational risks, the legal and financial structure underlying real money investors is likely to pose fewer obstacles if they were to pursue holdout strategies.

While asset managers have negotiated fiercely in previous sovereign bond restructurings, they have so far not been a major obstacle to international debt workouts. At the same time, drawing the line between negotiation tactics and early-stage holdout strategies may become increasingly difficult going forward.[71] Asset managers are likely to feature as regular participants in international restructuring procedures, and the implications for the resolution of sovereign debt crises could be mixed. On the one hand, real money funds may take an active role in steering creditor committees and working towards a fast and sustainable outcome, thereby resolving some of the collective action issues that have plagued numerous bond restructuring in the past.[72] On the other, asset managers may opt for tough line vis-à-vis the government by threatening non-participation in a restructuring deal, thereby delaying or even thwarting its conclusion.[73]

5.2.4. Retail Investors

The rise of retail holdouts in sovereign debt workouts is a recent phenomenon, as the Greek PSI of 2012 and the Argentine debt crisis in the early 2000s have illustrated.[74] The common narrative that vulture funds make up the majority of plaintiffs in sovereign debt trials is, thus, only partly true.[75] As Schumacher[76] shows, the average holdout rate in the course of the Argentine debt restructuring was 27.9% in retail bonds as compared to 17.1% in professional bonds, suggesting that retail investors may even be more inclined than professional creditors to hold out. Indeed, as Buchheit and Daly note, '[u]npersuaded (but not necessarily litigious) and unsophisticated creditors may decline to participate in a sovereign debt workout and find themselves tagged with the epithet "holdout".'[77]

Retail investors can be referred to as 'investors who invest small amounts of money for herself rather than on behalf of anyone else.'[78] They are the opposite of institutional investors, which invest money for the clients against the payment of a fee. While this definition lacks accuracy, it captures all those litigants who are not specialized distressed-debt investors that engage in litigation (i.e., vulture holdouts). Therefore, retail investors are 'unspecialised creditors of sovereigns, who (i) are neither institutional investors nor hedge funds and (ii) hold small amounts of sovereign debt.'[79]

Due to the size of their investment, retail holdouts are, in most cases, unable to obstruct sovereign debt restructurings. Nonetheless, with sovereign debt becoming an increasingly attractive investment for private individuals, their participation in a sovereign debt workout has gained importance. Besides the difference in size of holdings, retail investors are typically not represented in creditor committees.[80] This could undermine their bargaining power compared to large institutional investors, as the latter can align their demands and speak in a single voice with the sovereign.

Negotiations between the IIF and Greece in the run-up to the debt swap of 2012 served as a case in point. While the IIF was at all times of the crisis around the green table, smaller retail investors were typically not involved. As a result, retail investors may be incentivized to hold out not because they seek preferential treatment but rather because they are confronted with a fait accompli: a restructuring deal brokered between the sovereign issuer and a number of big institutional investors. When one compares the organization of plaintiffs in holdout suits against Argentina and Greece, it appears that bondholders representation in the TFA allowed Argentine retail investors to leverage their bargaining power vis-à-vis the government as well as file mass claims before the ICSID.[81] The establishment of an Argentine Bond Restructuring Agency (ABRA) pursued similar objectives: they enabled small bondholders to surrender their bonds to ABRA in exchange for certificates issued by ABRA.[82] ABRA would then represent the participating bondholders in the restructuring negotiations, although bondholders also retained the option to reverse the exchange at any time prior to the conclusion of a restructuring agreement.[83]

Argentina ultimately decided to settle with nearly 50,000 Italian retail holdouts in April 2016, paying them 150% of the original principal amount of the defaulted bonds.[84] Conversely, in the context of the Greek PSI, retail holdouts largely filed individual claims before domestic courts and the ICSID. Notably, more than 6,000 bondholders collectively filed suit against Greece in Greece – a case that ended up before the ECtHR.[85] However, while the vulture funds that targeted English law bonds were paid in full, years of litigation left retail holdouts empty-handed.

In this context, the dichotomy between retail holdouts and vulture holdouts became obvious: while vulture holdouts strategically targeted those Greek debt securities that bestowed upon them a higher degree of protection, retail holdouts were stuck with Greek law bonds with weak legal remedies against the sovereign. The latter failed to anticipate the sell-off of Greek bonds, did not want to realize their losses, or underestimated the financial risks associated with holding on to the bonds.

Another reason why retail investors can end up in a holdout position is the lack of regulatory incentives to participate in voluntary debt workouts and the absence of a special relationship with the issuing government that could encourage the conclusion of a mutually acceptable deal. Consequently, retail holdouts may be more inclined to engage in litigation against the sovereign borrower than institutional investors, such as banks or insurance companies.[86] In addition, some retail investors may be overly reliant on the capability and benevolence of their financial advisors when buying a stake in the sovereign debt of a (foreign) state. Indeed, misinformation about credit risks and weak consumer protection have meant that retail investors often spend a significant amount of their wealth on ostensibly safe sovereign debt instruments only to realize that states may also run out of money.[87]

While further empirical evidence would be valuable, the Argentine and the Greek crises confirmed that retail investors may be drawn into a sovereign debt restructuring for a variety of reasons, ranging from encouraging investment advice by domestic financial institutions to speculative behaviour. Rarely, however, do they pose the same risks of disruption as specialized and aggressive vulture funds, and have thus been subject to far less scrutiny from policymakers.

5.2.5. Commodity Traders

Commodity traders operate in one of the most opaque and complex markets in the world.[88] Like the market itself, their operations are shrouded in secrecy, and they usually prefer it to stay that way.[89] While commodity traders do not typically engage in financing operations to sovereign nations, extending loans to countries in exchange for long-term commodity purchases has become an important practice, with the pertinent instruments being known as resource-backed loans (RBLs).[90] The most common form of RBL is prefinancing, where the loan is repaid by the sale of a commodity in a different fiscal year.[91] Commodity traders typically collaborate with banks and insurers to arrange prefinancing deals.[92]

RBLs have been extended to numerous governments over the past few decades, including Chad, Cuba, Jamaica, Kazakhstan, Russia, and several sub-Saharan African nations, such as Congo Republic.[93] Given that commodity traders have provided financing to countries that lost access to almost all other sources of funding, White refers to them as 'lenders of last resort.'[94] However, as the IMF highlighted in 2020,[95] while the extent of RBLs to developing countries is substantial, data is scarce[96]; like the commodity trading business itself, financing operations behind it remain largely in the dark.

An increasingly debated issue is whether commodity traders[97] may act as holdouts in public debt restructurings. Like other creditors, commodity traders can end up in a restructuring, notably because their claims are often not tradeable. However, given the absence of both rules and practice in dealing with RBLs by commodity traders in a restructuring, it is by no means certain that they will be a particularly difficult type of creditor to deal with. What seems clear is that several specific characteristics of this type of lending are likely to complicate future debt restructurings and increase the likelihood that commodity traders may not be folded into the existing process:

- First, RBLs are inherently opaque and often hidden.[98] RBLs signed by the Republic of Congo only came to the public's knowledge when the country needed to seek IMF assistance; the debt-to-GDP ratio had to be adjusted upward by a whopping 50%.[99] Often, RBLs are subject to confidentiality clauses, which aim at preventing the debtor from disclosing the loan, including in the context of a debt restructuring.[100] Even in the absence of such clauses, transparency in the RBL market is a major concern, as such loans tend to be concluded without Parliamentary approval and are not subject to the same level of oversight as other public debt instruments.[101]

- Second, and related to the first point, resource rich sovereign debtors often borrow funds via SOEs, such as oil or mining companies, whose finances are managed outside the ordinary budgetary process. While it can make perfect sense to rely on SOEs to manage the extraction and sale of resources, it adds a layer of complexity if a significant share of a country's public debt is incurred via such off-budget entities.[102] Trading firms argue that they have a contract with the SOE rather than the state and that, therefore, 'negotiations are held with the trading firm and the banks to restructure the agreement.'[103]
- Third, RBLs typically lack contractual restructuring mechanisms, such as majority restructuring provisions or pari passu clauses.[104] Consequently, RBLs may need to be restructured separately, potentially undermining inter-creditor parity by requiring the debtor government to strike side deals and treat commodity traders more favourably than other lenders. Moreover, the absence of contractual tools is of particular concern if an RBL is provided by a syndicate that is more prone to collective action problems or is assigned to new creditors specialized in holdout strategies.[105] A commodity trader may decide to sell its stake in an RBL to a specialized fund in the secondary market for a discount – the buyer could then avail itself of the contractual advantages provided by the terms of the RBL loan with the goal of obtaining a more favourable restructuring outcome.
- Fourth, collateralization of RBLs provides additional leverage to a potential holdout in comparison to traditional private sector lenders, which lend on an unsecured basis.[106] The collateralization of the loan may foster incentives to pay back the commodity trader before all other creditors, given that their debts are linked to the country's key revenue streams.[107] As the OECD observes, this could make RBLs de facto senior debt that is repaid before debts owed to other creditors.[108] While the commodity trader would not hold out in the narrow sense, the country may decide not to include them in the restructuring perimeter, or if the country seeks to implement a comprehensive debt restructuring, the features of RBLs could provide significantly more leverage to the trader than other (unsecured) lenders.
- Fifth, commodity traders are not members of groups representing traditional lenders, such as the IIF, creating additional obstacles with respect to the coordination between them and other creditors.[109] Relatedly, commodity traders have not been included in the debt service suspension discussions in the context of the COVID-19 pandemic; despite the significant amount of debt owed to them via RBLs, commodity traders are not part of the Africa Private Creditor Working Group.[110]
- Sixth, prefinancing deals involve several parties besides the commodity trader, such as insurers and banks.[111] Indeed, while the trader takes the lead in originating and structuring the transaction, it ultimately acts as an intermediary between the exporter that receives the credit and the wider banking

> community.[112] Hence, in a restructuring scenario, collective action problems may arise both between different members of the syndicate of banks as well as between the trader and individual (or several) banks. For instance, depending on the specific contractual arrangement, banks – and potential assignees – may have to consent to a restructuring of an RBL, potentially giving rise to holdout behaviour that delays the settlement of a debt workout.

Even though there are few publicly known cases where commodity traders, or other parties to an RBL, employed holdout tactics to thwart restructurings, the specific legal and financial structure of RBLs described earlier harbours holdout risks. The existing – largely circumstantial – evidence of uncooperative behaviour paints a blurred picture.[113] Thus, considerable uncertainty remains as to how commodity traders will be included in future debt workouts.[114]

Overall, commodity traders are unlikely to pose a similar risk to restructuring operations as vulture funds, not only because their business model differs substantially but also because financing is a corollary of trading rather than the other way around.[115] At the same time, the complex financing structure, the lack of transparency, the likely absence of CACs and other contractual restructuring tools, as well as the risk of assignments to other creditors could undermine ongoing and future restructuring efforts in countries that have significantly increased the share of RBLs of the total size of debt.[116]

5.3. Official Sector Holdouts

Official sector creditors, such as sovereign states or their instrumentalities,[117] have rarely held out from debt restructuring deals and, perhaps not surprisingly, have received limited coverage in the literature.[118] At least two explanations may be offered for their reluctance to pursue sovereigns either inside or outside of court:

- First, the emergence of official sector holdouts is a recent phenomenon that has not been fully digested yet by the international financial community. Indeed, the Paris Club has established an impressive track record in coordinating rich bilateral lenders during restructurings. With the changing creditor landscape, however, the procedure overseen by the Club has been put under strain.
- Second, the distinction between official sector and private sector creditors, respectively, is not always clear-cut. Traditionally, the official sector has been understood to comprise sovereign lenders, the IMF, and the World Bank.[119] However, no legal instrument or authority exists that defines different types of creditors or delineates the boundaries between them.[120] A bilateral lender may have ample political or economic motives to disguise its holdings of another state's debt.[121]

The Paris Club's membership is currently limited to 22 permanent sovereign lenders, whose share of total official sector lending has steadily declined during the past two decades.[122] New players have entered the stage, including countries like China,[123] India, Kuwait, Saudi Arabia and Taiwan, all of which are not members of the Paris Club but provide a significant share of bilateral financing.[124] As Bredenkamp et al note, '[there] has been a dramatic shift in the "official" creditor base, with various "non-traditional" creditors growing in importance,' as 'non-Paris Club creditors have become the dominant source of official bilateral financing.'[125]

None of the new significant lenders has expressed a clear interest in joining the Paris Club, though several large bilateral lenders have obtained observer status.[126] There are at least two reasons for the reluctance to upgrade to full membership. First, as Viterbo suggests, certain bilateral lenders may desire a relationship with the borrower at arm's length, exhibiting a deferential approach towards the borrower's internal economic affairs, including its debt sustainability.[127] Second, joining the Club, which is dominated by creditors that often have small stakes in the restructuring, would force them into a principle-based negotiation framework in which it becomes harder to pursue one's own interests.[128]

At least in theory, however, both lenders that are members of the Paris Club and such that are not may act as holdouts in government debt restructuring. Whether or not such holdout behaviour has disruptive effects depends on the size of the creditors' claims and whether the sovereign debtor can afford to accumulate arrears to that holdout.[129] In that regard, the interplay between Paris Club procedures and the IMF's non-toleration policy for official sector arrears is key. For decades, the Fund has not tolerated any arrears to official sector creditors, which differs from the policy of lending into arrears towards private creditors.[130] Since 2015, however, the Fund may also lend if there is *no* Paris Club agreement or if such agreement is not representative, and if the relevant official bilateral creditor either consents to the IMF proceeding despite the arrears or meets three specific requirements under the LIOA.[131]

The new LIOA policy, which enables the Fund to lend in the face of official sector holdouts, was motivated by at least two developments. First, the previously mentioned proliferation of non–Paris Club creditors meant that there may not be a Paris Club agreement that is representative and the IMF could rely on, with official creditors obtaining a veto over Fund financing.[132] Second, in the context of Ukraine's 2015 government debt restructuring, one of the country's biggest creditors, Russia, refused to participate. Since prevailing Fund policy would have given Russia a de facto veto over the IMF financing,[133] the IMF adopted its policy and allowed for lending despite the existence of official arrears under narrow circumstances.[134]

The Fund-supported program went ahead, and Ukraine remained in arrears to Russia on the Eurobond up to this day. To remedy the default, Russia filed a lawsuit against Ukraine before English courts, inter alia claiming that Ukraine had not negotiated in good faith.[135] In 2017, the UK High Court rejected a full trial, arguing that Ukraine has 'no justiciable defence.'[136] More specifically, the presiding Justice Blair found that Russia held a valid contractual claim, against which Ukraine could not invoke defences pertaining to alleged violations of international law by the Russian government. However, in September 2018, in a surprising twist, the Court of Appeal for England and Wales reversed the High Court's judgment.[137] The case is still pending for appeal to the UK Supreme Court at the time of writing.

Notes

1 See Chapter 1.2.4. 'Holdout Creditor Problems in Sovereign Debt Restructurings.'

2 For a statistical overview of litigation against HIPCs, see IMF, 'Heavily Indebted Poor Countries Initiative and Multilateral Debt Relief Initiative – Statistical Update' (15 December 2014) <www.elibrary.imf.org/view/journals/007/2014/089/article-A001-en.xml> accessed 2 November 2021. For background, also see Mark A Walker and Bathelemy Fay, 'Sovereign Debt Renegotiation: Restructuring The Commercial Debt Of HIPC Debtor Countries' (2010) 73(4) Law and Contemporary Problems 317, 318, noting this:

> [t]he shortcomings of the debt sustainability analysis underpinning the HIPC Initiative may help explain why a number of commercial creditors of HIPC debtors have resorted to litigation to collect on their claims rather than participate alongside official and other creditors in the HIPC Initiative.

3 Lee Buchheit, Guillaume Chabert, Chanda DeLong, and Jeromin Zettelmeyer, 'How to Restructure Sovereign Debt: Lessons from Four Decades' in Ali Abbas, Alex Pienkowski, and Ken Rogoff (eds), *Sovereign Debt: A Guide for Economists and Practitioners* (Oxford: Oxford University Press, 2019).345.

4 See Chapter 1.2.5. 'The Evolution of Sovereign Debt Restructuring Practice.'

5 See, for example, Chris Heitzig, Aloysius Uche Ordu, and Lemma Senbet, 'Sub-Saharan Africa's Debt Problem' (*Brookings Africa Growth Initiative*, October 2021) <www.brookings.edu/wp-content/uploads/2021/10/COVID-and-debt.pdf> accessed 2 November 2021.

6 The discussion of different types of holdout creditors usually includes an analysis of the distinct legal features of different debt instruments that these creditors hold.

7 For a seminal piece on this type of holdout, see Jill Fisch and Caroline Gentile, 'Vultures or Vanguards: The Role of Litigation in Sovereign Debt Restructuring' (2004) 53(1) Emory Law Journal 1047.

8 See, for evidence, Sebastian Horn, Carmen Reinhart, and Chrisoph Trebesch, 'Hidden Defaults' (2022) World Bank Policy Research Working Paper No 9925, 10 <https://openknowledge.worldbank.org/bitstream/handle/10986/36965/Hidden-Defaults.pdf?sequence=1&isAllowed=y> accessed 2 April 2022 (noting that 'the data show clearly that China's large state-owned banks very rarely agree to provide deep debt relief to their debtors').

9 For many, see John AE Pottow, 'Mitigating the Problem of Vulture Holdout: International Certification Boards for Sovereign Debt Restructurings' (2013) Law and Economics Working Paper 81, 7 <http://repository.law.umich.edu/cgi/viewcontent.cgi?article=1191&context=law_econ_current> accessed 2 November 2021; Jonathan I Blackman and Rahul Mukhi, 'The Evolution of Modern Sovereign Debt Litigation: Vultures, Alter Egos, and Other Legal Fauna' (2010) 73(4) Law and Contemporary Problems 47.

10 Mauro Megliani, *Sovereign Debt: Genesis, Restructuring, Litigation* (Berlin: Springer, 2015) 509 (further noting that '[t]he [vulture fund] scheme was replicated in the 1960s with reference to the bonds issued by Greece in the 1920s and unpaid since 1941').

11 For an overview, see Cephas Lumina, 'Curbing "Vulture Fund" Litigation' in Ilias Bantekas and Cephas Lumina (eds) *Sovereign Debt and Human Rights* (Oxford:

Oxford Scholarship Online, 2019) 498–513 (concluding that '[t]he story of vulture funds is a story of insatiable greed' and as follows:

> [t]he proliferation of vulture fund litigation underscores the need for more robust domestic legislation and strengthened intergovernmental efforts, which should include key jurisdictions where vulture funds litigate, through which vulture funds will not be allowed to operate (or at least have no incentive to operate) outside formal debt restructuring processes.

12 Fisch and Gentile (n 7) 1045 define 'vulture funds' as 'investment funds, particularly hedge funds and mutual funds, that purchase the debt of countries, or companies, that are in financial distress.' Buchheit et al (n 3) characterize them as follows:

> [v]ulture investors may approach a sovereign debt restructuring with malice aforethought; they often intend from the outset to reject a negotiated settlement and to seek a preferential recovery at the sharp end of a lawsuit. Aggressive recovery strategies of this kind have sometimes significantly disrupted the orderly resolution of sovereign debts, prompting debtor countries to develop techniques to counter such behaviour.

13 See Rodrigo Olivares-Caminal, 'Sovereign Default: More Business Opportunities' (2010) 55 The Hedge Fund Journal <https://thehedgefundjournal.com/sovereign-default-more-business-opportunities/> accessed 2 November 2021 (noting that '[h]oldouts will usually be specialists in distressed debt – vulture funds.').

14 See Lumina (n 11) 504 (citing studies by the World Bank and the IMF suggesting that 'the potential impact of court judgments varied from less than 0.5 per cent of the debtor country's GDP to 49 per cent, in the case of Liberia').

15 For the definition, see Robert E Scott, Mitu Gulati, and Stephen J Choi, 'Hidden Holdouts: Contract Arbitrageurs and the Pricing of Collective Rights' (July 2018) NYU Law & Economics Research Paper Series No 8 <https://papers.ssrn.com/sol3/papers.cfm?abstract_id=3203949> accessed 2 November 2021.

16 Greece's decision to pay off a significant share of holdouts in English law bonds in 2012 serves as a case in point. See Chapter 3 'Holdout Creditor Problems and Domestic Law Debt: The Greek Debt Restructuring in Courts and Tribunals (2012–2020).' Also see Buchheit et al (n 3) 13 (noting that 'the holdout creditor prospers only if all or most of its fellow creditors agree to provide debt relief to the sovereign; the more debt relief, the better, from the standpoint of the holdout').

17 In other words, if everyone employs vulture tactics, the business model would become obsolete. Buchheit et al (n 3) 5 describe this conundrum as follows:

> [t]he sovereign debtor will lack the resources to pay all of its debts on their original terms; that is essentially the definition of financial distress. Turning all or any significant part of those claims into court judgments does not alter this hard fact. The sovereign will not have the money to pay all claims in full regardless of whether the claimants transform themselves from simple creditors into judgment creditors.

18 Cristina Kirchner, 'Address by Cristina Kirchner at UN General Assembly' (24 September 2014) <www.cfkargentina.com/address-by-cristina-kirchner-at-un-general-assembly-2014/> accessed 2 November 2021.

19 Merion Jones, 'Vulture Funds Threat to Developing World' *BBC Newsnight* (London, 14 February 2007).

20 See *NML Capital Limited v Argentina*, Appeal judgment, [2011] UKSC 31, [2011] 2 AC 495, [2011] 3 WLR 273, ILDC 1805 (UK 2011), (2011) 147 ILR 575, 6 July 2011, United Kingdom; Supreme Court [SC].

21 Law on combating against the activities of vulture funds (Belgium [be]) ['Belgian Vulture Fund Law']. The Belgian law was controversial. No doubt, it responds

scholars have repeatedly called for more determined (legislative) action against vulture litigation. See Joseph E Stieglitz and Martin Guzman, 'A Rule of Law for Sovereign Debt' (*Project Syndicate*, 15 June 2015) <www.project-syndicate.org/commentary/sovereign-debt-restructuring-by-joseph-e-stiglitz-and-martin-guzman-2015–06?barrier=accessreg> accessed 2 November 2021. Wozny, for example, remarks that '[t]he Belgian Laws do not resolve the problems posed by vulture funds in a thoughtful way and other countries should be sceptical in adopting a model that follows the Belgian model.' Lucas Wozny, 'National Anti-Vulture Funds Legislation: Belgium's Turn' (2017) 2 Columbia Business Law Review 697, 744. The UN Human Rights Council took a more positive stance, welcoming the fact that the Belgian law 'implements a key recommendation contained in a [Human Rights Council] resolution.' See U.N. Human Rights Office of the High Commissioner, 'Belgian Legislation Against Vulture Funds Should Be Preserved – UN Rights Expert Urges' (*Press release*, 15 June 2006) <www.ohchr.org/EN/NewsEvents/Pages/DisplayNews.aspx?NewsID=20106&LangID=E> accessed 2 November 2021.

22 See, for an overview, Human Rights Council, 'Draft Progress Report on the Activities of Vulture Funds and the Impact on Human Rights' (2015) Advisory Committee (15th session) A/HRC/AC/15/CRP.1 <www.ohchr.org/Documents/HRBodies/HRCouncil/AdvisoryCom/Session17/A_HRC_33_54.docx> accessed 21 January 2021.

23 Ibid.

24 What is considered 'immoral' by the Belgian lawmaker is the financial gain the vulture fund may obtain by buying at a discount during the crisis and being paid the full face value of the bond. Increasingly granular financial markets data should allow for a better assessment regarding the actual discount holdouts paid.

25 The following criteria are listed in the Law: (i) the debtor was insolvent at the time of the debt buyback; (ii) the creditor is based in a tax haven; (iii) the creditor has a track record in litigation; (iv) the creditor refused to take part in debt restructuring efforts; (v) the creditor used its position of force to obtain advantages in the proceedings or contracts; (vi) the impact the reimbursement may have on the debtor's socio-economic situation. See Belgian Vulture Fund Law (n 21).

26 For an overview, see Astrid Iversen, 'Holdout Creditor Litigation' (2015) University of Oslo Faculty of Law Legal Studies Research Paper Series No 2015–13, 20, 35 <https://papers.ssrn.com/sol3/papers.cfm?abstract_id=2613280> accessed 2 November 2021.

27 HM Treasury, 'Government Acts to Halt Profiteering on Third World Debt Within the UK' (*Press release*, 2011) <www.gov.uk/government/news/government-acts-to-halt-profiteering-on-third-world-debt-within-the-uk> accessed 2 November 2021. Thus, the UK Act would, for instance, not apply if vulture funds were to sue countries like Argentina and Greece.

28 See Iversen (n 26). For a recent in-depth analysis of the Belgium law against vultures, also compare Jacques Richelle, 'Belgian 2015 Anti-Vulture Funds Law' (*Strelia Lawyers*, February 2016) <www.strelia.com/sites/strelia.com/files/strelia_-_belgian_2015_anti-vulture_funds_law.pdf> accessed 2 November 2021, concluding this:

> [e]xcept for State debt held in the Euroclear system, the Anti-Vulture Funds Law will probably have a limited impact since (i) Belgian courts are unlikely to be competent with respect to foreign debt payment issues and (ii) attempts to enforce foreign judgements and attach foreign States' assets located in Belgium should be limited.

Also see Wozny (n 21) (noting that 'national legislatures have increasingly begun to exhibit a preference for adopting national legislative solutions to this issue').

29 Human Rights Council Advisory Committee, 'Thirty-Third Session A/HRC/33/54' (September 2016) <www.ohchr.org/EN/HRBodies/HRC/AdvisoryCommittee/Pages/VultureFunds.aspx> accessed 2 November 2021.

30 Ibid. The Council describes their tactics as follows: Vulture funds: (i) target sovereign States with distressed economies and frequently with weak capacity for legal defence; (ii) operate and take advantage of the lack of regulation of the secondary market; (iii) refuse systematically to participate in orderly and voluntary debt restructuring processes; (iv) sue the country for reimbursement of the full value of the bond, plus interest and delay penalties; (v) chase the country to enforce the judgment; (vi) obtain exorbitant profits; and (vii) operate in jurisdictions where bank secrecy rules apply.

31 Elaine Moore, John Paul Rathbone, and Vivianne Rodrigues, 'Argentina Faces Fresh Default' *Financial Times* (New York, 16 August 2014).

32 Robin Wigglesworth, 'Gramcery Reaps Argentina Bond Windfall' *Financial Times* (New York, 2 August 2016).

33 Renae Merle, 'How One Hedge Fund Made $2 Billion from Argentina's Economic Collapse' *Washington Post* (Washington, DC, 29 March 2016).

34 See Julian Schumacher, *Enforcement in Sovereign Debt Markets* (PhD thesis, Humboldt University, Berlin 2015) unpublished manuscript, 145.

35 For distressed debt investing in the corporate (debt) market, see Edith S Hotchkiss and Robert M Mooradian, 'Vulture Investors and the Market for Control of Distressed Firms' (1997) 43 Journal of Financial Economics 401 (finding that vulture investors add value by disciplining managers of distressed firms.).

36 Even in the early days of sovereign debt litigation, it required specific skills or a specific business model in order to be victorious against the debtor. Hence, holding out was not considered attractive to mainstream creditors. See Ran Bi, Marcos Chamon, and Jeromin Zettelmeyer, 'The Problem That Wasn't: Coordination Failures in Sovereign Debt Restructurings' (2011) IMF Working Paper No 11/265 <www.imf.org/external/pubs/ft/wp/2011/wp11265.pdf> accessed 2 November 2021.

37 See Stuart C Gilson, Kose John, and Larry HP Lang, 'Troubled Debt Restructurings – An Empirical Study of Private Reorganization of Firms in Default' (1990) Journal of Financial Economics 315.

38 Just in 2014, the Argentine USD-denominated bonds rallied to a yield of more than 19%, resulting in a substantial increase of Argentina's refinancing costs. See Nicole Hong, 'Argentina's Bond Yields Lure Back Buyers' *The Wall Street Journal* (New York, 19 March 2014).

39 Goldman Sachs, an investment bank, has been criticized for purchasing almost USD3 billion in Venezuelan debt (more specifically, bonds issued by the state-owned oil company) at a moment in time when the country's default probability for the coming months is estimated to stand north of 90% (July 2017). Goldman acquired the bonds for 31 cents on the dollar, reflecting the high level of riskiness markets attach to these instruments. The Economist, 'Goldman Sachs Is Criticised for Buying Venezuelan Bonds' *The Economist* (London, 1 June 2017) (noting that protesters gathered outside Goldman's headquarters in New York, lamenting that the investment bank thereby supports a brutal and cash-strapped regime).

40 Anna Gelpern, 'Sovereign Debt: Now What' (2016) 41(2) Yale Journal of International Law Online 45.

41 See, for example, Katharina Pistor, 'A Legal Theory of Finance' 41(2) Journal of Comparative Economics 315 (describing how this kind of speculative investment behaviour led to the insolvency of MF Global in 2011).

42 For the seminal paper, see Andrew Haldane and Jörg Scheibe, 'IMF Lending and Creditor Moral Hazard' (2004) Bank of England Working Paper No 216 <www.bankofengland.co.uk/archive/Documents/historicpubs/workingpapers/2004/wp216.pdf> accessed 2 November 2021. Empirical evidence bolsters the existence of this phenomenon, suggesting that speculative creditors have benefited greatly from IMF bailouts in the past.

43 For a discussion of the role of CDS in sovereign debt restructurings before the Greek debt restructuring of 2012, see IMF, 'Sovereign Debt Restructuring – Recent Developments and Implications for the Fund's Legal and Policy Framework' (26 April 2013) 16 <www.imf.org/external/np/pp/eng/2013/042613.pdf> accessed 2 November 2021 (noting that the first case in which a sovereign CDS was triggered was Ecuador in 2008, when President Rafael Correa refused to meet an interest payment; the settlement resulted in a recovery rate of 31.75% for those who could not obtain a bond for physical delivery to settle their contracts via cash).

44 Anna Gelpern and Mitu Gulati, 'CDS Zombies' (2012) 13 European Business Organization Law Review 347.

45 See Chapter 2.2.1.1.3. 'NML Capital v Argentina.'

46 Daniel Bases, 'For Argentina Holdout Fund, a Decade's Pursuit May Pay Off' *Reuters* (London, 2 December 2012) <www.reuters.com/article/argentina-debt-elliott-idUSL1E8MU9NK20121202> accessed 2 November 2021.

47 This is why domestic insolvency and reorganization laws mandate the equal treatment of all creditors, establish clear priorities among creditors, and halt legal action against the debtor until all assets are distributed in accordance with the prescribed procedure. The international financial system, however, lacks such process, thus providing those willing to engage in lengthy litigation and arbitration with the opportunity to do so and potentially reap enormous benefits.

48 That holdout problems inform policy decision in current debt crises has been confirmed recently when the US Congress passed the Puerto Rico Oversight, Management and Economic Stability Act (PROMESA) law. This law expressly prohibits creditors from suing the insolvent country for debt repayment, anticipating holdout creditor problems in the wake of restructuring Puerto Rico's unsustainable debt. See, for example, DLA Piper, 'PROMESA Becomes Law: All Business in Puerto Rico Will Be Affected – Top Points About This Sweeping Rescue Package' (*DLA Piper Government Affairs Alert*, 5 July 2016) <www.dlapiper.com/en/us/insights/publications/2016/07/promesa-becomes-law/> accessed 2 November 2021.

49 See IMF, 'Sovereign Debt Restructuring – Recent Developments and Implications for the Fund's Legal and Policy Framework' (26 April 2013) <www.imf.org/external/np/pp/eng/2013/042613.pdf> accessed 2 November 2021.

50 Syndicates may be divided into *direct syndicates* (each individual bank retains several responsibility for the obligations assumed singularly towards the borrowing State) and *participation syndicates* (one bank alone – the lead bank – enters into the agreement with the borrower). For an in-depth analysis of the syndicated loan market for sovereign borrowers, see Megliani (n 10) 165 et seq.

51 Udabir Das, Michael Papaioannou, and Christoph Trebesch, 'Sovereign Debt Restructurings 1950–2010: Literature Survey, Data and Stylized Facts' (2012) IMF Working Paper, WP/12/203 <www.imf.org/external/pubs/cat/longres.aspx?sk=26190.0> accessed 2 November 2021.

52 Mark Stumpf, 'Sovereign Commercial Bank Restructuring Agreements: Should Bond Innovations or Other Modifications Be Adopted? (2018) 13(3) Capital Markets Law Journal 392, 394–395 (further adding that 'restructuring agreements were therefore negotiated with the full knowledge that holdout creditors were a real and present problem').

53 See Rory Macmillan, 'Towards a Sovereign Debt Workout System' (1995–1996) 16 Northwestern Journal of International Law & Business 57, 72.

54 See, in particular, *Argentina and Banco Central de la República Argentina v Weltover Incorporated and ors,* Final appeal, Docket No 91–763, 504 US 607 (1992), ILDC 1924 (US 1992), 112 S Ct 2160 (1992), 119 L Ed 2d 394 (1992), (1995) 100 ILR 510, 12 June 1992, United States; Supreme Court [US].

55 Macmillan (n 53) 72–73.

56 Ibid, noting this:

> [the sharing clause] mandated that any recovery in an action by a single creditor had to be shared with all of the other creditors of the loan agreement, thereby significantly reducing the recovery of the single creditor bringing the action.

Moreover, the sharing clause is typically absent in sovereign bonds governed by a fiscal agency agreement, which explains why the bulk of holdout litigation occurred in this asset class.

57 See Lee Buchheit, 'The Sharing Clause as a Litigation Shield' (1990) 9(10) International Financial Law Review 15–16 (also noting, however, that '[the] protection [from the sharing clause] is regrettably not all-encompassing, [since] large segments of a sovereign's external debt may not be covered by formal restructuring arrangements into which helpful little sharing clauses can be inserted').

58 Ibid.

59 Philip Power, 'Sovereign Debt: The Rise of the Secondary Market and Its Implication for Future Restructurings' (1996) 64(4) Fordham Law Review 2701.

60 IMF, 'The Evolution of Public Debt Vulnerabilities in Lower Income Countries' (February 2020) IMF Policy Papers 19 <www.imf.org/~/media/Files/Publications/PP/2020/English/PPEA2020003.ashx> accessed 2 November 2021.

61 Ibid (noting that '[t]he "all-in" cost of a syndicated loan would also include additional fees charged by the leading bank and financial advisors. If backed by a guarantee, the cost would also include the indemnity fee').

62 Stumpf (n 52) and IMF, 'The International Architecture for Resolving Sovereign Debt Involving Private-Sector Creditors – Recent Developments, Challenges, Reform Options' (2020), IMF Policy Papers, 38 <www.imf.org/en/Publications/Policy-Papers/Issues/2020/09/30/The-International-Architecture-for-Resolving-Sovereign-Debt-Involving-Private-Sector-49796> accessed 2 November 2021.

63 The lack of regulatory oversight may be exacerbated by the fact that some members of a banking syndicate are state-owned banks that are subject to special legal frameworks.

64 The BIS understands real money investors as comprising mutual funds, pension funds, insurance and reinsurance companies, and endowments. See BIS, 'Glossary' (December 2016) <www.bis.org/statistics/glossary.htm?&selection=302&scope=Statistics&c=a&base=term> accessed 2 November 2021.

65 At the same time, some investment funds have started to rely on debt financing strategies against the backdrop of unconventional monetary policies; see Fernando Avalos, Ramon Moreno, and Tania Romero, 'Leverage on the Buy Side' (2015) BIS Working Papers No 517 <www.bis.org/publ/work517.pdf> accessed 21 November 2021.

66 For an overview, see Georgia Bush, Carlos Canon, and Daniel Gray, 'Emerging Market Capital Flows: The Role of Fund Manager Portfolio Allocation' (2021) Banco de Mexico Working Papers No. 2021–113 <www.banxico.org.mx/publications-and-press/banco-de-mexico-working-papers/%7BF21B341C-067A-8583-0755-AC73B792ED51%7D.pdf> accessed 12 September 2021.

67 Oliver West, 'EM Real Money Should Take on Restructuring Rep Risk' *Global Capital* (London, 13 August 2020) <www.globalcapital.com/article/28muaqiq94joecdu9a9kw/emerging-markets/latam/em-real-money-should-take-on-restructuring-rep-risk> accessed 2 November 2021 (noting that '[r]eal money investors have historically avoided the reputational risk involved in participating in sovereign debt restructurings').

68 For instance, in the 2015 Ukraine debt restructuring, the asset manager Franklin Tempelton was the largest private creditor; see Anna Gelpern, 'Ukraine's Bond Restructuring: Surgery, Conspiracy, and Campaign' (2015) Peterson Institute for International Economics, Realtime Economic Issues Watch <www.piie.com/blogs/

realtime-economic-issues-watch/ukraines-bond-restructuring-surgery-conspiracy-and-campaign> accessed 2 November 2021.

69 Ibid ('[t]he average person does not differentiate between Paul Singer's Elliott and Larry Fink's BlackRock, so even the most socially conscious fund can find its reputation tarred by the behaviour of the opportunists').

70 Buchheit et al in Ali Abbas, Alex Pienkowski, and Ken Rogoff (eds), *Sovereign Debt: A Guide for Economists and Practitioners* (Oxford: Oxford University Press, 2019) 328-364..

71 During the restructurings of Ecuadorian and Argentine securities in 2020, for instance, real money investors held the largest share of bonds and were, for one of the first times, the key interlocutors for the respective governments during the negotiations. Oliver West and Ross Lancaster, 'Real Money to the Fore as Lat Am Pair Usher in New Era of Sov Debt Workouts' *Global Capital* (London, 6 August 2020) <www.globalcapital.com/article/28muafl03lb49y9ird8n4/emerging-markets/latam/real-money-to-the-fore-as-lat-am-pair-usher-in-new-era-of-sov-debt-workouts> accessed 2 November 2021.

72 Commentators broadly considered that the Ecuadorian debt restructuring of 2020, in which asset managers held a significant share of the private debt, was successful due to the swift implementation of a debt reduction. See Andres De La Cruz and Ignacio Lagos, 'CACs at Work: What Next? Lessons from the Argentine and Ecuadorian 2020 Debt Restructurings' (2021) 16(2) Capital Markets Law Journal 226.

73 Indeed, at the early stages of the Argentine restructuring negotiations in 2020, it seemed as if private creditors, such as the asset manager BlackRock, would be willing to hold out for as long as the government did not meet its demands. See Jorge Fontevecchia, 'Martín Guzmán: The Reality Facing Argentina Was Not Understood by Creditors' *Buenos Aires Times* (Buenos Aires, 13 June 2020).

74 See Chapter 2 'Holdout Creditor Problems and Foreign Law Debt' and Chapter 3 'Holdout Creditor Problems and Domestic Law Debt: The Greek Debt Restructuring in Courts and Tribunals (2012–2020).'

75 See, for this narrative, for example, Marcus Miller and Dania Thomas, 'Sovereign Debt Restructuring: The Judge, the Vultures and Creditor Rights' (2007) 30(10) The World Economy 1491. Also see Mauro Megliani, 'Vultures in Courts: Why the UNCTAD Principles on Responsible Financing Cannot Stop Litigation' (2015) 28 Leiden Journal of International Law 849.

76 Schumacher (n 34) 125.

77 Lee Buchheit and Elena Daly, 'Minimising Holdout Creditors: Carrots in Rosa Lastra and Lee Buchheit (eds), *Sovereign Debt Management* (Oxford: Oxford University Press, 2014) 5.

78 The Free Financial Dictionary, 'Retail Investor' <http://financial-dictionary.thefreedictionary.com/retail+investor> accessed 2 November 2021.

79 Retail investors often commit significant amounts of their overall savings to government bonds, some in a speculative manner but most to provide for a safe investment that offers steady returns.

80 See, for example, Jeromin Zettelmeyer, Christoph Trebesch, and Mitu Gulati, 'The Greek Debt Restructuring: An Autopsy' (2013) 28(75) Economic Policy 513.

81 See Chapter 2.3.1.1. 'Abaclat and Others v Argentine Republic' (discussing mass claims arbitration against Argentina by Italian bondholders represented through the TFA).

82 See IMF, 'The Restructuring of Sovereign Debt – Assessing the Benefits, Risks, and Feasibility of Aggregating Claims' (September 2003) IMF Legal Department, 24 <www.imf.org/external/np/pdr/sdrm/2003/090303.pdf> accessed 2 November 2021.

83 Ibid 24–25.

84 See Task Force Argentina (TFA), 'Task Force Argentina Announces Final Argentina Settlement for Italian Bondholders' (*Press Release*, 22 April 2016) <www.tfargentina.

it/download/TFA%20Comunicato%2022%20aprile%202016_eng.pdf> accessed 2 November 2021.

85 See Chapter 3.5.1. 'Court of Justice of the EU (CJEU).'

86 For ample empirical evidence Schumacher (n 34)119.

87 See, for example, Luigi Oliveri, 'Italian Banks Unload Argentine Bonds in Italy; Investigation Blocked' (*Executive Intelligence Review*, 11 March 2005) <http://larouchepub.com/other/interviews/2005/3210luigi_olivieri.html> accessed 2 November 2021. Also see World Bank Group, 'Debt Transparency in Developing Countries' (2021) 67 <https://documents.worldbank.org/en/publication/documents-reports/documentdetail/743881635526394087/debt-transparency-in-developing-economies> accessed 2 December 2021 (noting that 'RBLs are heavily concentrated in a few countries where they represent a substantial share of the relevant countries' borrowings.'); Ricardo Soares de Oliveira and Olivier Vallee, 'The Republic of Congo Is a "Dark Debt" Pioneer' *Foreign Policy* (Washington, DC, 21 May 2021) (describing Congo's RBL deals).

88 See Kate Kelly, *The Secret Club That Runs the World* (New York: Penguin Random House, 2015).

89 Javier Blas and Jack Farchy, *The World For Sale: Money, Power, and the Traders Who Barter the Earth's Resources* (Oxford: Oxford University Press, 2021).

90 See for an overview, David Mihalyi, Aisha Adam, and Jyhjong Hwang, 'Resource-Backed Loans: Pitfalls and Potential' (*Natural Resource Governance Institute*, February 2020) <https://resourcegovernance.org/sites/default/files/documents/resource-backed-loans-pitfalls-and-potential.pdf> accessed 2 November 2021. Such resource-backed loans (RBL) can serve different functions, such as payment in kind, as source of an income revenue stream to make repayments or as an asset that serves as collateral.

91 The IMF has for instance defined 'prefinancing' in the context of Congo's oil-backed loans as follows:

> [p]refinancing is defined as a loan backed by oil, that is, advances of money to the debtor by the lender made on the basis of an undertaking that the debtor will surrender to the creditor at a future date the equivalent in oil of the loan plus interest and other fees; the loan is repaid by the sale of the oil in a different fiscal year.

See IMF, 'Republic of Congo: 2004 Article IV Consultation and New Staff-Monitored Program – Staff Report; Staff Statement; Public Information Notice on the Executive Board Discussion; and Statement by the Executive Director for the Republic of Congo' IMF Country Report No 04/232 (July 2004) <www.imf.org/external/pubs/ft/scr/2004/cr04232.pdf> accessed 2 November 2021.

92 See Trafigura, 'Prepayments Demystified' (January 2020) <www.commoditiesdemystified.info/pdf/Prepayments_Demystified_CommoditiesDemystified.pdf> accessed 2 November 2021.

93 Blas and Farchy (n 89). One of the most famous cases is Jamaica, which received funding from Marc Rich & Co., a major commodity trader in the 1970s and 1980s, to send a team to the Winter Olympics. See Natasha White, 'Cool Runnings, Commodity Traders and Global Capital – a Review of "The World for Sale"' (*Global Witness*, 8 April 2021) <www.globalwitness.org/en/blog/cool-runnings-commodity-traders-capital/> accessed 2 November 2021. Total RBLs between 2004 and 2016 amounted to 65% of Congo's GDP and 128% of its total government debt stock as of 2016; see Mihalyi et al (n 90) 30 and de Oliveira and Vallee (n 87).

94 Natasha White, 'Commodity Traders: Lenders of Last Resort for Africa's Oil-Producers' (*Global Witness*, 3 July 2019) <www.globalwitness.org/en/blog/commodity-traders-lenders-of-last-resort/> accessed 2 November 2021.

95 IMF (n 62).

96 The most complete dataset so far is provided by Mihalyi et al (n 90), who show that 52 RBLs were signed between 2004 and 2018 in sub-Saharan Africa and Latin America

(14 countries in total), with a value of USD164 billion. However, this dataset includes only seven loans from commodity traders, while the rest of the loans was provided by governments, SOEs, or policy banks.

97 It should be noted that commodity traders are contentious creditors, not least due to possible governance and corruption concerns; see White (n 94) (noting that '[i]n the early 2000s, the French state-owned oil company Elf Aquitaine employed them in Congo to enrich its secret funds and provide huge unaccountable revenue streams to those in power').

98 As the OECD, for instance, noted 'oil-backed loans are hard to oversee and are typically off-budget – even if they end up being the state's responsibility when crisis strikes – significantly adds to the danger that these funds might be misappropriated or diverted.' See OECD, 'The Impact of Coronavirus (COVID-19) and the Global Oil Price Shock on the Fiscal Position of Oil-Exporting Developing Countries' (30 September 2020) OECD Policy Responses to Coronavirus (COVID-19) <www.oecd.org/coronavirus/policy-responses/the-impact-of-coronavirus-covid-19-and-the-global-oil-price-shock-on-the-fiscal-position-of-oil-exporting-developing-countries-8bafbd95/> accessed 2 November 2021.

99 See World Bank Group (n 87) and OECD (n 98). Also see Federico Lupo-Pasini, 'Hidden Sovereign Finance' (2021) 16(2) Capital Markets Law Journal 165.

100 See IMF (n 91).

101 See OECD (n 98) (highlighting that '[c]ollateralised loan agreements are characterised by their greater opacity, including lending terms and fees that are often undisclosed' and that '[r]esource-backed loans are often excluded from countries' official debt statistics or databases, and only more recently have these type of loans been brought on the agenda by initiatives like the Extractive Industries Transparency Initiative (EITI)').

102 And, as research by NGOs shows, creates ample opportunities for corruption, well protected from the public eye and international policymakers. See, for example, Public Eye, 'Gunvor in Congo' (September 2017) <https://gunvorincongo.publiceye.ch/> accessed 2 November 2021 (reporting about Gunvor's dealings with Congo's *Société nationale des pétroles congolais* (SNPC), which led to a criminal trial and the sentencing of a Gunvor employee for bribery, fraud, and embezzlement).

103 Trafigura (n 92) (conceding, however, that '[o]n occasion such negotiations form part of a wider debt restructuring by the country concerned, including the wider creditor community and international financial institutions').

104 See Natasha White, 'Hey, Big Lenders' (*Global Witness*, 30 November 2018) <www.globalwitness.org/en/blog/hey-big-lenders/> accessed 2 November 2021 (noting that '[t]raditional debt contracts contain clauses on collective action and equal treatment, and are generally a known entity,' but that '[s]uch clauses may not exist in traders' contracts, which are private and vary by case').

105 For instance, the Anglo-Swiss trading firm's 2015 loan to Chad takes the form of a syndicated loan, with a total amount of USD1 billion, of which Glencore's portion is USD347 million. See Alonso Soto, 'Glencore Under Pressure from IMF to Rework Chad Loan' *Bloomberg* (New York, 17 June 2020) <www.bloomberg.com/news/articles/2021-06-17/pressure-piles-on-chad-private-creditors-after-g-20-relief-deal> accessed 2 November 2021.

106 White describes the issues as follows:

> Moreover, as traders' loans are often secured against oil, they are deemed more 'senior' to others, meaning they rank above other, unsecured creditors in the restructuring hierarchy. The presence of traders as lending institutions therefore makes coordination around debt restructuring more challenging.

See White (n104).

107 To be sure, the actual enforcement of collateral agreements remains subject to considerable uncertainty and is likely to require the commodity trader to have physical control over the relevant asset. In this regard, Mihalyi et al assert that '[l]enders can seize these assets if the government stops servicing the loan, for example, where specific cargoes are assigned as security to a commodity trader.' See Mihalyi et al (n 90) 42.

108 OECD (n 98).

109 See ibid and Mihalyi et al (n 90).

110 OECD (n 98) (hence, the OECD has been urging the international community that '[a]n agreement between private creditors to suspend debt service payments should also include commodity trading companies, given their growing importance as lenders to oil-exporting developing countries').

111 See Jenny Strasburg and Margot Patrick, 'Glencore Oil Deals Could Bite Banks' *Wall Street Journal* (4 October 2015).

112 Trafigura (n 92).

113 See Sum-Jim Ho, 'Sovereign Debt Column: Is This Time Different for Sub-Saharan Africa?' (Winter 2019–2020) 10 Cleary Gottlieb Emerging Markets Restructuring Journal <www.clearygottlieb.com/-/media/files/emrj-materials/issue-10-winter-2019_2020/sovereign-debt-column–is-this-time-different-for-subsaharan-africa-pdf.pdf> accessed 2 November 2021 (discussing the restructuring of Glencore debt in Chad).

114 Julia Payne, 'Trafigura Completes Congo Republic Oil Loan Restructuring' *Reuters* (London, 23 March 2021).

115 This is at least how commodity traders themselves would characterize it; see Trafigura (n 92).

116 For some data points, see World Bank Group (n 87).

117 For instance, the ECB was accused of acting as holdout investor in the Greek PSI after it had received a preferential treatment by the Greek government. See, for the court case on the ECB's carve-out in the Greek 2012 restructuring, Chapter 3.5.1.1. 'Accorinti v ECB.' For a broader analysis of potential holdout problems in the context of euro area sovereign debt restructurings, see Sebastian Grund and Filip Grle, 'The European Central Bank's Public Sector Purchase Programme (PSPP), the Prohibition of Monetary Financing and Sovereign Debt Restructuring Scenarios' (2016) 41(6) European Law Review 781.

118 See, for example, Hancen Yu, 'Official Bondholder: A New Holdout Creature in Sovereign Debt Restructuring After Vulture Funds' (2017) 16 Washington University Global Studies Law Review 535 (noting that '[d]uring the recent Ukraine-Russia sovereign bond dispute, a new type of holdout creditor immerged – one that is potentially immune from these contractual arrangements'); Gelpern (n68) 2 ('Russia was the biggest holdout in Ukraine's debt restructuring, and is in its fifth year of suing Ukraine on the bonds in English courts').

119 By contrast, the private sector typically comprises financial institutions, non-financials, as well as households. Institutional private creditors are typically represented by the IIF, which negotiates on behalf of the private sector community with the distressed sovereign and other stakeholders.

120 The IMF has sought to differentiate between private and official lenders for the purpose of its own policies, which are, however, not binding to creditors or debtors outside an IMF program context.

121 Moreover, modern capital markets allow a sovereign to hold debt on its own account, through a state-owned entity, a central bank, development banks, or in multiple other ways.

122 Notably, one of the biggest bilateral sovereign lenders, China, is not a member of the Paris Club and, thus, not bound by its principles.

123 As several studies show, China has become the largest creditor to emerging market and developing economies, dwarfing most Paris Club lenders. See, for example,

Horn et al (n 11) and Anna Gelpern, Sebastian Horn, Scott Morris, Brad Parks, and Christoph Trebesch, 'How China Lends: A Rare Look into 100 Debt Contracts with Foreign Governments' (May 2021) Peterson Institute for International Economics Working Paper 21–7; <www.piie.com/publications/working-papers/how-china-lends-rare-look-100-debt-contracts-foreign-governments> accessed 2 November 2021; Chorzempa and Adnan Mazarei, 'Improving China's Participation in Resolving Developing-Country Debt Problems' (May 2021) Peterson Institute for International Economics, Policy Brief 21–10 <www.piie.com/publications/policy-briefs/improving-chinas-participation-resolving-developing-country-debt-problems> accessed 2 November 2021.

124 Viterbo (n 29) 101. Similarly, the IMF observed, '[l]arge emerging economies like China, Brazil and India, and other non-Paris Club creditors that provide significant bilateral official financing such as Saudi Arabia, now account for the major share of official bilateral claims on low-income countries.' See IMF, 'Reforming the Fund's Policy on Non-Toleration of Arrears to Official Creditors' (2015) IMF Policy Papers, 11 <www.imf.org/external/np/pp/eng/2015/101515.pdf> accessed 2 November 2021.

125 Hugh Bredenkamp, Ricardo Hausmann, Alex Pienkowski, and Carmen Reinhart, 'Challenges Ahead' in Abbas et al (n 70).

126 This said, the G20 Common Framework for Debt Treatments beyond the Debt Service Suspension Initiative provides for a new forum to coordinate the restructuring of claims by official lenders that are not members of the Paris Club, including some of the new major creditors, that are owed to 73 low-income countries. See G20, 'Statement at the Extraordinary G20 Finance Ministers and Central Bank Governors' Meeting' (Riyadh, 13 November 2020) <www.imf.org/-/media/Files/News/news-articles/english-extraordinary-g20-fmcbg-statement-november-13.ashx> accessed 2 November 2021. The Common Framework was approved in November 2020 during the Riyadh G20 Summit in response to the COVID-19 pandemic; however, at the day of this writing, there has not been a successful conclusion to a debt restructuring under the Common Framework. Time will tell whether the Common Framework has the potential to overcome coordination problems among official sector creditors, although it has been off to a rocky start and the IMF as well as other stakeholders have pushed to step up the Framework by expanding its scope to middle-income countries and including a standstill when a sovereign applies for debt treatment under the Common Framework. See Kristalina Georgieva and Ceyla Pazarbasioglu, 'The G20 Common Framework for Debt Treatments Must Be Stepped Up' (*IMF Blog*, 2 December 2021) <https://blogs.imf.org/2021/12/02/the-g20-common-framework-for-debt-treatments-must-be-stepped-up/> accessed 2 December 2021.

127 Viterbo (n 29) 101.

128 Ibid (Viterbo notes that '[t]his situation might give rise to creditor coordination problems and possibly to holdout behaviours among official creditors').

129 Arrears to official sector creditors are not uncommon, though they are generally discouraged by IFIs, such as the IMF; see IMF (n 124)..

130 Ibid 2. Two important exceptions existed, however: The IMF may provide financing as long as Paris Club agreements are adequately representative or the Executive Director representing the bilateral lender would consent to the IMF financing despite the existence of arrears. According to the Fund's policies, a Paris Club agreement is adequately representative if 'it covers a majority of total financing contributions from official bilateral creditors over the program period.'

131 Ibid 5, noting this:

> the Fund would consider lending into arrears owed to an official bilateral creditor only in circumstances where all the following criteria are satisfied: (i) prompt financial support from the Fund is considered essential, and the member is pursuing appropriate policies; (ii) the debtor is making good faith efforts to reach

> agreement with the creditor on a contribution consistent with the parameters of the Fund-supported program – ie, that the absence of an agreement is due to the unwillingness of the creditor to provide such a contribution; and (iii) the decision to provide financing despite the arrears would not have an undue negative effect on the Fund's ability to mobilize official financing packages in future cases.

132 Ibid 13, noting this:

> [t]he proposed change in the Fund's arrears policy – which in its current form can result in each official bilateral creditor having a veto over Fund lending decisions – will help reduce this risk by making it harder for noncontributing creditors to receive full payment on their debt at the expense of contributing creditors.

133 This was because the IMF considered Russia's claim to be official, even if structured as bond. See IMF, 'Status of Ukraine's Eurobond held by the Russian Federation' (11 December 2015) <http://www.imf.org/external/pubs/ft/scr/2015/cr15344.pdf> accessed 2 November 2021.

134 See Maximilian Hess, 'Bond of War – Russian Geo-Economics in Ukraine's Sovereign Debt Restructuring' (2018) Foreign Policy Research Institute <www.fpri.org/wp-content/uploads/2018/09/rpe-5-hess-final-.pdf> accessed 2 November 2021. For a legal review of the Ukraine-Russia bond dispute, including the subsequent litigation in English courts, see, for example, Anna Gelpern, 'Russia's Contract Arbitrage' (2014) 9(3) Capital Markets Law Journal 308; Mark Weidemaier, 'Contract law and Ukraine's $3 Billion Debt to Russia' (2016) 11 Capital Markets Law Journal 244; Mark Weidemaier, 'Ukraine Wins Appeal in Russian Bond Case' (*Credit Slips*, 14 September 2018) <www.creditslips.org/creditslips/2018/09/ukraine-wins-appeal-in-russian-bond-case.html#more> accessed 2 November 2021.

135 Gelpern (n 134) 309–312.

136 *Law Debenture Trust Corporation plc v Ukraine*, [2017] EWHC 655 (Comm), [2017] QB 1249, [2017] 3 WLR 667, [2017] WLR(D) 226, 29 March 2017, United Kingdom; England and Wales; High Court [EWHC]; Queen's Bench Division [QBD]; Commercial Court.

137 See Jane Croft and Roman Olearchyk, 'Ukraine-Russia Bond Dispute Set for Full English Trail' *Financial Times* (London, 14 September 2018).

6 Concluding Remarks

Despite the claim by Citibank's former Chairman Walter Wriston that 'countries never go bankrupt,'[1] states' public debts have in the past and will in the future reach unsustainable levels. However, irreconcilable political and economic interests abound; the international community has so far proven reluctant to implement a legal framework that regulates the rights and interests of creditors and debtors in the event of a sovereign default. Sovereign debt and its restructuring are, thus, largely founded on a non-system, as discussed in Chapter 1. While the existing architecture for debt restructurings at the international level has, at times, functioned better than many authors would suggest[2], the risk of disruption by both old and new holdout creditors remains real.

This book analysed holdout creditor problem against the backdrop of the two largest sovereign debt restructurings in history, the Greek debt workout of 2012 and the Argentine restructurings of 2005 and 2010. The two operations gave rise to a multitude of formidable legal problems that, on several occasions, seemingly overwhelmed judges and arbitrators. Thousands of lawsuits in the wake of Argentina and Greece, the most seminal of which were covered in this book, have circumscribed the perimeter for future public debt restructurings and underscored the different doctrinal approach to dealing with holdout creditor claims under foreign and domestic law instruments, respectively.

As Chapter 2 showed, holdout problems are likely to remain more pressing in the *foreign law* debt context, notably since courts in Europe and the US have all but eliminated adjudicatory immunity and most other defences to debt repayment. Judges in New York went even further, demonstrating their willingness to entertain unconventional contractual interpretations to provide litigious creditors with injunctive remedies capable of coercing a sovereign into granting preferential treatment. Moreover, ICSID arbitration decisions in the sovereign debt context have become increasingly inconsistent in the sovereign debt context, as illustrated by the divergent outcomes of ICSID proceedings related to Greece and Argentina, further exacerbating legal uncertainty.

At the same time, traditional enforcement channels remain constrained both as a matter of law and practice: central bank reserves on accounts with the FRBNY and the BIS are essentially immune from attachment, and courts in France and Germany have raised the bar to attaching assets within their jurisdiction that are

DOI: 10.4324/9781003361879-6

not evidently used for commercial purposes by the sovereign. Notwithstanding the limited risks for seizures, however, sovereign debt litigation may still cut a sovereign off from access to international credit markets. Any sovereign deciding to renege on its foreign law–governed debt instruments will, therefore, need to carefully consider the vulnerability of its assets to seizure attempts by holdouts and craft a smart restructuring strategy to avoid being blocked from access to foreign capital flows.

The Greek case, discussed in Chapter 3, demonstrated that the reorganization of a private debt stock governed by *domestic law* provides the sovereign debtor with considerably more flexibility and discretion. But as the ECtHR made clear, legal engineering has its limits. Introducing a legislative device that would result in the extinction of bondholders' repayment rights would run into serious obstacles under constitutional law, while a market-based solution that gives creditors a say over the restructuring plan proposed was deemed an appropriate interference with their rights. Moreover, as multiple lawsuits in Austrian and German courts have shown, the enforcement of domestic law claims in foreign courts raises complex jurisdictional questions, which tend to overlap with the assessment of the debtor country's immunity in those courts.

As Chapter 4 on the lessons from Greece and Argentina suggested further research is needed that delineates the increasingly blurry lines between domestic and foreign law restructuring as a matter of judicial practice. Sovereigns will have to continue to navigate murky procedural and substantive law doctrines while creditors can rarely be assured that they will ultimately succeed in court. Indeed, the subject of holdout litigation remains complex and prone to simplification or politicization. Hard-and-fast rules are few and far between, and the integration of economic imperatives, political preferences, and legal limits poses challenges that municipal courts and international tribunals cannot, and indeed should not, resolve on their own.

Finally, Chapter 5 discussed different types of holdout creditors. Against the backdrop of increasingly diverse funding sources for governments, new private and official sector holdouts will emerge and potentially haunt debt restructurings, adding complexity to an already opaque process. I thus refrained from asking, let alone answering, the question of which type of architecture reform should be pursued; many authors have presented possible solutions, and policymakers have made significant progress in closing some of the loopholes. Yet the ever-evolving nature of modern sovereign finance will require flexibility in addressing holdout creditor problems. And it is beyond doubt that those engaged in the resolution of future debt crises will need to look in the rear-view mirror and heed the most important lessons from Argentina and Greece.

Notes

1 See Ross Buckley, 'The Bankruptcy of Nations: An Idea Whose Time Has Come' (2009) 43(3) The International Lawyer 1189 (positing that 'Wriston's reasoning was utterly fallacious').

2 See Ran Bi, Marcos Chamon, and Jeromin Zettelmeyer, 'The Problem That Wasn't: Coordination Failures in Sovereign Debt Restructurings' (2011) IMF Working Paper No 11/265, 1 <www.imf.org/external/pubs/ft/wp/2011/wp11265.pdf> accessed 2 November 2021 (noting that '[even though] there was a widespread expectation [in the early 1990s] that debt renegotiation would become far more difficult compared to the bank-led process of preceding decades, . . . surprisingly that has not been the case').

Bibliography

Books

Abbas, Ali, Alex Pienkowski, and Ken Rogoff, *Sovereign Debt: A Guide for Economists and Practitioners* (Oxford: Oxford University Press, 2019).

Allen, Franklin, Elena Carletti, and Mitu Gulati (eds), *Institutions and the Crisis* (Florence: European University Institute, 2018).

Amtenbrink, Fabian, Christoph Herrmann, and Rene Repasi (eds), *The EU Law of the Economic and Monetary Union* (Oxford: Oxford University Press, 2020).

Audit, Matthias, *Insolvabilité des États et Dettes Souveraines* (Paris: LDGJ, 2011).

Bankas, Ernest, *The State Immunity Controversy in International Law – Private Suits Against Sovereign States in Domestic Courts* (Berlin: Springer, 2005).

Bantekas, Ilias, and Cephas Lumina (eds), *Sovereign Debt and Human Rights* (Oxford: Oxford Scholarship Online, 2019).

Binder, Christina, Ursula Kriebaum, August Reinisch, and Stephan Wittich, *International Investment Law for the 21st Century. Essays in Honour of Christoph Schreuer* (Oxford: Oxford University Press, 2009).

Blas, Javier, and Jack Farchy, *The World For Sale: Money, Power, and the Traders Who Barter the Earth's Resources* (Oxford: Oxford University Press, 2021).

Bohoslavsky, Juan Pablo, and Jemej Letnar Cernic (eds), *Making Sovereign Financing and Human Rights Work* (London: Bloomsbury, 2014).

Borchard, Edwin, and Justus S Hotchkiss, *State Insolvency and Foreign Bondholders: General Principles* (New Haven: Yale University Press, 1951).

Braga, Carlos, and Gallina Vincelette, *Sovereign Debt and the Financial Crisis* (Washington, DC: The World Bank, 2011).

Brunnermaier, Markus, Harold James, and Jean-Pierre Landau, *The Euro and the Battle of Ideas* (Princeton: Princeton University Press, 2016).

Dolzer, Rudolf, and Christoph Schreuer, *Principles of International Investment Law* (Oxford: Oxford University Press, 2012).

Douglas, Zachary (ed), *The Foundations of International Investment Law: Bringing Theory into Practice* (Oxford: Oxford University Press, 2014).

Durlauf, Steven, and Lawrence Blime (eds), *The New Palgrave Dictionary of Economics* (London: Palgrave Macmillan, 2009).

Dyson, Kenneth HF, *States, Debt, and Power: 'Saints' and 'Sinners' in European History Integration* (Oxford: Oxford University Press, 2014).

Edwards, Sebastian, *Capital Controls and Capital Flows in Emerging Economics: Policies, Practices, and Consequences* (Chicago: Chicago University Press, 2007).

———. *American Default: The Untold Story of FDR, the Supreme Court, and the Battle Over Gold* (Princeton: Princeton University Press, 2018).

Eichengreen, Barry, Ricardo Hausmann, and Ugo Panizza, *Other People's Money* (Chicago: University of Chicago Press, 2005).

Fox, Hazel, and Philippa Webb, *The Law of State Immunity* (Oxford: Oxford University Press, 2013).

Gallagher, Kevin P, *The Clash of Globalizations – Essays on the Political Economy of Trade and Development* (New York: Anthem Press, 2013).

Garner, Bryan A, *Black's Law Dictionary* (London: Thomson Reuters, 2014, 10th ed).

Ginsburg, Tom, Mark D Rosen, and Georg Vanberg, *Constitutions in Times of Financial Crises* (Cambridge: Cambridge University Press, 2019).

Gopinath, Gita, Elhanan Helpman, and Kenneth Rogoff (eds), *Handbook of International Economics* (Amsterdam: Elsevier, 2014).

Grant, John P, and J Craig Barker (eds), *Encyclopaedic Dictionary of International Law* (Oxford: Oxford University Press, 2009, 3rd ed).

Guzman, Martin, Jose Antonio Ocampo, and Joseph Stieglitz (eds), *Too Little, Too Late: The Quest to Resolve Sovereign Debt Crises* (New York: Columbia University Press, 2016).

Haskell, John D, and Akbar Rasulov (eds), *New Voices and Perspectives in International Economic Law* (Berlin: Springer, 2020).

Herman, Barry, José Antonio Ocampo, and Shari Spiegel (eds), *Overcoming Developing Country Debt Crises* (Oxford: Oxford University Press, 2010).

Jekewitz, Jürgen (ed), *Des Menschen Recht zwischen Freiheit und Verantwortung: Festschrift für Karl Josef Partsch zum 75. Geburtstag* (Berlin: Duncker & Humblot, 1989).

Kelly, Kate, *The Secret Club That Runs the World* (New York City: Penguin Random House, 2015).

King, Jeff, *The Doctrine of Odious Debt in International Law – A Restatement* (Cambridge: Cambridge University Press, 2016).

Krueger, Anne, *A New Approach to Sovereign Debt Restructuring* (Washington, DC: IMF, 2002).

Kupeylants, Hayk, *Sovereign Defaults Before Domestic Courts* (Oxford: Oxford University Press, 2018).

Lastra, Rosa, and Lee Buchheit (eds), *Sovereign Debt Management* (Oxford: Oxford University Press, 2014).

Lorz, Sigrid, *Auslandische Staaten vor Deutschen Zivilgerichten: Zum Spannungsverhaltnis Von Staatenimmunitat Und Recht Auf Zugang Zu Gericht* (Tuebingen: Mohr Siebeck, 2017).

Megliani, Mauro, *Sovereign Debt: Genesis, Restructuring, Litigation* (Berlin: Springer, 2015).

Muller, Sam, *International Organizations and Their Host States: Aspects of Their Legal Relationship* (Amsterdam: Martinus Nijhoff, 1995).

Müller, Matthias, *Staatsbankrott und private Gläubiger* (Baden-Baden: Nomos, 2015).

Olivares-Caminal, Rodrigo, *Legal Aspects of Sovereign Debt Restructuring* (London: Sweet & Maxwell, 2009).

Olson, Mancur, *The Logic of Collective Action: Public Goods and the Theory Of Groups* (Cambridge: Harvard University Press, 1965).

Paulus, Christoph (ed), *A Debt Restructuring Procedure for Sovereigns – Do We Need a Legal Procedure?* (London: Hart, 2014).

Petch, Tolek, *Legal Implications of the Euro Zone Crisis* (Amsterdam: Kluwer, 2014).

Peters, Anne (ed), *Max Planck Encyclopaedia of Public International Law* (Oxford: Oxford University Press, 2020).

Peters, Anne, Evelyne Lagrange, Stefan Oeter, and Christian Tomuschat (eds), *Immunities in the Age of Global Constitutionalism* (The Hague: Brill Nijhoff, 2014).

Rault, Charlotte, *The Legal Framework of Sovereign Debt Management* (Berlin: Nomos, 2017).

Reinhart, Carmen, and Kenneth Rogoff, *This Time Is Different: Eight Centuries of Financial Folly* (Princeton: Princeton University Press, 2009).

Reinisch, August (ed), *The Privileges and Immunities of International Organisations in Domestic Courts* (Oxford: Oxford University Press, 2011).

Rieffel, Lex, *Restructuring Sovereign Debt: The Case for Ad Hoc Machinery* (Washington, DC: Brookings Institution Press, 2003).

Ringbom, Henrik (ed), *Jurisdiction Over Ships: Post-UNCLOS Developments in the Law of the Sea* (Amsterdam: Brill, 2015).

Roos, Jerome, *Why Not Default? The Political Economy of Sovereign Debt* (Princeton: Princeton University Press, 2019).

Roubini, Nouriel, and Brad Setser, *Bailouts or Bail-Ins? Responding to Financial Crises in Emerging Economies* (Washington, DC: Peterson Institute for International Economics, 2004).

Sachs, Jeffrey (ed), *Volume 1: The International Financial System: Developing Country Debt and Economic Performance* (Chicago: University of Chicago Press, 1989).

Schier, Holger, *Towards a Reorganisation System for Sovereign Debt* (Leiden/Boston: Martinus Nijhoff Publishers, 2007).

Schreuer, Christoph, Loretta Malintoppi, August Reinisch, and Anthony Sinclair, *The ICSID Convention* (Cambridge: Cambridge University Press, 2009, 2nd ed).

Schumacher, Julian, *Enforcement in Sovereign Debt Markets* (PhD thesis, Humboldt University, Berlin, 2015) unpublished PhD book.

Spiro, David E., *The Hidden Hand of American Hegemony: Petrodollar Recycling and International Markets* (Ithaca: Cornell University Press, 1999).

Strong, Stacie, *Class, Mass, and Collective Arbitration in National and International Law* (Oxford: Oxford University Press, 2013).

Sturzenegger, Frederico, and Jeromin Zettelmeyer, *Debt Defaults and Lessons from a Decade of Crises* (Cambridge: MIT Press, 2007).

Szodruch, Alexander, *Staateninsolvenz und Private Gläubiger: Rechtsprobleme des Private Sector Involvement bei staatlichen Finanzkrisen im 21. Jahrhundert* (Berlin: Berliner Wissenschaftsverlag, 2010).

Tooze, Adam, *Crashed: How a Decade of Financial Crises Changes the World* (New York: Penguin Random House, 2018).

Verdier, Pierre-Hughes, *Global Banks on Trial: U.S. Prosecutions and the Remaking of International Finance* (Oxford: Oxford University Press, 2020).

Viterbo, Annamaria, *Sovereign Debt Restructuring: The Role and Limits of Public International Law* (Turin: Giappichelli, 2020).

Waibel, Michael, *Sovereign Debt Before International Courts and Tribunals* (Cambridge: Cambridge University Press, 2011).

Wolfrum, Rüdiger, *Max Planck Encyclopaedia of Public International Law* (Heidelberg: Oxford University Press, 2007, online version).

Wood, Philipp, *The Law and Practice of International Finance* (London: Sweet & Maxwell, 2008) 163.

Yang, Xiaodong, *State Immunity in International Law* (Cambridge: Cambridge University Press, 2012).

Netanella Tani, Zahavi, *Sovereign Debt: Analyses and Remedies* (PhD thesis, 2005) unpublished manuscript.

Journal Articles and Commentaries

Alfaro, Laura, Noel Maurer, and Faisal Ahmed, 'Gunboats and Vultures: Market Reaction to the "Enforcement" of Sovereign Debt' (2010) 73 Law and Contemporary Problems 39.

Alvarez, Jose E, and Gustavo Topalian, 'The Paradoxical Argentina Cases' (2012) 6(3) World Arbitration & Mediation Review 491.

Asonuma, Tamon, and Christoph Trebesch, 'Sovereign Debt Restructuring: Preemptive or Post-Default' (2016) 14(1) Journal of the European Economic Association 175.

Audit, Matthias, 'Sovereign Bonds and National Relativism: Can New York Law Contracts Safely Cross the Atlantic?' (2014) 9(2) Capital Markets Law Journal 177.

Beess und Chrostin, Jessica, 'Sovereign Debt Restructuring and Mass Claim Arbitration Before the ICSID, the Abaclat Case' (2012) 53(2) Harvard International Law Journal 505.

Benish, Kevin D, 'Crystallex Int'l Corp. v Bolivarian Rep. Venez. (3D Cir.)' (2021) 60(2) International Legal Materials 147.

Bianco, Giuseppe, 'European Union's Investment Agreements and Public Debt' (2017) 2 European Business Law Review 119.

Blackman, Jonathan, and Rahul Mukhi, 'The Evolution of Modern Sovereign Debt Litigation: Vultures, Alter Egos, and Other Legal Fauna' (2010) 73(4) Law and Contemporary Problems 47.

Blackman, Jonathan, Carmine Boccuzzi, William Lawrence, Jarrett Perlow, Fahad Habib, Jeffrey Robins, Karen Woody, Heather Van Slooten Walsh, Phillip Dye Jr, Justin Marlles, Dawna Gardner, Vitali S Rosenfeld, Rahul Mukhi, and Alida Lasker, 'International Litigation' (2007) 42 The International Lawyer 415.

Blom, Jasper, 'The Institute of International Finance: From Poacher to Gatekeeper' (2021) 23(1) Business and Politics 153.

Blumrosen, Alexander, and Fleur Maelt-Deraedt, 'NML Capital Ltd. v Republic of Argentina' (2013) 107(3) The American Journal of International Law 638.

Boggio, Luca, 'Investors and Sovereign Debt Restructurings: The Protection of Financial Property before International Courts and Arbitrators' (2018) 15(2) Manchester Journal of International Economic Law 143.

Bolton, Patrick, and Olivier Jeanne, 'Structuring and Restructuring Sovereign Debt: The Role of a Bankruptcy Regime' (2007) 115(6) Journal of Political Economy 905.

Bradley, Michael, Elisabeth de Fontenay, Irving Aturo de Lira Salvatierra and Mitu Gulati, 'Pricing Sovereign Debt: Foreign versus Local Parameters' (2017) 24 European Financial Management 261.

Bratton, William W, 'Pari Passu and A Distressed Sovereign's Rational Choices' (2004) 53 Emory Law Journal 823.

Buchheit, Lee, 'The Sharing Clause as a Litigation Shield' (1990) 9(10) International Financial Law Review 15.

———. 'Cross-Border Lending: What's Different this Time' (1995) 16(1) Northwestern Journal of International Law & Business 44.

———. 'Changing Bond Documentation: The Sharing Clause' (1998) 17 International Financial Review 17.

———. 'The Search for Intercreditor Parity' (2002) 8(1) Law and Business Review of the Americas 73.

———. 'Trustees Versus Fiscal Agents for Sovereign Bonds' (2018) 13(3) Capital Markets Law Journal 410.

Buchheit, Lee, and Jeremiah S Pam, 'The Pari Passu Clause in Sovereign Debt Instruments' (2004) 53 Emory Law Review 870.

Buchheit, Lee, and Mitu Gulati, 'Sovereign Bonds and the Collective Will' (2002) 53 Emory Law Journal 1324.

———. 'Responsible Sovereign Lending and Borrowing' (2013) 73 Law and Contemporary Problems 63.

———. 'Restructuring Sovereign Debt After Argentina' (2017) 12 (2) Capital Markets Law Journal 224.

———. 'Sovereign Debt Restructuring in Europe' (2018) 9(1) Global Policy 65.

Buckley, Ross, 'The Facilitation of the Brady Plan: Emerging Markets Debt Trading from 1989 to 1993' (1997) 21 Fordham International Law Journal 1802.

———. 'The Transformative Potential of a Secondary Market: Emerging Markets Debt Trading from 1983 to 1989' (1997) 21(4) Fordham Journal of International Law 1152.

———. 'The Bankruptcy of Nations: An Idea Whose Time Has Come' (2009) 43(3) The International Lawyer 1189.

Carletti, Elena, Paolo Colla, Mitu Gulati, and Steven Ongena, 'The Price of Law: The Case of Eurozone Collective Action Clauses' (2021) 34(12) The Review of Financial Studies 5933.

Chevry, Jonathan, '*Poštová banka, a.s. and ISTROKAPITAL SE v Hellenic Republic*, ICSID Case No. ARB/13/8 (Poštová banka v Greece)' (2016) 15 World Trade Review 169.

Choi, Steven J, and Mitu Gulati, 'Contract as Statute' (2006) 104 Michigan Law Review 1129.

———. 'An Empirical Study of Securities Disclosure Practice' (2006) 80 Tulane Law Review 1023.

Choi, Stephen J, Mitu Gulati, and Eric A Posner, 'Pricing Terms in Sovereign Debt Contracts: A Greek Case Study with Implications for the European Crisis Resolution Mechanism' (2011) 6(2) Capital Markets Law Journal 163.

Cohen, Robert A, 'Sometimes a Cigar Is Just a Cigar: The Simple Story of Pari Passu' (2011) 40 Hofstra Law Review 11.

Craig, Paul, and Menelaos Markakis, 'Gauweiler and the Legality of Outright Monetary Transactions' (2016) 41(1) European Law Review 241.

Cruces, Jan, and Tim Samples, 'Settling Sovereign Debt's "Trial of the Century"' (2016) 31 Emory International Law Review 5.

De La Cruz, Andres, and Ignacio Lagos, 'CACs at Work: What Next? Lessons from the Argentine and Ecuadorian 2020 Debt Restructurings' (2021) 16(2) Capital Markets Law Journal 226.

Delaume, Georges R, 'Three Perspectives on Sovereign Immunity – Public Debt and Sovereign Immunity: The Foreign Sovereign Immunities Act of 1976' (1977) 71(3) The American Journal of International Law 399.

Dewachter, Hans, Leonardo Iania, Marco Lyrio, and Maite de Sola Perera, 'A Macro-Financial Analysis of the Euro Area Sovereign Bond Market' (2015) 50 Journal of Banking & Finance 308.

Dimri, BM, 'The Arrest of Argentine Warship "ARA Libertad": Revisiting International Law Governing Warships, Sovereign Immunity, and Naval Diplomatic Roles' (2013) 7(3) Journal of Defence Studies 97.

Drelichmann, Mauricio, and Hans-Joachim Voth, 'Lending to the Borrower from Hell: Debt and Default in the Age of Philip II' (2011) 121 The Economic Journal 1205.

Eichengreen, Barry, 'Restructuring Sovereign Debt' (2003) 17(4) Journal of Economic Perspectives 75.

Engelen, Christian, and Johann Graf Lambsdorff, 'Hares and Stags in Argentinean Debt Restructuring' (2009) 78 Journal of International Economics 141.

Euliss, Richard, 'The Feasibility of the IMF's Sovereign Debt Restructuring Mechanism: An Alternative Statutory Approach to Mollify American Reservations' (2003) 19(1) American University International Law Review 107.

Fisch, Jill, and Caroline Gentile, 'Vultures or Vanguards: The Role of Litigation in Sovereign Debt Restructuring' (2004) 53(1) Emory Law Journal 1047.

Gaillard, Emmanuel, and Ilija Mitrev Penushliski, 'State Compliance with Investment Awards' (2020) 35(3) ICSID Review 540.

Gallagher, Kevin, 'Financial Crisis and International Investment Agreements: The Case of Sovereign Debt Restructuring' (2012) 3(3) Global Policy 362.

Gelpern, Anna, 'Contract Hope and Sovereign Redemption' (2013) 8(2) Capital Markets Law Journal 132.

———. 'Russia's Contract Arbitrage' (2014) 9(3) Capital Markets Law Journal 308.

———. '*NML Capital, Ltd. v Republic of Argentina* and the Changing Roles of the *Pari Passu* and Collective Action Clauses in Sovereign Debt Agreements' (2015) 53 Columbia Journal of Transnational Law 396.

———. 'Sovereign Debt: Now What' (2016) 41(2) Yale Journal of International Law Online 45.

Gelpern, Anna, and Mitu Gulati, 'CDS Zombies' (2012) 13 European Business Organization Law Review 347.

Ginsberg, Simon, Ellen, and Q Monty Crawford, 'The Impact of Republic of Argentina v NML Capital, Ltd.: Why the Supreme Court's Ruling Against Argentina Avoided a Host of Unintended, Negative Consequences' (2015) 30(1) Maryland Journal of International Law 55.

Giroud, Sandrine, 'Enforcement Against State Assets and Execution of ICSID Awards in Switzerland: How Swiss Courts Deal with Immunity Defences' (2012) 30 ASA Bulletin 4.

Goldman, Samuel E, 'Mavericks in the Market: The Emerging Problem of Hold-Outs in Sovereign Debt Restructuring' (2000) 5 UCLA Journal of International Law & Foreign Affairs 159.

Grund, Sebastian, 'Restructuring Government Debt Under Local Law: The Greek Case and Implications for Investor Protection in Europe' (2017) 12(2) Capital Markets Law Journal 253.

———. 'The Legal Consequences of Sovereign Insolvency – A Review of Creditor Litigation in Germany Following the Greek Debt Restructuring' (2017) 24(3) Maastricht Journal of Comparative and European Law 399.

———. 'Enforcing Sovereign Debt in Court – A Comparative Analysis of Litigation and Arbitration Following the Greek Debt Restructuring of 2012' (2017) 1 University of Vienna Law Review 34.

———. 'The Greek Debt Crisis and Sovereign Debt Litigation in Austrian Courts' (2018) 21(1) Austrian Review of International and European Law Online 131.

Grund, Sebastian, and Filip Grle, 'The European Central Bank's Public Sector Purchase Programme (PSPP), the Prohibition of Monetary Financing and Sovereign Debt Restructuring Scenarios' (2016) 41(6) European Law Review 781.

Gulati, Mitu, and Lee Buchheit, 'Use of the Local Law Advantage in the Restructuring of European Sovereign Bonds' (2018) 3(2) University of Bologna Law Review 172.

Gulati, Mitu, and George Triantis, 'Contracts Without Law: Sovereign Versus Corporate Debt' (2007) 75 University of Cincinnati Law Review 977.

Gulati, Mitu, and Jeromin Zettelmeyer, 'Making a Voluntary Greek Debt Exchange Work' (2012) 7(2) Capital Markets Law Journal 169.

Gourinchas, Pierre-Oliver, Thomas Philippon, and Dimitri Vayanos, 'The Analytics of the Greek Crisis' (2016) 31(1) NBER Macroeconomics Annual 1.

Hagan, Sean, 'Designing a Legal Framework to Restructure Sovereign Debt' (2005) 36 Georgetown Journal of International Law 299.

Halverson Cross, Karen, 'The Extraterritorial Reach of Sovereign Debt Enforcement' (2015) 12 Berkeley Business Law Journal 111.

Hancen, Yu, 'Official Bondholder: A New Holdout Creature in Sovereign Debt Restructuring After Vulture Funds' (2017) 16 Washington University Global Studies Law Review 535.

Hébert, Benjamin, and Jesse Schreger, 'The Costs of Sovereign Default: Evidence from Argentina' (2017) 107(10) American Economic Review 3119.

Hotchkiss, Edith S, and Robert M Mooradian, 'Vulture Investors and the Market for Control of Distressed Firms' (1997) 43 Journal of Financial Economics 401.

Hudes, Karen, 'Coordination of Paris and London Club Reschedulings' (1985) 17(3) New York University Journal of International Law and Politics 553.

Jamnejad, Maziar, and Michael Wood, 'The Principle of Non-Intervention' (2009) 22(2) Leiden Journal of International Law 345.

Kahan, Marcel, 'The Scope of Section 316(b) After *Marblegate*' (2018) 13(2) Capital Markets Law Journal 136.

Kalaitzake, Manolis, 'The Political Power of Finance: The Institute of International Finance in the Greek Debt Crisis' (2017) 45(3) Politics & Society 389.

Kaplan, Jesse, 'Collective Action and the Competence of Courts: The Lessons from NML v Argentina' (2014) 1 Stanford Journal of Business and Finance Law 30.

Keegan, S Drake, 'The Rise and Fall of Exit Consents' (2014) 64 Duke Law Journal 1589.

Kerber, Markus, 'Sargnägel auf dem Anlegerschutz? – Anmerkungen zur Legalisierung der Zwangsumschuldung der Gläubiger griechischer Staatsanleihen durch die Urteile des EGMR vom 21.7.2016 und des EuGH vom 15.11.2018' (2019) 29 Wirtschafts & Bankrecht 395.

Kraska, James, 'The "ARA Libertad" (*Argentina v Ghana*). ITLOS Case No. 20 Provisional Measures' (2013) 107 The American Journal of International Law 1.

Krueger, Anne O, and Sean Hagan, 'Sovereign Workouts: An IMF Perspective' (2005) 6(1) Chicago Journal of International Law 203.

Krugman, Paul, 'Financing v Forgiving a Debt Overhang' (1988) 29 Journal of Development Economics 253.

Ku, Julian G, 'Don't Cry for Sovereign Debtors: Why Argentina's Defeat in US Courts Does Not Justify a Sovereign Debt Treaty' (2014) 36 University of Pennsylvania Journal of International Law 433.

Lupo-Pasini, Federico, 'Hidden Sovereign Finance' (2021) 16(2) Capital Markets Law Journal 165.

Macmillan, Rory, 'Towards a Sovereign Debt Workout System' (1995–1996) 16 Northwestern Journal of International Law & Business 57.

Manuelides, Yannis, 'Debtor Creditor Engagement in Sovereign Restructurings' (2018) 13(3) Capital Markets Law Journal 427.

———. 'Using the Local Law Advantage in Today's Eurozone (with Some References to the Republic of Arcadia and the Mamatas Judgment)' (2019) 14(4) Capital Markets Law Journal 469.

Manzo, Alejandro Gabriel, 'Enforceability of Judgments Against Sovereign States: Critical Analysis of the NML vs. Argentina Injunction' (2018) 14(2) Revista Direito GV 682.

Megliani, Mauro, 'Vultures in Courts: Why the UNCTAD Principles on Responsible Financing Cannot Stop Litigation' (2015) 28 Leiden Journal of International Law 849.

Miles, William, 'The Pricing of Risk in Emerging Credit Markets: Bonds Versus Loans' (2000) 6(2) International Advances in Economic Research 221.

Miller, Marcus, and Dania Thomas, 'Sovereign Debt Restructuring: The Judge, the Vultures and Creditor Rights' (2007) 30(10) The World Economy 1491.

———. 'Eurozone Sovereign Debt Restructuring: Keeping the Vultures at Bay' (2013) 29(4) Oxford Review of Economic Policy 745.

Mitchener, Kris, and Marc Weidenmier, 'Supersanctions and Sovereign Debt Repayment' (2010) 29(1) Journal of International Money and Finance 19.

Montanaro, Francesco, 'Case Comment *Poštová Banka SA and Istrokapital SE v Hellenic Republic* – Sovereign Bonds and the Puzzling Definition of "Investment" in International Investment Law' (2015) 30(3) ICSID Review 549.

Monteleone, Theresa, 'A Vulture's Gamble: High-Stakes Interpretation of Sovereign Debt Contracts in NML Capital Ltd v Republic of Argentina' (2014) 8(2) Capital Markets Law Journal 159.

Nakajima, Kei, 'Parallel Universes of Investment Protection? A Divergent Finding on the Definition of Investment in the ICSID Arbitration on Greek Sovereign Debts' (2017) 15(3) The Law & Practice of International Courts and Tribunals 472.

Neumann, Thore, 'NML Capital Ltd and EM Limited v Bank for International Settlements and Debt Enforcement Office Basel-Stadt' (2010) Oxford Reports on International Law in Domestic Courts (ILDC) 1547.

Olivares-Caminal, Rodrigo, 'Sovereign Bonds: A Critical Analysis of Argentina's Debt Exchange Offer' (2008) 10(1) Journal of Banking Regulation 28.

———. 'Understanding the *Pari Passu* Clause in Sovereign Debt Instruments: A Complex Quest' (2009) 43(3) The International Lawyer 1217.

———. 'The Pari Passu Interpretation in the Elliott Case: A Brilliant Strategy but an Awful (Mid-Long Term) Outcome?' (2011) 40(1) Hofstra Law Review 39.

———. 'The Definition of Indebtedness and the Consequent Imperilling of the *pari passu*, Negative Pledge and Cross Default Clauses in Sovereign Debt Instruments' (2017) 12(2) Capital Markets Law Journal 164.

Oosterlinck, Kim, 'Sovereign Debt Defaults: Insights from History' (2013) 29(4) Oxford Review of Economic Policy 697.

Ostransky, Josef, 'Sovereign Default Disputes in International Treaty Arbitration: Jurisdictional Considerations and Policy Implications' (2015) 3(1) Groningen Journal of International Law 27.

Paliouras, Vassilis, 'The Right to Restructure Sovereign Debt' (2017) 20 Journal of International Economic Law 115.

Panizza, Ugo, Federico Sturzenegger, and Jeromin Zettelmeyer, 'The Economics and Law of Sovereign Debt and Default' (2009) 47(3) Journal of Economic Literature 651.

Park, Stephen K, and Tim R Samples, 'Tribunalizing Sovereign Debt: Argentina's Experience with Investor-State Dispute Settlement' (2017) 50 Vanderbilt Journal of Transnational Law 1033.

Peters, Anne, 'Die funktionale Immunität internationaler Organisationen und die Rechtsweggarantie; zugleich Anmerkung zur Entscheidung des schweizerischen Bundesgerichts zur Immunität der Bank für Internationalen Zahlungsausgleich (BIZ) vom 12 Juli 2010 (BGE 136 III 379, 5A 360/2010)' (2011) 21 Revue Suisse de Droit International et Européen 397.

Poon, Arthur, 'Place of Performance Under Article 7(1) Brussels I Recast' (2021) 70(3) International and Comparative Law Quarterly 635.

Porzecanski, Aturo, 'From Rogue Creditors to Rogue Debtors: Implications of Argentina's Default' (2005) 6 Chicago Journal of International Law 311.

Power, Philip, 'Sovereign Debt: The Rise of the Secondary Market and Its Implication for Future Restructurings' (1996) 64(4) Fordham Law Review 2701.

Power, Vincent, 'Ships, Sovereign Immunity and the Subtleties of the Brussels I Regulation: Case C-641/18 LG and Others v Rina SpA, Ente Registro Italiano Navale: Ships, Sovereign Immunity and the Subtleties of Brussels I: Rina Case Note' (2021) 28(3) Maastricht Journal of European and Comparative Law 419.

Reinhart, Carmen, Vincent Reinhart, and Kenneth Rogoff, 'Public Debt Overhangs: Advanced Economy Episodes Since 1800' (2012) 26(3) Journal of Economic Perspectives 69.

Raffer, Kunibert, 'Applying Chapter 9 Insolvency to International Debts: An Economically Efficient Solution with a Human Face' (1990) 18(2) World Development 301.

Reeves, William Harvey, 'The Foreign Sovereign Before United States Courts' (1970) 38(3) Fordham Law Review 455.

Reinhart, Carmen, and Kenneth Rogoff, 'The Forgotten History of Domestic Debt' (2011) 121(552) The Economic Journal 319.

Reinisch, August, 'European Court Practice Concerning State Immunity from Enforcement Measures' (2006) 17(4) European Journal of International Law 803.

Robinson, Thomas E, 'The Peculiar Case of the ARA Libertad: Provisional Measures and Prejudice to the Arbitral Tribunal's Final Result' (2015) 20 Harvard Negotiation Law Review 265.

Rogoff, Kenneth, and Jeromin Zettelmeyer, 'Bankruptcy Procedures for States: A History of Ideas, 1976–2001' (2002) 49(3) IMF Staff Papers 470.

Rosenfeld, Friedrich, 'Mass Claims in International Law' (2013) 4(1) Journal of International Dispute Settlement 159.

Rudolf, Beate, and Nina Hüfken, 'Joined Case Nos. 2 BvM 1–5/03 & BvM 1–2/06' (2007) 101(4) The American Journal of International Law 857.

Sachs, Jeffrey, 'Do We Need an International Lender of Last Resort?' (20 April 1995) Frank D Graham Lecture at Princeton University, on file with author.

Samples, Tim R, 'Rogue Trends in Sovereign Debt: Argentina, Vulture Funds, and Pari Passu Under New York Law' (2014) 35(1) Northwestern Journal of International Law & Business 49.

Sandrock, Otto, 'The Case for More Arbitration When Sovereign Debt Is to Be Restructured: Greece as an Example' (2012) 23 The American Review of International Arbitration 507.

Schill, Stephan, 'Der völkerrechtliche Staatsnotstand in der Entscheidung des BVerfG zu Argentinischen Staatsanleihen – Anachronismus oder Avantgarde?' (2008) 68 ZaöRV 45.

Schramm, Dorothee, 'Enforcement and the Abolition of Exaquatur Under the 2012 Brussels I Regulation' (2013/14) 15 Yearbook of Private International Law 143.

Schwarcz, Steven, 'Sovereign Debt Restructuring: A Bankruptcy Reorganization Approach' (2000) 85 Cornell Law Review 956.

———. 'Sovereign Debt Restructuring and English Governing Law' (2017) 12 Brooklyn Journal of Corporate, Financial & Commercial Law 73.

Scott, Hal, 'How Would a New Bankruptcy Regime Help?' (2002) 33(1) Brookings Papers on Economic Activity 334.

Shutter, Andrew, 'Barbados Sovereign Debt Restructuring 2018–2019 – Like the Island, Small but Perfectly Formed' 15(2) Capital Markets Law Journal 250 (2020).

Singer, Michael, 'Abandoning Restrictive Sovereign Immunity: An Analysis in Terms of Jurisdiction to Prescribe' (1985) 26 Harvard International Law Journal 1.

Steinkamp, Sven, and Frank Westermann, 'The Role of Creditor Seniority in Europe's Sovereign Debt Crisis' 29(79) Economic Policy 495 (2014).

Stolper, Antonia, and Sean Dougherty, 'Collective Action Clauses: How the Argentina Litigation Changed Sovereign Debt Markets' (2017) 12(2) Capital Markets Law Journal 239.

Szczudlik, Katarzyna Barbara, 'Mass Claims Under ICSID' (2015) 4(2) Wroclaw Review of Law, Administration & Economics 70.

Tarullo, Daniel K, 'The Role of the IMF in Sovereign Debt Restructuring' (2005) 6(1) Chicago Journal of International Law 287.

Tomz, Michael, and Mark Wright, 'Empirical Research on Sovereign Debt and Default' (2013) 5 Annual Review of Economics 247.

Tsibanoulis, Dimitris, and Iakovos Anagnostopoulos, 'The Greek PSI and the Litigation Surrounding It' (2014) 2 International Review of Financial Services 18.

Viterbo, Annamaria, 'Supranational Creditors: A Threat to the Equal Status of Bondholders?' (2015) 10(2) Capital Markets Law Journal 193.

Waibel, Michael, 'Opening Pandora's Box: Sovereign Bonds in International Arbitration' (2007) 101 American Journal of International Law 711.

Walker, Mark A, and Bathelemy Fay, 'Sovereign Debt Renegotiation: Restructuring the Commercial Debt of HIPC Debtor Countries' (2010) 73(4) Law and Contemporary Problems 317.

Weidemaier, Mark, 'Sovereign Immunity and Sovereign Debt' (2014) 1 University of Illinois Law Review 68.

———. 'Contract Law and Ukraine's USD 3 bn Debt to Russia' (2016) 11(2) Capital Markets Law Journal 244.

———. 'Restructuring Euro Area Sovereign Debt: Have the Options Narrowed?' (2020) 6(1) Journal of Financial Regulation 125.

Weidemaier, Mark, and Anna Gelpern, 'Injunctions in Sovereign Debt Litigation' (2014) 31(1) Yale Journal on Regulation 189.

Weidemaier, Mark, and Mitu Gulati, 'The Relevance of Law to Sovereign Debt' (2015) 11 Annual Review of Law and Social Science 395.

———'Necessity and the Covid-19 Pandemic' (2020) 15(3) Capital Markets Law Journal 277.

Weller, Marc-Philippe, and Pauline Grotz, 'Staatsnotstand bei Staatsanleihen' (2015) 20 Juristenzeitung 989.

Wheeler, Christopher, and Amir Attaran, 'Declawing the Vulture Funds: Rehabilitation of a Comity Defence in Sovereign Debt Litigation' (2003) 39 Stanford Journal of International Law 253.

Wirtz, Alison, 'Bilateral Investment Treaties, Holdout Investors, and Their Impact on Grenada's Sovereign Debt Crisis' (2015) 16(1) Chicago Journal of International Law 249, 253.

Witte, Andreas, 'Greek Bond Haircut: Public and Private International Law and European Law Limits to Unilateral Sovereign Debt Restructuring' (2012) 9(3) Manchester Journal of International Law 307.

Wood, Michael, 'Do International Organizations Enjoy Immunity Under Customary International Law' (2014) (10)(2) International Organizations Law Review 287.

Wozny, Lucas, 'National Anti-Vulture Funds Legislation: Belgium's Turn' (2017) 2 Columbia Business Law Review 697.

Wright, Mark, 'Sovereign Debt Restructuring: Problems and Prospects' (2012) 2(1) Harvard Business Law Review 166.

Xava, Miranda, 'Life After Debt – The Greek PSI and Its Aftermath' (2013) 14(1) World Economics 81.

Zettelmeyer, Jeromin, Christoph Trebesch, and Mitu Gulati, 'The Greek Debt Restructuring: An Autopsy' (2013) 28(75) Economic Policy 513.

Newspaper Articles

Atkins, Ralph, 'ECB Avoids Forced Losses on Greek Bonds' *Financial Times* (London, 16 February 2012).

Balzli, Beat, 'How Goldman Sachs Helped Greece to Mask Its True Debt' *Spiegel Online* (Hamburg, 8 February 2010) <www.spiegel.de/international/europe/greek-debt-crisis-how-goldman-sachs-helped-greece-to-mask-its-true-debt-a-676634.html>.

Bases, Daniel, 'For Argentina Holdout Fund, a Decade's Pursuit May Pay Off' *Reuters* (London, 2 December 2012) <www.reuters.com/article/argentina-debt-elliott-idUSL1E8MU9NK20121202>.

Celarier, Michelle, 'Singer Takes Victory Lap in Debt Feud' *New York Post* (New York, 30 October 2012).

Chambers, Alex, and Lefteris Papadimas, 'Athens, Creditor Group Turn Up Heat on Greek Bondholders' *Reuters* (London, 6 March 2012) <www.reuters.com/article/us-greece-bonds-idUSTRE82412N20120306>.

Cotterill, Joseph, 'Choose Your Own Adventure, Sovereign Debt Trial of the Century Edition' *Financial Times Alphaville* (London, 8 February 2013) <https://ftalphaville.ft.com/2013/02/08/1379162/choose-your-own-adventure-sovereign-debt-trial-of-the-century-edition/>.

Croft, Jane, and Roman Olearchyk, 'Ukraine-Russia Bond Dispute Set for Full English Trail' *Financial Times* (London, 14 September 2018).

De Oliveira, Ricardo Soares, and Olivier Vallee, 'The Republic of Congo Is a "Dark Debt" Pioneer' *Foreign Policy* (Washington, DC, 21 May 2021).

Dobson, Paul, and Abigail Moses, 'ECB Greek Plan May Hurt Bondholders While Triggering Debt Swaps' *Bloomberg* (London, 17 February 2012) <www.bloomberg.com/news/articles/2012-02-17/ecb-plan-to-shield-its-greek-bonds-may-subordinate-some-holders-ubs-says>.

Economist, The, 'Argentina's Default – Foreign Creditors Join the Pyre' *The Economist* (London, 3 January 2002).

———. 'An Illusory Haven – What Lessons Should Investors Learn from the Argentine and Greek Restructurings? *The Economist* (London, 20 April 2013).

———. 'As We Forgive Our Debtors' *The Economist* (London, 16 June 2015).

———. 'At Last' *The Economist* (London, 5 May 2016).

———. 'Goldman Sachs Is Criticised for Buying Venezuelan Bonds' *The Economist* (London, 1 June 2017).

Elliott, Larry, 'Argentina Debt Crisis Fears Grow After US Supreme Court Ruling' *The Guardian* (London, 16 June 2014).

Elliott, Lee, 'Stop Debt Vultures, Demands Brown' *The Guardian* (London, 6 May 2002).

Fontevecchia, Andrea, 'The Real Story of How a Hedge Fund Detained a Vessel in Ghana and Even Went for Argentina's "Air Force One"' *Forbes Markets* (New York, 10 May 2012) <www.forbes.com/sites/afontevecchia/2012/10/05/the-real-story-behind-the-argentine-vessel-in-ghana-and-how-hedge-funds-tried-to-seize-the-presidential-plane/>.

Fontevecchia, Jorge, 'Martín Guzmán: The Reality Facing Argentina Was Not Understood by Creditors' *Buenos Aires Times* (Buenos Aires, 13 June 2020).

Hiltzik, Michael, 'Argentina Is Cautionary Tale as US Debates Debt Limit' *Los Angeles Times* (Los Angeles, 15 January 2013).

Hong, Nicole, 'Argentina's Bond Yields Lure Back Buyers' *The Wall Street Journal* (New York, 19 March 2014).

Institute of International Finance (IIF), 'By-Laws' (January 2020) <www.iif.com/Portals/0/Files/general/2020_IIF_Bylaws.pdf?ver=2020-02-27-151109-237>.

Jones, Merion, 'Vulture Funds' Threat to Developing World' *BBC Newsnight* (London, 14 February 2007).

Landon, Thomas, 'Bet on Greek Bonds Paid Off for "Vulture Fund"' *New York Times* (New York, 15 May 2012).

Liptak, Adam, 'Argentina's Debt Appeal Is Rejected by Supreme Court' *The New York Times* (New York, 16 June 2014).

Matezou, Renee, 'In About-Face, Greece Pays Bond Swap Holdouts' *Reuters* (London, 15 May 2012) <www.reuters.com/article/us-greece-bond-idUSBRE84E0MY20120515>.

Merle, Renae, 'How One Hedge Fund Made $2 Billion from Argentina's Economic Collapse' *Washington Post* (Washington, DC, 29 March 2016).

Millan, Carolina, 'Argentina Haunted by Default Legacy as German Suit' *Bloomberg* (New York, 27 September 2016) <www.bloomberg.com/news/articles/2016-09-27/argentina-still-haunted-by-default-legacy-as-german-suit-looms>.

Mitchell, Jason, 'Argentina Settles Majority of Claims Filed with ICSID' *Euromoney* (New York, 6 July 2007) <www.euromoney.com/article/b132237ncc2ync/argentina-settles-majority-of-claims-filed-with-icsid>.

Moore, Elaine, John Paul Rathbone, and Vivianne Rodrigues, 'Argentina Faces Fresh Default' *Financial Times* (New York, 16 August 2014).

Oloixarac, Pola, 'Argentina vs. The Vultures' *The New York Times* (New York, 19 September 2014).

Payne, Julia, 'Trafigura Completes Congo Republic Oil Loan Restructuring' *Reuters* (London, 23 March 2021).

Smith, David, 'Seized Argentinian Sailing Ship Leaves Ghana' *The Guardian* (London, 20 December 2012).

Sreeharsha, Vinod, 'Argentina's Senate Allows Payment to Bondholders' *The New York Times* (New York, 31 March 2016).

Story, Louise, Landon Thomas, and Nelson Schwartz, 'Wall St. Helped to Mask Debt Fuelling Europe's Crisis' *New York Times* (New York, 13 February 2010).

Strasburg, Jenny, and Margot Patrick, 'Glencore Oil Deals Could Bite Banks' *Wall Street Journal* (New York, 4 October 2015).

Watson, Katy, 'Argentina Defaults for Second Time' *BBC News* (London, 31 July 2014) <www.bbc.com/news/business-28578179>.

Wearden, Greaeme, 'Greece Debt Crisis: Timeline' *The Guardian* (London, 5 May 2010).

Wernau, Julie, and Taos Turner, 'Argentina Sells $2.75 Billion of 100-Year Bonds' *Wall Street Journal* (New York, 19 June 2017).

West, Oliver, 'EM Real Money Should Take on Restructuring Rep Risk' *Global Capital* (London, 13 August 2020) <www.globalcapital.com/article/28muaqiq94joecdu9a9kw/emerging-markets/latam/em-real-money-should-take-on-restructuring-rep-risk>.

West, Oliver, and Ross Lancaster, 'Real Money to the Fore as Lat Am Pair Usher in New Era of Sov Debt Workouts' *Global Capital* (London, 6 August 2020) <www.globalcapital.com/article/28muafl031b49y9ird8n4/emerging-markets/latam/real-money-to-the-fore-as-lat-am-pair-usher-in-new-era-of-sov-debt-workouts>.

Wigglesworth, Robin, 'Gramcery Reaps Argentina Bond Windfall' *Financial Times* (New York, 2 August 2016).

Wolf, Martin, 'Holdouts Give Vultures a Bad Name' *Financial Times* (London, 2 September 2014).

Online Sources

Acker, Kevin, Deborah Brautigam, and Yufan Huang, 'Debt Relief with Chinese Characteristics' (June 2020) SAIS-CARI Working Paper Series No 39 <https://static1.squarespace.com/static/5652847de4b033f56d2bdc29/t/60353345259d4448e01a37d8/1614099270470/WP+39+-+Acker%2C+Brautigam%2C+Huang+-+Debt+Relief.pdf>.

Allen, Craig, 'Law of the Sea Tribunal Resoundingly Affirms the Sovereign Immunity of Warships and Orders Ghana to Release Argentine Tall Ship ARA Libertad' (*Opinio Juris*, 15 December 2012) <http://opiniojuris.org/2012/12/15/law-of-the-sea-tribunal-resoundingly-affirms-the-sovereign-immunity-of-warships-and-orders-ghana-to-release-argentine-tall-ship-ara-libertad/>.

Allen & Overy, 'Argentina Settles Five Investment Treaty Awards' (7 November 2013) <https://perma.cc/NW3Q-VLRZ>.

Asonuma, Tamon, Gerardo Peraza, Kristine Vitola, and Takahiro Tsuda, 'Sovereign Debt Restructurings in Belize: Achievements and Challenges Ahead' (July 2014) IMF Working Paper WP14/32 <www.imf.org/external/pubs/ft/wp/2014/wp14132.pdf>.

Atteritano, Andrea, 'Immunity of States and Their Organs: The Contribution of Italian Jurisprudence Over the Past Ten Years' (2008) Contribution to the Annual Conference of the Italian Association of Law and Economics <www.sidi-isil.org/wp-content/uploads/2010/12/1_02_atteritano1.pdf>.

Audit, Matthias, 'Sovereign Bonds by Law: Can a State Debt be Non-Contractual?' (Presentation at the Interdisciplinary Sovereign Debt Research and Management Conference, Geneva, 5–6 October 2017) <www.dropbox.com/s/5wv34c4cxz0u8sj/3C_Matthias%20Audit_Debtcon2%20-%20Non%20contractual%20state%20debt%20%206%20oct%202017.%20V3%20pptx.pdf?dl=0>.

Avalos, Fernando, Ramon Moreno, and Tania Romero, 'Leverage on the Buy Side' (2015) BIS Working Papers No 517 <www.bis.org/publ/work517.pdf>.

Bank for International Settlements (BIS), 'Glossary' (December 2016) <www.bis.org/statistics/glossary.htm?&selection=302&scope=Statistics&c=a&base=term>.

———. 'Central and Government Debt Securities Markets' (2020) <www.bis.org/statistics/c4.pdf>.

———. 'About the BIS – Overview' <www.bis.org/about/index.htm?m=1%7C1>.

Barbados, 'Barbados-Law Bonds Invitation Memorandum' (5 November 2019) <www.oblible.com/Prospectus/www.oblible.com__USP48864AQ80.pdf>.

Beers, David, and Jamshid Mavalwalla, 'Database of Sovereign Defaults, 2017' (June 2017) Bank of Canada Technical Report No 101 <www.bankofcanada.ca/2014/02/technical-report-101/>.

Bi, Ran, Marcos Chamon, and Jeromin Zettelmeyer, 'The Problem that Wasn't: Coordination Failures in Sovereign Debt Restructurings' (2011) IMF Working Paper No. 11/265 <www.imf.org/external/pubs/ft/wp/2011/wp11265.pdf>.

Bianco, Giuseppe, 'How Neutral Is the Law of Sovereign Debt' (2017) 9(3) ESIL Conference Paper Series (ESIL Research Forum, Granada, 30–31 March 2017) <https://papers.ssrn.com/sol3/papers.cfm?abstract_id=3045246>.

Bini Smaghi, Lorenzo, 'Private Sector Involvement: From (Good) Theory to (Bad) Practice' (6 June 2011) Speech by Mr Lorenzo Bini Smaghi, Member of the Executive Board of the European Central Bank at the Reinventing Bretton Woods Committee, Berlin <www.ecb.europa.eu/press/key/date/2011/html/sp110606.en.html>.

———. 'The European Debt Crisis' (17 October 2011) Speech by Mr Lorenzo Bini Smaghi, Member of the Executive Board of the European Central Bank, at the Atlantik-Brücke Event, Meeting of Regional Group Frankfurt, Frankfurt am Main <www.bis.org/review/r111026c.pdf>.

Blom, Jasper, 'What We Can Learn from the Institute of International Finance' (*Open Democracy*, 24 January 2019) <www.opendemocracy.net/en/banking-on-public-power-what-we-can-learn-from-institute-of-international-finance/>.

Bossu, Wouter, Cory Hillier, and Wolfgang Bergthaler, 'Local Currency Bond Markets Law Reform: A Methodology for Emerging Markets and Developing Economies' (2020) IMF Working Paper Series WP/20/258 <www.imf.org/en/Publications/WP/Issues/2020/11/20/Local-Currency-Bond-Markets-Law-Reform-A-Methodology-for-Emerging-Markets-and-Developing-49905>.

Bradlow, Daniel, 'Prudent Debt management and Lessons from the Mozambique Constitutional Council' (*AfronomicsLaw*, 5 August 2020) <https://papers.ssrn.com/sol3/papers.cfm?abstract_id=3676342>.

Brahms, Lisa, 'Legitimacy of Global Governance of Sovereign Default: The Role of International Investment Agreements' (2013) Working Papers by the Center for International Political Economy No 16 <www.polsoz.fu-berlin.de/polwiss/forschung/oekonomie/ipoe/index.html>.

Buchheit, Lee, 'Sovereign Debt Restructuring: The Legal Context' (2013) BIS Papers No 72 – Sovereign Risk: A World Without Risk-Free Assets? (Proceedings of a seminar on Sovereign Risk Including Contributions by Central Bank Governors and Other Policy-Makers, Market Practitioners and Academics, Basel, 8–9 January 2013) <www.bis.org/publ/bppdf/bispap72.pdf>.

Buchheit, Lee, and Mitu Gulati, 'Greek Debt: The Endgame Scenarios' (April 2011) unpublished manuscript <http://scholarship.law.duke.edu/faculty_scholarship/2380/>.

Bush, Georgia, Carlos Canon, and Daniel Gray, 'Emerging Market Capital Flows: The Role of Fund Manager Portfolio Allocation' (2021) Banco de Mexico Working Papers No 2021–113 <www.banxico.org.mx/publications-and-press/banco-de-mexico-working-papers/%7BF21B341C-067A-8583-0755-AC73B792ED51%7D.pdf>.

Chorzempa, Martin, and Adnan Mazarei, 'Improving China's Participation in Resolving Developing-Country Debt Problems' (May 2021) Peterson Institute for International Economics, Policy Brief 21–10 <www.piie.com/publications/policy-briefs/improving-chinas-participation-resolving-developing-country-debt-problems>.

Clifford Chance, 'Enforcement Against State Assets: France's Latest Contribution to the Argentinean Saga' (April 2013) Briefing Note <www.cliffordchance.com/

content/dam/cliffordchance/briefings/2013/04/cour_de_cassation_decisions_on_state_immunity.pdf>.

———. 'Sovereign Debt Restructuring – Proposed Amendment to New York Banking Law Through New Article 7' (May 2021) <www.cliffordchance.com/content/dam/cliffordchance/briefings/2021/05/sovereign-debt-restructuring-proposed-amendment-to-new-york-banking-law-through-new-article-7.pdf>.

Club de Paris, 'The Six Principles' (2016) <www.clubdeparis.org/en/communications/page/the-six-principles>.

Cordella, Tito, and Andrew Powell, 'Preferred and Non-Preferred Creditors' (March 2021) IDB Working Paper Series 1215 <https://publications.iadb.org/publications/english/document/Preferred-and-Non-Preferred-Creditors.pdf>.

Costabile, Nicolas, 'Argentina: From International Market isolation to Promising Opportunities for Investors' (*Commercial Dispute Resolution News*, 27 September 2016) <www.cdr-news.com/categories/arbitration/6733-argentina-from-international-market-isolation-to-promising-opportunities-for-investors>.

Cuniberti, Gilles, 'Sovereign Immunities and the Scope of the Brussels Ibis Regulation After Rina and SHAPE' (*The European Association of Private International Law*, 9 February 2021) <https://eapil.org/2021/02/09/sovereign-immunities-and-the-scope-of-the-brussels-ibis-regulation-after-rina-and-shape/>.

Das, Udabir, Michael Papaioannou, and Christoph Trebesch, 'Sovereign Debt Restructurings 1950–2010: Literature Survey, Data and Stylized Facts' (2012) IMF Working Paper, WP/12/203 <www.imf.org/external/pubs/cat/longres.aspx?sk=26190.0>.

De Santis, Roberto A, 'The Euro Area Sovereign Debt Crisis – Safe Haven, Credit Rating Agencies and the Spread of the Fever From Greece, Ireland and Portugal' (2012) ECB Working Paper Series No 1419 <www.ecb.europa.eu/pub/pdf/scpwps/ecbwp1419.pdf?20b5463a06e46d4321d81b1f8fb1990f>.

DLA Piper, 'PROMESA Becomes Law: All Business in Puerto Rico Will Be Affected – Top Points About This Sweeping Rescue Package' (*DLA Piper Government Affairs Alert*, 5 July 2016) <www.dlapiper.com/en/us/insights/publications/2016/07/promesa-becomes-law/>.

Dreger, Joana, 'Why Is Sovereign Debt Restructuring a Challenge? The Case of Greece' (2012) Bruges European Economic Policy Briefings 24/2012, 21 <http://aei.pitt.edu/58456/>.

Emerging Markets Traders Association (EMTA), 'Creditor Engagement Clauses – Pro's and Con's' (2 March 2015) <www.emta.org/print.aspx?id=9257>.

Erce, Aitor, Enrico Malluci, and Mattia Picarelli, 'A Journey in the History of Sovereign Defaults on Domestic Law Public Debt – Sovereign Histories' (2021) Universidad Publica de Navarra Working Paper D.T. 2108 <https://www2.unavarra.es/gesadj/CyD5/depEconomia/documentos-trabajo/2021/WP2108.pdf>.

Euler, Dimitij, 'Switzerland's Department of Foreign Affairs Endorsed BGH Decision (BGE 136 III 379) Not to Lift Bank of International Settlement's (BIS) Immunity Due to an Attempt of NML Capital to Freeze USD300m (£186m) on Argentina's Bank Accounts' (*Young ICCA Blog*, 3 December 2012) <www.youngicca-blog.com/switzerlands-department-of-foreign-affairs-endorsed-federal-supreme-court-decision-bge-136-iii-379-not-to-lift-bank-of-international-settlements-bis-immunity-due-to-an-attempt-of/#_ftn9>.

European Central Bank (ECB), 'ECB Announces Expanded Asset Purchase Programme' (22 January 2015) <www.ecb.europa.eu/press/pr/date/2015/html/pr150122_1.en.html>.

———. 'Debt Sustainability Analysis for Euro Area Sovereigns: A Methodological Framework' (April 2017) Occasional Paper Series No 185 <www.ecb.europa.eu/pub/pdf/scpops/ecbop185.en.pdf?abccaa198c0d791777fe3dfb148873f5>.

European Commission, 'The Economic Adjustment Programme for Greece' (2010) Occasional Papers 61 <http://ec.europa.eu/economy_finance/publications/occasional_paper/2010/pdf/ocp61_en.pdf>.

———. 'Compliance Report ESM Stability Support Programme for Greece' (July 2018) Fourth Review <https://ec.europa.eu/info/sites/default/files/economy-finance/compliance_report_4r_2018.06.20.docx.pdf>.

European Stability Mechanism (ESM), 'Explainer on EFSF Medium-Term Debt Relief Measures for Greece' (*Press release*, 22 November 2018) <www.esm.europa.eu/press-releases/explainer-efsf-medium-term-debt-relief-measures-greece>.

European Union, 'Court of Justice of the European Union (CJEU)' (2018) About the EU <https://europa.eu/european-union/about-eu/institutions-bodies/court-justice_en>.

Eurostat, 'Provision of Deficit and Debt Data for 2008 – Second Notification' (*Newsrelease Euroindicators*, October 2009) <https://ec.europa.eu/eurostat/documents/2995521/5074630/2-22102009-ap-en.pdf/490aa296-ccc7-4714-91c5-b5c8ddb73948?version=1.0>.

Federal Reserve Bank of New York, 'Services for Central Banks and International Institutions' (October 2015) <www.newyorkfed.org/aboutthefed/fedpoint/fed20>.

Financial Markets Law Committee, 'Pari Passu Clauses – Analysis of the Role, Use and Meaning of Pari Passu Clauses in Sovereign Debt Obligations as a Matter of English Law' (April 2015) <www.fmlc.org/uploads/2/6/5/8/26584807/fmlc_paper_analysing_the_role,_use_and_meaning_of_pari_passu_clauses_in_sovereign_debt_obligations_as_a_matter_of_english_law.pdf>.

Franklin Templeton, 'The Evolution of China's Lending to Emerging Markets' (April 2021) <www.franklintempleton.com/content-ftthinks/common-pdf/fixed-income/evolution-of-china-lending-to-emerging-markets-us.pdf>.

Freshfields Bruckhaus Deringer, 'NML v Argentina: Supreme Court Tightens Waiver of Sovereign Immunity Test' (2 July 2013) Client Briefing <www.lexology.com/library/detail.aspx?g=3b63767e-0978-452e-a447-20ff566c92b4#15>.

Group of Twenty (G20), 'Statement at the Extraordinary G20 Finance Ministers and Central Bank Governors' Meeting' (*Riyadh*, 13 November 2020) <www.imf.org/-/media/Files/News/news-articles/english-extraordinary-g20-fmcbg-statement-november-13.ashx>.

Garcia-Bolivar, Omar, 'Defining an ICSID Investment: Why Economic Development Should be the Core Element' (*Investment Treaty News*, 13 April 2012) <www.iisd.org/itn/2012/04/13/defining-an-icsid-investment-why-economic-development-should-be-the-core-element/>.

Gayner, Oliver, 'Case Comment: NML Capital Limited v Republic of Argentina [2011] UKSC 31' (*UKSC Blog*, 22 July 2011) <http://ukscblog.com/case-comment-nml-capital-limited-appellant-v-republic-of-argentina-respondent-2011-uksc-31/>.

Gelpern, Anna, 'After Argentina' (2005) Peterson Institute for International Economics Policy Briefs No PB05-02 <https://piie.com/publications/policy-briefs/after-argentina>.

———. 'Hard, Soft, and Embedded: Implementing Principles on Promoting Responsible Sovereign Lending and Borrowing' (2012) Georgetown Law Faculty Publications and Other Works 1860 d<https://scholarship.law.georgetown.edu/facpub/1860/>.

———. 'Sovereign Damage Control' (2013) Peterson Institute of International Economics Policy Brief 13–12 <https://piie.com/publications/pb/pb13-12.pdf>.

———. 'Ukraine's Bond Restructuring: Surgery, Conspiracy, and Campaign' (2015) Peterson Institute for International Economics, Realtime Economic Issues Watch <www.piie.com/blogs/realtime-economic-issues-watch/ukraines-bond-restructuring-surgery-conspiracy-and-campaign>.

———. 'Examining Belt and Road: The Lending Practices of the People's Republic of China and Impact on the International Debt Architecture' (18 May 2021) Testimony Before the House Committee on Financial Services, Subcommittee on National Security, International Development and Monetary Policy <https://docs.house.gov/meetings/BA/BA10/20210518/112661/HHRG-117-BA10-Wstate-GelpernA-20210518.pdf>.

Gelpern, Anna, Sebastian Horn, Scott Morris, Brad Parks, and Christoph Trebesch, 'How China Lends: A Rare Look into 100 Debt Contracts with Foreign Governments' (May 2021) Peterson Institute for International Economics Working Paper 21–27 <www.piie.com/publications/working-papers/how-china-lends-rare-look-100-debt-contracts-foreign-governments>.

Georgieva, Kristalina, and Ceyla Pazarbasioglu, 'The G20 Common Framework for Debt Treatments Must Be Stepped Up' (*IMF Blog*, 2 December 2021) <https://blogs.imf.org/2021/12/02/the-g20-common-framework-for-debt-treatments-must-be-stepped-up/>.

Glinavos, Ioannis, 'Casenote: Decision 1116–1117/2014 (21.3.14) of the Greek Council of State (Συμβούλιο της Επικρατείας)' (2014) unpublished manuscript <https://papers.ssrn.com/sol3/papers.cfm?abstract_id=2445568>.

Goldmann, Matthias, 'Human Rights and Sovereign Debt Workouts' (April 2014) unpublished manuscript <www.academia.edu/5561607/Human_Rights_and_Sovereign_Debt_Workouts>.

Grandaubert, Victor, 'France Legislates on State Immunity from Execution: How to Kill Two Birds with One Stone?' (*EJIL: Talk*, 23 January 2017) <www.ejiltalk.org/france-legislates-on-state-immunity-from-execution-how-to-kill-two-birds-with-one-stone/>.

Grgir, Aida, Zvonimir Mataga, Matija Longar, and Ana Vilfan, 'The Right to Property Under the European Convention on Human Rights' (2007) Human Rights Handbooks of the European Council No 10 <https://rm.coe.int/168007ff5>.

Grigorian, David, Trevor Alleyne, and Alejandro Guerson, 'Jamaica Debt Exchange' (2012) IMF Working Paper WP/12/244 (October 2012) <www.imf.org/external/pubs/ft/wp/2012/wp12244.pdf>.

Gulati, Mitu, and George Vanberg, 'Paper Tigers (or How Much Will Courts Protect Rights in a Financial Crisis?)' (2018) SSRN <https://papers.ssrn.com/sol3/cf_dev/AbsByAuth.cfm?per_id=365684>.

Hagan, Sean, 'Sovereign Debt Restructuring: The Centrality of the IMF's Role' Peterson Institute for International Economics Working Paper 20–13 (July 2020) <www.piie.com/system/files/documents/wp20-13.pdf>.

Haldane, Andrew, and Jörg Scheibe, 'IMF Lending and Creditor Moral Hazard' (2004) Bank of England Working Paper No 216 <www.bankofengland.co.uk/archive/Documents/historicpubs/workingpapers/2004/wp216.pdf>.

Heitzig, Chris, Aloysius Uche Ordu, and Lemma Senbet, 'Sub-Saharan Africa's Debt Problem' (*Brookings Africa Growth Initiative*, October 2021) <www.brookings.edu/wp-content/uploads/2021/10/COVID-and-debt.pdf>.

The Hellenic Republic, 'Invitation Memorandum' (24 February 2012) <http://ftalphaville.ft.com/files/2012/02/Reg_S_Invitation_Memorandum.pdf>.

Hess, Maximilian, 'Bond of War – Russian Geo-Economics in Ukraine's Sovereign Debt Restructuring' (2018) Foreign Policy Research Institute <www.fpri.org/wp-content/uploads/2018/09/rpe-5-hess-final-.pdf>.

HM Treasury, 'Government Acts to Halt Profiteering on Third World Debt Within the UK' (*Press Release*, 2011) <www.govuk/government/news/government-acts-to-halt-profiteering-on-third-world-debt-within-the-uk>.

Ho, Sum-Jim, 'Sovereign Debt Column: Is This Time Different for Sub-Saharan Africa?' (Winter 2019–2020) 10 Cleary Gottlieb Emerging Markets Restructuring Journal <www.clearygottlieb.com/-/media/files/emrj-materials/issue-10-winter-2019_2020/sovereign-debt-column-is-this-time-different-for-subsaharan-africa-pdf.pdf>.

Horn, Sebastian, Carmen Reinhart, and Chrisoph Trebesch, 'Hidden Defaults' (2022) World Bank Policy Research Working Paper No 9925 <https://openknowledge.worldbank.org/bitstream/handle/10986/36965/Hidden-Defaults.pdf?sequence=1&isAllowed=y>.

Hornbeck, John, 'Argentina's Defaulted Sovereign Debt: Dealing with the "Holdouts"' (6 January 2013) Congressional Research Service 5.

Human Rights Council, 'Draft Progress Report on the Activities of Vulture Funds and the Impact on Human Rights' (2015) Advisory Committee (15th Session) A/HRC/AC/15/CRP.1 <www.ohchr.org/Documents/HRBodies/HRCouncil/AdvisoryCom/Session17/A_HRC_33_54.docx>.

———. 'Thirty-Third Session A/HRC/33/54' (September 2016) <www.ohchr.org/EN/HRBodies/HRC/AdvisoryCommittee/Pages/VultureFunds.aspx>.

International Capital Markets Association (ICMA), 'ICMA Sovereign Bond Consultation Paper', December 2013 <https://www.icmagroup.org/assets/documents/Maket-Practice/Regulatory-Policy/Sovereign-Debt-Information/ICMA-Sovereign-Bond-Consultation-Paper-79801-5-863-v1-8-161213.pdf>

International Centre for the Settlement of Investment Disputes (ICSID), 'Venezuela Submits a Notice under Article 71 of the ICSID Convention' (*News Releases*, 26 January 2012) <https://icsid.worldbank.org/news-and-events/news-releases/venezuela-submits-notice-under-article-71-icsid-convention> accessed 2 November 2021.

Internal Evaluation Office (IEO), 'The IMF's Role in Greece in the Context of the 2010 Stand-By Arrangement' (2016) Background Paper BP/16–02/11 <www.ieo-imf.org/ieo/files/completedevaluations/EAC__BP_16-02_11__The_IMFs_Role_in_Greece_in_the_Context_of_the_2010_SBA.PDF>.

———. 'The IMF and the Crises in Greece, Ireland, and Portugal: An Evaluation by the Independent Evaluation Office' (8 July 2016) IEO Report <www.ieo-imf.org/ieo/pages/CompletedEvaluation267.aspx>.

International Monetary Fund (IMF), 'The Restructuring of Sovereign Debt – Assessing the Benefits, Risks, and Feasibility of Aggregating Claims' (September 2003) IMF Legal Department, 24 <www.imf.org/external/np/pdr/sdrm/2003/090303.pdf>.

———. 'Republic of Congo: 2004 Article IV Consultation and New Staff-Monitored Program – Staff Report; Staff Statement; Public Information Notice on the Executive Board Discussion; and Statement by the Executive Director for the Republic of Congo' (July 2004) IMF Country Report No 04/232 <www.imf.org/external/pubs/ft/scr/2004/cr04232.pdf>.

———. 'Iraq – First Review Under the Stand-By Arrangement and Financing Assurances Review Staff Report; Staff Supplement; Press Release on the Executive Board Discussion; and Statement by the Executive Director for Iraq' (2008) <www.elibrary.imf.org/view/journals/002/2008/303/article-A001-en.xml>.

———. 'Europe and IMF Agree €110 Bn Financing Plan with Greece' (*IMF Survey Online*, 2 May 2010) <www.imf.org/external/pubs/ft/survey/so/2010/car050210a.htm>.

———. 'Sovereign Debt Restructuring – Recent Developments and Implications for the Fund's Legal and Policy Framework' (26 April 2013) <www.imf.org/external/np/pp/eng/2013/042613.pdf>.

———. 'Strengthening the Contractual Framework to Address Collective Action Problems in Sovereign Debt Restructuring' (2014) IMF Policy Papers <www.imf.org/external/np/pp/eng/2014/090214.pdf>.

———. 'Heavily Indebted Poor Countries Initiative and Multilateral Debt Relief Initiative – Statistical Update' (15 December 2014) <www.elibrary.imf.org/view/journals/007/2014/089/article-A001-en.xml>

———. 'Progress Report on Inclusion of Enhanced Contractual Provisions in International Sovereign Bond Contracts' (March 2015) IMF Staff Report <www.imf.org/external/np/pp/eng/2015/091715.pdf>.

———. 'The Fund's Lending Framework and Sovereign Debt – Further Considerations' (April 2015) <www.imf.org/~/media/Websites/IMF/Imported/external/np/pp/eng/2015/_040915pdf.ashx>.

———. 'Debt Sustainability Analysis' (November 2015) <www.imf.org/external/pubs/ft/dsa/>.

———. 'Reforming the Fund's Policy on Non-Toleration of Arrears to Official Creditors' (December 2015) IMF Policy Paper <www.imf.org/external/np/pp/eng/2015/101515.pdf>.

———. 'Status of Ukraine's Eurobond Held by the Russian Federation' (11 December 2015) <http://www.imf.org/external/pubs/ft/scr/2015/cr15344.pdf>.

———. 'Argentina: 2016 Article IV Consultation-Press Release; Staff Report; and Statement by the Executive Director for Argentina' (October 2016) IMF Country Report No 16/346 <www.imf.org/en/Publications/CR/Issues/2016/12/31/Argentina-2016-Article-IV-Consultation-Press-Release-Staff-Report-and-Statement-by-the-44386>.

———. 'Greece – Ex-Post Evaluation of Exceptional Access Under the 2012 Extended Arrangement – Press Release; Staff Report; and Statement by the Executive Director for Greece' (February 2017) IMF Country Report No 17/44 <www.imf.org/en/Publications/CR/Issues/2017/02/07/Greece-Ex-Post-Evaluation-of-Exceptional-Access-Under-the-2012-Extended-Arrangement-Press-44636>.

———. 'Fourth Progress Report on the Inclusion of Enhanced Contractual Provisions in International Sovereign Bonds' (March 2019) <www.elibrary.imf.org/view/journals/007/2019/008/article-A001-en.xml>.

———. 'The Evolution of Public Debt Vulnerabilities in Lower Income Countries' (February 2020) IMF Policy Paper <www.imf.org/~/media/Files/Publications/PP/2020/English/PPEA2020003.ashx>.

———. 'The International Architecture for Resolving Sovereign Debt Involving Private-Sector Creditors – Recent Developments, Challenges, Reform Options' (2020) IMF Policy Paper <www.imf.org/en/Publications/Policy-Papers/Issues/2020/09/30/The-International-Architecture-for-Resolving-Sovereign-Debt-Involving-Private-Sector-49796>.

———. 'Joint World Bank-IMF Debt Sustainability Framework for Low-Income Countries' (17 March 2021) Factsheet <www.imf.org/en/About/Factsheets/Sheets/2016/08/01/16/39/Debt-Sustainability-Framework-for-Low-Income-Countries>.

———. 'Questions and Answers on Sovereign Debt Issues' (8 April 2021) <www.imf.org/en/About/FAQ/sovereign-debt#Section%205>.

———. 'Fiscal Monitor – Strengthening the Credibility of Public Finances' (October 2021) <www.imf.org/en/Publications/FM/Issues/2021/10/13/fiscal-monitor-october-2021>.

———. 'Issues in Restructuring of Sovereign Domestic Debt' (November 2021) <www.imf.org/-/media/Files/Publications/PP/2021/English/PPEA2021071.ashx>.

International Relations Committee of the ECB Task Force on IMF and Global Financial Governance Issues, 'The IMF's Role in Sovereign Debt Restructurings'

(September 2021) ECB Working Paper No 262, 22 <www.ecb.europa.eu/pub/pdf/scpops/ecb.op262~f0e9e1e77e.en.pdf> accessed 2 November 2021.

Iversen, Astrid, 'Holdout Creditor Litigation' (2015) University of Oslo Faculty of Law Legal Studies Research Paper Series No 2015–13 <https://papers.ssrn.com/sol3/papers.cfm?abstract_id=2613280>.

Kahn, Robert, 'Venezuela on the Edge' (*Council of Foreign Relations Blog*, 23 February 2013) <www.cfr.org/blog/venezuela-edge>.

Khan, Ashraf, 'Legal Protection: Liability and Immunity Arrangements of Central Banks and Financial Supervisors' (2018) IMF Working Paper WP/18/176 <www.imf.org/en/Publications/WP/Issues/2018/08/02/Legal-Protection-Liability-and-Immunity-Arrangements-of-Central-Banks-and-Financial-46086>.

Kirchner, Cristina, 'Address by Cristina Kirchner at UN General Assembly' (24 September 2014) <www.cfkargentina.com/address-by-cristina-kirchner-at-un-general-assembly-2014/>.

Kleiman, Elie, and Julie Spinelli, 'NML v Argentina: Supreme Court Tightens Waiver of Sovereign Immunity Test' (July 2013) Freshfields Bruckhaus Deringer Client Briefing <www.internationallawoffice.com/Newsletters/Litigation/France/Freshfields-Bruckhaus-Deringer-LLP/NML-v-Argentina-Supreme-Court-tightens-waiver-of-sovereign-immunity-test>.

Koutras, Andreas, 'A Better Translation of Bondholders Act 4050' (*Andreas Koutras Blog*, March 2012) <http://andreaskoutras.blogspot.com.au/2012/03/better-tarnslation-of-bondholders-act.html>.

Ku, Julian, 'Here Comes That Frivolous Argentina ICJ Claim! Oh, and They Have No Jurisdiction Either!' (7 August 2014) <http://opiniojuris.org/2014/08/07/comes-frivolous-argentina-icj-claim-oh-jurisdiction-either/>.

Lane, Philip, and Gian Maria Milesi-Ferretti, 'International Financial Integration in the Aftermath of the Global Financial Crisis' (2017) IMF Working Paper WP/17/115 <www.imf.org/en/Publications/WP/Issues/2017/05/10/International-Financial-Integration-in-the-Aftermath-of-the-Global-Financial-Crisis-44906>.

Lockman, Michael, 'Pari Passu Undone: Game-Changing Decisions for Sovereigns in Distress' (2017) 3 Emerging Markets Restructuring Journal <www.clearygottlieb.com/~/media/cgsh/files/2017/publications/emrj-spring-2017/pari-passu-undone-gamechanging-decisions-for-sovereigns-in-distress.pdf>.

Mandeng, Ousmène Jaques, 'Intercreditor Distribution in Sovereign Debt Restructuring' (2004) IMF Working Paper, WP/04/183, 18 <www.imf.org/external/pubs/ft/wp/2004/wp04183.pdf>.

Mankowski, Peter, 'The Saga of the Greek State Bonds and Their Haircut: Hellas Triumphans in Luxemburg, Really?' (*Conflict of Laws.net*, 22 November 2018) <https://conflictoflaws.net/2018/the-saga-of-the-greek-state-bonds-and-their-haircut-hellas-triumphans-in-luxemburg-really/>.

Markakis, Menelaos, 'ECtHR Rules on Greek Debt Restructuring' (*Oxford Human Rights Hub*, 30 July 2016 <http://ohrh.law.ox.ac.uk/european-court-of-human-rights-rules-on-greek-debt-restructuring/>.

Mihalyi, David, Aisha Adam, and Jyhjong Hwang, 'Resource-Backed Loans: Pitfalls and Potential' (February 2020) Natural Resource Governance Institute <https://resourcegovernance.org/sites/default/files/documents/resource-backed-loans-pitfalls-and-potential.pdf>.

Myrvin, Anthony, Gregorio Impavido, and Bert van Selm, 'Barbados' 2018–19 Sovereign Debt Restructuring – A Sea Change?' (February 2020) IMF Working Paper

No. 20/34 <www.imf.org/en/Publications/WP/Issues/2020/02/21/Barbados-201819-Sovereign-Debt-RestructuringA-Sea-Change-49044>.

Oliveri, Luigi, 'Italian Banks Unload Argentine Bonds in Italy; Investigation Blocked' (*Executive Intelligence Review*, 11 March 2005) <http://larouchepub.com/other/interviews/2005/3210luigi_olivieri.html>.

Organisation for Economic Cooperation and Development, 'The Impact of Coronavirus (COVID-19) and the Global Oil Price Shock on the Fiscal Position of Oil-Exporting Developing Countries' (30 September 2020) OECD Policy Responses to Coronavirus (COVID-19) <www.oecd.org/coronavirus/policy-responses/the-impact-of-coronavirus-covid-19-and-the-global-oil-price-shock-on-the-fiscal-position-of-oil-exporting-developing-countries-8bafbd95/>.

Pagoulatos, George, 'Greece After the Bailouts: Assessment of a Qualified Failure' (2018) Hellenic Observatory Discussion Papers on Greece and Southeast Europe Paper No 130 <www.lse.ac.uk/Hellenic-Observatory/Assets/Documents/Publications/GreeSE-Papers/GreeSE-No130.pdf>.

Papademos, Lucas, 'The Pitfalls of EZ Sovereign Debt Restructuring' (*VoxEU*, 26 October 2011) <https://voxeu.org/article/greek-debt-restructuring-perils-and-promises>.

Paris Club, 'Annual Report 2008' 14 <www.clubdeparis.org/sections/communication/rapport-annuel-d/annual-report-2008/downloadFile/file/AnnualReport2008.pdf>.

Peterson, Luke, 'Argentina and Ghana Announce Settlement of Arbitration Over Detained Warship' (*Kluwer Arbitration Blog*, 28 September 2013) <http://kluwerarbitrationblog.com/2013/09/28/argentina-and-ghana-announce-settlement-of-arbitration-over-detained-warship-ara-libertad/>.

Posner, Eric, and Glen Weyl, 'A Solution to the Collective Action Problem in Corporate Reorganization' (2013) University of Chicago Coase-Sandor Institute for Law & Economics Research Paper No 653 <https://papers.ssrn.com/sol3/papers.cfm?abstract_id=2321904>.

Porzecanski, Aturo C, 'Behind the Greek Default and Restructuring of 2012' (2014) MPRA Paper No 44166, 9 <https://mpra.ub.uni-muenchen.de/44166/1/Behind_the_Greek_Default_and_Restructuring_of_2012.pdf>.

Pottow, John AE, 'Mitigating the Problem of Vulture Holdout: International Certification Boards for Sovereign Debt Restructurings' (2013) Law and Economics Working Paper 81, 7 <http://repository.law.umich.edu/cgi/viewcontent.cgi?article=1191&context=law_econ_current>.

Powell, Andrew, 'Bipolar Debt Restructuring: Lessons from LAC' (*Vox Lacea*, 24 February 2017) <http://vox.lacea.org/?q=debt-lessons-LAC>.

Prieto, Gustavo, 'Ecuador Returns to the ICSID Convention: A Brief Assessment of Its Decade-Long International Investment Law "Exit Strategy" ' (*EJIL: Talk*, 19 July 2021) <www.ejiltalk.org/ecuador-returns-to-the-icsid-convention-a-brief-assessment-of-its-decade-long-international-investment-law-exit-strategy/>.

Public Eye, 'Gunvor in Congo' (September 2017) <https://gunvorincongo.publiceye.ch/>.

Richelle, Jacques, 'Belgian 2015 Anti-Vulture Funds Law' (*Strelia Lawyers*, February 2016) <www.strelia.com/sites/strelia.com/files/strelia_-_belgian_2015_anti-vulture_funds_law.pdf>.

Ritter, Raymond, 'The Principles for Stable Capital Flows and Fair Debt Restructuring in Emerging Markets' (April 2009) ECB Occasional Paper Series No 103 <www.ecb.europa.eu/pub/pdf/scpops/ecbocp103.pdf>.

Rylatt, Jake, 'Sitting, Waiting, Wishing: Argentina Initiates Sovereign Default Claim Before the ICJ' (*Cambridge International Law Journal Blog*, 10 August 2014) <http://

cilj.co.uk/2014/08/10/sitting-waiting-wishing-argentina-initiates-sovereign-default-claim-international-court-justice-requesting-usa-consent-jurisdiction/>.

Sachs, Jeffrey, 'Do We Need an International Lender of Last Resort' (April 1995) Frank D Graham Lecture at Princeton University <www.cibid.harvard.edu/archive/hiid/papers/intllr.pdf>.

Sawhney, Isabelle, 'The Hidden Law Guiding the Sovereign's Use of Exit Consents' (27 April 2019) SSRN <https://papers.ssrn.com/sol3/papers.cfm?abstract_id=3363957>.

Schadler, Susan, 'Living with Rules: The IMF's Exceptional Access Framework and the 2010 Stand-By Arrangement with Greece' (8 July 2016) IEO Report <www.ieo-imf.org/ieo/files/completedevaluations/EAC__BP_16-02_08__Living_with_Rules_-_The_IMF_s_Exceptional_Framework_and_the_2010_SBA_with_Greece.PDF>.

Schlegl, Matthias, Christoph Trebesch, and Mark Wright, 'Sovereign Debt Repayments: Evidence on Seniority' (*VoxEU*, 11 August 2015) <http://voxeu.org/article/sovereign-debt-repayments-evidence-seniority>.

Schumacher, Julian, Christoph Trebesch, and Henrik Enderlein, 'Sovereign Defaults in Court' (2018) ECB Working Paper Series No 2135 <www.ecb.europa.eu/pub/pdf/scpwps/ecb.wp2135.en.pdf>.

Schumacher, Julian, and Beatrice Weder di Mauro, 'Diagnosing Greek Debt Sustainability: Why Is It so Hard?' (Fall 2015) Brookings Papers on Economic Activity 280 <www.brookings.edu/wp-content/uploads/2016/06/SchumacherTextFall15BPEA.pdf>.

Scott, Robert E., Mitu Gulati, and Stephen J Choi, 'Hidden Holdouts: Contract Arbitrageurs and the Pricing of Collective Rights' (July 2018) NYU Law & Economics Research Paper Series No 18–27 <https://papers.ssrn.com/sol3/papers.cfm?abstract_id=3203949>.

Stieglitz, Joseph E, and Martin Guzman, 'A Rule of Law for Sovereign Debt' (*Project Syndicate*, 15 June 2015) <www.project-syndicate.org/commentary/sovereign-debt-restructuring-by-joseph-e-stiglitz-and-martin-guzman-2015–06?barrier=accessreg>.

Strickland, Tim, 'Sovereign Debt Restructuring: Recent Issues and Reforms' (2014) Reserve Bank of Australia Bulletin, December – Quarter 73 <www.rba.govau/publications/bulletin/2014/dec/pdf/bu-1214-9.pdf>

Sushama, Deepu Jojo, 'Mass Claims in Investment Arbitration – The Need of the Hour' (*Kluwer Arbitration Blog*, 4 March 2015) <http://kluwerarbitrationblog.com/2015/03/04/mass-claims-in-investment-arbitration-the-need-of-the-hour/>.

Task Force Argentina (TFA), 'Task Force Argentina Announces Final Argentina Settlement for Italian Bondholders' (*Press Release*, 22 April 2016) <www.tfargentina.it/download/TFA%20Comunicato%2022%20aprile%202016_eng.pdf>.

The Republic of Italy, 'USD 2,000,000,000, 5.375% Notes due 2017' (18 January 2006) Prospectus Supplement to Prospectus <www.bourse.lu/security/US465410BS63/115975>.

Trafigura, 'Prepayments Demystified' (January 2020) <www.commoditiesdemystified.info/pdf/Prepayments_Demystified_CommoditiesDemystified.pdf>.

UNCTAD, 'Principles on Responsible Sovereign Lending and Borrowing (PRSLB)' (2012) <www.unctad.info/upload/Debt%20Portal/Principles%20drafts/SLB_Principles_English_Doha_22-04-2012.pdf>.

United Mexican States, 'USD 110,000,000,000, Global Medium-Term Notes, Series A' (*Base Prospectus*, 3 February 2016) <www.bourse.lu/programme/Programme-Mexico/2395>.

United States Securities and Exchange Commission, 'Annual Report of the Republic of Argentina' (2009) 153 <www.sec.gov/Archives/edgar/data/914021/000090342310000550/roa-18k_0927.htm>.

Walter, Stephan, 'The Aftermath of the CJEU's Kuhn Judgment – Hellas Triumphans in Vienna, Really' (*ConflictofLaws*, 12 February 2019) <https://conflictoflaws.net/2019/the-aftermath-of-the-cjeus-kuhn-judgment-hellas-triumphans-in-vienna-really/>.

Weidemaier, Mark, 'Venezuela Is Like . . . PDVSA's Alter Ego, and Vice Versa?' (*Credit Slips*, 17 August 2017) <www.creditslips.org/creditslips/2017/08/venezuela-is-like-any-other-shareholder.html#more>.

———. 'Ukraine Wins Appeal in Russian Bond Case' (*Credit Slips*, 14 September 2018) <www.creditslips.org/creditslips/2018/09/ukraine-wins-appeal-in-russian-bond-case.html#more>.

White, Natasha, 'Hey, Big Lenders' (*Global Witness*, 30 November 2018) <www.globalwitness.org/en/blog/hey-big-lenders/>.

———. 'Commodity Traders: Lenders of Last Resort for Africa's Oil-Producers' (*Global Witness*, 3 July 2019) <www.globalwitness.org/en/blog/commodity-traders-lenders-of-last-resort/>.

———. 'Cool Runnings, Commodity Traders and Global Capital – a Review of 'The World for Sale' (*Global Witness*, 8 April 2021) <www.globalwitness.org/en/blog/cool-runnings-commodity-traders-capital/>.

World Bank Group, 'Debt Transparency in Developing Countries' (2021) <https://documents.worldbank.org/en/publication/documents-reports/documentdetail/743881635526394087/debt-transparency-in-developing-economies>.

Xafa, Miranda, 'Lessons from the 2012 Greek Debt Restructuring' (*VoxEU*, 25 June 2014) <http://voxeu.org/article/greek-debt-restructuring-lessons-learned>.

Zampolli, Fabrizio, 'Sovereign Debt Management as an Instrument of Monetary Policy: An Overview' (May 2012) BIS Papers No 65 <www.bis.org/publ/bppdf/bispap65f_rh.pdf>.

Statutes, Treaties, and Judicial Authorities

International Treaties and Conventions

Agreement between the Swiss Federal Council and the Bank for International Settlements to determine the Bank's legal status in Switzerland of 10 February 1987 (text as amended effective 1 January 2003 by the exchange of letters of 18 December 2002/13 January 2003).

Articles of Agreement of the International Monetary Fund (as amended) (International Monetary Fund [IMF]) 2 UNTS 39, UN Reg No I-20, TIAS 1501, 60 Stat 1401, 3 Bevans 1351.

Articles of Agreement of the International Bank for Reconstruction and Development (International Bank for Reconstruction and Development [IBRD]) 2 UNTS 134, UN Reg No I-20, TIAS 1502, 60 Stat 1440, 3 Bevans 1390.

Charter of the United Nations (done at San Francisco, United States, on 26 June 1945) (United Nations [UN]) 1 UNTS XVI, 59 Stat 1031, TS 993, 3 Bevans 1153, 145 BSP 805, 892 UNTS 119.

Chinese-Greek BIT of 1992 <https://edit.wti.org/document/show/59648dac-d963-4e94-92a2-dcfadbeb86c5?textBlockId=50709ec6-3dce-4619-aaae-e45899706555&page=1>.

Comprehensive Economic and Trade Agreement between Canada, of the One Part, and the European Union [and its Member States] of the Other Part [2017] OJ L11/23.

Convention on Jurisdictional Immunities of States and their Property (United Nations [UN]) UN Doc A/RES/59/38, Annex, UN Doc A/59/508.

Convention on the Law of the Sea (United Nations [UN]) 1833 UNTS 3, UKTS 81 (1999), UN Doc A/Conf.62/122, UN Reg No I-31363.

Convention on the Recognition and Enforcement of Foreign Arbitral Awards (United Nations [UN]) 330 UNTS 3, 21 UST 2517.

Convention on the Settlement of Investment Disputes Between States and Nationals of Other States (International Centre for Settlement of Investment Disputes [ICSID]) 575 UNTS 159, UN Reg No I-8359, 17 USTS 1270, TIAS 6090, UKTS 25 (1967) Cmnd 3255.

Convention respecting the Bank for International Settlements 104 LNTS 441.

Draft Articles on Jurisdictional Immunities of States and Their Property adopted by the Commission at its forty-third session in 1991 (Final Outcome) (International Law Commission [ILC]) UN Doc A/46/10, 13, (1991) II(2) UNYBILC 13.

European Convention on State Immunity (Council of Europe) ETS No 74, 1495 UNTS 181, UN Reg No I-25699.

Greek-Slovak BIT of 1991 <https://investmentpolicy.unctad.org/international-investment-agreements/treaties/otheriia/1815/greece – slovakia-bit-1991->.

International Convention for the Unification of Certain Rules of Law relating to Bills of Lading (as amended) 120 LNTS 155, Reg No LoN-2764.

Treaty Establishing the European Stability Mechanism (European Union [EU], (Brussels, 2 February 2012).

United Nations General Assembly Resolution 69/319: Basic Principles on Sovereign Debt Restructuring Processes (United Nations General Assembly [UNGA]) UN Doc A/RES/69/319.

Vienna Convention on Diplomatic Relations (United Nations [UN]) 500 UNTS 95, (1972) 23 UST 3227, TIAS No 7502, UN Reg No we-7310.

Vienna Convention on the Law of Treaties (United Nations [UN]) 1155 UNTS 331.

Domestic and EU Statutes

Act No 2016–1691 of 9 December 2016 on the Fight Against Missing Morality (*Loi De La Lutte Contre Les Manquements À La Probité*) (France [fr]).

Austrian Organic Law on the General Rights of Citizens of 21 December 1867 (*Staatsgrundgesetz über die allgemeinen Rechte der Staatsbürger*) (Austria [at]).

Charter Of Fundamental Rights Of The European Union (European Union [EU]) [2000] OJ C364/1, [2007] OJ C303/1, [2012] OJ C326/391.

Council Regulation on jurisdiction and the recognition and enforcement of judgments in civil and commercial matters (Council of the European Union) No 44/2001/EC, [2001] OJL12/1.

Debt Relief (Developing Countries) Act (United Kingdom 2010 c.22 [gb]).

Law on combating against the activities of vulture funds (Belgium [be]).

Loi n° 91–650 du 9 juillet 1991 portant réforme des procédures civiles d'exécution (France [fr]).

Regulation of the European Parliament and of the Council on the service in the Member States of judicial and extrajudicial documents in civil or commercial matters (service of documents), and repealing Council Regulation (EC) No 1348/2000 (European Parliament) (Council of the European Union) 1393/2007/EC, [2007] OJ L324/79.

Regulation of the European Parliament and of the Council on jurisdiction and the recognition and enforcement of judgments in civil and commercial matters (European Parliament) (Council of the European Union) 1215/2012/EU, [2012] OJ L351/1.

Swiss Code 281.1 of 11 April 1889 on Debt Enforcement and Bankruptcy (*Bundesgesetz über Schuldbetreibung und Konkurs*) (Switzerland) [ch]).

International and European Courts

Court of Justice of the EU (CJEU)

Accorinti v European Central Bank, Judgment, Case T-79/13, [2015] Court of Justice of the European Union [CJEU]; GC of the European Union [EGC].

ECB v Slovenia, Judgment, reference for a preliminary ruling, Case C-316/19, ECLI:EU:C:2020:1030, [2020] OJ C187/59, 17 December 2020, Court of Justice of the European Union [CJEU]; European Court of Justice [ECJ].

Fahnenbrock v Hellenic Republic, Opinion of the Advocate General, Joined Cases C-226/13, C-245/13, C-247/13 and C-578/13, [2014], 9th December 2014, Court of Justice of the European Union [CJEU]; European Court of Justice [ECJ].

Fahnenbrock v Hellenic Republic, Judgment, reference for a preliminary ruling, Case C-226/13, Case C-245/13, Case C-247/13, Case C-578/13, ECLI:EU:C:2015:383, [2015] OJ C270/2, 11th June 2015, Court of Justice of the European Union [CJEU]; CJEU [ECJ]; CJEU (1st Chamber).

Gauweiler and ors v Deutscher Bundestag, Judgment, reference for a preliminary ruling, Case C-62/14, ECLI:EU:C:2015:400, 16th June 2015, Court of Justice of the European Union [CJEU]; European Court of Justice [ECJ]; European Court of Justice (Grand Chamber).

Hellenic Republic v Kuhn, Judgment, Case C-308/17, ECLI:EU:C:2018:911, 15th November 2018, Court of Justice of the European Union [CJEU]; European Court of Justice [ECJ]; European Court of Justice (1st Chamber).

Hellenic Republic v Kuhn, Opinion of the Advocate General, Case C-308/17, ECLI:EU:C:2018:528, [2018], 4th July 2018, Court of Justice of the European Union [CJEU]; European Court of Justice [ECJ].

Harald Kolassa v Barclays Bank plc, Case C-375, ECLI:EU:C:2015:37, [2015] 28th January 2015, Court of Justice of the European Union [CJEU]; European Court of Justice [ECJ].

K Chrysostomides & Co and Others v Council and Others, Case T-680/17, Court of Justice of the European Union [CJEU], GC of the European Union [EGC].

Ledra Advertising Limited v European Commission and European Central Bank, Judgment, Case C-8/15 P, Case C-9/15 P, Case C-10/15 P, ECLI:EU:C:2016:701, OXIO 191, 20th September 2016, Court of Justice of the European Union [CJEU]; European Court of Justice [ECJ]; European Court of Justice (Grand Chamber).

LTU v Eurocontrol, Judgment, reference for a preliminary ruling, Case C-29/76, ECLI:EU:C:1976:137, [1976], 14th October 1976, Court of Justice of the European Union [CJEU]; European Court of Justice [ECJ].

Nausicaa Anadyomène and Banque d'escompte v ECB, Judgment, Case T-749/15, [2017], 24th January 2017, Court of Justice of the European Union [CJEU]; European General Court [EGC].

Pringle v Government of Ireland and ors, Judgment, reference for a preliminary ruling, Case C-370/12, ECLI:EU:C:2012:756, [2013] OJ C26/15, ILEC 053 (CJEU 2012), 27th November 2012, Court of Justice of the European Union [CJEU]; European Court of Justice [ECJ].

Rina SpA v Ente Registro Italiano Navale, Judgment, Case C-641/18, ECLI:EU:C:2020:349, [2020], 7th May 2020, Court of Justice of the European Union [CJEU]; European Court of Justice [ECJ].

Rina SpA v Ente Registro Italiano Navale, Opinion of Advocate General, Case C-641/18, ECLI:EU:C:2020:3, [2020], 14th January 2020, Court of Justice of the European Union [CJEU]; European Court of Justice [ECJ].

Supreme Site Services GmbH and Others v Supreme Headquarters Allied Powers Europe, Case C-29/76, ECLI:EU:C:2020:638 [2020], 3rd September 2020, Court of Justice of the European Union [CJEU]; European Court of Justice [ECJ].

Weiss and ors, Judgment, Case C-493/17, ECLI:EU:C:2018:1000, 11th December 2018, Court of Justice of the European Union [CJEU]; European Court of Justice [ECJ].

European Court of Human Rights

Al-Adsani v United Kingdom, Merits, App No 35763/97, ECHR 2001-XI, IHRL 2981 (ECHR 2001), [2001] ECHR 761, (2002) 34 EHRR 11, (1987) 12 BHRC 88, (2003) 123 ILR 24, 21st November 2001.

Bramelid and Malmström v Sweden, Admissibility, App No 8588/79, App No 8589/79, (1982) 29 DR 76, [1982] ECHR 16, (1983) 5 EHRR 249, (1983) 5 EHRR CD278, (1986) 8 EHRR 116, 12th October 1982, European Commission on Human Rights (historical).

James and ors v United Kingdom, Merits, App No 8793/79, Case No 3/1984/75/119, A/98, IHRL 55 (ECHR 1986), [1986] ECHR 2, (1986) 8 EHRR 123, [1986] RVR 139, (1987) 75 ILR 396, 21st February 1986.

Malysh and ors v Russian Federation, Admissibility, App No 30280/03, 11th February 2010, European Court of Human Rights [ECHR].

Mamatas v Greece, App No 63066/14, App No 64297/14, App No 66106/14, 21st July 2016, European Court of Human Rights [ECHR].

Waite and Kennedy v Germany, Merits, App No 26083/94, ECHR 1999-we, IHRL 3200 (ECHR 1999), OXIO 272, [1999] ECHR 13, (1999) 30 EHRR 261, (1999) 118 ILR 121, [1999] 6 BHRC 499, 18th February 1999, European Court of Human Rights [ECHR]; Grand Chamber [ECHR].

International Tribunal for the Law of the Sea

ARA Libertad (Argentina v Ghana), Case No. 20, Request for the Prescription of Provisional Measures, 15 December 2012.

International Centre for the Settlement of Investment Disputes

Abaclat and ors v Argentina, Decision on jurisdiction and admissibility, ICSID Case No ARB/07/5, IIC 504 (2011), despatched 4th August 2011, World Bank; International Centre for Settlement of Investment Disputes [ICSID].

Abaclat and ors v Argentina, Dissenting Opinion of Professor Georges Abi-Saab, ICSID Case No ARB/07/5, 28th October 2011, World Bank; International Centre for Settlement of Investment Disputes [ICSID].

Abaclat and ors v Argentina, Procedural order no 17, ICSID Case No ARB/07/5, IIC 815 (2013), 8th February 2013, World Bank; International Centre for Settlement of Investment Disputes [ICSID].

Abaclat and ors v Argentina, Settlement agreement dated 21 April 2016, ICSID Case No ARB/07/5, World Bank; International Centre for Settlement of Investment Disputes [ICSID].

Abaclat and ors v Argentina, Consent award, ICSID Case No ARB/07/5, IIC 905 (2016), despatched 29th December 2016, World Bank; International Centre for Settlement of Investment Disputes [ICSID].

Alemanni and 74 others v Argentina, Decision on jurisdiction and admissibility, ICSID Case No ARB/07/8, IIC 666 (2014), despatched 17th November 2014, World Bank; International Centre for Settlement of Investment Disputes [ICSID].

Ambiente Ufficio SpA v Argentina, Decision on jurisdiction and admissibility; dissenting opinion of Santiago Torres Bernárdez, ICSID Case No ARB/08/9, 2nd May 2013, World Bank; International Centre for Settlement of Investment Disputes [ICSID].

CMS Gas Transmission Company v Argentina, Application for annulment and request for stay of enforcement of arbitral award, ICSID Case No ARB/01/8, IIC 66 (2005), 8th September 2005, World Bank; International Centre for Settlement of Investment Disputes [ICSID].

Československa obchodní banka AS v Slovakia, Decision on objections to jurisdiction, ICSID Case No ARB/97/4, (1999) 14 ICSID Rev-FILJ 251, IIC 49 (1999), (2002) 5 ICSID Rep 330, 24th May 1999, World Bank; International Centre for Settlement of Investment Disputes [ICSID].

Deutsche Bank AG v Sri Lanka, Final award, ICSID Case No ARB/09/02, IIC 578 (2012), despatched 31st October 2012, United Nations [UN]; World Bank; International Centre for Settlement of Investment Disputes [ICSID].

Fedax NV v Venezuela, Award, ICSID Case No ARB/96/3, IIC 102 (1998), (2002) 5 ICSID Rep 200, (1998) 37 ILM 1391, (1999) XXIVa YB Com Arb 39, 9th March 1998, World Bank; International Centre for Settlement of Investment Disputes [ICSID].

LG&E Energy Corporation and ors v Argentina, Award, ICSID Case No ARB/02/1, IIC 295 (2007), despatched 25th July 2007, World Bank; International Centre for Settlement of Investment Disputes [ICSID].

Marfin Investment Group Holdings SA, Alexandros Bakatselos and others v Republic of Cyprus, ICSID Case No ARB/13/27, Notice of Dispute, despatched 23rd January 2013, World Bank; International Centre for Settlement of Investment Disputes [ICSID] (on file with author).

Mitchell v Congo, the Democratic Republic of the, Award, ICSID Case No ARB/99/7, IIC 965 (2004), despatched 9th February 2004, World Bank; International Centre for Settlement of Investment Disputes [ICSID].

Poštová banka as and Istrokapital SE v Greece, Award, ICSID Case No ARB/13/8, IIC 679 (2015), despatched 9th April 2015, World Bank; International Centre for Settlement of Investment Disputes [ICSID].

Poštová Banka AS and Istrokapital SE v The Hellenic Republic, Decision on Poštová Banka's application for partial annulment of the award, ICSID Case no ARB/13/8, IIC 854 (2016), despatched 29th September 2016, World Bank; International Centre for Settlement of Investment Disputes [ICSID].

Salini Costruttori SpA and Italstrade SpA v Morocco, Decision on jurisdiction, ICSID Case No ARB/00/4, IIC 206 (2001), (2004) 6 ICSID Rep 398, (2004) 6 ICSID Rep 400, (2003) 42 ILM 609, (2002) 129 Clunet 196, 16th July 2001, despatched 23rd July 2001, United Nations [UN]; World Bank; International Centre for Settlement of Investment Disputes [ICSID].

International Court of Justice

Certain Norwegian Loans, *France v Norway*, Judgment, jurisdiction; separate opinion of Judge Lauterpacht, ICJ GL No 29, [1957] ICJ Rep 9, [1957] ICJ Rep 34, ICGJ 175 (ICJ 1957), 6th July 1957, United Nations [UN]; International Court of Justice [ICJ].

Jurisdictional Immunities of the State, *Germany v Italy*, Judgment, ICGJ 434 (ICJ 2012), 3rd February 2012, United Nations [UN]; International Court of Justice [ICJ].

Permanent Court of Arbitration

Romak SA (Switzerland) v Uzbekistan, Final Award, ICGJ 462 (PCA 2009), PCA Case No AA280, 26th November 2009, Permanent Court of Arbitration [PCA].

Russian Claim for Interest on Indemnities (Damages Claimed by Russia for Delay in Payment of Compensation Owed to Russians Injured During the War of 1877–1878), *Russia v Turkey*, Award, (1961) XI RIAA 421, ICGJ 399 (PCA 1912), (1912) 1 HCR 547, 11th November 1912, Permanent Court of Arbitration [PCA].

Permanent Court of International Justice

French Company of Venezuelan Railroads Case, *France v Venezuela*, (1962) X RIAA 285, 31st July 1905, Mixed Claims Commission (France-Venezuela).

Payment of Various Serbian Loans Issued in France, *France v Kingdom of the Serbs, Croats, and Slovenes, Judgment*, Judgment No 14, PCIJ Series A No 20, ICGJ 260 (PCIJ 1929), 12th July 1929, League of Nations (historical) [LoN]; Permanent Court of International Justice (historical) [PCIJ].

Société Commerciale de Belgique, Belgium v Greece, Judgment, PCIJ Series A/B No 78, ICGJ 331 (PCIJ 1939), 15th June 1939, League of Nations (historical) [LoN]; Permanent Court of International Justice (historical) [PCIJ].

Domestic Courts

Argentina

Galli, Hugo Gabriel y otro c. Poder Ejecutivo Nacional s/amparo, Judgment, G 2181 XXXIX, 5th April 2005, Argentina; National Supreme Court of Justice [CSJN].

Austria

GS v Hellenic Republic, Appeal judgment, 4 Ob 233/19x, 21st February 2020, Austria; Supreme Court of Justice [OGH].

L v Hellenic Republic I, Appeal judgment, 10 Ob34/16x, 25 April 2017, Austria; Supreme Court of Justice [OGH].

L v Hellenic Republic II, Appeal judgment, 10 Ob103/18x, 22 January 2019, Austria; Supreme Court of Justice [OGH].

RB and TB v Hellenic Republic, Interlocutory appeal judgment, 4Ob227/13f, ILDC 2214 (AT 2014), 20th May 2014, Austria; Supreme Court of Justice [OGH].

RE v Hellenic Republic, Appeal judgment, 8 Ob125/15p, 25th November 2015, Austria; Supreme Court of Justice [OGH].

RB and GB v Hellenic Republic, Appeal judgment, 4 Ob 163/15x, 16th January 2016, Austria; Supreme Court of Justice [OGH].

TW v Hellenic Republic, Appeal judgment, 8 Ob67/15h, 30th July 2015, Austria; Supreme Court of Justice [OGH].

Belgium

Elliott Associates, L.P., General Docket No. 2000/QR/92 (Cour d'Appel [CA] [Court of Appeal] Bruxelles, 8ème ch. 26 September 2000).

République d'Argentine v NML Capital, n C.11.0688.F, 22 November 2012, Belgium, Cour de cassation [Cass].

France

NML Capital Limited v Argentina, Appeal judgment, Case No 09–72 057, 867, (2012) 139 JDI 668, 28th September 2011, France; Court of Cassation [Cass]; Civil Division.

Société NML Capital Limited v Argentina and Air France, No 11–13–323, 28th March 2013, France; Court of Cassation [Cass]; Civil Division.

Germany

Argentine Necessity Case, *K and ors v Argentina* (represented by President Néstor Kirchner), Order of the Second Senate, 2 BvM 1/03, 2 BvM 2/03, 2 BvM 3/03, 2 BvM 4/03, 2 BvM 5/03, 2 BvM 1/06, 2 BvM 2/06, BVerfGE 118, 124, ILDC 952 (DE 2007), NJW 2007, 2610, (2010) 138 ILR 1, (2007) 4 AJIL 857, 8th May 2007, Germany; Constitutional Court [BVerfG].

BGH, Beschluss vom 04.10.2005 – VII ZB 9/05, 4th October 2005, Germany; Federal Court of Justice [BGH].

BGH, Beschluss vom 25.11.2010 – VII ZB 120/09, 25th November 2010, Germany; Federal Court of Justice [BGH].

BGH, Urteil vom 24.02.2015 – XI ZR 193/14, XI ZR 193/14, NJW 2015, 2328, 24th February 2015, Germany; Federal Court of Justice [BGH].

BGH, Urteil vom 08.03.2016 – VI ZR 516/14, VI ZR 516/14, NJW 2016, 1659, 8th March 2016, Germany; Federal Court of Justice [BGH].

BGH, Urteil vom 19.12.2017 – XI ZR 796/16, 19th December 2017, Germany; Federal Court of Justice [BGH].

BVerfG, Beschluss vom 06.12.2006–2 BvM 9/03, 6th December 2006, Germany; Constitutional Court [BVerfG].

BVerfG, Urteil vom 3.7.2019–2 BvR 824/15, 2 BvR 825/15, Second Senate, 3 July 2019, Germany; Constitutional Court [BVerfG].

BVerfG, Urteil vom 6.5.2020–2 BvR 331/18, Second Senate, 6th May 2020, Germany; Constitutional Court [BVerfG].

LG (Frankfurt), Urteile vom 30.03.2015–2–1 S 108/14, 204/14, 280/14, 30th March 2015; Germany; Frankfurt am Main; District Court [LG].

OLG (Frankfurt), Urteil vom 18.09.2014–16 U 41/14, 18 September 2014, Germany; Hesse; Frankfurt am Main; Higher Regional Court [OLG].

OLG (Köln), Urteil vom 12.05.2016–8 U 44/15, 8 U 44/15, ZIP 2016, 40, WM 2016, 1590, 12th May 2016, Germany; North Rhine-Westphalia; Cologne; Higher Regional Court [OLG].

OLG (Oldenburg), Urteil vom 15.04.2016–13 U 43/15, 18th April 2016, Germany; Lower Saxony; Oldenburg; Higher Regional Court [OLG]

OLG (Schleswig), Urteil vom 07.07.2016–5 U 84/15, 7th July 2016, Germany; Schleswig-Holstein; Higher Regional Court [OLG].

Italy

Borri v Argentina, Request for a ruling on jurisdiction, Case No 11225, Order No 6532/2005, ILDC 296 (IT 2005), (2005) 88 Riv Dir Int 856, 27th May 2005, Italy; Supreme Court of Cassation.

Ferrini v Germany, Appeal decision, Decision No 5044/2004, ILDC 19 (IT 2004), (2004) 87 Riv Dir Intern 539, (2005) 99 AJIL 242, (2006) 128 ILR 658, 11th March 2004, Italy; Supreme Court of Cassation.

Switzerland

BGer, Urteil vom 12.07.2010–5A.360/2010, *NML Capital Limited and EM Limited v Bank for International Settlements and Debt Enforcement Office Basel-Stadt*, Final appeal judgment, 5A.360/2010, BGE 136 III 379, ATF 136 III 379, ILDC 1547 (CH 2010), 12th July 2010, Switzerland; Federal Supreme Court [BGer].

Groupement d'Entreprises Fougerolle v European Organization for Nuclear Research (CERN), BGE 118 Ib 562, 21st December 1992, Switzerland; Federal Supreme Court [BGer].

United Kingdom

AIC Ltd v Federal Government of Nigeria [2003] EWHC 1357 (QB).

Assenagon Asset Management SA v Irish Bank Resolution Corp Ltd (formerly Anglo Irish Bank Corp Ltd), 27th July 2012, United Kingdom; England and Wales; High Court [EWHC] 2090; Chancery Division [ChD].

NML Capital Limited v Argentina, Appeal judgment, [2011] UKSC 31, [2011] 2 AC 495, [2011] 3 WLR 273, ILDC 1805 (UK 2011), (2011) 147 ILR 575, 6th July 2011, United Kingdom; Supreme Court [SC].

Law Debenture Trust Corporation plc v Ukraine, [2017] EWHC 655 (Comm), [2017] QB 1249, [2017] 3 WLR 667, [2017] WLR(D) 226, 29th March 2017, United Kingdom; England and Wales; High Court [EWHC]; Queen's Bench Division [QBD]; Commercial Court.

Trendtex Trading Corporation v Central Bank of Nigeria, Appeal decision, ILDC 1735 (UK 1977), [1977] 1 QB 529, [1977] 1 All ER 881, [1977] 2 WLR 356, (1979) 64 ILR 111, 13th January 1977, United Kingdom; England and Wales; Court of Appeal [CA]; Civil Division [EWCA Civ].

United States of America

Allied Bank International v Banco Credito Agricola de Cartago and ors, Case No 225, Docket 83–7714, 757, 758 F 2d 516 (2d Cir 1985), 77 ALR Fed 281, (1985) 24 ILM 762, 18th March 1985, United States; Court of Appeals (2nd Circuit) [2d Cir].

Argentina and Banco Central de la República Argentina v Weltover Incorporated and ors, Final appeal, Docket No 91–763, 504 US 607 (1992), ILDC 1924 (US 1992), 112 S Ct 2160 (1992), 119 L Ed 2d 394 (1992), (1995) 100 ILR 510, 12th June 1992, United States; Supreme Court [US].

Argentina v NML Capital Limited, Appeal judgment, Docket No 12–842, 573 US ___ (2014), ILDC 2201 (US 2014), 134 S Ct 2250 (2014), 189 L Ed 2d 234 (2014), 16th June 2014, United States; Supreme Court [US].

Argentina v NML Capital Limited, Brief of Amicus Curiae Euroclear Bank SA/NV in Support of Petitioner, Docket No 13–990, 24th March 2014, United States; Supreme Court [US].

Banco Credito Agricola de Cartago v Allied Bank International, No 85–146, 473 US 934 (1985), 23rd September 1985, United States; Supreme Court [US].

Elliott Associates LP v Panama, No 96 Civ 5514(DC), 975 F Supp 332 (SDNY 1997), 10th September 1997, United States; New York; District Court for the Southern District of New York [SDNY].

Elliott Associates LP v Banco de la Nación and Peru, 194 FRD 116 (SDNY 2000), 2000, United States; New York; District Court for the Southern District of New York [SDNY].

EM Limited and NML Capital Limited v Argentina, No 05–1525-cv, 131 Fed Appx 745 (2d Cir 2005), 13th May 2005, United States; Court of Appeals (2nd Circuit) [2d Cir].

EM Limited and NML Capital Limited v Argentina, No 11–4065-cv (L), 695 F 3d 201 (2d Cir 2012), 20th August 2012, United States; Court of Appeals (2nd Circuit) [2d Cir].

EM Limited and NML Capital Limited v Banco Central De La República Argentina and Argentina, Opinion, 720 F Supp 273 (SDNY 2010), 7th April 2010, United States; New York; District Court for the Southern District of New York [SDNY].

EM Limited and NML Capital Limited v Banco Central De La República Argentina and Argentina, Appeal judgment, ILDC 2495 (US 2015), 800 F 3d 78 (2nd Cir 2015), 31st August 2015, United States; Court of Appeals (2nd Circuit) [2d Cir].

FG Hemisphere Assocs. v Republique du Congo, 455 F 3d 575 (5th Cir 2006), 10th July 2006, United States; Court of Appeals (5th Circuit) [5th Cir].

First National City Bank v Banco Para el Comercio Exterior de Cuba, No 81–984, 462 US 611 (1983), 103 S Ct 2591 (1983), (1983) 22 ILM 840, 17th June 1983, United States; Supreme Court [US].

Libra Bank Limited v Banco Nacional de Costa Rica, Decision on motion for summary judgment, 570 F Supp 870 (SDNY 1983), (1984) 78 AJIL 443, 6th July 1983, United States; New York; District Court for the Southern District of New York [SDNY].

Lightwater Corporation Limited v Argentina, No 02 Civ 3804 (TPG), No 02 Civ 3808 (TPG), No 02 Civ 5932 (TPG), 14th April 2003, United States; New York; District Court for the Southern District of New York [SDNY].

LNC Investments, Inc v Banco Central de Nicaragua, No 00–7610, 228 F3d 423 (2d Cir 2000), 20th September 2000, United States; Court of Appeals (2nd Circuit) [2d Cir].

Jam et al v International Finance Corporation, 27th February 2019 (No 17–1011, 139 S. Ct. 759 (2019)), OXIO 474, Supreme Court [US]; United Nations [UN]; International Finance Corporation [IFC].

NML Capital Limited v Argentina I, Opinion, Nos 02 Civ 3804, 02 Civ 3808, 02 Civ 4124, 02 Civ 5432, 02 Civ 2507, 02 Civ 8528, 02 Civ 8845 (TPG), 29th March 2005, United States; New York; District Court for the Southern District of New York [SDNY].

NML Capital Limited v Argentina II, 12th September 2008, United States; New York; District Court for the Southern District of New York [SDNY].

NML Capital Limited v Argentina III, No 08 Civ 6978 (TPG), No 09 Civ 1707 (TPG), No 09 Civ 1708 (TPG), 7th December 2011, United States; New York; District Court for the Southern District of New York [SDNY].

NML Capital Limited v Argentina IV, No 08 Civ 6978 (TPG), 23rd February 2012, United States; New York; District Court for the Southern District of New York [SDNY].

NML Capital Limited v Argentina V, 699 F3d 246, 26th October 2012, United States; Court of Appeals (2nd Circuit) [2d Cir].

NML Capital Limited v Argentina VI, Docket No 08 Civ 6978, 21st November 2012, United States; New York; District Court for the Southern District of New York [SDNY].

NML Capital Limited v Argentina VII, Docket No 12–105, 1st March 2013, United States; Court of Appeals (2nd Circuit) [2d Cir].

NML Capital Limited v Argentina VIII, Opinion affirming orders of the district court, 727 F 3d 230 (2d Cir 2013), 23rd August 2013, United States; Court of Appeals (2nd Circuit) [2d Cir].

NML Capital Limited and EM Limited v Banco Central de la República Argentina, 652 F 3d 172 (2d Cir 2011), 5th July 2011, United States; Court of Appeals (2nd Circuit) [2d Cir].

Pravin Banker Associates Limited v Banco Popular del Peru and Peru, 895 F Supp 660 (SDNY 1995), 24th August 1995, United States; New York; District Court for the Southern District of New York [SDNY].

Pravin Banker Associates Limited v Banco Popular del Peru and Peru, Docket No 96–7183, 109 F 3d 850 (2d Cir 1997), 65 USLW 2640, 25th March 1997, United States; Court of Appeals (2nd Circuit) [2d Cir].

Perry v United States, 294 US 330, [1935] 18th February 1935, United States; Supreme Court [US].

Stolt-Nielsen S A v AnimalFeeds Int'l Corp, 559 US 662, [2010] 9th December 2009, United States; Supreme Court [US].

The Export-Import Bank of the Republic of China v Grenada, 2013 US Dist LEXIS 117740, 19th August 2013, United States; New York; District Court for the Southern District of New York [SDNY].

Walker International Holdings v Republic of Congo, 395 F3d 229 (5th Cir 2004), 22nd December 2004, United States; Court of Appeals (5th Circuit) [5th Cir].

Weltover Incorporated and ors v Argentina and Banco Central de la Argentina, Appeal judgment, 941 F 2d 145 (2d Cir 1991), 13th August 1991, United States; Court of Appeals (2nd Circuit) [2d Cir].

White Hawthorne LLC v Argentina, 2016 US Dist LEXIS 177895, 2016, United States; New York; District Court for the Southern District of New York [SDNY].

Index

Note: page numbers in *italics* indicate a table.

Abaclat v Argentina 56–59, 62, 125; risk recognition 64
Abi-Saab, Georges (dissenting opinion) 58–59
absolute sovereign immunity, principle (demise) 2
Accorinti v ECB 109–110, 118
accrued interest rates, forgiveness 6
acta iure gestionis 48–49, 103, 105, 114–115, 145
acta iure imperii 41, 48–49, 103, 105, 114–115
adjudicatory sovereign immunity 47–50
Allied Bank International v Banco Credito Agricola de Cartago 33
Ambiente Ufficio v Argentine Republic 56, 59–60, 63–64, 125
ARA Libertad 45–46, 53–54
Argentina: Argentina-Italy BIT 57; creditors, injunctive relief 35; debt moratorium 39; debt restructuring, 33; election (2016), impact 65; immunity, SDNY denial 42; international financial market return 65; jurisdiction immunity claim 48; Lock Law 31–32; pari passu clause, drafting 55; sovereign bond arbitration, impact 60–61; sovereign immunity, waiver 34; sovereignty, US court decisions (interference) 46–47; territorial link 64
Argentina and Banco Central de la República Argentina v Weltover Incorporate and ors (decision) 104
Argentina holdout 142; arbitration 56–65; lawsuits, settling 65–68; litigation 32
Argentina-Italy BIT 57
Argentina Necessity Case 38
Argentine Bond Restructuring Agency (ABRA), establishment 163
Argentine debt exchanges, impact 7
Argentine debt restructuring 3, 31–32; bondholder negotiations (2010) 32; courts/tribunals, relationship 31; debt swap (2005) 31–32; holdout litigation 32
asset management funds (real money investors) 161–162
asset manager, holdout investor actions (impossibility) 161–162
attachment, central bank reserves immunity 51–53
Aurelius Capital (holdouts) 158
Austria: Greek sovereign debt enforcement, hypothetical problems 108–109; holdout creditor litigation 105–107; OGH judgments 105–107

Banco Central de la República Argentina (BRCA): funds, attachment 44; funds, BIS transfer 45; sovereignty, waiver 34
Banec test 34–35, 52
banking syndicates, moral suasion/ regulatory pressure 161
Bank of International Settlements (BIS), currency reserve (Argentine holdings) 44
banks, international foreign loan market involvement 160–161
bilateral debt, restructuring 7
Bilateral Investment Treaty (BIT): Argentina-Italy BIT 57; differences 56; Germany-Sri Lanka BIT 120; Greece-Slovakia BIT 118–119; host state breach 65; negotiation/signing 58; obligations 61; States parties, agreement 58; Switzerland, holdout litigation 120

bondholders: debtor country payment 54; property rights, GBA interference (ECtHR assessment) 113; rights protection clauses 101
bonds: face value, market value (contrast) 117; nation payments, failure 33
Borri v Argentina 41, 48–49; Italian Supreme Court decision 104
Brady Plan 12, 160–161
Brussels I Regulation 104–106; Article 1(1) 105; Article 7(1) 106; Article 17(2) 105–106; inapplicability 116; jurisdiction 116; questions, applicability 111; usage 108
Brussels I (recast) Regulation, Article 7(1) 116
Bundesgerichtshof (BGH): Argentina repayment obligations 145; decisions 39–40; Germany, holdout creditor litigation 102–104; international jurisdiction focus 51; Second Chamber of the Constitutional Court ruling 40
Bundesverfassungsgericht (BVerfG): decision 38–39, 40–41; Germany, holdout creditor litigation 104

carrots/sweeteners, creditor participation encouragement 7
central bank reserves: assets protection 2; immunity 51–53
central banks, immunity 52
choice-of-forum clauses: absence (Greek bonds) 102; benefit 116
Collective Action Clause (CAC): absence 166; German law, relationship 147; insertion, benefit (ECtHR conclusion) 117; resemblance 100; Retrofit 144; retrofitting 117; use 11
collective action problems, occurrence 165
collective voting mechanism, retrofitting 101
commercial activity exception 47–49
commercial sovereign acts, delineation 47
commodity traders, operation 164–166
Corte Suprema di Cassazione 41, 145–146
Cour de Cassation (French Supreme Court): execution immunity 145; execution measures, dismissal 43; NML litigation 43–44; tax claims, attachment (prohibition) 51
Court of Appeals for the Second Circuit, pari passu clause interpretation 37
Court of Justice of the European Union (CJEU) 109–112; jurisprudence, impact 146
COVID-19 pandemic, impact 147
credit default swaps (CDSs), vulture holdout positions 159
creditor: attachment, public claims immunity 50–51; classes/ranking/priority 8–9; participation, carrot/sweetener encouragement 7
cross-border sovereign debt restructuring 32

debtor-in-possession (DIP) financing, concept 9
debt payment obligations, suspension 101
debt rescheduling/reprofiling 6
debt restructuring: deal 32; debt rescheduling, contrast 6–7; methods 6–7; scope 7–9; techniques 7
debt sustainability analysis (DSA), probabilistic approach (IMF) 5
Dionysius I, sovereign default origin 1
diplomatic immunity, principle 43
diplomatic instrumentalities, assets protection 2
distressed-debt instruments, yield 158
domestic bankruptcy, debtor-in-possession (DIP) financing concept 9
domestic government debt restructurings, immunity defence 146
domestic law debt, holdout creditor problems (relationship) 98
domestic law restructurings, sovereign immunity 107–108
domestic sovereign debt restructuring, foreign sovereign debt restructuring (contrast) 7–8
Drago-Porter-Convention 1–2

elite issuers, creditworthiness 144
Elliott Associates LP v Panama litigation 35
Elliott Management (vulture fund) 159
EMEs: external commercial debt 9–10; sovereign debt distress, risk 4; sovereign defaults 160
EM v BRCA litigation 34, 52
enforcement, immunity 50–54
English law-governed syndicated loans, usage 160
English law securities, bondholder rights protection clauses 101
Euro Area sovereign debt restructurings, Eurosystem claims (preferential treatment) 118
European Central Bank (ECB), investor legitimate expectations (nonviolation) 110

European Convention on State Immunity (ESCI) 115
European Court of Human Rights (ECtHR) 112–113; sovereign bonds clarification 117
European courts: Greece holdout litigation 109–118; judicial challenges 113–114; sovereign debt restructurings 113–114
Eurosystem claims, preferential treatment 118
Exceptional Access Policy framework, IMF 6–7
Export-Import Bank of the Republic of China, Grenada lawsuit 55–56

Fahnenbrock v Hellenic Republic 104, 110–111, 114
Fedax NV v Venezuela 59, 61–63
Federal Reserve Bank of New York (FRBNY) 34–35; foreign exchange reserves deposits 51–52
financial markets, globalization 3
Fiscal Agency Agreement (FAA), pari passu clause (breach) 36
foreign courts: holdout creditor litigation 102–109; sovereign debt enforcement 47–56
foreign judgements, recognition 47, 49–50
foreign law debt 180; holdout creditor problems, relationship 31; restructurings, domestic law debt restructurings (holdout contrast) 142
Foreign Sovereign Immunities Act (FSIA): property, US location (requirement) 50; statutory rules 48; violations 37–38
France, holdout litigation 42–44
free-rider problem 159
French Law Against Breaches of Probity *(Loi De La Lutte Contre Les Manquements Á La Probite)*, Article 60 (impact) 51
French Supreme Court. *See Cour de Cassation*
funds, BCRA transfer 45

G20 Common Framework for Debt Treatments 12
Germany, Greek sovereign debt enforcement 108–109
Germany, holdout creditor litigation 102–104; BGH judgments 102–104; BVerfG judgment 104
Germany, holdout litigation 38–41; *Bundesgerichtshof* (BGH) decisions 39–40; *Bundesverfassungsgericht* (BVerfG) decisions 38–39, 40–41
Germany v Italy (ICJ ruling) 145–146
global bond issuance, commercial activity (Italian court recognition) 48
government debt operations, asset manager holdout investor actions (impossibility) 161–162
Gramercy (holdouts) 158
Greece: bondholders, losses 102; bonds, choice-of-forum clauses (absence) 102; crisis, resolution/measures 112; debt crisis 98; debt exchanges, impact 7; debtor, (quasi-)contractual relationship 106; debt restructuring 98, 99–101; debt restructuring negotiations 99–100; debt securities, repayment (invocation) 103; foreign law bonds, restructuring 100; governing law, role 143; haircut, decisions 112; Institute of International Finance, negotiations 163; bonds, holdouts (impact) 102; bonds, restructuring 100–101; Parliament, statutory collective action mechanism 100; public debt, restructuring 110; restructuring measures 114; restructuring methods 100; rollover risk, capital flow cessation (impact) 99; sovereign debt crisis 98–99; sovereign debt enforcement, hypothetical problems 108–109; sovereign immunity 103
Greece holdout 142; arbitration 118–121; arbitration, interim conclusions 120–121; claims, *Poštová banka* tribunal adjudication 64; creditor litigation 102–109; litigation, interim conclusions 113–118
Greece-Slovakia BIT 118–119
Greek Bondholder Act 4050/2012 (GBA): adequacy/necessity 112; adoption 110–111; investor claim reduction 117; legal challenges 106; sovereign act, decision 107–108; statutory collective action mechanism 100
Greek Civil Code, Article 321 106
Greek Constitution, PSI violation 112
Greek Council of the State, bondholder conclusions 112
Greek Government Bonds (GGBs), Poštová banka contractual relationship 119
Greek government bonds, terms/conditions 143
Greek law 2198/1994 144

Greek Private Sector Involvement (Greek PSI) 100; holdout litigation, resolution 114; implementation 102; lawfulness 112; lawsuits 114; OGH case law 104; review 114
Greek State: bonds management, civil statute 115–116; securities, contractual relationship 111–112
Groupment d'Entreprises Fougerolle v European Organization for Nuclear Research (CERN) 53

haircut: decisions 112; impact 161–162
hedge funds, speculative holdout litigation (Greek government expectation) 3
Hellenic Republic v Kuhn decision 106–108, 111–112, 114–116
High Court of Accra, Statement of Claim 45–46
holdout creditor problems 9–10; domestic law debt, relationship 98; foreign law debt, relationship 31; interim conclusions 107–109
holdouts creditors: arbitration, interim conclusions 60–65; behaviour, negative effects 159; contract leveraging 11; genealogy 155, *156*; identity, knowledge 160; litigation 102–109; litigation, interim conclusions 113–118; negotiations, completion 65; pari passu injunction, equipping 55; problems, Greece restructuring methods 100; problems, incidence (reduction) 7; proliferation 155–156
host state, development (contribution) 61–62

immunity defence: circumvention, third-party injunctions 54–56; scope, definition (problem) 146
Institute of International Finance (IIF): commodity trader, nonmembership 165; debt restructuring negotiation role 99–100; Greece, negotiations 163
instruments, recovery (maximization) 6
intercreditor equity 10
intergovernmental international financial institutions, preferred creditor status 8–9
International Centre for Settlement of Investment Disputes (ICSID): arbitration decisions 180; arbitration, impact 61; claimants, settlements 56; creditor-friendly interpretation 118–119; investment definition 58; jurisdiction 60
International Centre for Settlement of Investment Disputes (ICSID) Convention: Article 25 119; Article 52 120; investment decision 58; jurisdiction 61–65; qualified silence 59
international comity, defence 33
International Court of Justice (ICJ): jurisdiction, acceptance 46–47; litigation 46–47; Statute, Article 38 329
International Debt Commission creation, Group of 77 proposal 11
"International Debt Restructuring Agency," establishment 11
International Financial Institution (IFI), preferred creditor status enjoyment 8–9
international financial market, Argentina return 65
international *lex specialis,* absence 38–39
International Monetary Fund (IMF): financing 9; non-toleration policy 11, 167; SDRM 11; stand-by arrangement, Executive Board approval 99
International Tribunal for the Law of the Sea (ITLOS): litigation 45–46, Argentina appeal 46; case, outcome 53–54
investment: duration 62–63; ICSID definition 58; protection 59; risk 63
Italian bondholders, security entitlements 58; Argentina (settlement) 163
Italian Supreme Court *(Corte Suprema di Cassazione),* litigation 41–42
Italy, holdout litigation 41–42

judicial enforcement channels2
judicial reconciliation, political change (impact) 66
jurisdiction *ratione personae* 58

Kuhn decision *see Hellenic Republic v Kuhn*

Less Developed Countries (LDC) borrowers, lawsuits 160
lenders of last resort (LOLR), IMF/ESM financing 9
Lending Into Official Arrears (LIOA) requirements 167
Lightwater v Argentina 33, 48
LNC v Nicaragua 51
Lock Law (Ley 26,017) 31

London Club 160; ad hoc approach exception 12
loss reinstatement clauses 7
lower-rated sovereigns, local currency bond issuance 144
Low-Income Countries (LICs): debt vulnerabilities 161; external commercial debt 9–10; sovereign debt distress, risk 4

Mamatas v Greece 107, 112–113; cesura 147–148; ECtHR ruling/decision 104, 114, 116; local law restructuring 148; perspective 117; risk-based approach, introduction 117; rule of law, violation 148
mass claims: admissibility 64–65; jurisdiction 58
Mexico, Tequila crisis 11
mixed activity conundrum 47–49
monetary damages, remedy (ineffectiveness) 37
moratoriums 6
multilateral creditors, preferred creditor status (enjoyment) 8–9
multilateral debt, restructuring 7

Nausicaa Anadyomène and Banque d'escompte vo ECB 118
New York law-governed syndicated loans, usage 160
NML Capital: holdouts 158; SDNY injunction 65–66
NML Capital v Argentina 35–38, 42, 159; partial summary judgment, motion (granting) 36
NML Capital v Argentina II 43–44, 51
NML litigation, US Supreme Court interpretation 37
NML v Argentina 35; implications 55; United Kingdom Supreme Court (UKSC) decision 42
NML v Argentina (UK) 49–50
NML v BIS 53
non-commercial sovereign acts, delineation 47
non-contractual liability, claims 106
non-Paris Club bilateral lenders, inclusion 155–156
non-payment, threats 7
non-restructured bondholders, payment 56

Oberster Gerichtshof (Austrian Supreme Court) (OGH): final judgment 114; holdout creditor litigation judgments 105–107; plaintiff case refutation 146; sovereign immunity denial 103
official sector creditors, private sector creditors (distinction) 166
official sector holdouts 166–168; emergence 166
ordre public (Austria) 107, 109

pacta sunt servanda, principle (application) 2
Pakistan, restructuring 11
par in parem non habet imperium (principle) 2
pari passu clause: Argentina violations, SDNY claims 36, 66; breach 36; Court of Appeals for the Second Circuit interpretation 36; interpretation 35, 66
pari passu injunction: holdout invocation 55; target 55
Paris Club 7; ad hoc approach exception 12; debt relief 11; membership, limitation 166–167; negotiations, success 11; non-Paris Club bilateral lenders, inclusion 155–156
petrodollars, channeling 2–3
post-default arbitration 56
post-Greek PSI litigation 143
Poštová banka v Hellenic Republic: arbitration 119–120; award 121; tribunal, holdout claims adjudication 64
Pravin Banker Associates Limited v Banco Popular del Peru and Peru 33
pre-emptive restructurings 5
preferred creditor status (PCS), enjoyment 8–9
prefinancing deals, party participation 165–166
principal haircut 6
private creditor committees, negotiation stage role 6
private sector: creditors, official sector creditors (contrast) 166; holdouts 157–166; market participants, impact 109
Private Sector Involvement (PSI): implementation 100, 102; option, problem 99; violation 112
proportionality, principles (breach) 110
Protocol No 1 ECHR, Article 1 107
public debt: New York/English law governance 145; sustainability, IMF Executive Board definition 4
public law-based instruments, impact 144

ratable payment, understanding 55
ratione materiae, establishment 119
ratione personae jurisdiction: absence 57; tribunal assessment 58
real money investors, leverage (absence) 161
Regulation (EC) No 1393/2007, Article 1(1) interpretation 110
reprofiling 6
Republic of Congo, RBLs (signing) 164–165
reputational risks 162
resource-backed loans (RBLs): collateralization, leverage (providing) 165; contractual restructuring mechanisms, absence 165; legal/financial structure, description 166; opacity/hiddenness 164–165; restructuring 166
restructurings: ad hoc process 5–6; deal, non-participation threat 162; outcome 7
retail holdouts, rise 162–164; settlements 68
Rina SpA v Ente RegistroItaliano Navale decision 115
Romak v Uzbekistan 63
Russia, international law violations 167–168

Salini test: criteria/decision 57, 59; rejection, ICSID jurisdiction (relationship) 61–65; revival 121
sector lending, significance (loss) 3
Service of Documents Regulation 111, 115
Settlement Agreement, Task Force Argentina (TFA) signing 68
short-term interbank lines, recovery 160
sovereign bondholders, property right guarantees 116–118
sovereign bonds: arbitration 60–61; arbitration, mass claims (admissibility) 64–65; investment 57–58; legal basis 144–145; legal disputes, increase 3; purchase 64
sovereign borrower (defaults), vulture funds (options) 158–159
sovereign creditors, property rights (protection) 146–148
sovereign debt: developments 2–3; distress, risk 4; experts, impact 109; instruments, legal basis 143–145; overview 1; risk sentiment, deterioration 161; total volume, world GDP (comparison) 1; trial, timeline *67*
sovereign debt enforcement 47–56, 108; *NML* decision, impact 35
sovereign debtors: funds borrowing, SOEs (usage) 165; recalcitrance, rendering 55
sovereign debt restructuring 1, 3–12; alternative 158; closing stage 6; definition/types 4–5; domestic sovereign debt restructuring, foreign sovereign debt restructuring (contrast) 7–9; future 155; governing law, role 142–143; hampering 159; holdout creditor problems 9–10; initiation stage 6; legal/transactional aspects 5–9; negotiation stage 6; practice, evolution 10–12; principles/processes 5–6; process, stages 6
sovereign defaults, rulings 113–114
sovereign immunity 145–146; jurisdiction, link 114–116
sovereign loan restructurings 160
sovereign nation, restructuring right 12
State-Owned Enterprises (SOEs): borrowing 10; usage 165
statute-based instruments, impact 144
Statute of the BIS, Article 55(2) 44–45
statutory restructuring mechanism, voting requirement 100
sticks (coercive elements) 7
Supreme Court of the US (SCOTUS), NML litigation role 37
Swiss Federal Supreme Court (SFSC), litigation 44–45
Switzerland, holdout litigation 44–45
Switzerland-Uzbekistan BIT 120
syndicated bank loans: majority restructuring provisions (absence) 161; sovereign funding source 2–3

territorial link 64
third-party injunctions 54–56
trader doctrine, promulgation 145–146
Trendtex v Nigeria 49, 52

Ukraine, Russia lawsuit 167–168
UK State Immunity Act (SIA) 42, 50
unilateral European sovereign bond restructurings, sovereign bondholders (property right guarantees) 116–117
United General Assembly, Resolution on the Basic Principles on Sovereign Debt Restructuring Processes 146
United Kingdom Debt Relief (Developing Countries) Act 158
United Kingdom, holdout litigation 42

United Kingdom Supreme Court (UKSC) decision 42
United Nations, Basic Principles on Sovereign Debt Restructuring Processes 11
United Nations Conference on Trade and Development (UNCTAD) initiative 40–41; German law, relationship 147
United Nations Convention on State Immunity (UNCSI): Article 10, impact 145–146; Article 19(c), impact 51; financial transaction 48; immunity clarification 44
United Nations Convention on the Law of the Sea (UNCLOS): Article 32 54; Ghana violation 46
United Nations Human Rights Council, vulture funds definition 158
United States District Court for the Southern District of New York (SDNY): Argentina immunity denial 42; BRCA, funds holding 34; injunction 47; money judgments 35–36; NY Judiciary Law applicability, declining 33; pari passu violation, absence 56; payment orders, obtaining 44; precedent 66
United States, holdout litigation 32–38
US banking system, petrodollars (channeling) 2–3
US Bankruptcy Code, chapters 9/11 11
US Generalized System of Preferences, trade benefits 68
US Supreme Court, *Argentina v NML* 46

value recovery instruments 7
Vienna Convention on Diplomatic Relations (VCDR) 43
vulture funds 33, 156–159; Belgium Parliament definition 157–158; declaratory judgment 34; Lord Philipps opinion 157; manifest disproportion, focus 158; threat 157; United Nations Human Rights Council definition 158
vulture holdouts: settlements 65–66; sovereign debt enforcement (curbing) 158; targets 163

Waite and Kennedy v Germany 45
Washington Convention 64; Article 25 121; consultation 59
Weiss and ors 118
White Hawthorne, LLC v Republic of Argentina 66
World Bank funding, access 68
Wriston, Walter 180
Wymvoulio tis Epikrateias 112

Zahlungsdrehscheibe (international global payments platform) 45

For Product Safety Concerns and Information please contact our EU
representative GPSR@taylorandfrancis.com
Taylor & Francis Verlag GmbH, Kaufingerstraße 24, 80331 München, Germany

www.ingramcontent.com/pod-product-compliance
Lightning Source LLC
LaVergne TN
LVHW021125300926
849160LV00010B/866

* 9 7 8 1 0 3 2 4 2 2 3 6 7 *